JAPANESE DRAMA AND CULTURE IN THE 1960s

JAPANESE DRAMA AND CULTURE IN THE 1960s

The Return of the Gods

DAVID G. GOODMAN

An East Gate Book

M. E. Sharpe, Inc.
Armonk, New York
London, England

An East Gate Book

Copyright © 1988 by David Gordon Goodman

Available in the United Kingdom and Europe from M. E. Sharpe, Publishers, 3 Henrietta Street, London WC2E 8LU.

Library of Congress Cataloging-in-Publication Data

Japanese drama and culture in the 1960's.

    1. Japanese drama—20th century—Translations into English.
2. English drama—20th century—Translations from Japanese.
3. Japanese drama—20th century—History and criticism. 4. Theater—
Japan—History—20th century. I. Goodman, David G., 1946–
PL782.E5J37   1988   895.6′25′08   88-3053
ISBN 0-87332-477-3
ISBN 0-87332-478-1 (pbk.)

Printed in the United States of America

TO THE MEMORY OF
David Lester Gordon
Killed on Saipan
June 11, 1944

*

Norman Hirsh Gordon
Killed in Holland
August 26, 1944

*

And Their Mother
Sarah Davidson Gordon
(1894–1987)

The story is told of an automaton constructed in such a way that it could play a winning game of chess, answering each move of an opponent with a countermove. A puppet in Turkish attire and with a hookah in its mouth sat before a chessboard placed on a large table. A system of mirrors created the illusion that this table was transparent from all sides. Actually, a little hunchback who was an expert chess player sat inside and guided the puppet's hand by means of strings. One can imagine a philosophical counterpart to this device. The puppet called "historical materialism" is to win all the time. It can easily be a match for anyone if it enlists the services of theology, which today, as we know, is wizened and has to keep out of sight.

Walter Benjamin
"Theses on the Philosophy of History"

Contents

Preface and Acknowledgments

This book describes aspects of Japanese drama and culture in the 1960s. It presents English translations of five Japanese plays representative of the period; and it accounts for those plays, showing how they were related to and at the same time revealed their psychohistorical context.

All of the translations in this collection except *Find Hakamadare!* first appeared in *Concerned Theatre Japan* (*CTJ*), an English-language theatre journal I edited in Tokyo from 1969 to 1973. I have revised the translations, some more than others, and added commentary to make the texts more comprehensible to the English reader. The commentary is intended as a continuous discourse on theatre in Japan in the 1960s, and readers may wish to consider it as such.

I owe a debt of gratitude to all those who made *Concerned Theatre Japan* possible, especially to Fujimoto Kazuko, my wife, co-editor, and partner in every sense. Oyobe Katsuhito was responsible for the design and physical production of the magazine and was the third member of our editorial troika. Tsuno Kaitarō participated as a contributing editor, and indeed this anthology builds upon ideas he first presented in our introductory issue. Mikoshiba Shigeru was our photographer; and Andy Graham, Beth Kodama, and Pauline Sasaki all generously donated their time to help with the arduous tasks of typing and copy-editing.

Concerned Theatre Japan was initiated as part of the activities of Theatre Center 68/69 (today known as the Black Tent Theatre 68/71), and without the cooperation of all its members, it would never have been possible. Satoh Makoto, Saeki Ryūkō, and Yamamoto Kiyokazu deserve special thanks.

Koike Kazuko and Komiya Kiyoshi helped provide what little advertising income we had. All of the authors who allowed us to publish their work did so without remuneration.

The manuscript was completed with the support of a grant from the National Endowment for the Humanities. I am grateful to the Center for East Asian and Pacific Studies at the University of Illinois for allowing me to take the 1985–86 academic year away from my teaching obligations and for furnishing me with a grant to have my original translations typed onto floppy disks for easier editing and revision. My exceedingly able teaching assistant, Tsuneko Nakazawa, helped with this task.

JAPANESE DRAMA AND CULTURE IN THE 1960s

Introduction

> What holds a movement together? Any movement, not even a
> movement, a group of people, say, or a family, or a nation or a
> civilization? Something must. Do you know? Or you? Or you?
>
> Arnold Wesker, *Their Very Own and Golden City*[1]

The sixties in Japan were a period of intense eschatological reflection. Profound questions regarding ultimate ends were being asked in many artistic media. The plays written during this period reflect this trend, which resulted from the profound historical trauma of defeat in the Second World War, reactivated and exacerbated by the failure of the struggle to prevent renewal of the United States-Japan Mutual Security Treaty in 1960. Disillusioned with both the left-wing political and modern theatre movements, younger theatre people embarked upon a self-conscious attempt to develop an alternative historical mythology that could animate a comprehensive new movement in politics and the arts.

The mood of modern Japanese theatre in the 1960s can be understood from *Wesker 68*,[2] a festival of British playwright Arnold Wesker's work sponsored by an *ad hoc* consortium of theatre troupes from the full spectrum of Japanese modern theatre.[3] Wesker was flown in from England to deliver a lecture, to participate in symposia on the future of the theatre, and to attend performances of *The Wesker Tril-*

3

ogy. Although Wesker did not see it, his play on the vicissitudes of utopian projects, *Their Very Own and Golden City*, was also performed by a newly formed company that called itself "Theatre Center 68" after Wesker's own "Centre 42."[4] Members of this company included Tsuno Kaitarō (who directed), Satoh Makoto, and Saeki Ryūkō.[5] With the possible exception of the Moscow Art Theatre's performances in Tokyo in 1958, nothing like *Wesker 68* had ever taken place in modern Japanese theatre. Few playwrights experience in their lifetime the kind of celebration that the thirty-six-year-old Wesker enjoyed during the festival.

What was the nature of Wesker's appeal? He was born in 1932 in London's East End, the son of Jewish immigrants from Hungary and Russia, and his plays are marked by a disillusionment with Stalinist Communism and by a quest for a humane means to realize a New Jerusalem. These were precisely the issues that concerned modern Japanese theatre in the 1960s. It was Arnold Wesker's quest for an alternative, non-Stalinist form of political movement rooted in Jewish millenarianism that drew Japanese theatre people to his work.[6]

Origins of the Shingeki Movement

The name given to orthodox modern drama in Japan is *shingeki*, literally, "new theatre." Shingeki developed not as an extension of traditional Japanese theatre forms but through a rupture with them. What characterized shingeki and distinguished it from *kabuki* and *nō* drama was its ambition to produce a thoroughly realistic theatre in the spirit of Ibsen and Chekhov, and its desire to eschew what it regarded as the "irrationality" of premodern theatre forms.

The transition to modern Japanese drama was more than a shift from presentational to realistic technique, however. As in the West, where "modernism" meant "the replacement of religious certainty and moral absolutes by skepticism, doubt, agnosticism, and intellectual relativism,"[7] Japan's modern theatre was characterized by a similar alienation from the traditional cosmology. It is no coincidence that early shingeki plays depict the decline of traditional patterns of belief. Tsubouchi Shōyō's *En-no-Gyōja* (*En the Ascetic*, 1913) describes the decline of religious values in a decadent time and offers a transhistorical, Nietzchean *übermensch* as an antidote; and Kikuchi Kan's *Madman on the Roof* (*Okujō no kyōjin*, 1916) ridicules traditional religious practices.[8] Shingeki as we know it today thus originated in a rupture with classical theatre and with the premodern imagination it embodied.

The premodern imagination that informed kabuki overflowed with gods and demons of every description. Indeed, for most of its history, the appearance of a god on the stage was the *sine qua non* of Japanese theatre.[9] Such a theophany was and remains virtually indispensable in nō.[10] And apparitions teem in kabuki, from early works like *Gempei narukami denki* (1689), which later won distinction as one of the "Eighteen Great Kabuki Plays" (*kabuki jūhachiban*),[11] to Tsuruya Namboku IV's immensely popular *Tōkaidō Yotsuya kaidan* (Ghost Story of Yotsuya on the Tōkaidō), completed in 1825.[12] Even ostensibly secular kabuki classics like *Chūshingura*,[13] critic Maruya Saiichi has argued, represent permutations of traditional patterns of belief.[14] At the end of the nineteenth century, when the first experiments with Western-style theatre were made, the gods' hegemony over Japanese theatre may have been attenuated, but it remained essentially unchallenged.[15]

What shingeki sought to do above all was to supplant this god-infested premodern imagination. There were many attempts to do this within the framework of traditional theatre, "to remodel Kabuki as a pseudo nineteenth-century European theatre of Realism."[16] These attempts failed to produce the desired results, however, and by the early 1920s, they had all but been abandoned.[17]

The need for shingeki to make a complete break with tradition was stated most emphatically by Osanai Kaoru (1881–1928). Osanai had tried for years to reform kabuki, but he despaired of ever succeeding and, in 1924, founded the Tsukiji Little Theatre (*Tsukiji shōgekijō*) to give Japan its first truly modern theatre, free from kabuki's influence. The Tsukiji marked the beginning of the orthodox shingeki movement as we know it today.[18]

Osanai's exhortation to his actors in 1926 accurately reflects the attitude of the young shingeki movement toward traditional theatre:

> Above all, the enemy we must fight against in our effort to establish the
> *national* theatre we hold as our ideal is the traditional theatre, that is,

kabuki drama. . . . We must first wage war on this *tradition.* We must destroy *kabuki* patterns, we must create *our own distinct theatre art,* new and free.[19]

By the late 1930s, Osanai's goal had been achieved: shingeki had been established as a purely realistic theatre crowned by the psychological realism of Kishida Kunio and the socialist realism of Kubo Sakae.

The Evolution of the Shingeki Movement

Kubo's *Land of Volcanic Ash* is of particular interest to us because its career illustrates the evolution of the shingeki movement in the period prior to 1960.[20] First staged in 1938 in an atmosphere of intense political repression, the play attempted "a unification of scientific theory and poetic form"[21] and was viewed by its generation as an heroic attempt to counter the rising tide of fanatic ultranationalism with science and rationality. The comments of renowned political scientist Maruyama Masao, who attended the original production of the play, make this clear:

> The play appeared at a time when people like me were very pessimistic about the future of the social sciences, and so [the main character] Amamiya's struggle to maintain his integrity as a scientist really moved me. Any impulse I may have had to criticize the organization of the play or the acting became secondary, and I remember inexplicably breaking into tears as I watched.[22]

Land of Volcanic Ash and the ideal of socialist realism it epitomized dominated the shingeki imagination until the early 1960s. It was one of the first plays produced after the war, and it was restaged again in 1961.[23] By 1969, however, forty-three years after Osanai had exhorted his actors to reject kabuki, a newly formed theatre troupe could rail against shingeki in almost exactly the same terms:

> Ultimately it is our intention to destroy shingeki as an art, shingeki as a system, and in its place present before you a concrete alternative contemporary theatre. . . . What we lack in money we will make up for with our wits, and where we lack experience we will rely on a new sensitivity and

concrete acts; we will explore modes of expression different from shingeki, different production systems, different ways of organizing ourselves, different ways of relating to our audience.[24]

A number of theatre troupes similarly hostile to shingeki appeared
during the 1960s.[25] They constituted a countermovement in Japanese
theatre history that I call the "post-shingeki movement."[26] They rejected shingeki, which appeared to them to have become, in Harold
Rosenberg's phrase, "a tradition of the new." As critic Tsuno Kaitarō
explained at the time:

> Shingeki has become historical; it has become a tradition in its own right.
> The problem of the younger generation has been to come to terms with
> this tradition. For us, modern European drama [which shingeki has
> sought to emulate] is no longer some golden ideal as yet out of reach. It is
> instead a pernicious, limiting influence. Beneath Shingeki's prosperous
> exterior there is decadence. It has lost the antithetic élan that character-
> ized its origins. Shingeki no longer maintains the dialectical power to
> negate and transcend; rather, it has become an institution that itself
> demands to be transcended.[27]

The post-shingeki movement sought to destroy the shingeki epitomized by *Land of Volcanic Ash* as both a system and as an art. As a
system, shingeki had changed radically since its straitened days of
resistance before the war. The evolution of the troupe that originally
staged *Land of Volcanic Ash*, known after the war as *Mingei* (The
People's Art Theatre), illustrates the point.

> In 1950, when the present Mingei was formed, it consisted of 12 members:
> 11 actors and one director. By 1960, this small group had expanded into a
> company of 119 members: 51 actors, 13 directorial members, 16 manage-
> ment workers, plus 39 apprentices, producing 16 plays a year, performing
> 240 nights. In the next 10 years, however, that is by 1970, Gekidan Mingei
> grew into an organisation of 250 members, producing 10 plays a year, with
> performances on 600 nights. To understand the enormous scale of this
> expansion, we can compare these figures to those of the two leading
> companies in England, the National Theatre and the Royal Shakespeare
> Company. In both cases the number of acting members of the companies is
> kept around forty.[28]

Historian Thomas R. H. Havens corroborates the post-shingeki rebels' charge that a loss of creative vitality accompanied the expansion of the shingeki system:

> Companies that were barely alive in 1950 and conscientiously pursuing their own stage idioms in 1960 had become substantial businesses with a far-flung but reliable clientele by 1980, often no longer able to innovate or give their playwrights even an atelier production.[29]

Critics of shingeki viewed the loss of creativity as more than a by-product of the movement's success, however. In the 1960s, *Land of Volcanic Ash* and the kind of realism it epitomized came to be regarded by the younger generation as nothing less than an expression of Stalinist totalitarianism. Kan Takayuki, a representative critic, put it this way:

> The realism . . .that is the orthodox theory of the shingeki movement clearly has as its tacit premise a specific ideology of culture and art (not simply the ideology of socialism or communism but the revolutionary theory descended from the official dogma of the International Communist Movement before the war) that relates and commits one to the historical stage at which the transition from capitalism to socialism (the revolution) has arrived. As such, it is naturally antagonistic to all "avant-garde" tendencies in the arts that might be considered virulent or destructive, and it indicates a theory of art that remains within the frame of Socialist Realism (in its contemporary revisionist guise) that would repress all such tendencies.[30]

In short, the realism of *Land of Volcanic Ash*, which had thrilled audiences in the 1930s as a bold attempt to deal with the world in rational, scientific terms, appeared to young theatre practitioners around 1960 to be little more than Stalinist dogma.

The Security Treaty Crisis of 1960

The 1960 demonstrations against renewal of the U.S.-Japan Mutual Security Treaty were a major turning point in Japanese intellectual life. For young people in the theatre, the change was characterized by disillusionment with postwar Japanese democratic institutions, a break with the Old Left, and, most concretely, by a quest for alternatives to shingeki orthodoxy.

Marxism and the Hegelian conception of an ineluctable historical dialectic it subsumed were fundamental to this orthodoxy. As intellectual historian Fujita Shōzō has pointed out, Communism for the Japanese was not just another ideology; it was the prerequisite of Japanese intellectual modernity.[31] Lifton, Katō, and Reich concur:

> Marxism supplied Japanese intellectuals not only with a political ideology to combat social injustice but also with an intellectual tool for systematic analysis of their contemporary situation against a broad historical background. They experienced Marxism both as political idealism and social science—and in many cases as a form of religious dogma.[32]

To reject Marxism as the recanters (*tenkōsha*) of the 1930s did was to turn one's back, not simply on Communism, but on science, rationalism, in a word, on modern civilization and to surrender to the murky mythologies of militarist ultranationalism.[33]

After World War Two, as before, the shingeki movement was dominated by the left wing. Led by Marxists like Kubo Sakae, the shingeki movement had distinguished itself during the war years by its reticence to collaborate;[34] and for a period after 1945, it seemed that for this reason "shingeki [would become] the center, not only of the theatre world, but of all of Japanese culture."[35]

Institutionally, also, the left wing dominated the shingeki movement. While it was briefly patronized by commercial promoters like Tōhō and Shōchiku in the immediate postwar period, the shingeki movement soon refused to make the compromises required to become a viable commercial enterprise, and it was quickly thrown back on its own resources.

In order to deal with this economic crisis, a number of innovations were made. Of particular importance was the formation of the Workers' Theatre Council, *Rōen*,[36] in cooperation with the Japanese Communist Party (JCP). *Rōen*, which continues to function today, was modeled after the prewar German *Volksbühne*. It organized audiences for shingeki productions through JCP-controlled or -influenced labor unions.[37]

In Japan as elsewhere, Khrushchev's 1956 revelations of Stalin's crimes troubled left-wing intellectuals and had no small impact on the theatre. Critic Obase Takuzō, for example, writing on the occasion of the 1961 production of *Land of Volcanic Ash*, called the play "a monument to failure," referring to the failure of Marxism and the proletarian literary movement from which the play had emerged;[38] and one of the most influential plays of the time was *Dirty Hands*, Sartre's polemic on Stalinism.[39]

These doubts notwithstanding, opposition to the Security Treaty temporarily united the left wing. Even members of the anti-JCP faction of the student youth movement (*Zengakuren*) like playwright Fukuda Yoshiyuki and actor Kanze Hideo felt they had no choice but to continue their alliance with the JCP through the Security Treaty crisis.[40] Political realities necessitated compromise, but equally important, no viable alternative to Marxist orthodoxy, either in politics or in the theatre, yet existed. Disaffected as young theatre people like Fukuda and Kanze were with the interlocking Old Left and shingeki elites, they felt an alliance with them in the Conference of Modern Theatre Artists (*Shingekijin kaigi*) was preferable to the alternatives: acquiescence or futile, renegade opposition. As soon as the Security Treaty crisis ended, however, so did the tenuous unity within the ranks of the modern theatre movement, and the post-shingeki movement began.[41]

Five Representative Post-Shingeki Plays

The drama created during the 1960s by the disgruntled graduates of the Security Treaty struggle differed significantly from modern drama as it had been previously written and performed. Before the decade was over, their innovations would revolutionize the meaning of modern drama in Japan.

Post-shingeki drama has two main characteristics. First, it is characterized by the identification of a character or characters with an archetypal, transhistorical figure (a god) into whom they metamorphose; and, second, by a concern with the interrelated questions of personal redemption (salvation of the individual) and social revolution (salvation of the world).

At the center of each of the plays in this collection is an incidence of metamorphosis. Fukuda Yoshiyuki's *Find Hakamadare!* (*Hakamadare wa doko da*, 1964) describes how a band of oppressed peasants in medieval Japan identify with Hakamadare, their Robin Hood-like redeemer, depose him when he turns out to be a corrupt and ruthless villain, and assume his identity once he is dead. As the playwright points out in his introduction to the play, Hakamadare was not one man but a transhistorical figure whose name came to symbolize popular resistance to authority. "Thus it was," he explains, "that numberless robbers claiming to be Hakamadare continued to appear down to the sixteenth century."

Akimoto Matsuyo's *Kaison the Priest of Hitachi* (*Hitachibō Kaison*, 1965) depicts in realistic detail how a young man living in 1961 is metamorphosed into a twelfth-century warrior named Kaison, an immortal figure who is reputed to wander throughout Japan doing endless penance for sins committed centuries ago.

In *My Beatles* (*Atashi no Beatles*, 1967), Satoh Makoto shows how hoary archetypes can take very modern form. Teenagers metamorphose here into the Beatles, who in turn are understood to be manifestations of the archetypal "unexpected visitors" (*marebito*) who are fundamental to Japanese art and folk religion.

Similarly, in Kara Jūrō's *John Silver: The Beggar of Love* (*John Silver: Ai no kojiki*, 1970), lonely urbanites identify with a vengeful peg-legged seaman named John Silver, buccaneer of Manchuria, who wanders eternally seeking the immortal Orchid Flower, his one true love.

Finally, in *The Dance of Angels Who Burn Their Own Wings* (*Tsubasa o moyasu tenshi-tachi no butō*, 1970), by Satoh Makoto and three other playwrights, members of a modern motorcycle gang identify with the main actors in the French Revolution and assume their place in mankind's eternal quest for liberation.

If the central mechanism of identification and metamorphosis is the same in each of these plays, so is their central concern. Each deals with the interrelated problems of personal redemption and social revolution. *Kaison*, for example, describes the existential situation treated in most post-shingeki plays: release from the crushing pressures of history through identification with a transhistorical archetype. Apotheosis into Kaison enables the war orphan Keita to escape from history into mythic time and to divest himself of the excruciating burden of guilt he has carried with him since the war.

Fukuda's *Hakamadare* illustrates the post-shingeki movement's disaffection with Stalinism and its fascination with alternative forms of millenarianism. In the play, Hakamadare is Stalin, and when the peasants kill him, taking his problematic mantle upon themselves, they set off to realize what they call "The Hakamadarean Age," when the dead will be restored to life and perfect justice will prevail on earth.

Satoh's *Beatles* and Kara's *John Silver* treat the legacy of Japanese imperialism in Asia. Satoh's play describes how subliminal archetypes shape contemporary fantasies, precluding both revolution and personal salvation. Feeling moribund and devoid of purpose, Kara's characters long to return to the swashbuckling days of Japan's international piracy, when they felt truly alive. Kara accounts for the continuing need for salvific visions despite their political consequences.

In a sense, *The Dance of Angels* is the culminating work of this period, for it proposes an abandonment of the mechanism of identification and metamorphosis. Written as a critique of Peter Weiss's *Marat/Sade*, the play dismisses Weiss's concept of revolution as "simplistic" and "petit bourgeois." It places the concept of revolution in a theological context and proposes an alternative model that intentionally resembles the messianic revolutionism of Walter Benjamin, where revolution and redemption are identified.[42] Here, revolution/redemption are not the end of a historical process; instead every moment in time is a narrow gate through which the Messiah (revolution) might enter.

The Need for a Transcendent Vision

It is clear from the empirical evidence of the plays themselves that powerful forces were at work in Japanese culture in the 1960s, forces that made the most profound eschatological issues matters of immediate, urgent concern. Any discussion of Japanese drama during this period must account for this phenomenon.

As I have argued in my book *After Apocalypse: Four Japanese Plays of Hiroshima and Nagasaki*,[43] one of the major motives behind significant experimentation in Japanese drama in the postwar period was the need felt by diverse playwrights to find an effective means to deal with the atomic bomb experience. Here I will only summarize the argument I present at length in that book.

By the late 1940s, it was already clear that the purely realistic dramaturgy shingeki had developed could not encompass the full scope of the modern Japanese experience. The claustrophobic psychological realism of Kishida Kunio had never concerned itself with society or historical events. Socialist realism had of course been concerned with society and history; but in *Land of Volcanic Ash*, Kubo Sakae had spent 300 pages describing the dynamics of life in a tiny agricultural community in Hokkaido. Using the same techniques, how many pages would it take to treat the disaster of the Second World War, or even a single event during that war, the bombing of Hiroshima? In my view, it was the inability of shingeki realism, in either its socialist or psychological variety, to deal satisfactorily with events like the atomic bombings and the entire war experience for which they were a synecdoche that led to some of the most significant experimentation in postwar Japanese playwriting.

Of particular interest in plays about Hiroshima and Nagasaki is the need playwrights obviously felt to give the victims some form of "symbolic immortality,"[44] to integrate them into a transcendent order that would explain their lives and validate their deaths. This need explains the unmistakable resurgence of religious thought and imagery that characterized these plays, from the Pure Land Buddhism of Hotta Kiyomi's *The Island* (*Shima*, 1955) and the Catholicism of Tanaka Chikao's *The Head of Mary* (*Maria no kubi*, 1959) to the Shintoism of Satoh Makoto's post-shingeki *Nezumi Kozō: The Rat* (*Nezumi kozō jirokichi*, 1969).

As in plays dealing with the atomic experience, the works collected in this volume are products of the need to formulate symbolic immortality in the post-Hiroshima age. All of the mysterious, godlike figures who appear in these plays, from Kaison to John Silver, from Hakamadare to the Beatles, are immortals: transhistorical figures, identification with whom promises eternal life.

Kaison the Priest of Hitachi formulates with especial clarity the problem that post-shingeki plays treat. That problem has been stated most eloquently in another context by Mircea Eliade:

> And in our day, when historical pressure no longer allows any escape, how can man tolerate the catastrophes and horrors of history—from collective deportations and massacres to atomic bombings—if beyond them he can glimpse no sign, no transhistorical meaning; if they are only the blind play of economic, social, or political forces, or, even worse, only the result of the "liberties" that a minority takes and exercises directly on the stage of universal history?[45]

Eliade's question is precisely the one that post-shingeki dramatists were trying to answer. And it is precisely this transhistorical meaning that Keita seeks when he identifies with the immortal Kaison. Irrevocably separated by the war from all that is dear to him, paralyzed by fear, and feeling himself sinking into insanity, Keita calls desperately on the immortal Kaison, who answers his prayer for salvation. Kaison not only connects him with his departed mother but integrates him into the great stream of Japanese history; he mobilizes Keita, in the last scene literally putting him back on his feet; and he restores to him a sense of meaning in life.

Kaison is no abstraction; he is no metaphor. A bona fide deity from the Japanese pantheon, he actually appears on the stage, walking, talking, and interacting with mortal men. By making Kaison appear on the stage, Akimoto broke decisively with shingeki orthodoxy and established the basic method of post-shingeki drama.

The reappearance of gods like Kaison on stage after a fifty-year hiatus was greeted by Japanese theatre-goers with foreboding rather than with joy. Salvation by Kaison meant that the hoary archetypes that had always ruled the Japanese imagination were still active, that they still maintained a powerful hold on the Japanese mind. It meant that the constellation of beliefs and feelings that had informed the Japanese emperor system and wartime institutions were still alive,[46] and that the facade of Japan's postwar democracy was but a thin veneer. Kaison's reappearance meant that nothing, or close to nothing, stood between the Japanese and the subliminal impulses that had led to the near-annihilation of the Second World War.

Satoh Makoto and Kara Jūrō explore the implications of this conclusion in their work. In *My Beatles*, Satoh made the startling discovery that gods like Kaison not only continue to control the imagination of Japanese young people, but that they take contemporary form: rock idols like the Beatles. As John Lahr recognized fourteen years after Satoh wrote his play, the Beatles were "local divinities" who fulfilled a "shamanistic" function.[47] In the Japanese context, this had more than metaphorical significance: it meant that all those subliminal cultural forces responsible for Japanese imperialism, specifically the colonization and exploitation of Korea and its legacy in Satoh's own generation, were still active and powerful.

In *John Silver: The Beggar of Love*, Kara Jūrō amplified this theme. To avoid the deadening sense of meaninglessness that characterized their postwar existence, the Japanese might very well turn once more to international piracy. Not only did Kara recognize this as a distinct possibility, but he presents it as a viable, reasonable alternative to anomie and symbolic death. Kara's ex-pirates reminiscing about their lives of blood and gore in Manchukuo are not significantly different from ex-Nazis reminiscing about "the good old days" of *sturm und drang*, when their lives were filled with vision and purpose. Kara's play is morally ambiguous and intentionally provocative. It asks a question many in his audience could not answer: Why not?

The Dance of Angels answers the question. It argues that certain, perhaps all, grand revitalizing schemes endanger human survival. It suggests that our continuing quest for salvation from the human condition, for redemption and revolution, risks total annihilation of the human species. The play recommends that if we are to survive, we must stop dreaming, that because it leads ineluctably to atrocities like Auschwitz and Hiroshima, we must end our quest for revolution/redemption, the ultimate vivifying scenario—or at the very least revolutionize what our concepts of revolution and redemption mean.[48]

Toward a Theory of the Development of Modern Japanese Drama

The post-shingeki movement was a countermovement in Japanese theatre history. It was an attempt to reestablish contact with the premodern imagination that had been taboo since shingeki's rupture with kabuki in order to deal more effectively with the questions posed by the modern Japanese experience. The most obvious characteristic of this movement was the shared need to reinject the gods, "grotesque abstractions of the subliminal impulses of the modern Japanese imagination,"[49] into modern Japanese theatre. It was not a movement in the sense of a centrally organized enterprise, but in the sense that a number of disparate groups and personalities responded simultaneously in a more or less similar fashion to a commonly perceived need. The movement did not seek merely to return to the past; it was not atavistic. It was dialectical, seeking to recapture and reaffirm the past in order to negate and transcend it. As Tsuno Kaitarō put it:

> We feel that although Shingeki's break with classical No and Kabuki was both justified and inevitable, it nonetheless cut us off from the sources of our traditions and trapped us within the restrictive confines of a static, bourgeois institution. Today we are seeking to reaffirm our tradition, but not as our predecessors did in the years leading up to the war. To them, reaffirming traditional values meant an atavistic and uncritical reinstatement of a fictitious, idealized past. We, on the other hand, are attempting to reaffirm our tradition, even when we find it distasteful, in order to deal directly and critically with it. Our hope is that by harnessing the energy of the Japanese popular imagination we can at once transcend the enervating cliches of modern drama and revolutionize what it means to be Japanese.[50]

Many scholars have pointed out that the Tokugawa period (1600–1868) was a period of secularization in Japanese history. Lifton, Katō, and Reich write, for example, that "the Japanese as a people were secularized even before industrialization began in the late nineteenth century. . . ."[51] Although there is substantial evidence to support this view, it is also true that the ostensible secularism of the Tokugawa period pertains to popular disillusionment with established religions, particularly Buddhism, and that folk religion continued to be both important and vigorous.[52] Not only did the early and mid-nineteenth century see the establishment of significant new religions like the Kurozumi, Konkō, and Tenri sects, which were based on folk beliefs;[53] but folk religion also informed the arts. As Ouwehand has shown in his analysis of the popular catfish prints known as *namazu-e*, for example, folk religion in the Tokugawa period was a profound and pervasive force with distinct millenarian implications.[54]

When Tsuno and others in the post-shingeki movement speak of a dialectical return to the Japanese popular imagination, it is to the imagination molded by this folk religion to which they are referring. The popularity during the 1960s of the late Tokugawa artist Ekin exemplifies the resurgence of interest in Tokugawa folk culture that took place at this time;[55] and the post-shingeki movement exulted in constant references to the Tokugawa period, overlapping Tokugawa and contemporary events using the kabuki technique of *mitate* (camouflaging politically sensitive or otherwise taboo material in an earlier historical period).[56]

In its quest for a "modern" theatre, shingeki had, for better or worse, severed the connection between the theatre and the premodern folk imagination, the "irrationality" of the kabuki theatre. It established instead a purely realistic theatre modeled after the work of Ibsen and Chekhov. As I have already said, this was to all appearances a secular theatre, devoid of the plethora of gods and demons that had teemed on the kabuki stage. But as in the Tokugawa case, the secular facade of modern theatre concealed a particular mythological, if not exactly theological, formulation.[57]

I will leave a detailed description of the way post-shingeki critics understood the mythological formulation of shingeki to a later chapter of this volume. Suffice it here to say that that formulation involved the two main intellectual currents that informed the modern Western drama that shingeki playwrights sought to emulate, Christianity and Marxism; and that these two currents shared, at least in their modern interpretation, a common root in Hegelian philosophy.

Christianity had a profound influence on modern Japanese theatre. Kishida Kunio was influenced by the devoutly Catholic Jacques Copeau;[58] Tanaka Chikao and Fukuda Tsuneari both identify themselves as Catholic;[59] and Takeda Kiyoko argues that left-wing dramatist Kinoshita Junji should be viewed as an apostate Christian writer.[60] Yashiro Seiichi is a practicing Christian;[61] and I have argued that Satoh Makoto, who received his early education in Christian schools, has been motivated by his ambivalence toward Christianity.[62] In short, the influence of Christianity on modern Japanese drama has been extensive,[63] and Christians have been overrepresented among Japanese playwrights.[64]

I have already described the influence of Marxism on modern Japanese drama. In various modulations, Marxism dominated the shingeki movement from the collapse of the Tsukiji Little Theatre troupe following Osanai Kaoru's death in 1928 into the 1960s.

As Walter Benjamin concluded, however, theology is the unacknowledged puppeteer that has animated Marxism's historical materialism,[65] and so the post-shingeki movement's rejection of shingeki orthodoxy was simultaneously a rejection of its implicit mythological formulation, its faith in a unified, dialectical historical process leading ineluctably to either revolution (Marxism) or redemption (Christianity). However, post-shingeki critics objected to the way this formulation "dichotomizes external history and the individual inner world" and reduces "history ... to the very Hegelian simplicity we have hoped to escape."[66] They recognized, as Walter Benjamin had, that "the storm of historical progress led not to utopia but to renewed barbarism";[67] and they consciously sought to replace the Hegelian-Marxist myth with a more humane one. Thus, as shingeki had done with kabuki before it, the post-shingeki movement's ultimate goal was to challenge and supplant, not just the external forms of shingeki, but its underlying mythological formulation.

Through their dialectical encounter with the premodern Japanese popular imagination, post-shingeki playwrights developed an alternative formulation, a new myth that they hoped would animate a new movement in politics and the arts. That alternative formulation is exemplified in the plays collected in this volume. It consisted most essentially of (1) a nontragic, anti-Hegelian dramaturgy that refused to dichotomize external history and the individual inner world and that viewed spiritual redemption and political revolution as inextricably linked phenomena; (2) a revalorization of Japanese cultural experience, even (or perhaps especially) in its aberrant forms; and (3) an emphasis on "movement" that was manifest in the use of mobile tent theatres and other nontraditional theatre spaces.[68]

Each of these tenets had far-reaching implications. Post-shingeki's nontragic dramaturgy was simultaneously a nontragic reading of history and a rejection of the Hegelian construction implicit in shingeki, which required assimilation to an absolute historical dialectic. Reaffirming and revalidating Japanese cultural particularity replaced the dogma of humanistic universalism with a more dynamic appreciation of the range of human experience and possibility. And the emphasis on nontraditional theatre spaces freed small troupes from dependency on the bureaucracy of Rōen (and the Old Left that controlled it), making it possible for them to travel through the country and have national impact. More profoundly, the use of tent theatres and the emphasis on "mobility," "motion," and "the movement" in the writing and thinking of the time were expressions of the desperate need to break out of the sense of paralysis and impotence young people had experienced as a result of the failure of the 1960 Security Treaty struggle.[69]

Post-Shingeki Drama and Culture in the 1960s

The decade of theatrical experimentation described in this volume culminates in 1970, when both *The Beggar of Love* and *The Dance of Angels* were performed. Nineteen-seventy was also the year Mishima Yukio committed ritual suicide (*seppuku*) at the headquarters of the Japanese Self-Defense Forces in Tokyo, after having tried to incite the troops to rise up, overthrow the democratically constituted government, and restore the emperor to power. The post-shingeki movement and Mishima's suicide are related, and understanding the relationship helps us understand the nature of Japanese culture during this period.

Mishima's suicide was an attempt to address the same problem that post-shingeki drama was trying to solve. That problem was a sense that life in postwar Japan was empty and meaningless because it was divorced from the bedrock of Japanese culture. The sense of meaninglessness originated in Japan's defeat in the Second World War. Defeat was traumatic because it had discredited the institutions and values for which millions of Japanese had just given their lives, in particular the emperor system, its institutional expressions, and the philosophical and mythological systems of thought that informed it.[70] Henceforth, what should the Japanese live and die for? It was a question not easily answered.

The Security Treaty crisis of 1960 reactivated and exacerbated this problem for the Japanese. The overwhelming task of reconstruction had demanded total concentration in the decade and a half following the war. But by 1960, Japan was poised to begin its period of unprecedented economic growth (*kōdo seichō*), and people had the time to reflect on their values and cultural priorities. It was at precisely this historical moment that the demonstrations opposing renewal of the U.S.-Japan Mutual Security pact took place.

> There were 223 *demo* [demonstrations] involving an estimated 961,000 people in Tokyo between April 1959 and July 1960. Their size ranged from several hundred to a maximum claim by leftists of 330,000. After May 19, daily *demo* in Tokyo ranged from a few thousand to upwards of 135,000.[71]

With these daily demonstrations keeping it constantly in the news, and with the active participation of the nation's intellectuals and academics, the Security Treaty crisis captivated the imagination of the entire nation and severely tested Japan's democratic institutions. When the Treaty was allowed to renew itself automatically on June 19, the event was, to say the least, anticlimactic.[72] A feeling of helplessness and impotence spread among the demonstrators, particularly the anti-JCP students (*Zengakuren-ha*), who regarded the outcome as an all but unmitigated defeat.[73]

Many of the young people who went on to create the post-shingeki movement were members of this faction. Their sense of helplessness and impotence reactivated and exacerbated the sense of meaninglessness that was the legacy of the war; and, as we have seen, it was this sense of meaninglessness that the post-shingeki movement sought to address.[74]

Nineteen-sixty was also a turning point for Mishima Yukio, who, we are told, "became totally absorbed in the events."[75] The previous year, he had published *Kyōko no ie* (*Kyōko's House*), a book critics had not liked but which, nonetheless, revealed more of Mishima's inner life than had any work since *Confessions of a Mask* (*Kamen no kokuhaku*, 1949). In *Kyōko no ie*, Mishima had invented a series of alter egos who frequented a salon presided over by a woman named Kyōko, whose name means "mirror." In other words, in Kyōko's house, the various facets of Mishima's personality were reflected. One of these, a boxer who, after an injury ends his career, joins an ultranationalist group, was the persona Mishima chose for himself after 1960.

In retrospect, this choice became clear almost immediately after the demonstrations, with the publication of Mishima's short story "Patriotism" (*Yūkoku*) in December 1960. The story concerns a fictitious event related to the coup d'état attempted by young Japanese army officers on February 26, 1936. That event was the ritual suicide performed by a young army lieutenant who, unable to reconcile his human feelings toward the rebels and his duty to his army unit, which he felt certain would be mobilized to put down the rebellion, chooses to take his own life. With "Patriotism," Mishima embarked on the road to his own suicide ten years later; and with it he solved the problem of meaninglessness in postwar Japan, the problem of what or whom one should die for, the question of who or what could best guarantee symbolic immortality. Mishima's solution is revealed in the story: "In the radiant, bridelike figure of his white-robed wife the lieutenant seemed to see a vision of all those things he had loved and for which he was to lay down his life—the Imperial Household, the Nation, and the Army Flag."[76]

Mishima's solution, elaborated in such volumes as *Bunka bōei ron* (*On the Defense of Culture*, 1968), wherein he asserted that the emperor was and always had been the *sine qua non* of Japanese culture and that the defense of Japanese culture necessarily entailed defending the Imperial Institution, was precisely the kind of "atavistic and uncritical reinstatement of a fictitious, idealized past"[77] that the post-shingeki movement had assiduously and studiously avoided. Nevertheless, this atavistic fiction served its purpose: it allowed Mishima to identify his personal need to die with pervasive questions regarding the source of transcendental meaning that faced his society.

My purpose here is not to analyze Mishima's life or his death,[78] but only to point out that he was responding to the same shared cultural and psychological needs as the post-shingeki movement—only Mishima's solution was atavistic and solipsistic while the post-shingeki movement was dialectical and engaged.[79]

Ōe Kenzaburō was responding to similar psychocultural needs when he wrote *A Personal Matter* (*Kojinteki na taiken*, 1964) and *Hiroshima Notes* (*Hiroshima nōto*, 1965). The books are closely linked. Written simultaneously, Ōe intended them to be published on the same day.[80] Both books concern holocaust experiences: Ōe's personal holocaust, the birth of his brain-damaged first child; and the holocaust that enveloped Hiroshima. In these experiences, Ōe perceived an alternative to the ideologies of humanism and tragedy. In both books, Ōe rejects humanism and seeks a rationale for movement and political action in existential experience. He defines humanism as that attitude which allows people to remain indifferent to the suffering of others;[81] and he travels to Hiroshima looking for a "humanism beyond popular humanism—a new humanism sprouting from the misery of Hiroshima."[82]

Like post-shingeki drama, *A Personal Matter* and *Hiroshima Notes* are concerned with the question of movement and potency, sexual and political, in the postwar and post–1960 era. *A Personal Matter* concerns sexual potency. The main character, Bird, gradually recovers from sexual impotence precipitated by the birth of his "monster baby," and as he does so he also recovers the ability to deal with the reality of his brain-damaged son. The prominent references to nuclear testing in the book[83] establish the relationship with *Hiroshima Notes*, which deals with the question of political potency, what constitutes and justifies effective political action in the post-Hiroshima age. In the end, with deceptive simplicity, Ōe concludes "that reality compels you to live properly when you live in the real world."[84]

Similarly, Ōe's 1971 novella *The Day He Himself Shall Wipe My Tears Away* (*Mizukara waga namida o nuguitamō hi*) deals with the emperor system and severely criticizes the work and thought of Mishima Yukio. According to Michiko Wilson, "That the death of Mishima galvanized the composition of *My Tears* is no secret. . . . The work is [Ōe's] challenge, as a writer, to 'the cultural tradition headed by the Emperor System.' . . . "[85] In even later works, like Ōe's 1983 cogitation on William Blake, the author takes up explicitly the metaphysical and theological themes that were the legacy of the 1960s.[86]

The questions and concerns that precipitated the emergence of the post-shingeki movement were thus pervasive in the 1960s, and an understanding of the post-shingeki movement helps us understand Japanese culture during this period. But we can go beyond the 1960s with the insights we gain from the post-shingeki movement. In an essay entitled "The Liberation of Japanese Ghosts," for example, Mori Jōji, a professor of English literature at Waseda University and an authority on Kenneth Burke, argues,

> As social institutions, systems of government, and the law are "modernized," or "democratized" [in Japan], the antimodern "ghost impulse" becomes more and more pervasive in the works of our best authors. Many of the masterpieces by modern Japanese writers [like Kawabata, Tanizaki, and Mishima] are masked varieties of ghost tales. . . . The term [ghost] is presented here as a tool of analysis to deal simultaneously with three factors in literature, the archetypal, the aesthetic, and the sociopsychological. If we accept the idea that modern Japanese literature is haunted— archetypally, aesthetically, and psychologically—by ghosts as defined here, then we may regard that literature also as an attempt to liberate these ghosts.[87]

The post-shingeki movement was quite literally a movement "to liberate Japanese ghosts," not to affirm them, but to acknowledge and negate them. Mori is arguing that in the realm of the novel this attempt to liberate Japanese ghosts (or gods)—to come to terms with death anxieties and provide artistic forms that could contain and express them—had been going on since the Meiji period. Mori's work suggests that the post-shingeki movement, far from being an aberration, was very much within the mainstream of modern Japanese life and literature.

The Relevance of the Post-Shingeki Movement

There is a remarkable scene in Satoh's *Nezumi Kozō: The Rat*, where the souls of the dead stream back and repossess the living. All duration is abolished; history ceases to exist. There is only the eternal present, a hell where human beings are condemned to eternal and escalating fits of self-destructive violence.[88]

There was an intense sense of urgency to the post-shingeki movement. It derived from the conviction that unless the Japanese could come to terms with the subliminal impulses of their culture, then the souls of the dead would indeed stream back to repossess the living, that unless the Japanese achieved a degree of self-transcendence, ceased in some fundamental way to *be* Japanese, they would be condemned to repeat *ad infinitum* the debacle of national destruction they had experienced in World War Two.[89]

This helps explain two special features of post-shingeki drama. First, in these plays "salvation" is virtually indistinguishable from damnation. Identification with and apotheosis into Kaison or Silver or the Beatles means abandoning historical time and responsibility and being sucked into the maelstrom of eternal redundancy. Second, the theme of ceasing to be Japanese runs throughout the plays. In *Kaison*, Hidemitsu concludes that the only way to resist Yukino's call, the siren's call of ahistorical being, is to leave Japan. In *My Beatles*, Chong tries desperately to shed his Japanese identity. In *The Beggar of Love*, the message is that to continue being Japanese will entail a repetition of the dreams of salvation responsible for past atrocities; that to prevent a repetition of past atrocities, the Japanese must cease being

Japanese. And *The Dance of Angels* defines the role of the theatre as a means to revolutionize the imagination and achieve self-transcendence.

These plays are Japanese and thus principally concerned with Japanese dilemmas. But their message has far-reaching implications for us all. The plays suggest that the root of our self-destruction, should it come, will lie in our own imagination. These plays argue that if we are to survive, we must alter the structure of our imagination and achieve self-transcendence, that we must cease in fundamental ways to be the people we are. And they attempt to develop a practical method to alter the imagination and achieve that transcendence.

The message and method of post-shingeki drama has relevance for us in America. In a perceptive review of the film *Platoon*, which depicts the Vietnam War, William Adams described what this relevance might be.

> "I keep thinking," Michael Herr writes in *Dispatches*, "about all the kids who got wiped out by seventeen years of war movies before coming to Vietnam to get wiped out for good. . . . We'd all seen too many movies. . . ." It is a wonderful and horrible epigram. . . . Herr is surely right that many of those who fought in Vietnam cut their teeth on Audie Murphy and John Wayne, who were *our* Achilles and Aeneas, ancient longings in modern form. But Herr had, I think, something even more serious and bitterly ironic in mind; it was our imagination that killed us . . . we were seduced by notions of personal and collective heroism, prepared for destruction by dazzling images of virtue that were ultimately, and merely, deadly.[90]

Audie Murphy and Achilles, John Wayne and Aeneas. Identification with cultural archetypes in modern garb. It is our imagination that killed us in the past, and it is our imagination that will kill us in the future. Post-shingeki drama presents this message and a suggested program of action. It has relevance for us all.

Notes

Unless otherwise noted, all Japanese works cited were published in Tokyo.

1. Arnold Wesker, *The Kitchen, The Four Seasons, Their Very Own and Golden City*, revised ed. (Harmondsworth, Middlesex, England: Penguin Books, 1981), pp. 143–144.

2. *Wesker 68* took place from October 30 through November 16, 1968. Wesker's plays were performed in Nagoya, Niigata, Morioka, Kyoto, and Osaka in addition to Tokyo.

Three issues of a special *Wesker 68* newspaper, beautifully designed by Hirano Kōga, were published on August 31 (two issues) and October 25, 1968. The newspaper published excerpts from Wesker's political and theatrical writing, articles on the festival itself, and pieces on other aspects of the theatre, such as the Living Theatre's return to the United States in September 1968 after a four-year European exile.

I was involved tangentially in *Wesker 68*. I drafted the letter inviting Wesker to Japan, corresponded with the playwright in England before and after his visit, and contributed to the *Wesker 68* newspaper.

3. Among the troupes that took part were Haiyūza, Bungakuza, Mingei, Sanjūnin-kai, Seihai, Henshin, and Shinjinkai. Representatives of these troupes staged *The Wesker Trilogy*.

4. *Their Very Own and Golden City* was performed from June 18 through 25 in Tokyo, followed by performances in Kyoto, Osaka, Nagoya, and Yokohama.

5. Theatre Center 68 was originally an association of three troupes, Rokugatsu gekijō (The June Theatre), Jiyū gekijō (The Freedom Theatre), and Hakken-no-kai (The Association of Discovery). It was actually Rokugatsu gekijō (named to commemorate the June 1960 demonstrations) that performed the play.

6. George Steiner has explained the complex relationship between Jews and Marxism that informs Wesker's work: "The implication of the European and Russian Jew in Marxism had natural causes. As has often been said, the dream of a secular millennium—which is still alive in Georg Lukács and the master historian of hope, Ernst Bloch—relates the social utopia of communism to the messianic tradition. For both Jew and communist, history is a scenario of gradual humanization, an immensely difficult attempt by man to become man.... But from Eduard Bernstein to Pasternak, the involvement of the Jewish personality in communism and the Russian Revolution follows an ironic pattern. Nearly invariably it ends in dissent or heresy.... As Stalinism turned to nationalism and technocracy ... the revolutionary intelligentsia went to the wall. The Jewish Marxist, the Trotskyite, the socialist fellow-traveller were trapped in the ruins of utopia. The Jew who had joined communism in order to fight the Nazis, the Jewish communist who had broken with the party after the purge trials, fell into the net of the Hitler-Stalin pact." (George Steiner, *Language and Silence* [Harmondsworth, Middlesex, England: Penguin Books, 1969], pp. 127–128.)

7. Irving Howe, ed., *Classics of Modern Fiction* (New York: Harcourt, Brace and World, 1968), p. 5.

8. An English translation of Kikuchi's play is included in Donald Keene, ed., *Modern Japanese Literature* (New York: Grove Press, 1956), pp. 278–287.

9. The best short description of the continuity of Japanese theatre and folk religion is Jacob Raz, "Chinkon—From Folk Beliefs to Stage Conventions: Certain Recurring Folkloristic Elements in Japanese Theatre," *Mask und Kothurn* (1981), 27(1):5–18.

10. Frank Hoff and Willi Flindt, "The Life Structure of Noh: An English Version of Yokomichi Mario's Analysis of the Structure of Noh," *Concerned Theatre Japan* (1973), II(3–4):214 and *passim*.

11. A translation is included in James Brandon, *Kabuki: Five Classic Plays* (Cambridge, MA: Harvard University Press, 1975).

12. Refer to the chapters on kabuki in Donald Keene, *World Within Walls: Japa-*

nese Literature of the Pre-Modern Era, 1600–1867 (New York: Grove Press, 1976), pp. 438–476. Keene gives useful summaries of *Narukami* on pp. 440–441 and 568–569; and of *Yotsuya kaidan* on pp. 468 and 569–570.

13. Donald Keene, trans., *Chūshingura: The Treasury of Loyal Retainers* (New York: Columbia University Press, 1971).

14. Maruya Saiichi, *Chūshingura to wa nani ka* (Kōdansha, 1984). Maruya argues that *Chūshingura* is based on the ancient Japanese belief in evil spirits (*akuryō shinkō*).

15. I do not mean to imply that there are no "realistic" dramas in the classical theatre repertory. *Genzai nō* and *sewamono* are categories of realistic plays in the nō and kabuki repertories respectively.

16. A. Horie-Webber, "Modernisation of the Japanese Theatre: The Shingeki Movement," in W. B. Beasley, ed., *Modern Japan: Aspects of History, Literature, and Society* (Berkeley: University of California Press, 1977), p. 155.

17. The failure of attempts to modernize Kabuki is summarized in J. Thomas Rimer, *Toward a Modern Japanese Theatre: Kishida Kunio* (Princeton: Princeton University Press, 1974), chapter 2, "Modernization or Westernization: The Movement for a Modern Theatre in Japan before 1925," pp. 7–55.

18. See Brian Powell, "Japan's First Modern Theatre—The Tsukiji Shōgekijō and Its Company, 1924–1926," *Monumenta Nipponica* (1975), 30(1):69–85; and John Allyn, Jr., "The Tsukiji Little Theatre and the Beginnings of Modern Theatre in Japan" (Ph.D. diss., University of California-Los Angeles, 1970).

19. *Osanai Kaoru zenshū*, vol. 6 (Kyoto: Rinsen shoten, 1975), pp. 459–460. Emphasis in the original.

20. Kubo Sakae, *Land of Volcanic Ash*, tr. David G. Goodman, East Asia Papers 40 (Ithaca, NY: Cornell China Japan Program, 1986).

21. Kubo Sakae, *Shingeki no sho* (Shinchōsha, 1955), p. 43.

22. Quoted in *Gendai nihon gikyoku senshū*, vol. 9 (Hakusuisha, 1955), pp. 409–410.

23. *Haiyūza* produced Part One in 1948. The 1961 production was by the *Mingei* (People's Art) troupe.

24. Quoted in Senda Akihiko, "Kaisetsu," *Gendai nihon gikyoku taikei*, vol. 8 (San'ichi shobō, 1972), pp. 418–419.

This was the manifesto of Theatre Center 68/69, issued at a press conference conducted at *Jiyū gekijō* (The Freedom Theatre) on September 10, 1969. The manifesto reflects the thinking of the founding members of the troupe, including Satoh Makoto, Tsuno Kaitarō, and Saeki Ryūkō.

I also participated in this news conference as a founding member of the troupe and as editor of *Concerned Theatre Japan*, its English-language periodical. See *Asahi shimbun*, evening edition, September 24, 1969.

25. I have described four of these troupes in *Theatre Companies of the World*, ed. William C. Young and Colby H. Kullman (Westport, CT: Greenwood Press, 1986), pp. 110–125.

26. "Post-shingeki movement" is an adaptation of Senda Akihiko's coinage, *datsu shingeki undō*. (Senda Akihiko, *Hirakareta gekijō* [Shōbunsha, 1976], p. 119.) The most common term for this movement in the 1960s and 70s was *angura*, a perversion of "underground [theatre]." A slightly more descriptive term is *shōgekijō undō* or little theatre movement, which referred to the small storefront theatres many of the troupes employed.

27. Tsuno Kaitarō, "The Tradition of Modern Theatre in Japan," tr. David G. Good-

man, *The Canadian Theatre Review*, Fall 1978, p. 11.

Frank Hoff has explained how the reaffirmation of the premodern imagination by post-shingeki troupes in the 1960s affected acting. See "Killing the Self: How the Narrator Acts, *Asian Theatre Journal* (Spring 1985), II(1):1-27.

28. Horie-Webber, "Modernisation of the Japanese Theatre," pp. 148-149. The evolution of the Shinkyō troupe into Mingei is actually more complex than I am making it seem. A chart illustrating the various steps in the process appears as an appendix to Sugai Yukio, *Shingeki sono butai to rekishi, 1906-* (Kyūryūdō, 1967), no page number given.

29. Havens, *Artist and Patron in Postwar Japan: Dance, Music, Theater, and the Visual Arts, 1955-1980* (Princeton: Princeton University Press, 1982), p. 161. Havens' chapter on theatre is a valuable guide to the forces that shaped orthodox shingeki in the postwar period.

30. Kan Takayuki, *Sengo engeki: shingeki wa norikoerareta ka*, Asahi senshō 178 (Asahi shinbunsha, 1981), p. 86.

31. Fujita Shōzō, "Shōwa hachinen o chūshin to suru tenkō no jōkyō," in Shisō no kagaku kenkyūkai, ed., *Kyōdō kenkyū tenkō*, vol. 1 (Heibonsha, 1959), p. 35.

32. Robert Jay Lifton, Shūichi Katō, and Michael R. Reich, *Six Lives, Six Deaths: Portraits from Modern Japan* (New Haven: Yale University Press, 1979), p. 177.

33. On *tenkō*, see Kazuko Tsurumi, *Social Change and the Individual: Japan Before and After Defeat in World War II* (Princeton: Princeton University Press, 1970). This book is particularly useful because it compares and contrasts radicals in the 1930s and 1960s.

34. Kubo Sakae, *Land of Volcanic Ash*, pp. 12-13.

35. Okuno Takeo, "Kaisetsu," *Gendai nihon gikyoku taikei*, vol. 1 (San'ichi shobō, 1971), p. 453. See also my essay, "Shingeki Under the Occupation," in *The Occupation of Japan: Arts and Culture* (Norfolk: MacArthur Memorial, forthcoming).

36. Short for *Kinrōsha engeki kyōgikai.*

37. For more on *Rōen*, see Havens, *Artist and Patron in Postwar Japan*, pp. 152-158.

38. Obase Takuzō, "Idainaru haiboku no kinenhi," *Shingeki*, November 1961, pp. 2-12.

39. Sartre's play was staged by the Waseda Theatre Study Group (*Waseda engeki kenkyūkai* or *Waseda gekiken*) in late 1960. It was the Group's first production following the climax of the Security Treaty struggle in June. Tsuno Kaitarō codirected, and many others associated with the post-shingeki movement were involved.

40. I describe their reasoning at length in my introduction to *Find Hakamadare!* below.

41. These are the theatrical and political origins of the post-shingeki movement. The history of modern Japanese theatre is complex, however, and there have been important playwrights like Miyoshi Jūrō, who have opposed the orthodox shingeki movement and others, like Mishima Yukio, for whom it was irrelevant. Nevertheless, what I have described is, I believe, the mainstream of modern Japanese drama.

The same thing is true for the period of the 1960s. The five plays translated here are representative of the period. They are by writers, all of whom are still active, who shaped Japanese drama and changed it irrevocably. Other playwrights, notably Terayama Shūji, Betsuyaku Minoru, and Shimizu Kunio, were also influential and deserve attention in another context.

42. The thought of Walter Benjamin is directly relevant to the post-shingeki movement and particularly to the work of those involved with the Black Tent Theatre (Theatre Center) 68/71. As editor-in-chief of Shōbunsha, Tsuno Kaitarō was responsible for publishing Benjamin's complete works in Japan; and Satoh Makoto has quoted Benjamin frequently in epigraphs to his plays. See *Abe Sada no inu* (Abe Sada's Dogs; Shōbunsha, 1976); *Kinema to kaijin* (The Phantom of the Cinema; Shōbunsha, 1976); and *Blanqui-goroshi shanhai no haru* (The Killing of Blanqui, Spring in Shanghai; Shōbunsha, 1979). Benjamin also inspired Satoh's *Yoru to yoru no yoru* (Night of Night's Night; Shōbunsha 1981).

43. David G. Goodman, ed. and trans., *After Apocalypse: Four Japanese Plays of Hiroshima and Nagasaki* (New York: Columbia University Press, 1986).

44. The term "symbolic immortality" was coined by Robert Jay Lifton to describe the "compelling and universal inner quest for a continuous symbolic relationship between our finite individual lives and what has gone before and what will come after. It is a search for symbolizing continuities, despite the discontinuities of death." (Lifton, Katō, and Reich, *Six Lives, Six Deaths*, pp. 7 and *passim*.)

Lifton has developed a theory of human psychology and its relationship to culture and history based on what he sees as humanity's quest for symbolic immortality. The major statement of this theory is Robert Jay Lifton, *The Broken Connection: On Death and the Continuity of Life* (New York: Simon and Schuster, 1979). Lifton describes this theory more succinctly in his article, "The Sense of Immortality: On Death and the Continuity of Life," in Robert Jay Lifton, ed., *Explorations in Psychohistory* (New York: Simon and Schuster, 1974), pp. 271–287.

45. *The Myth of the Eternal Return, Or, Cosmos and History*, tr. Willard R. Trask, Bollingen Series 46 (Princeton: Princeton University Press, 1971), p. 151.

46. Critic Kogarimai Ken explicitly identified Kaison with the emperor system. See Kogarimai Ken, *Hyōi to kamen* (Serika shobō, 1972), pp. 74–75.

47. John Lahr, "The Beatles Considered," *The New Republic*, December 2, 1981, p. 22. I quote Lahr in full in the epigraph to my introduction to *My Beatles*.

48. Lifton has shown how both nuclear weapons and the Nazi death camps are expressions of the quest for revitalization and, paradoxically, the conquest of death. See Robert Jay Lifton and Richard Falk, *Indefensible Weapons: The Political and Psychological Case Against Nuclearism* (New York: Basic Books, 1982), pp. 3–125; and Robert Jay Lifton, *The Nazi Doctors: Medical Killing and the Psychology of Genocide* (New York: Basic Books, 1986).

49. Ōzasa Yoshio, *Dōjidai engeki to gekisakka-tachi* (Geki shobō, 1980), p. 25.

50. "The Tradition of Modern Theatre in Japan," p. 19.

51. Lifton, Katō, and Reich, *Six Lives, Six Deaths*, p. 199.

52. Hori Ichirō has written on the survival and institutionalization of Japanese folk religion in the modern period. See Hori, "The New Religions and the Survival of Shamanic Tendencies," *Folk Religion in Japan: Continuity and Change*, ed. Joseph M. Kitagawa and Alan L. Miller (Chicago: University of Chicago Press, 1968), pp. 217–251.

53. See Hori, *Folk Religion in Japan*, pp. 224–238.

54. "The pressure of social unrest and dissatisfaction within the *collectivum* of the folk culture, and the expectation of a new, ideal time [*naori-yo* and *miroku-yo*], increased by the catalyzing tension of a collectively and numinously experienced earthquake disaster, found an outlet in the religiously-charged representations of the collective medium of namazu [catfish] prints. . . . Now, the striking thing is that these prints,

which are *in form* entirely *profane* are peopled by the essentially sacred, ambivalent trickster figure of the namazu, and the content of the representations—embodied in and 'acted' by this namazu-trickster—is often dressed in forms of seemingly profane *humour* and *personification* on the human level." (C. Ouwehand, *Namazu-e and Their Themes: An Interpretative Approach to Some Aspects of Japanese Folk Religion* [Leiden: E. J. Brill, 1964], pp. 238–239. Emphasis in the original.)

55. See Hirosue Tamotsu, "Ekin," *Concerned Theatre Japan* (Summer 1970), I(2):101–124. A film about Ekin, *The Scandalous Adventures of Buraikan (Buraikan)*, with a screenplay by Terayama Shūji and directed by Shinoda Masahiro, was also released in 1970.

56. Satoh's *Nezumi Kozō: The Rat* is a good example. For the text and an analysis of this play, see my *After Apocalypse*, pp. 249–319. Many of Kara's plays, including *Yui Shōsetsu* and *Koshimaki Osen*, also exemplify this phenomenon.

57. Although not exactly, my notion of an "underlying mythological formulation" corresponds to concepts that have been proposed by others. It corresponds, for example, to what Foucault calls an *episteme*, the "positive unconscious of knowledge" that governs science and the arts in a given age. (Michel Foucault, *The Order of Things: An Archaelogy of the Human Sciences* [London: Tavistock, 1970], p. xi.)

It corresponds also to one sense of what Kuhn means by a paradigm, "the entire constellation of beliefs, values, techniques, and so on shared by members of a given community." (Thomas S. Kuhn, *The Structure of Scientific Revolutions*, 2nd ed. [Chicago: University of Chicago Press, 1962, 1970], p. 175.)

Kan has already used Kuhn's term in his history of postwar Japanese theatre. He argues that the transition from shingeki to post-shingeki represented a "paradigm shift" in modern Japanese theatre. (Kan, *Sengo engeki*, pp. 11–13 and *passim*.) I agree with Kan, but I wish to probe into the mythological and theological roots of the overt changes he describes.

In this sense, my idea of an "underlying mythological formulation" corresponds most closely to the approach taken by LaFleur, who adapts Foucault's concept of an *episteme* to the Japanese context. LaFleur argues that medieval Japan was governed by a Buddhist *episteme* and that the medieval period in Japan can be defined as the "epoch during which the basic intellectual problems, the most authoritative texts and resources, and the central symbols were all Buddhist." (William R. LaFleur, *The Karma of Words: Buddhism and the Literary Arts in Medieval Japan* [Berkeley: University of California Press, 1983], p. 9.)

I am not comfortable with either the term *"episteme"* or "paradigm"; nor can what I am identifying be conveniently described with adjectives like "Buddhist" or "Christian." I do share LaFleur's approach, however, in relating and interrelating literary texts with a shared, underlying, and basically religious substratum that I call, for lack of a better term, a mythological formulation.

58. Saeki argues, in fact, that Kishida's views on the theatre were almost completely derived from Copeau. See Saeki Ryūkō, "Kishida Kunio o yomu," *Hōkō no shukusai* (Asahi shuppansha, 1986), especially pp. 413–418. See also J. Thomas Rimer, *Toward A Modern Japanese Theatre: Kishida Kunio* (Princeton: Princeton University Press, 1974), pp. 59–60. Kishida came under Copeau's influence in the period that culminated in the French director's conversion to Catholicism in 1925.

59. See Tanaka's *The Head of Mary* and my discussion of his work in *After Apocalypse*, pp. 105–181. Regarding Fukuda, see Benito Ortolani, "Fukuda Tsuneari: Mod-

ernization and Shingeki," in Donald H. Shively, ed., *Tradition and Modernization in Japanese Culture* (Princeton: Princeton University Press, 1971), p. 474 and *passim*; and Fukuda Tsuneari and Takeuchi Yoshimi, "Gendaiteki jōkyō to chishikijin no sekinin," *Tenbō*, September 1965, p. 25.

60. Takeda Kiyoko, "Kinoshita Junji ni okeru genzai ishiki," *Haikyōsha no keifu*, Iwanami shinsho 862 (Iwanami shoten, 1973), pp. 139–217. See also Kinoshita Junji, *Between God and Man*, tr. Eric J. Gangloff (Tokyo University Press, 1979), and my review of the work in *The Journal of the Association of Teachers of Japanese* (1978), XIV(2):214–219.

61. See, for example, Yashiro Seiichi, *Kami, hito, soshite ai* (Seibunsha, 1977).

62. David G. Goodman, "Satoh Makoto and the Post-Shingeki Movement in Japanese Contemporary Theatre" (Ph.D. diss., Cornell University, 1982), pp. 94–95.

63. *Kindai nihon kiristokyō bungaku zenshū*, vol. 12 (Kyōbunkan, 1981), an anthology of Japanese Christian plays, contains works by eight more authors, none of whom I have mentioned, including Mushakōji Saneatsu, Akutagawa Ryūnosuke, Arishima Takeo, Masamune Hakuchō, Miyoshi Jūrō, and Katō Michio.

64. Christians comprise less than one percent of the Japanese population.

65. See the epigraph to this volume.

Richard Wolin explains Benjamin's parable as follows: "By way of this parable Benjamin seeks to call attention to the fact that historical materialism—especially in face of its manifest failure to meet the threat of fascism in the 1930s—remains in and of itself incapable of providing humanity with the full range of wisdom and understanding necessary to surmount the realm of historical necessity. This explicit return to the Messianic philosophy of history of his early work . . . signifies not a hasty appeal, made in an hour of historical despair, to a suprahistorical redeemer, but instead an acknowledgment of the fact that in its reliance on the Enlightenment myth of historical progress, historical materialism has remained a prisoner of the same logic it wanted to transcend." (Richard Wolin, *Walter Benjamin: An Aesthetic of Redemption* [New York: Columbia University Press, 1982], pp. 260–261.)

66. *Ika suru jikan*, pp. 76–77; "The Eternal Recanter," *Concerned Theatre Japan*, II(1–2):112.

67. Wolin, *Walter Benjamin*, p. 269.

68. The post-shingeki movement is often referred to as the "little theatre movement" (*shōgekijō undō*). Theatre Center 68/71 (also known as the Black Tent Theatre) and Kara's red tent are the most prominent examples of mobile tent theatres. Both are still in use.

69. See, for example, the original prospectus for Theatre Center 68/71 in *Concerned Theatre Japan* (Autumn 1970), I(3):13–15. See also the "Document" and "Conversation" in *Concerned Theatre Japan* (Winter-Spring, 1971), I(4):28–52, which communicate a sense of the excitement and liberation that accompanied the production of *The Dance of Angels Who Burn Their Own Wings*, the first play produced in Theatre Center 68/71's black tent.

70. Hori writes, "One of the most significant religious phenomena in Japan after World War II has been a sudden rise of new religious movements. Sprouting up like mushrooms after a rain, they amounted to more than seven hundred sects at the peak. . . . This phenomenon should be understood as a response to the acute anomie into which the Japanese people were thrown by defeat and occupation." (Hori, *Folk Religion in Japan*, pp. 217–218.)

Lifton, Katō, and Reich describe this "anomie" as an "undermining or at least weakening of virtually all forms of symbolic immortality among the Japanese, especially emperor-centered cultural chauvinism and deification of various political-national institutions." (Lifton, Katō, and Reich, *Six Lives, Six Deaths*, p. 16.)

71. George R. Packard III, *Protest in Tokyo: The Security Treaty Crisis of 1960* (Westport, CT: Greenwood Press, 1978), p. 262.

72. Here is what happened: "On May 19, Socialist Diet members staged a sit-in in the Lower House in an effort to prevent the opening of the session and police were called in to remove them. The same night, a little after midnight, remaining conservatives, in a dubious parliamentary maneuver, voted to extend the session and then, with no protest, quickly passed the treaty. The government's strong-arm tactics aroused immediate response from the press as well as large numbers of university students and professors, labor leaders, and politicians, who denounced the ruling Liberal Democratic party—and Prime Minister Kishi Nobusuke—as deceitful and antidemocratic.

"Protests escalated rapidly, and on June [15], 1,000 demonstrators were injured in clashes with the special riot police and a female student, Kamba Michiko, was trampled and died. On June 19, 300,000 demonstrators gathered outside the Diet and demanded its dissolution, but that midnight, one month after the treaty's unusual approval by parliament, the agreement automatically went into effect." (Lifton, Katō, and Reich, *Six Lives, Six Deaths*, p. 255.)

73. Packard, *Protest in Tokyo*, pp. 327–328.

74. Ōzasa, *Dōjidai engeki to gekisakka-tachi*, p. 34.

75. Lifton, Katō, and Reich, *Six Lives, Six Deaths*, p. 255.

76. Mishima Yukio, "Patriotism," tr. Geoffrey W. Sargent, *Death in Midsummer*, ed. Donald Keene (New York: New Directions, 1966), p. 111.

77. Mishima was a disciple of the Japanese Romantic School (*Nihon roman-ha*) to which Tsuno was referring in his statement. See Lifton, Katō, and Reich, *Six Lives, Six Deaths*, pp. 245–246 and 257.

78. In addition to the chapter on Mishima already cited in Lifton, Katō, and Reich, *Six Lives, Six Deaths*, pp. 231–274; see John Nathan, *Mishima: A Biography* (Boston: Little, Brown and Co., 1974) for a thorough analysis of the Mishima phenomenon.

79. Mishima's solution may also prove to be dangerous. See Ian Buruma, "A New Japanese Nationalism," *The New York Times Magazine*, April 12, 1987, pp. 23–29; 38. I do not agree with Buruma's conclusions, but I share with him a belief that Japanese neonationalism should be taken seriously.

80. Ōe Kenzaburō, *Teach Us to Outgrow Our Madness*, tr. John Nathan (New York: Grove Press, 1974), p. xvii.

81. *A Personal Matter*, tr. John Nathan (New York: Grove Press, 1969), p. 64; and *Hiroshima Notes*, tr. Toshi Yonezawa (Tokyo: YMCA Press, 1981), pp. 106–107.

82. Ōe, *Hiroshima Notes*, p. 76.

83. Ōe, *A Personal Matter*, pp. 152–153; 193–194, for example.

84. Ōe, *A Personal Matter*, p. 213.

85. Michiko N. Wilson, *The Marginal World of Ōe Kenzaburo: A Study in Themes and Techniques* (Armonk, NY: M. E. Sharpe, 1986), pp. 81–82.

86. Ōe Kenzaburō, *Atarashii hito yo mezame yo* (Kōdansha, 1983).

87. Mori Jōji, "The Liberation of Japanese Ghosts," in Jack Bailey, ed., *Listening to Japan* (New York: Praeger, 1973), pp. 23; 27. Mori has also published a full-length study of modern Japanese literature in Japanese under the equivalent title, *Nihon no yūrei*

no kaihō (Shōbunsha, 1974).

88. *After Apocalypse*, pp. 310–316.

89. Ōe makes a similar suggestion in *A Personal Matter*, p. 194, where he speculates about the possible existence of "lemming people" who hope for human annihilation. "In fact," Ōe writes, "[Bird] was aware of a black-hearted lemming presence whispering through himself."

90. William Adams, *"Platoon*: Of Heroes and Demons," *Dissent*, Summer 1987, p. 383.

Lifton also analyzes what he calls the "John Wayne thing" in Robert Jay Lifton, *Home from the War—Vietnam Veterans: Neither Victims nor Executioners* (New York: Simon and Schuster, 1973), pp. 219-220 and *passim*.

FIND HAKAMADARE!

Commentary

> It is too early to know—but it will be interesting to observe—whether the "ampo spirit" [of the 1960 demonstrations] finally takes root in the popular culture, or whether these efforts were a kind of leftist *gagaku* with symbols and appeal exclusively for the leftist cultural elite.
>
> George R. Packard III (1966)[1]

Writing in the early 1970s, Ellis S. Krauss answered Packard's question in the affirmative: "The experience of the 1960 treaty crisis was so salient as to create a generation of students who, to this day, are referred to as the 'Ampo generation' and whose leaders' names became household words in Japan."[2]

Post-shingeki drama derived its immediate impetus from the political experience of 1960. It grew out of the need to develop new goals and patterns of movement that could supplant the discredited Stalinist style of the Old Left. It raised fundamental questions about the ultimate goals of the left-wing movement and reflected the evolving thought of the New Left in the 1960s.

Seigei: The Youth Art Theatre

In November 1959, twenty members of the third graduating class of the Mingei drama school joined playwright Fukuda Yoshiyuki, nō actor

Kanze Hideo, and composer Hayashi Hikaru to found *Seigei*, the Youth Art Theatre.[3] The troupe became one of the most important spawning grounds for the post-shingeki movement. Three of the playwrights represented in this anthology (Fukuda, Kara, and Satoh) were affiliated with this troupe, and it produced pioneering works, including Fukuda's *Find Hakamadare!* and Betsuyaku Minoru's *The Elephant* (*Zō*, 1962).[4]

Kanze recalls how the troupe was created:

> Seigei was born out of the frustration felt by the young theatre people who were part of the *Shingekijin kaigi* (Conference of Modern Theatre Artists) that was formed to participate in the anti-United States-Japan Mutual Security Treaty struggle. They were frustrated because of the way the demonstrations were being organized and conducted by the old guard. As soon as things started getting serious, we were always told to disperse and go home. I was always in the demonstrations and felt frustrated, too. As far as the theatre itself was concerned, I found the productions of the big companies like Haiyūza and Mingei boring and irrelevant.[5]

The 1960 renewal of the U.S.-Japan Mutual Security Treaty is one of the most significant issues in postwar Japanese history.[6] For months, the nation was convulsed by debate over whether the Treaty should be renewed. Massive protests culminated on June 15, 1960, when demonstrators forced their way into the Diet compound and one of their number, Kamba Michiko, was killed.

The Security Treaty debate concerned whether Japan should in effect ally itself with the West by renewing the agreement that permits U.S. military bases on Japanese soil. The alternative proposed by the Old Left, principally the Japanese Communist Party (JCP), seemed to the younger generation merely to substitute an alliance with the Soviet Union for the existing relationship with the West, a prospect they found at least as repugnant. Instead, the young demonstrators envisioned a neutral and nonaligned position for Japan, both politically and culturally. The post-shingeki movement was an expression of this desire to create an independent Japanese culture.

The shingeki establishment was closely allied with the JCP. Many of the members of the movement, if not actually Party members, were sympathetic with the Party and its goals. Furthermore, the Party had helped shingeki survive after the war. Through Rōen, the JCP had helped organize audiences for shingeki productions in exchange for prepackaged cultural programs that enhanced the Party's image and furthered its policies.

The frustration Kanze describes resulted from the inability of the members of Seigei to accept Party discipline during the 1960 demonstrations. The troupe allied itself instead with the anti-JCP "mainstream" faction of *Zengakuren*, the Japanese student movement, and clad in identical blue neckerchiefs, spearheaded the shingeki contingent in the demonstrations. This boldness made Seigei seem heroic to younger theatre people and "Trotskyite" to the shingeki establishment.[7]

Kanze's sense that the theatrical activities of the major shingeki troupes were irrelevant to contemporary concerns also relates to shingeki's relationship with the Communist movement. Orthodox shingeki had been dominated by socialist realism since the 1930s. Surveying the works of dramatic theory translated and published in Japan in the 1940s and 50s, for example, Kan Takayuki found a heavy emphasis on Russian and Soviet theory. According to Kan, only one volume of Brecht's theatre essays was published during this period, and the heterodox ideas of Piscator, Reinhardt, and Meyerhold, not to mention the legacy of expressionism and surrealism, were largely ignored.[8]

To Kan and others of his generation, therefore, "realism" was not simply one style of theatre among many, but a pernicious ideology that actively sought to repress all heterodox tendencies.[9] This helps to explain the deep and acrimonious split that developed between orthodox shingeki and its young opponents: Seigei appeared Trotskyite to the leaders of the shingeki movement, and orthodox shingeki appeared Stalinist to them.

Document Number 1

Political dissent influenced the repertory of Seigei. The troupe mounted its first production in October 1960. Alongside two prewar plays very much in the shingeki tradition, the troupe staged Fukuda Yoshiyuki's *Kiroku nambaa 1* (Document Number 1), which dramatized the troupe's experience in the recent demonstrations.[10]

Document Number 1 represents a pivotal moment in the history of the Japanese modern theatre movement. Fukuda had begun his playwriting career in the mainstream of the shingeki movement. His first major work, *Nagai bohyō no retsu* (A Long Row of Tombstones, 1957), was written under the influence of Kubo Sakae and Kinoshita Junji.[11] It was an accomplished historical drama that portrayed the events surrounding the dismissal of liberal economist Kawai Eijirō from the faculty of Tokyo Imperial University in the late 1930s. In the spirit of *Land of Volcanic Ash* and Kinoshita's *Fūrō* (Turbulent Times), the play addresses questions of individual integrity and academic freedom in a repressive age.

Fukuda has described *Document Number 1* and its relation to the 1960 demonstrations. His account is worth quoting at length.

> On June 15, at the height of the 1960 struggle against the Mutual Security Treaty, a group of protestors organized around members of the shingeki movement was attacked by a band of right-wingers.[12] I was standing on top of a loudspeaker truck at the time, clutching a microphone. Somebody somewhere had dreamed up a policy of "passive dispersal," and I had been put in the unenviable position of implementing that policy even as I opposed it. It's fair to say that I discovered the members of the newly formed Youth Art Theatre as comrades at that moment. They were acting on the basis of the thesis that "you should do everything that is required of you and then go ahead on your own." I was functioning on the same basis, and eventually Kanze Hideo joined us. That about sums up what happened.
>
> After the excitement of the Security Treaty crisis quieted down, we resumed preparations for the our first production. The program was to be *Umi no yūsha*, Kikuchi Kan's adaptation of *Riders to the Sea*, and Kinoshita Mokutarō's *Izumiya somemonoten* (Izumiya Dye Shop), but as I watched the rehearsals, I suggested that we also include a *schprechchor*.[13] I interviewed members of the troupe about their experiences during the demonstrations and wrote *Document Number 1* in a matter of days. . . .
>
> The *Izumiya Dye Shop* deals with [the attempt by anarchists and socialists to assassinate Emperor Meiji in 1910]. As the play ended, the curtain was lowered, only to be raised again immediately. Naturally, the stage was still filled with the *Izumiya* set, and the actors were still in their costumes. One of the actors turned to the audience, thanked them for coming to the theatre, and said that he'd like to explain how the troupe came into being. As he was speaking, the set was being dismantled by the other actors who, as they removed their makeup, joined him in addressing the audience. Of course, the actors used their real names and described their personal experiences, my fictional embellishments not compromis-

ing the essential truthfulness of their accounts. As the discussion progressed, there were scenes for free discussion and for ensemble movement; the content of the debate alternated between fantasy and documentary plays-within-the-play; and the actors oscillated freely between "themselves" and their numerous "roles." In this way, the documentary record of the troupe up to that day simultaneously became an account of the anti-Security Treaty struggle. . . .

Document Number 1 . . . was the direct result of my experience of the 1950s and of the 1960 demonstrations. I had written *Fuji sanroku* (The Foot of Mt. Fuji) [with Fujita Asaya] in 1953 and *A Long Row of Tombstones* in 1957, but it was only with *Document Number 1*, written for Seigei, that I developed a real sense of my own direction as a playwright. . . .

Even though I was not really capable of dealing with it consciously at the time, what was present there was the idea, or rather the feeling, that the members of the troupe were the real heroes of the theatre. In Seigei there was no special directorial contingent; the actors all fulfilled that function in turn, and so in *Document Number 1* the actors were the masters of the stage in every sense. . . . In the idiom of his times, Trotsky referred to "the masses" as "steam," "the energy that makes things move." . . . I came to conceive of actors as being akin to those masses. . . .

Change worthy of the name always takes place when the spontaneous energy of the masses transcends all leadership. Social change occurs when the flow of spontaneous feeling and instinct, at times erupting into anarchistic violence, is united with a similarly spontaneous organizational or systematic component. If one is an optimist and believes in the continuity of this sort of movement, that is anarchism. On the other hand, as Trotsky says in the introduction to his *History of the Russian Revolution*, "Without a guiding organization the energy of the masses would dissipate like steam not enclosed in a piston-box." Nevertheless, he continues, "what moves things is not the piston or the box, but the steam."[14]

In short, *Document Number 1* introduced a new formulation of the theatre that grew out of the political experience of 1960 and that challenged every aspect of shingeki orthodoxy. In place of socialist realism, Seigei introduced a presentational style inspired by Bertolt Brecht.[15] Unlike shingeki, where the text was central, Seigei's actors were conceived as the basic force driving the entire theatrical enterprise, and their relationship with the audience was no longer construed as that of edifier to edified, as had been the case in orthodox shingeki, but of equals engaged in a dialogue. Involvement in the demonstrations and the use of agitprop techniques had established, at least in principle, the possibility of performing theatre outside the proscenium stage, and the new emphasis on spontaneity and independence that grew out of the rejection of bureaucratic Party discipline was quickly translated into a rejection of the bureaucratic company system that characterized troupes like Mingei.

Find Hakamadare!

Fukuda wrote *Find Hakamadare!* in two weeks in April 1964. Seigei staged the play in May. It was directed by Kanze Hideo with music by Hayashi Hikaru.

The play concerns a group of impoverished peasants living some time between the ninth and the sixteenth century who set out to find their long-awaited savior, a Robin Hood-like outlaw named Hakamadare. Since they don't know who or where Hakamadare is, they decide to attract his attention by impersonating him. They hope that he will hear of their activities and be angered enough to come after them. In the meantime, they act as they imagine Hakamadare would, stealing from the rich and giving to the poor. Eventually, the real Hakamadare does appear, but he is not the benevolent redeemer they had expected. He is instead a cynical, rapacious tyrant. Given the choice between their dream and reality, the peasants choose their dream. Rather than submit to Hakamadare, who is authentic but flawed, they decide to adhere to their ideal, which, though fantasy, is perfect. They kill Hakamadare and continue their quest.

Find Hakamadare! is a critique of Stalinism and embodies the same philosophy about popular movements that Fukuda expressed in his account of *Document Number 1. Hakamadare no tō* is the Japanese expression for what I have translated as "Hakamadare's band." *Tō* is the Japanese word for political party, and so it is clearer in the original text than in the translation that Fukuda is talking about alternative conceptions of "the Party."

The real Hakamadare represents Stalinism, the amoral party of real politics and undiluted power.[16] In Act Seven, after he makes his identity known, Hakamadare describes his plan to bring all the peasants who are impersonating him under his control and create a vast and powerful party organization. This party organization will have two contingents: a public contingent that will be moral and nurture the good will of the masses, and a clandestine contingent that will use any means to amass power. The public contingent will enhance the party's image and the morale of its adherents; the clandestine contingent will pursue the party's ultimate goal of seizing control of the state.

The peasants are horrified by Hakamadare's cynicism. They had seen themselves and the party as part of a moral crusade, so when Hakamadare tries to coerce them into rejecting their ideal and submitting to his "reality," they rebel. They refuse to submit to the tyranny of party discipline or the cult of one man's personality. Theirs is the real party, a party of the masses, spontaneous popular energy harnessed by an equally spontaneous organizational component.[17]

Sources and Interpretations

As Fukuda writes in his introductory comments, *Find Hakamadare!* is based on medieval Japanese legends. Fukuda acknowledges elsewhere, however, that the real inspiration for the play came from the literature of modern China.[18] A story by Ma Shitu called "Searching for the Red Army" (*Zhao hong jun*) was of particular importance. The story concerns a peasant named Wang Tianlin who, having heard of a band of righteous outlaws called the Red Army, sets out to join them. He wanders aimlessly until he meets other peasants who share his aspiration, and they begin announcing themselves as the Red Army in the hope that the real Red Army will hear of them and make contact. Their hopes are not realized, however, and eventually they are surrounded by the Kuomintang and destroyed. Only Wang survives. He joins the Kuomintang, where he goes to work as a cook and continues to search for the Red Army. The story is told by a Communist agent who has infiltrated the Kuomintang and hears Wang's tale. After completing his story, Wang Tianlin turns to the agent and says, "But now my quest is over. I have found the Red Army: it is you."[19]

Another source of inspiration was *Ninja bugeichō* (Ninja Chronicles), the multivolume comic-book epic created by Shirato Sanpei between 1959 and 1962. Frederik Schodt has described the aspects of Shirato's work that fascinated Fukuda and his generation:

Ninja Bugeichō, with its stress on class consciousness and reform, had a special appeal to university students and intellectuals, who called its theme one of "historical materialism." Student newspapers printed commentaries on it and recommended that their readers learn from it. For many, *Ninja Bugeichō* became a substitute for reading Marx.[20]

Find Hakamadare! thus combines classical Japanese literary sources with contemporary political experience and pop art. It is more than a political fable, however. It is an exploration of the millenarian roots of modern Communism.

The theological, millenarian dimension of the play is unmistakable. The villagers first hear of Hakamadare from a dying priest. Each man receives the revelation of imminent salvation individually and nurtures his private vision until he discovers that everyone else shares his dream. The villagers discuss the prophecy, and although they differ on the details, they agree that with the arrival of Hakamadare, history as they have known it will cease and they will enter the "Hakamadarean Age" (*Hakamadare no yo*), when death will be overcome ("dead trees will put out leaves") and men will come to experience "bliss like they've never known." *Hakamadare no yo* intentionally echoes a millenarian Buddhist term, *Miroku no yo*, "the Age of Maitreya," the so-called Buddhist Messiah.[21] There will be a fundamental change in the order of being in the Hakamadarean Age, a change so radical that it cannot be anticipated on the basis of present experience. The believers do everything in their power to hasten the coming of Hakamadare, the messiah, but when he actually appears, he proves to be false. Rather than abandon their dream, they ignore the empirical evidence and continue to pursue their ideal.

Find Hakamadare! reveals that while the post-shingeki movement evolved out of the political experience of 1960 the question at its root was the relationship between revolution and redemption, utopia and millennium, politics and the messiah. In the plays that followed, this question was examined with increasing intensity and insight.

Notes

1. George R. Packard III, *Protest in Tokyo: The Security Treaty Crisis of 1960* (Princeton: Princeton University Press, 1966), p. 319.
2. Ellis S. Krauss, *Japanese Radicals Revisited: Student Protest in Postwar Ja-*

pan (Berkeley: University of California Press, 1974), p. 5.

3. *Seigei* is short for *Seinen geijutsu gekijō*.

4. Included in *After Apocalypse: Four Japanese Plays of Hiroshima and Nagasaki* (New York: Columbia University Press, 1986), pp. 183–248.

5. "Noh Business," *Concerned Theatre Japan* (Winter-Spring 1971), I(4):13. An abbreviated version of this interview also appeared in *The Drama Review* (Spring 1971), 15(3):185–192. The interview was conducted on November 29, 1970, by David G. Goodman, Fujimoto Kazuko, and Yamamoto Kiyokazu.

6. For a thorough discussion of the 1960 Security Treaty Crisis, see George R. Packard, *Protest in Tokyo*.

7. Kan, *Sengo engeki: Shingeki wa norikoerareta ka*, Asahi sensho 178 (Asahi shimbunsha, 1981), p. 150.

8. Kan, *Sengo engeki*, pp. 126–127.

9. See Kan's comment quoted in the introduction to this volume.

10. The text of this play may be found in *Dōjidai engeki* (June 1970), I(2):85–105.

11. Kinoshita was a disciple of Kubo and wrote his first play, *Fūrō* (Turbulent Times), under his influence. Kinoshita compares *Nagai bohyō no retsu* favorably to *Fūrō*, and Fukuda publicly acknowledges Kinoshita as his mentor. Kinoshita Junji, "*Nagai bohyō no retsu* ni tsuite," *Kinoshita Junji hyōron-shū*, vol. 5 (Miraisha, 1974), pp. 257–258. Fukuda Yoshiyuki, *Fukuda Yoshiyuki daini sakuhin-shū: oppekepe, hakamadare wa doko da* (San'ichi shobō, 1967), p. 253.

12. Packard recounts what happened. "At 5:15 P.M. on the opposite side of the compound, a scuffle broke out between a demonstrating Modern Drama Group (*Shingekidan*) and 200 rightists in the Renovation Action Corps (*Ishin Kōdōtai*) when the rightists drove their truck into the midst of the marchers." *Protest in Tokyo*, p. 295.

13. An agitprop choral drama.

14. Fukuda Yoshiyuki, "Shibai to minshū to," *Dentō to sōzō*, ed. Hirosue Tamotsu, *Dentō to gendai*, vol. 12 (Gakugei shorin, 1971), pp. 62–65.

This translation is from Leon Trotsky, *The Russian Revolution*, tr. Max Eastman (New York: Doubleday Anchor), p. xi.

15. Fukuda explicitly acknowledges his debt to Brecht and specifically to the German playwright's agitprop drama *The Measures Taken*. See "Shibai to minshū to," pp. 63–64. Significantly, *The Measures Taken*, which Brecht forbid to be performed shortly after he wrote it in 1930, was given its first full-scale production in Japan in 1980 under the direction of Satoh Makoto. For details of this production see the discussion between Satoh Makoto and Kanze Hideo, "Naze *shochi* ka" in *Shingeki*, (February 1981) 334:124–132.

16. It is interesting to note certain congruencies between Hakamadare and the young Stalin. Robert Tucker writes, for example, that as a student Stalin was deeply impressed by *The Patricide*, a novel by the Georgian romantic writer Alexander Kazbegi. Stalin identified with the novel's hero, Koba, and enjoyed being called by his name. Koba, like Hakamadare, leads a Robin Hood existence in the mountains. "Besides furnishing Soso [Stalin] with an idealized image of the hero as avenger," Tucker writes, the novel "conveyed to him the message that vindictive triumph is a cause to which a person can worthily devote his life."

Tucker also notes how the young Stalin tried to emulate Koba. Around 1905, "in various sections of the country, including Transcaucasia, fighting groups of the party carried out a series of 'expropriations,' i.e., armed robberies of banks, mail coaches, and so on. . . . While never a direct participant, [Stalin] functioned behind the scenes as the planner and organizer of various 'expropriations.'" See Robert C. Tucker, *Stalin as Revolutionary, 1879-1929* (New York: Norton, 1973), pp. 79-81 and 102-103. I am grateful to Christopher Phillips for bringing Tucker's book to my attention.

17. For an enlightening comparison with the American experience, see Richard Wright's description of his membership in the Communist Party excerpted in Richard Crossman, ed., *The God That Failed* (New York: Harper and Row, 1963), pp. 115-162. Vivian Gornick has also written an account of the American experience of Stalinism. See Vivian Gornick, *The Romance of American Communism* (New York: Basic Books, 1977), esp. pp. 3-27.

18. *Fukuda Yoshiyuki daini sakuhinshū*, pp. 251-252.

19. This account is based on Tsuno Kaitarō's retelling of the story in *Mon no mukō no gekijō* (Hakusuisha, 1972), p. 80.

20. Frederik L. Schodt, *Manga! Manga!: The World of Japanese Comics* (New York: Kodansha International, 1986), p. 71.

We published the first part of Shirato's *Red Eyes* (Akame, 1961) in my English translation in *Concerned Theatre Japan* (1971), II(1-2, part 2):19-87.

Saitō Ren's play *Red Eyes* (Akame, 1967), translated in the same issue of *Concerned Theatre Japan* (part 1):45-109, is based on this work, and its protagonist is modeled after Shirato. See also Saitō's "By Way of Introduction" in the same issue (part 1):36-44.

Saeki Ryūkō's critique of Saitō's play is quoted in the chapter on criticism below.

21. *Miroku no yo*, the age of Maitreya, was a phrase popular among the aristocracy in the Heian period and is found, for example, in the "Yūgao" chapter of *The Tale of Genji*, where Genji prays to be reborn in "the age of Maitreya" so his love for Yūgao may continue eternally. I am indebted to Miyata Noboru, "Various Types of Maitreya Belief in Japan" (unpublished ms., 1983), p. 9, for this insight.

Find Hakamadare!

A PLAY

by Fukuda Yoshiyuki

This translation of *Find Hakamadare!* (*Hakamadare wa doko da*) is based on the script as it appears in *Fukuda Yoshiyuki daini sakuhinshū* (*Oppekepe, Hakamadare wa doko da*) (San'ichi shobō, 1967). The text also appears in *Gendai nihon gikyoku taikei*, vol. 6 (San'ichi shobō, 1971). The play was first performed in 1964 by the Youth Art Theatre under the direction of Kanze Hideo.

CAST OF CHARACTERS

Old Bones
Villagers 1–7
Kogiku
Man
Sheriff (later, Former Sheriff)
Henchmen 1–3
Dream Beauties (Tall, Plump, Petite)
Dream Cattle, Horses, Villagers, etc.

Author's Introduction

According to the *Konjaku monogatari* and the *Uji shūi monogatari*, two medieval collections of popular tales, "a renowned Theefe" named Hakamadare preyed on the capital during the Heian period. The constabulary of the time was no match for this fearless and wily outlaw. Government-edited Japanese language textbooks published before World War II included the version from the *Konjaku monogatari*, which relates how the famous bandit was no match for the peerless warrior Fujiwara no Yasumasa (958–1036); but another version suggests that Hakamadare was none other than Yasumasa's brother Yasusuke, which, if true, would make Hakamadare all the more typical of the period, a bureaucrat by day, a bandit by night.

In all likelihood, Hakamadare was not one man. As the fame of the original outlaw grew, others impersonated him or claimed to be his heir. Hakamadare became so popular that his name developed a certain utility value; and it was only a matter of time before "Hakamadare" became synonymous with "righteous outlaw" and a symbol of popular resistance to authority. Thus it was that numberless robbers claiming to be Hakamadare continued to appear down to the sixteenth century.

The period of the play may therefore be any time from the ninth through the sixteenth century. An itinerant priest, starving and emaciated, has appeared in a poor farming village. Despite the ministrations of the villagers, he dies. Before he does so, however, he makes a prophecy: someday Hakamadare will arrive with his band to release the villagers from the savage oppression under which they toil. And it is at this point that our play begins.

The curtain opens in the darkness. A frigid wind is howling.
VOICE (*solemnly*):

> Winds of ignorance, clouds of strife.
> Bootless hopes for salvation rife.
> Sad the people, like withered grass.
> Even songbirds cry, "Alas!"

The lights come up. Villagers, the heroes of our play, appear.
VILLAGERS: Where are you, Hakamadare? Hakamadare, save us!

ACT 1
HOOFBEATS IN THE NIGHT

An impoverished farming village. Dusk.
Old Bones and the Seven Villagers stand before a freshly dug grave.
OLD BONES (*breaking the silence*): Aye, he was a good priest.
VILLAGERS (*together, with feeling*): Aye, that he was!
OLD BONES (*after a pause*): A pity he passed away!
VILLAGERS (*with feeling*): Aye, a pity indeed!
VILLAGER 1 (*after a pause*): I found him. It was dusk, like now. The setting sun had turned the clouds blood red. He was up on the mountain pass, lying on the ground, clutching his staff.
VILLAGER 4: Aye, and I carried him down to Old Bones' house. He didn't weigh more than a sack of dry leaves. I almost forgot I was carrying him!
VILLAGER 3: We all took turns nursing him, but it didn't do no good.
Villager 6 snivels. This is his response to almost every situation.
VILLAGER 2 (*a youth*): Worse luck! He traveled all this way only to draw his last breath in this godforsaken village in this godforsaken land!
VILLAGER 4: We wanted to feed him a little rice gruel, but there wasn't a grain of rice between us!
VILLAGER 7: And . . . and if the sheriff got wind of us helping an outsider, he'd've given us all a good drubbing and doubled our taxes to boot!
VILLAGER 2: No place to get sick, not this village, not this land! Better to die outright and have done with it!
VILLAGER 5 (*under his breath*): Aye, that's a fact!
Pause.
VILLAGERS 1 and 3 (*simultaneously*): But. . . .
The two men stare at each other in surprise. The others look at them. Villager 3 yields.
VILLAGER 1: But they say there are villages worse off than ours!
VILLAGER 2: You mean, where the sheriff is crueler?
VILLAGER 4: Where the baron is greedier?
VILLAGER 1: How could that be?
VILLAGER 3: That's what they say!
Villager 1 and Villager 3 eye each other curiously.

VILLAGER 3 (*to 2 and 4*): They say they're all like that!

VILLAGER 5: Who says?

VILLAGER 1 and VILLAGER 3 (*together*): No. . . . (*They stare at each other. Then speaking again in unison*): Nobody in particular. . . . (*They look quizzically at each other. Then again in unison*): Right? *Pause.*

VILLAGER 2 (*tentatively*): Well, if there are villages worse off than ours, nobody lives in them, I'll be bound!

OLD BONES: But they do!

Villagers look at Old Bones. Pause.

VILLAGER 4 (*tentatively*): But if they're worse off than us, how could they survive?

OLD BONES: But survive they do. Even in places worse than this.

VILLAGER 1 and VILLAGER 3: That's what they say. (*They look at each other and nod.*)

Pause.

VILLAGER (*staring at the others*): But just suppose there really are peasants worse off than us. What have they got to live for?

Pause.

VILLAGER 7: That some day, deep in the night. . . . (*He claps his hand over his mouth.*)

VILLAGER 4: Deep in the night, what?

VILLAGER 7: Nothing. Never mind.

VILLAGER 6: What's coming deep in the night?

VILLAGER 7: How . . . how should I know? Leave me alone!

VILLAGER 2 (*to Villager 6*): Nobody said anything was "coming." What do you know about this?

OLD BONES: All right, that's enough. (*He gets to his feet.*) Looks like you're all in on it anyway.

Pause.

VILLAGER 2: Don't look at me, Old Bones. I don't know nothing, not me. That's why I'm asking!

OLD BONES: A likely story! Who was it spent more time with the priest than anyone else? Who took him gruel with chestnuts when all he had was straw to chew?

VILLAGER 2: Ha! You think I believed that monk's rantings?

OLD BONES: The way I figure it, you claim not to believe because you want to believe so badly.

VILLAGER 2: That's crazy! I just wondered if everybody got told the same stuff as me, that's all.

OLD BONES: And if they did?

VILLAGER 2: I wondered if they was stupid enough to believe it.

OLD BONES: And if they was?

VILLAGER 2: Then . . . if they was, then I'd tell them: it's nothing but a pack of lies. The whole idea that "late one night, when the winds howl across the desolate fields. . . ." Who'd ever believe it!

VILLAGER 4: That's not right! "Desolate plains," he said. Plains, it was, not fields. I remember. "Late one night, when the winds howl across the desolate plains."

VILLAGER 6: You've got it all wrong! He didn't say howl; he said rage. "Late one night, when the winds rage," that was it.

OLD BONES: But you're all sure it was "late one night"?

VILLAGER 3: We'll hear the faint, clear sound of hoofbeats, that's what he said.

VILLAGERS (*all at once*): Aye! That was it! The sound of hoofbeats!

VILLAGER 1: They'll grow into an army, roaring like the sea!

VILLAGERS: Aye! Like the sea!

OLD BONES: Hm. And? . . .

VILLAGERS: It'll be Hakamadare!

Pause.

OLD BONES: Just as I suspected: everyone heard the same thing. The way I heard it, it went like this: An outlaw has appeared in the capital. He steals gold and jewels from the rich and gives everything to the poor.

VILLAGER 2: Aye, that's right! But it's a band of outlaws, not one man. They call themselves Hakamadare's band.

VILLAGER 3: No matter what tricks the sheriff tries, they slip through his fingers like shadows.

VILLAGER 4: And not just in the capital. In every village, in every province. They swoop down like the wind, then vanish without a trace!

VILLAGER 1: When Hakamadare and his band are gone, the barons and the sheriffs rule no more. A new world is born, and the people live in peace and contentment.

VILLAGER 5: If Hakamadare came, even a godforsaken village like this would be a paradise!

VILLAGER 6: Dead trees would put out leaves!

VILLAGER 3: Dogs would frolic and cows would low. Cocks would announce the dawn!

VILLAGER 7: Mothers' breasts would swell with milk. Children would grow plump and healthy!

VILLAGER 1: Late one night, Hakamadare and his band would arrive, and a new day would dawn, bringing bliss like we've never known! That's what the priest said.

VILLAGERS (*enthusiastically*): Aye, that's what he said!

Pause.

OLD BONES: No doubt about it: we all heard the same thing.

VILLAGERS: The same thing!

Pause.

VILLAGER 7: But. . . .

Villagers all look at Villager 7.

VILLAGER 7: Ne . . . never mind.

OLD BONES: Too good to be true, that's what you want to say, isn't it? A tale like that could only be a dream?

VILLAGER 1: But why would the priest lie to us on his deathbed?

VILLAGER 3: What would he gain?

VILLAGER 7: Nothing, that's what!

VILLAGER 6: I can't believe he'd ever deceive. . . . (*He weeps.*)

VILLAGER 4: He's right!

VILLAGER 5: I think so, too!

VILLAGER 7: Aye, but even so. . . .

Everyone looks at Villager 7.

OLD BONES: Even so what?

VILLAGER 7: Nothing, nothing. It's just that, well, it would be wonderful if Hakamadare came, but, the sheriff and his men are strong, that's all. They're strong and there's lots of them. Even Hakamadare wouldn't stand a. . . .

Pause.

VILLAGER 7 (*conscious of the disapproving eyes upon him*): I'm not saying he'd get caught. It's just that.... (*Seeing Villager 4 and Villager 2 rising menacingly to their feet*): Maybe I'm wrong. No, not maybe: I'm definitely wrong!

VILLAGER 2: Nobody can beat Hakamadare! Nobody! He and his band don't know the meaning of defeat!

VILLAGER 4: Aye! Bring on the sheriffs! Bring on the lords!

VILLAGER 2: When Hakamadare comes, I'll join him!

VILLAGER 4: Me too! I'll entreat him to let me join his band.

VILLAGER 2: I'm going to be one of Hakamadare's men, I am, and dash from village to village like the wind!

VILLAGER 4: We may be poor, but we want to help people who suffer like we do!

VILLAGER 5: But....

Everyone looks at Villager 5.

VILLAGER 5 (*with a desperate intensity*): How long will it be before Hakamadare comes?

Pause.

VILLAGER 1: He'll come. Don't worry, he'll come.

Pause.

VILLAGER 3: We'll just have to wait, be patient and wait. We've endured until now. We can wait a little longer.

VILLAGER 1: If Hakamadare's on his way, at least we have something to wait for!

VILLAGER 2: Aye! No matter what the sheriff does to us ...

VILLAGER 7: No matter what new taxes the baron dreams up ...

VILLAGER 4: Hakamadare's on his way!

VILLAGER 1: Let the sun parch the land; the rains wash away the seed; let winter freeze the mud so there's not a blade of grass or piece of bark to chew. There's nothing we can't stand!

VILLAGER 3: We'll just grit our teeth and wait. Because Hakamadare's on his way!

VILLAGERS (*with assurance*): Aye!

Villager 6 is overcome with emotion and weeps.

OLD BONES: I see. There's just one thing that bothers me. Why did the priest go out of his way to tell each of us the same thing separately?

Why did he warn us not to tell anyone else? We each tucked the legend of Hakamadare away in our hearts, where it grew. . . .

VILLAGER 3: I just thought it was too good to be true, Old Bones. I wanted it to be true so bad. . . .

OLD BONES: You were afraid it would turn out to be a lie if you told anyone else.

The villagers look at each other and laugh with a sense of self-recognition.

OLD BONES (*almost inaudibly*): There's no way to be sure if the priest was telling the truth. But we all want to believe it, so believe it we will. And as for waiting, we don't have much choice.

VILLAGER 1: What's that, Old Bones? What're you mumbling about?

OLD BONES: Nothing. Never you mind.

The sun has set.

Blackout.

The sound of the wind in the darkness. Then a solemn voice is heard.

VOICE:

> So long as sadness and despair
> Fill men's hearts everywhere,
> They'll wait for Hakamadare to alight,
> And dream of hoofbeats in the night.

The sound of a galloping steed. Gradually the hoofbeats grow into the roar of an advancing army. Then there is quiet.

Only the sound of the wind remains.

After a few moments:

VILLAGERS (*voices*): How much longer, Hakamadare? How much longer do we have to wait? How much longer?

The wind blows more fiercely than ever.

VOICE:

> True or false, the difference small
> To men with naught to lose at all.
> They strain the sound of hoofs to hear,
> The sword of justice drawing near.

ACT 2
IF THE REAL HAKAMADARE WON'T
COME, THEN . . .

A year later.

Voices can be heard shouting as the lights come up:

VILLAGER 2 (*in a state of high excitement*): Ha . . . Hakamadare's here!

VILLAGER 4 (*similarly*): He's come at last! Hakamadare's come at last!

Another place in the same remote village.

It is almost dawn. Flickering lights suggest a manor house burning in the distance.

The excited Villagers run about the stage overjoyed, shouting.

VILLAGER 2: They attacked the baron's manor last night! His son was killed; his retainers fled!

VILLAGER 4: They were up against Hakamadare, after all! They danced a pretty jig and ran for their lives!

VILLAGER 2: Look over there on the mountain! The manor house is going up in flames!

VILLAGER 1: Hakamadare's come at last!

VILLAGER 3: Just like the priest said!

VILLAGER 1: Hakamadare's come at last!

Pause. The Villagers gaze off in the direction of the manor house (over the heads of the audience would be good).

VILLAGER 1 (*delirious*): The baron's done for now!

VILLAGER 4 (*similarly*): Flowers will bloom!

VILLAGER 7 (*similarly*): Dogs will bay!

VILLAGERS (*in unison*): A new world will be born!

The Villagers sink to the ground, overwhelmed.

Without warning, Villager 6 bursts into tears, startling his fellows.

VILLAGER 1: This is no time to cry!

VILLAGER 6: I can't help. . . . (*He weeps.*)

VILLAGER 7 (*also bursting into tears*): Every night for the past year I've prayed, "Let this be the night I hear the hoofbeats!" I'd go to bed soon as the sun went down, and wake up in the middle of the night and listen. I'd try not to breathe; I'd strain my ears while I did my chores. When the sun came up, I'd fall into bed, exhausted. And then last night, last night of all nights! I fell asleep by the fire and . . . and. . . . (*He weeps.*)

VILLAGER 3 (*also bursting into tears*): I . . . I'm sorry! What can I say? I doubted Hakamadare would ever come! I began thinking the old priest deceived us! Forgive me, Hakamadare! I didn't mean it! (*He kowtows in the direction of the manor.*)

VILLAGER 1 (*dropping to his knees and bowing in the same direction*): Thank you, Hakamadare! Thank you! You don't know how long we've waited!

VILLAGER 2: Thank you, Hakamadare!

VILLAGER 4: We'll never be able to repay you, Hakamadare!

VILLAGER 3: Thank you! Oh, thank you!

Villager 6 weeps even louder than before.

Pause.

VILLAGER 2: Wait! Something isn't right!

VILLAGERS: What's that? What are you talking about? What do you mean something isn't right? How dare you talk that way about Hakamadare? (*The other villagers react similarly in turn.*)

VILLAGER 2 (*to Villager 4*): Listen, the manor house started burning a long time ago, didn't it?

VILLAGER 4: Aye, and it will collapse any minute.

VILLAGER 2: In other words, it's been quite a while, but Hakamadare still hasn't showed up.

VILLAGER 6: He's right! Where is Hakamadare?

VILLAGER 7: Where did he go?

Pause.

VILLAGER 1: That's just Hakamadare's way—he strikes, then vanishes like the wind.

VILLAGER 3: But we wanted to meet him . . .

VILLAGER 6: And say thank you at least . . .

VILLAGER 7: Let him know how we feel!

VILLAGERS: Aye! It's the truth!

VILLAGER 2: I was counting on seeing him!

VILLAGER 4: I was going to join his band!

VILLAGER 2: Now what am I going to do?

VILLAGER 7: Hakamadare may strike like the wind, but he can't have gotten far.

VILLAGER 2: Maybe we should go after him?

VILLAGER 1: But which way should we go?

VILLAGER 3: Hakamadare's like a whirlwind: there's no telling where he'll strike next.

The Villagers talk anxiously among themselves.

Villager 5 entered a few minutes ago, looking utterly exhausted. He speaks now for the first time.

VILLAGER 5: You've got it all wrong.

OLD BONES (*noticing him*): Gorōji! Where've you been?

VILLAGER 5: The manor.

VILLAGERS (*all at once*): The manor?! What was it like? Did you see Hakamadare? Did he have his band with him? What were they like?

VILLAGER 5: It wasn't Hakamadare.

VILLAGERS (*in confusion*): What?! What're you talking about? Gorōji, you're covered with blood! What happened?

VILLAGER 5: It wasn't Hakamadare, I said.

VILLAGER 4: You don't know what you're talking about! If it wasn't Hakamadare, then? . . .

VILLAGER 1: Then who set fire to the manor?

VILLAGER 5: I did.

VILLAGERS: What!?

VILLAGER 5: I did, I said. (*He begins to collapse even as he is speaks.*)

The Villagers rush to support him.

VILLAGERS (*all at once*): Take it easy! Don't stop now, Gorōji! Tell us what happened! I'm so confused! I don't know what to think anymore! Come on, Gorōji, speak up!

VILLAGER 5 (*shaking off the others*): Leave me alone! Get away! I'm a murderer! A murderer! (*He slumps to the ground.*)

OLD BONES (*signaling the others to be quiet*): All right, Gorōji, tell us what happened.

VILLAGER 5: The baron's son . . . I . . . I. . . .

The Villagers gasp.

OLD BONES (*gravely*): We know what you've been through. First they forced your sister into service at the manor, and when you went to beg for her release they took your wife. So you went again to beg for mercy, and this time they took your mother. Last night they finally allowed them back to the village, but they arrived in coffins. The rest of us pretended not to notice. We didn't know what to do.

VILLAGER 2: I just clenched my teeth and thought, "Wait till Hakamadare gets here!"

VILLAGER 5: That's just it! I went crazy last night! I sneaked into the manor house and killed the baron's son with my bare hands. Then I stood there and shouted at the top of my lungs: I'm Hakamadare! Hakamadare's come at last!"

VILLAGERS (*in tumult*): No!?

VILLAGER 5: And all the baron's men ran for their lives. They didn't even look at me!

The Villagers are stunned.

Pause.

OLD BONES: Then it wasn't Hakamadare?

VILLAGERS: Hakamadare didn't come?

Pause.

VILLAGER 7: What are we going to do? If they find out it wasn't Hakamadare! . . .

VILLAGER 1: He's right! Before the day's out, the sheriff and his men. . . .

VILLAGER 3: They'll be back!

VILLAGERS: What . . . what are we going to do? (*The Villagers all talk at once.*)

OLD BONES: All right, all right! Settle down! First of all, the sheriff and his men are headed for the great lord's manor. That's on the other side of the mountain, so it'll be nightfall before they get back, not before. We have all day to think of something, so just settle down! Settle down! All right. If Gorōji here was Hakamadare, it looks like we're not about to experience "bliss like we've never known."

VILLAGER 3: We'll be lucky if that's all it means!

VILLAGER 1: We're really in for it now!

VILLAGER 2: They'll punish the whole village!

VILLAGER 4: They'll hang the lot of us!

VILLAGER 7: It wasn't me! I didn't have anything to do with it!

VILLAGER 2: They'll hang you just the same.

VILLAGER 7: Now look what you've done, Gorōji!

VILLAGER 4: And before I had a chance to meet Hakamadare!
Villager 6 weeps.
VILLAGER 5 (*shouting in anguish*): I know! I'm sorry! It's all my fault!
   I'm to blame! Tie me up and turn me in! It's our only hope! Please!
   Old Bones, please!
OLD BONES: Not so fast, Gorōji. Listen to me, everyone. Are you really
   ready to hand Gorōji over to the sheriff?
Silence.
VILLAGER 5 (*still sitting stolidly on the ground*): I . . . when I was in the
   baron's manor, I was like a mad dog frothing at the mouth. I
   didn't care a wit for my life. I just slashed away at everything in
   sight. But then I escaped into the woods and waited for morning. I
   was drenched in sweat and began to shiver. I was covered with blood
   from head to toe, and it began to get sticky and hard. I got so scared,
   I thought I'd lose my mind! I realized I'd done something
   unforgivable! I'm a murderer! I'm a murderer who slew his lord,
   killed soldiers, and slaughtered sheriff's men by the score! I'm a
   murderer, and I'll never be able to look another man in the eye!
Pause.
VILLAGER 6: You poor! . . . (*He weeps.*)
VILLAGER 5 (*getting to his feet*): Farewell!
VILLAGERS: Gorōji! Where're you going, Gorōji?
Villager 5 starts walking away.
VILLAGER 1 (*stopping him*): Wait! Even if you're going to turn yourself
   in, the sheriff won't be back until evening.
VILLAGER 3 (*also stopping 5*): They'll punish the whole village anyway,
   even if you turn yourself in!
VILLAGER 7: If only Hakamadare would come!
Villager 5 finally breaks down and cries.
OLD BONES (*jumping to his feet*): That's it! That's it!
VILLAGERS: What? Old Bones, what're you talking about?
OLD BONES: Hakamadare *did* come!
VILLAGERS: What? What do you mean?
VILLAGER 7: Where?
OLD BONES (*indicating Villager 5*): Here! Think about it! Gorōji killed
   the baron's son and scared off the sheriff's men. That's just what
   Hakamadare would do, isn't it? You could say Gorōji did half of

Hakamadare's job for him. (*To Villager 5*): Hey, Gorōji! That makes you Hakamadare! You're half Hakamadare! (*To the Villagers*): You know, I've been watching you people. When you thought it was Hakamadare burned down the manor house, you're ready to jump for joy; but if Gorōji did the same thing, you act like he's the worst villain ever walked the face of the earth! (*To 5*): Don't worry, Gorōji, claiming you were Hakamadare was the smartest thing you ever did! If we keep quiet, no one'll ever suspect it wasn't the real Hakamadare. See, Hakamadare really *did* strike and vanish like the wind!

VILLAGER 1: The sheriff won't be that easy to fool, Old Bones.

VILLAGER 7 (*almost simultaneously*): They'll find out it was Gorōji for sure!

VILLAGER 3 (*similarly*): And if they find him, we're all done for!

VILLAGER 4 (*similarly*): They'll know it was an imposter!

VILLAGER 2 (*similarly*): They'll figure out it wasn't Hakamadare after all!

OLD BONES: No, they won't. They'll never find him.

VILLAGERS: Why not?

OLD BONES: Gorōji's only half Hakamadare, so he can't vanish like the wind, but he can go underground like a mole!

VILLAGER 1: But if Gorōji disappears, what's going to happen to the rest of us?

VILLAGER 2: Aye! The sheriff will come around wanting to know where he went!

OLD BONES: We'll disappear with him.

VILLAGERS: Disappear with him?

OLD BONES: What do you say we *all* became Hakamadare?

VILLAGERS (*after a brief pause*): Become Hakamadare?

OLD BONES: No matter how long we wait, it looks like Hakamadare isn't coming. That's all the more reason to become Hakamadare ourselves. Well? Don't just stand there with your mouths hanging open!

VILLAGERS (*in a panic*): But . . . but! . . .

OLD BONES: Listen: Gorōji did half of Hakamadare's job all by himself, didn't he? What would happen if we all did the same thing? Hakamadare's no superman. He's human, just like us. Well?

VILLAGER 1: But Old Bones, Gorōji claimed he was Hakamadare. The sheriff and his men let out a yelp and ran for their lives. That means. . . .

OLD BONES: We do the same thing. We all claim to be Hakamadare!

VILLAGERS: Now wait a minute, Old Bones!

OLD BONES: You mean you still don't understand? We've got to go into hiding whether we like it or not, right? Well then, why go half-way? We may never be like the real Hakamadare, but we can try. We can be followers in spirit. In other words, wherever we go, wherever ruthless barons oppress the weak, wherever the rich exploit the poor, . . .

VILLAGER 2 (*excitedly, while the other Villagers are still staring at Old Bones in speechless amazement*): We'll overwhelm them, is that it?

OLD BONES: We won't exactly "overwhelm" them. We're not really Hakamadare, remember? First we'll investigate careful as we can. We'll figure how we can get ourselves into the manor and how we can get the money out.

VILLAGER 2: Where to set fires to distract the sheriff, things like that?

OLD BONES: Right. We'll plan carefully and attack only when we're sure we'll succeed.

VILLAGER 4 (*becoming caught up in the idea*): Hakamadare wouldn't be so cautious. He'd strike like the wind!

OLD BONES: But don't forget, we're only imposters.

VILLAGER 2 and VILLAGER 4 (*nodding*): Oh, that's right!

VILLAGER 1 (*worried*): Wai . . . wait a minute, Old Bones. You're getting everybody excited, but . . . but what if the real Hakamadare finds out?

OLD BONES: That's the whole point! Listen, if the real Hakamadare gets wind that imposters are going around claiming to be him. . . .

VILLAGER 7: He'll blow his stack!

VILLAGER 3: He'll come after us!

OLD BONES: And we'll be able to meet him! The real Hakamadare we've been waiting for!

VILLAGER 1 (*impressed but not yet willing to go along*): And if we meet Hakamadare, we'll say, "We're sorry we used your name, but it was the only way we could think of to meet you."

VILLAGER 3 (*similarly*): "Please forgive us!" Like that?

OLD BONES: What do you say? Instead of sitting around here and waiting, it'd be a lot faster to go out and find Hakamadare ourselves. And the best way to do that is to let him find us!

VILLAGERS: He's right! He's got a point!

OLD BONES (*more convinced than ever*): Don't you see? We look like peasants. . . .

VILLAGER 6: But we are peasants!

OLD BONES: You still don't understand, do you? In our hearts we're Hakamadare, outlaws for justice!

VILLAGERS (*a minority*): Well, maybe. . . .

OLD BONES: Where's your sense of adventure? Come on! Aye!

VILLAGERS (*only 2 and 4 with enthusiasm, the rest reluctantly*): Aye!

OLD BONES (*excited*): That's the spirit! Now, it goes without saying that we don't want to take life unnecessarily, even if we're up against the sheriffs and their men. Wait a minute! In other words, we have to have certain rules to live by.

VILLAGER 2 (*excited*): Aye! And Hakamadare's rules are strict!

OLD BONES: Right then, are you ready?

VILLAGERS (*here and below, as before, only a minority with enthusiasm*): Aye!

OLD BONES: The rules are to be obeyed at all times. That's rule number one. All right?

VILLAGERS: Aye!

OLD BONES: Ruler number two: there will be no unnecessary taking of life, even if we're up against the sheriffs and their men. The real Hakamadare doesn't kill.

VILLAGERS: Aye!

OLD BONES: Be especially kind to women and children, just like the real Hakamadare. That's rule number three.

VILLAGERS: Aye!

OLD BONES: Rule number four's important. You ready for this? All booty's to be distributed among the poor.

VILLAGERS: Aye!

OLD BONES: We only take what we need to keep ourselves alive. That's rule number five.

VILLAGERS: Aye!

OLD BONES: But what about when we haven't been able to steal anything and we're starving ourselves? . . . We're not allowed to take so much as a potato from the people even then. This is where the rules get hard. If the villagers offer us something, . . .

VILLAGER 7: Then we can eat it?

OLD BONES: No, even if they offer us something, we don't just take it. If we haven't got anything to give them in return, then we help them in their fields to repay our debt. That's rule number six.

VILLAGERS: Aye!

VILLAGER 5 (*he has kept his peace but now shouts suddenly*): I can't go through with it!

OLD BONES: Why not, Gorōji?

VILLAGER 5: I could never be Hakamadare. I . . . I'm a murderer! I lost control and killed a man in cold blood! I wasn't thinking anything but how much I hated him. All I wanted was to kill! That's different from Hakamadare. What I did and Hakamadare are completely different! I'll never be able to look another man in the eye!

OLD BONES: Yes, you will. You'll be able to look men in the eye, and the Buddha too, once you meet Hakamadare. Once you meet the real Hakamadare and become a member of his band, everything will be forgiven. The murder you committed won't be murder anymore.

VILLAGER 5: If not murder, then what?

OLD BONES: Hakamadare's sword of justice wielded for the betterment of the world and mankind! How's that?

VILLAGER 5: But I killed him with my bare hands!

OLD BONES: All right, then: the fist of justice. Is that better?

Pause.

OLD BONES: They say if you're going to drink poison, take a deep draught.

Pause.

OLD BONES: Well? You with us or not, Gorōji?

VILLAGER 5: How long will it be before we meet the real Hakamadare?

OLD BONES: Don't worry. It won't be long. This time we're going out looking. (*To villagers*): Right?

VILLAGERS: Aye!

OLD BONES: Then what are we waiting for? Let's go!

VILLAGERS 2, 4, and 6 (*with spirit*): Aye! Aye!

Villagers 1, 3, and 7 hesitate. They remain unconvinced. And as the others give another spirited shout, Villager 6 also begins to lose his nerve.

VILLAGER 1: Old Bones!

VILLAGER 3: You . . . you really mean to go through with this?

VILLAGER 7: I'm scared!

VILLAGER 6: Me, too!

VILLAGER 2: Hey, you were just shouting with us!

VILLAGER 6: But I . . . I. . . . (*He bursts into tears.*)

OLD BONES (*losing patience*): Listen to me, all of you! Face it: this is our only chance. We don't have any choice!

Blackout.

(*The transition to the next scene should be expeditious, indicating that not much time has elapsed.*)

ACT 3
WITH THE SKY FOR A BLANKET AND
THE EARTH FOR A BED

Scene 1

A mountain pass. Darkness.

Villager 4 runs in. He is attired in modest travel gear, with a sickle and other paraphernalia stuck in his belt.

VILLAGER 4 (*looking around*): Anybody here? (*Pause.*) Guess not. We were to meet on this mountain pass by nightfall and set out from here. Old Bones said we'd attract less attention that way. But it looks like I'm the first one to arrive. Ha! And I was afraid I'd be late! Imposters or not, we're Hakamadare and his band, and we've got to act the part. I may not have a broadsword to thrust in my belt, but at least my sickle's sharp. In fact, I was so busy honing it, I lost track of time. (*He holds the sickle up to the night sky.*) Too bad the moon's not out; it'd glitter in the moonlight.

Villager 2 enters carrying a hoe and looking back over his shoulder. He almost collides with Villager 4, and the two men gawk at each other in surprise.

VILLAGER 4: Who . . . who's there!?

VILLAGER 2: Who . . . who's there, yourself!?

VILLAGER 4: That you, Jirōta?

VILLAGER 2: Shirōbei?

VILLAGER 4: You're late!

VILLAGER 2: What do you mean I'm late? I got here a long time ago. There was nobody around, so I went scouting.

VILLAGER 4: I guess that makes us the first. What happened to the others?

VILLAGER 2: Got cold feet, I'll bet.

VILLAGER 4 (*earnestly*): You think so?

VILLAGER 2: That's the way it looks.

As they are walking back toward center stage, Villager 3 peeks out of the underbrush.

VILLAGER 3 (*softly*): Heave-to!

VILLAGER 2 and VILLAGER 4: Ahhh! (*They collapse in terror. Then, recognizing 3*): Oh, it's you!

Villager 3 does not move or respond.

VILLAGER 2 (*getting to his feet*): You're late! Where've you been?

VILLAGER 4 (*also getting to his feet*): You trying to scare us out of our wits?

Villager 3 still does not move.

VILLAGER 2: What's got into you?

VILLAGER 4: You're making me nervous!

VILLAGER 3 (*softly*): Heave-to!

VILLAGER 4: Stop saying that!

VILLAGER 2: All this excitement gone to your head?

VILLAGER 3 (*abruptly*): You idiots! You forgot the agreement!

VILLAGER 2 and VILLAGER 4: What agreement?

VILLAGER 3: What Old Bones said: that whenever we regroup, we have to say the password. When I say "Heave-to!" you have to say "Heave-ho!" back.

VILLAGER 2: That's right! But. . . .

VILLAGER 4: But that's only after we begin our journey.

VILLAGER 3: What do you call this? We began our journey the minute we left our homes in the village. Now come on, say it. (*Softly*): Heave-to!

VILLAGER 2: But we already know each other!

VILLAGER 4: We can dispense with the formalities tonight, can't we?

VILLAGER 3: Hey, what's rule number one?

VILLAGER 2 and VILLAGER 4: To obey the rules at all times.

VILLAGER 3: All right then. (*Softly*): Heave-to!

VILLAGER 2 (*looking at 4, embarrassed*): Do we have to?

VILLAGER 3: Say it!

VILLAGER 2 and VILLAGER 4: All right! All right!

VILLAGER 4: Give us our cue again.

VILLAGER 3 (*nodding, in a low voice*): Heave-to!

VILLAGER 2 and VILLAGER 4 (*similarly*): Heave-ho!

VILLAGER 3: Jirōta? Shirōbei?

VILLAGER 2 and VILLAGER 4: Aye! It's us.

VILLAGER 3: All right then. Old Bones, Jirōta and Shirōbei are here!

OLD BONES: Good. (*He emerges from the undergrowth.*) You can come out now.

VILLAGERS: Aye!

There is a rustling sound, and the rest of the villagers emerge from the bushes.

VILLAGER 2 and VILLAGER 4: You . . . you been here all this time?

VILLAGER 3: Of course! We saw you coming.

VILLAGER 1: You tromped in here with your nose up in the clouds, babbling some nonsense. How could we miss you?

VILLAGER 7: It's important to set off on the right foot. That's what Old Bones wanted to teach us.

VILLAGER 6 (*already with tears in his voice*): Out of the goodness of his heart!

OLD BONES: Never mind about that. Now that we're all here, we'd better make tracks. Wait a minute! (*To 2 and 4*): What have you got there?

VILLAGER 2: This? It's my hoe, what's it look like?

VILLAGER 4: I brought my sickle. I honed it real good.

VILLAGER 2: I chose something with a long handle, to keep our enemies at a distance.

OLD BONES: Fools! We're supposed to be homeless peasants looking for work.

VILLAGER 2: What's wrong with a peasant carrying a hoe?

VILLAGER 4: Or a sickle?

OLD BONES: You just can't . . . I mean, you can't be so obvious about it!

VILLAGER 1: Old Bones is right. You look *too much* like peasants.

VILLAGER 3: Here, you take this pot, and you take this kettle.

Continuing their explanations, the Villagers load 2 and 4 down with pots and pans and other paraphernalia.

OLD BONES: All right then. We got out of the village before the sheriff and his men arrived. So far so good.

VILLAGERS: So far so good.

VILLAGER 3: Hold on a minute!

OLD BONES: What?

VILLAGER 3: Where's Gorōji?

OLD BONES: Gorōji? He was here a minute ago.

VILLAGER 3: Well, he's not here now.

VILLAGER 5 (*from up in a tree*): Up here!

The Villagers are startled.

VILLAGER 1: Hey, what're you doing up there?

VILLAGER 3: You crazy?

VILLAGER 5: I'm looking at the village.

VILLAGER 1: To see if the sheriff's come?

VILLAGER 5: No. Just taking a last look.

Without knowing exactly why, the Villagers all turn to face the village.

VILLAGER 6 (*sobbing*): Our village!

VILLAGER 3: Hey, it's bad luck to. . . .

VILLAGER 1: Leave him alone. He's entitled.

Pause.

OLD BONES: We've turned our back on everything we know. It's a long road we have before us. We'll walk from dawn to dusk, and when it's time to sleep, we'll have the sky for a blanket . . .

VILLAGER 2: Some blanket!

VILLAGER 4: Big enough to cover an army!

The Villagers laugh.

OLD BONES: And the earth for a bed.

VILLAGER 1: And hard as a rock, too!

VILLAGER 3: Who could ask for more?

Villagers laugh.

OLD BONES: Then, here we go!

VILLAGERS: Aye! (*They start walking, but . . .*)

VILLAGER 1: Wait a minute!

OLD BONES: What?

VILLAGER 1: Which way are we going?

OLD BONES: What difference does it make? We don't know where Hakamadare is, so there's no telling where our quest will lead us. We just have to begin.

VILLAGER 2: Old Bones is right. We'll attack the first evil miser we find.

VILLAGER 3: All misers are evil, stupid!

VILLAGER 6: Now boys, it's bad luck to start a journey with an argument.

The Villagers laugh.

OLD BONES: All right. Forward, march!

VILLAGERS: Aye!

They begin their trek.

If possible, the scenery should be changed while the Villagers are walking across the stage.

Music. The following song is sung during the transition to Scene 2:

> Here we go, don't be shy!
> Hakamadare you and I!
> Lending righteousness a hand!
> Seeking Hakamadare's band!
>
> We steal, yes it's true,
> Not for us, but for you!
> Let the downtrodden stand!
> We're Hakamadare's band!

Scene 2

Outside a manor.

The time should be spring.

The Villagers enter. They gather and confer. Then they scatter and infiltrate the manor compound.

After a brief interlude, they reassemble. They discuss their findings, then divide up into two or three groups. The main group forms itself into a human ladder and effortlessly surmounts the manor walls.

This all takes place in silence, with the staccato rhythm of time-lapse photography.

Shortly, the manor house is consumed in flames. There is shouting and chaos. The Villagers reappear and begin shouting:

VILLAGER 1: Look! There goes Hakamadare!

VILLAGER 2: Hakamadare, friend of the weak, defender of the poor!

VILLAGER 4: Hakamadare and his merry band!

VILLAGER 3: They made off with every bit of treasure in the baron's manor!

VILLAGER 5: They said they'd divide it among the people of the village!

VILLAGER 7: There'll be gold coins in every house by morning!

VILLAGER 6: Hakamadare's come at last!

OLD BONES: The smallest of them was six feet tall! They came riding out of nowhere and vanished like the wind!

VILLAGER 4 (*grabbing Old Bones*): Old Bones, Old Bones! Is that true? Did Hakamadare really come?

VILLAGER 7: That was quick!

VILLAGER 6: What a relief! Finally!

OLD BONES: You fools! I'm talking about us! I'm only making it sound like the real thing!

VILLAGER 2 (*entering at a run*): Old Bones, the sheriff's here!

VILLAGER 1: Run for it!

OLD BONES: No, stay where you are. We'll meet him here. Right here.

VILLAGER 3: What!

OLD BONES: Listen, do just as I tell you. First you say, "Good evening, my liege!"

VILLAGERS: Good evening, my liege.

OLD BONES: "Five hundred bandits with the faces of demons just rode by."

The Villagers haltingly repeat Old Bones' words.

OLD BONES: "They went thata way."

VILLAGERS: They went thata way.

OLD BONES: You just keep repeating that. Every time you see a sheriff.

VILLAGERS 1, 2, 3, and 5: Aye! We understand.

VILLAGERS 4, 6, and 7 (*their words overlapping 1, 2, 3, and 5*): Every time you see a sheriff.

VILLAGERS 1, 2, and 3 (*to 4, 6, and 7*): No! Stupid!

VILLAGER 5: Here he comes!

OLD BONES: All right, scatter! We'll meet at Three Pines.

VILLAGERS: Aye!

The Villagers scatter in silence.

The manor house burns to the ground.

Scene 3

A road.

It is autumn.

The Villagers saunter in.

OLD BONES: What say we rest here?

VILLAGERS: Aye! (*They sit.*)

VILLAGER 1: They sure gave us a hard time in that village last night!

VILLAGER 3: We did all right, I'd say.

VILLAGER 1: We did all right, but they still gave us a hard time.

VILLAGER 4: Aye, there we were distributing gold to the people when all of a sudden they started asking if the money was from Hakamadare.

VILLAGER 2: Nothing unusual in that. But then they wanted to know if we were Hakamadare!

VILLAGER 5: So I told them, absolutely not . . .

VILLAGER 6: We're imposters, I said, but no sooner were the words out of my mouth then they shouted . . .

VILLAGER 7: Imposters!? and began pummeling us with their fists!

VILLAGER 1: So we just threw down the money and ran!

The Villagers laugh.

VILLAGER 3: Aye, but we did all right even so.

The Villagers laugh again.

VILLAGER 5 (*looking offstage*): Hey, Old Bones!

OLD BONES (*entering at a leisurely pace*): It's about time! Here comes the posse now!

VILLAGER 2: They were quicker at the last village.

VILLAGER 4: Aye, but it took them longer at the village before that.

VILLAGER 1: Once they get used to chasing us, this'll be just about right.

A Sheriff with a curled mustache enters on horseback. He is attended by two Henchmen. At least that is the intention. In fact, three men link hands and carry the Sheriff between them. The man in front wears a horse head; the two behind wear the black hats appropriate to their role. The Henchmen may cover their faces if they like. The "horse" should be in almost constant motion.

SHERIFF (*clip-clopping past, then turning back*): Stay, churlish peasant knaves!

VILLAGERS: Yes, my liege?

SHERIFF: I would ask thee a question.

VILLAGERS: Yes, my liege.

SHERIFF: I'm probably wasting my breath.

VILLAGERS: Oh no, my liege.

SHERIFF: But I'm going to ask thee anyway, so consider thyselves lucky.

VILLAGERS: Yes, my liege.

SHERIFF: I'm doing this out of selfless beneficence.

VILLAGERS: Thank you, my liege!

SHERIFF: I expect straight answers, nothing less!

VILLAGERS: Yes, my liege.

VILLAGER 4 (*bored with this routine*): If you're looking for Hakamadare, he went thata way.

SHERIFF: What? Thata way? Giddyap! Giddyap!

He "gallops" away but immediately reins in his mount and returns.

SHERIFF: Wait a minute, wait a minute!

VILLAGER 4: Yes, my liege?

SHERIFF: I didn't ask thee anything yet!

VILLAGER 4: Yes, my liege, but. . . .

VILLAGER 1 (*restraining him*): Sorry, my liege. We didn't mean to give offense.

SHERIFF: Impudent swine! Come forward!

VILLAGER 4: Yes, my liege.

SHERIFF (*he urges his mount around Villager 4, whom he strikes with his whip*): You'll do.

VILLAGER 4: I will?

SHERIFF: As my guide and porter. Pick up my bags and follow me.

VILLAGER 4: Yes, my liege, but. . . .

Old Bones signals Villager 4 not to resist.

VILLAGER 4 (*understanding*): Yes, my liege. Thank you, my liege.

SHERIFF: Consider thyself privileged to serve.

VILLAGER 4: Yes, my liege.

SHERIFF: Forward, march!

*Sheriff, Horse, and Henchmen exit. Villager 4 follows. The rest of the
Villagers watch them go.*

VILLAGER 3: You think he'll be all right?

VILLAGER 1: Don't worry. Shirōbei can take care of himself.

VILLAGER 3: The other day he misread Old Bones' signal, you know.

VILLAGER 7: He thought the signal for "lay low" meant "charge"!

VILLAGER 2: And he rushed out all by himself. The sheriff and his men
didn't know what to do!

VILLAGER 7: I didn't either, but I yanked the rope taut across the road
just in time. The sheriff and his men tumbled off their horses like we
planned, but Shirōbei got caught too and landed on the ground with
them. And that wasn't exactly in the plan!

The Villagers laugh.

VILLAGER 3 (*frowning*): We couldn't just leave him there. We had to
risk our necks to save him!

VILLAGER 1: But everything turned out all right in the end. Don't be
too hard on him.

VILLAGER 3 (*in deadly earnest*): What do you mean? Of course we
should be hard on him! Getting the signals mixed up is as bad, if not
badder, than breaking the rules!

VILLAGER 6 (*anxiously*): Now, now, don't get excited!

VILLAGER 3 (*to 6*): Excited? Look who's talking! You and your over-
worked tear ducts!

VILLAGER 1 (*to 3*): All your talk isn't going to make him any more
cautious.

VILLAGER 2: Next time he'll get us into trouble by being too careful,
mark my words!

VILLAGER 3: The point is precision. We can't afford mistakes.

VILLAGER 1 (*to 3*): Precision? Then what do you mean, "bad, if not
badder"? That's supposed to be "bad, if not worse"!

VILLAGER 6 (*bursting into tears*): I just wanted to avoid an argument, that's all!

Old Bones has been gesticulating energetically for some time.

OLD BONES: Ah-hah!

The Villagers look at him in surprise.

VILLAGER 1: Ah-hah?

OLD BONES: I have to take a share of the blame for Shirōbei jumping out like that. You see, the signal that used to look like "charge!" was actually the signal for "retreat!" I was afraid somebody might get mixed up, so I switched them around. I guess I got carried away. From now on, this will mean "go!" (*He scratches his nose.*) And this will mean "wait!" (*He pulls his ear.*) Everybody got that? From now on, this is "go!"

VILLAGERS (*rubbing their noses*): Go!

OLD BONES: Right!

VILLAGERS (*pulling their ears*): Wait!

OLD BONES: Right! (*Putting his hand to his chest.*) And this will mean "scatter!"

While the Villagers are listening to these instructions, the Sheriff has returned in the same manner as before. That is, he appears mounted on the hands of his "Horse" and Henchmen. The horse continues to fidget nervously, rubbing its nose with its forelegs, etcetera.

SHERIFF: Stay, churlish peasant knaves!

VILLAGERS (*startled*): Ye . . . yes, my liege!

SHERIFF: What means all that, aged knave?

OLD BONES: Mean?

SHERIFF: Rubbing thine nose and pulling thine ears. Methinks thee comport thyself suspiciously!

OLD BONES: Oh, my liege, on the contrary! There's nothing in the least suspicious about it. There's a perfectly good explanation. It's so simple, there are hardly words to describe. . . .

SHERIFF: No words to describe?

OLD BONES: By the way, did you find Hakamadare?

VILLAGER 1: Did you capture the rascally thief so soon? Leave it to a right brave warrior like my liege!

VILLAGER 3: Must've been the mustache. It'll do it every time!

VILLAGER 2: One stern look and he dropped to his knees, begging for mercy!

SHERIFF: Silence! Hakamadare was nowhere to be seen. That churlish knave I hired as a guide led me on a wild goose chase for half an hour. I thought I recognized the path and found myself back here.

OLD BONES: Then you got closer than you think!

SHERIFF: What's that?

OLD BONES: Now that you mention it, what became of your guide?

SHERIFF: Him? I took my eyes off the wretch for one minute and he was gone!

VILLAGERS (*whispering to one another*): What do you think happened to that fool?

SHERIFF: Methinks ye swine grow suspiciouser by the minute! Aged knave, confess! Those hand movements are black magic, aren't they?

The Sheriff's Horse is fidgeting constantly now.

OLD BONES: Black magic? Heaven forbid, my liege! We are but homeless farmers wandering in search of work. It's the truth, I swear it!

SHERIFF: Enough of thine lies! What spell wast thou casting?

OLD BONES: Well, you see. . . .

SHERIFF: No words to describe it, eh? Well, if there be no words, it's my duty as sheriff to help thee find them! Thou rubbed thine nose. What meanst that?

At this signal, Villager 6 begins to leap out of the crowd, but the others restrain him.

VILLAGER 1: Only when Old Bones does it, stupid!

SHERIFF (*oblivious*): Thou pulled thine ears. What about that?

The Horse is more nervous than ever.

OLD BONES: Yes, my liege, you see, it means. . . .

SHERIFF: It means?

OLD BONES: You see, when I rub my nose like this. . . .

Just as Old Bones is about to signal with a flick of his nose, the horse rears, and the Sheriff tumbles to the ground in a heap. He groans and loses consciousness.

OLD BONES: Well, that takes care of him!

VILLAGER 4 (*voice only*): Just leave everything to me!

VILLAGER 3: Hey! It's him!

VILLAGER 1: Where are you?

VILLAGER 4: In here!

So saying, the "Horse" removes its head. It is Villager 4.

VILLAGER 4 (*loudly*): Hakamadare strikes again!

He poses heroically. The rest of the Villagers groan.

VILLAGER 1: Hey, how did you know the signal? It only just changed!

VILLAGER 4: Because I was watching, of course! From inside the horse!

VILLAGER 3: For once you didn't get mixed up.

VILLAGER 4: Listen, I may be forgetful, but even I can remember what happened two minutes ago!

The Villagers laugh.

The two Henchmen, who have thrown themselves on the ground before the Villagers, look up and remove their masks.

HENCHMAN 1: We're just peasants from a village near here.

HENCHMAN 2: Won't you let us join you? Won't you let us be, . . .

HENCHMAN 1 and 2: Members of Hakamadare's band!

The Villagers look at one another.

VILLAGER 4: I told them on the way. They say they don't care if we're imposters. They want to join us anyway.

VILLAGER 3: Absolutely not!

VILLAGER 1: Lots of people have asked us, but we've always said . . .

VILLAGER 2: "If you want to be *like* Hakamadare, then *be* Hakamadare . . ."

VILLAGER 7: "And quest for him yourself! And if you find him, . . ."

VILLAGER 6: "Let us know!"

VILLAGER 1: It may be wrong to pretend to be Hakamadare, but the more imposters there are, the better the chance that the real Hakamadare will hear of it!

OLD BONES: If one of us imposters meets the real Hakamadare, he can let the others know, and pretty soon all the imposters will know the true Hakamadare. And when that happens, the imposters won't be imposters anymore! The ranks of Hakamadare's band will swell beyond imagination!

VILLAGERS: Aye! That's just the way it will be!

HENCHMEN 1 and 2 (*who have been listening attentively*): But, there are only two of us!

VILLAGER 5 (*softly*): It doesn't matter if there's only one. You can still be Hakamadare.

Everyone looks at Villager 5.

VILLAGER 5 (*in the same low tone*): It'd be hard, but not impossible. If it was me, I might not have been able to make it alone. But since there are two of you, it'll be that much easier.

VILLAGER 1: You find others to join you. See?

Henchmen 1 and 2 nod.

VILLAGER 4: Good luck!

Henchmen 1 and 2 get to their feet and bow deeply. The Villagers return their bow.

Blackout.

ACT 4
IT WAS HAKAMADARE WHO SAVED YOU!

Snow should be falling.

In the mountains. Night.

Voices can be heard calling, "Heave-to!" while others respond like an echo, "Heave-ho!" The voices continue reverberating through the still, snow-covered hills. They gradually draw closer, and the lights come up.

Villager 7 enters walking backward, erasing his tracks in the snow as he does so. Sensing the presence of another human being, he drops to his knees.

VILLAGER 1 (*entering*): Heave-to!

VILLAGER 7: Heave-ho!

VILLAGER 1: That you, Shichibei?

VILLAGER 7: Aye!

VILLAGER 1: You all right?

VILLAGER 7: Not a scratch.

VILLAGER 1: Good. Old Bones, Shichibei's back!

OLD BONES (*entering*): It's all right, you can come out now.

The Villagers gather. Everyone is there except Villager 2.

VILLAGER 3: You cover your tracks?

VILLAGER 7: Didn't leave a trace.

OLD BONES: Everybody here, then?

VILLAGER 1: Everyone except Jirōta. But there's nothing to worry about. Jirōta can take care of himself.

OLD BONES: Hm. Well, we did all right for ourselves again tonight.

VILLAGERS: Aye! (*They laugh.*)

VILLAGER 4: Our reputation helps.

VILLAGER 7: Everywhere we go, people are talking about Hakamadare.

VILLAGERS: Aye! Everywhere! (*They laugh with pleasure.*)

VILLAGER 5: But. . . .

Everyone looks at Villager 5.

VILLAGER 5: They're only talking about us, not the real Hakamadare.

The Villagers fall silent.

VILLAGER 1: Gorōji's right. Sometimes we think, "Maybe this time it's for real!" and trace the rumor, but it always turns out to be us they're talking about.

VILLAGER 3: Once we were sure it was Hakamadare, but when we asked, it turned out to be those peasants we met who were impersonating Hakamadare themselves.

VILLAGER 7: They were copying us. Impersonating the impersonators!

VILLAGER 4: No, we're copying the real thing and so are they. They're copies of the original just like us.

VILLAGER 7: I don't get it.

VILLAGER 4: Why not? Listen, we're not just fakes, we're copies of the real thing. If that's so, then those that copy us. . . .

OLD BONES: The only thing that matters is that we haven't heard of anybody who's seen the real Hakamadare. Not a word.

The Villagers are silent.

VILLAGER 7: Do you think? . . .

Everyone looks at 7.

VILLAGER 7: Never mind. It's nothing.

VILLAGER 3: Do we think what?

VILLAGER 1: Shichibei, you worried that maybe the sheriff caught the real Hakamadare?

VILLAGER 3: The real Hakamadare wouldn't be so easy to catch!

VILLAGER 4: No sheriff could catch him!

VILLAGER 6: They can't even catch us!

Everyone laughs.

Silence.

VILLAGER 6 (*abruptly*): But supposing. . . .

VILLAGERS (*looking at 6*): Supposing what?

VILLAGER 6 (*shrinking back*): Nothing.

VILLAGER 4 (*standing threateningly over him*): Hey! You're worried that he's dead, aren't you!

VILLAGER 6: I never said that!

VILLAGER 4: That's what you meant! You've got a lot of nerve! Hakamadare wouldn't be so easy to kill!

VILLAGER 6 (*weeping*): That's not what I meant!

Everyone is silent. The snow continues to fall.

VILLAGERS (*simultaneously*): But if Hakamadare's. . . .

They look at each other and do not continue.

OLD BONES: You want to know what'll happen to us imposters if the real Hakamadare's gone, right? (*With conviction*): Don't worry! Hakamadare's alive and well, somewhere!

VILLAGERS (*with fervor*): Aye! We never doubted it!

OLD BONES: One thing's for certain, though: the real Hakamadare hasn't heard about us yet.

VILLAGER 1: We haven't done enough to attract his attention.

VILLAGER 4: We have to become more famous.

VILLAGER 3: More people have to hear about our exploits.

OLD BONES: We have to try harder.

VILLAGERS: Aye! Aye!

VILLAGER 1: Sh!

VILLAGER 3: What is it?

VILLAGER 1: Listen.

A voice can be heard: "Heave-to!"

VILLAGER 3: It's Jirōta!

VILLAGER 4: Heave-ho!

Villager 2 enters. He is carrying what appears to be a body over his shoulder.

VILLAGER 4: Jirōta, that you?

VILLAGER 2 (*breathing hard*): Aye!

VILLAGER 4: You took your time! What's that?

VILLAGER 1: Hey, it's a woman!

VILLAGERS (*getting to their feet*): What? A woman?

VILLAGER 3: Hey! Hey! You've broken the rules! How dare you?

VILLAGER 6: Now look what you've gone and done!

VILLAGER 2: Don't . . . don't be stupid! This is no woman. Look! She's only a child!

Villager 2 lays his burden on the ground, and the other Villagers examine it.

VILLAGER 1: It is sort of a small woman.

VILLAGER 7: Is she unconscious?

VILLAGER 2: No, just asleep. She fell asleep while I was carrying her.

VILLAGER 6: She's beautiful.

Everyone is silent.

VILLAGER 3 (*to 2*): It doesn't make any difference: you still broke the rules! Hakamadare's law says we steal gold and treasure but not people!

VILLAGER 2: I know the rules. But this is no person. You can't call her a person.

VILLAGER 3: Why not? That's the first I heard children aren't people!

VILLAGER 2: That's not what I mean. I mean, she was for sale, so. . . .

OLD BONES: For sale? You mean, the baron of that manor? . . .

VILLAGER 2: That's right. I got to know the baron's servants, and while I was in the manor house, I found out what the baron's been up to. He buys people from nearby villages and sells them to *other* villages far away.

OLD BONES: This child was one of them.

VILLAGER 2: That's right. The servants who spoke to me said . . . you know, the minute you mention you're from Hakamadare's band, . . .

VILLAGER 6: People confide in you and tell you all their troubles.

VILLAGER 7: Not only that, they tell you where the strong box is and where the guard is weak.

VILLAGER 4: They tell you everything you need to know. It sort of takes the fun out of it.

VILLAGERS: Aye!

VILLAGER 2: Anyway, the servants who confided in me said there was this little orphan girl without a friend in the world, and couldn't Hakamadare do something to save her.

OLD BONES: I see.

Quiet.

VILLAGER 2: So, anyway, I thought about it. We aren't allowed to take anything but gold and treasure — under any circumstances. But this child was being sold like a sack of potatoes, so. . . .

VILLAGER 1: In that case, Jirōta, if she's a sack of potatoes, we have to divide her among the villagers.

VILLAGER 2: Don't be stupid! We can't divide a human being!

VILLAGER 1: Let me get this straight. According to you, is she a person or a sack of potatoes?

VILLAGER 2: Well, I . . .

VILLAGER 3: The point is you broke the rules!

VILLAGER 2: But . . . in that case maybe we have to bend the rules.

VILLAGER 3: You can't be changing the rules any time you want to! Promises, maybe, but rules serve a larger purpose. Larger by a long shot!

VILLAGER 2: What "larger purpose"? What're you talking about?

VILLAGER 3: The . . . you know, what makes us who we are, the. . . . (*He looks to Old Bones for help.*) Right?

OLD BONES: Yes. The way I see it, it's like this. While this child was in the manor house, she was just like a sack of potatoes, so there's nothing wrong with our helping ourselves to her. Because she's not human, right? On the other hand, once Jirōta took her out of the manor house, she wasn't for sale anymore. She stopped being a sack of potatoes and became a person. She became human.

VILLAGER 2 (*overjoyed*): Right! That's right!

VILLAGER 3 (*cocking his head*): I still think he broke the rules.

VILLAGER 4: Hey, she's waking up!

Everyone watches the girl in silence.

The girl, Kogiku, opens her eyes and looks dazedly about.

KOGIKU (*suddenly frightened and clinging to Jirōta*): Save me!

VILLAGER 2: I already did! These are my friends. They may not look it, but they're part of Hakamadare's band just like me.

VILLAGER 4: That's us! (*Seeing Kogiku still quavering with fear*): There's nothing to be afraid of!

OLD BONES (*laughing*): You're safe now, child. Nobody's going to sell you to some faraway land. We'll take care of you until we can find someone trustworthy to look after you permanently. (*To the Villagers*): Agreed?

VILLAGERS: Aye!

KOGIKU: Where is he?

OLD BONES: Who?

KOGIKU: Hakamadare, where is he?

Pause.

KOGIKU: Hakamadare saved me, right? I know all about Hakamadare, I do. Granny told me. He's tall as a cedar, as a damsel fair. He rides a fiery steed. . . .

The Villagers are at a loss.

OLD BONES: He's not here.

Kogiku looks at him suspiciously.

OLD BONES: We don't know where he is. But we're all part of Hakamadare's band. We're his men. Even if we've never met him, that's who we are. We want to find Hakamadare, and that's why we're traveling like this. From now on, you're going to travel with us and look for the man who saved your life, Hakamadare. And when you find him, you can thank him for everything he's done. All right?

Kogiku still eyes him suspiciously.

Pause. The snow is falling harder now.

VILLAGER 1: Old Bones, if we don't get moving soon, we'll be buried alive.

OLD BONES: You're right. Come on, everybody!

VILLAGERS: Aye! (*They rise. Villager 2 hoists Kogiku to his shoulder.*)

VILLAGER 1: Which way should we go this time, Old Bones?

OLD BONES: Good question. Up to now we've slept during the day, when the sun was warm, and traveled at night. . . . (*Looking at the snowy sky*): But it looks like we'll have to hibernate for a while like bears and wild boar.

The Villagers troop off.

Music. Everyone sings.

> No flag do we follow,
> No one told us to go.
> Wandering o'er the land,
> We're Hakamadare's band!

How much farther do we go,
Searching high and low,
Through snow and sand,
Seeking Hakamadare's band?

*If possible, we should show the Villagers continuing their journey.
And here, an interlude.*

INTERLUDE

*The setting consists of a huge, gnarled pine tree, abstractly represent-
ed. The lights in the auditorium remain on. In fact, the entire scene
parodies the structure and staging of classical nō drama.*
    *Villager 1 and Villager 2 enter with a pot and a bucket. They seat
themselves on either side of the stage.*
VILLAGER 1: Yah! (*He strikes the bucket.*)
VILLAGER 2: Ohhh! (*He strikes the pot.*)
Old Bones, Villager 7, and Villager 5 enter.
OLD BONES, VILLAGER 7, and VILLAGER 5 (*together*):

If lies be true
And reality a dream
Then dream I will,
As others do! (*Repeat*)

OLD BONES: Over hills and through dales. . . .
VILLAGER 5: Past fields and villages. . . .
VILLAGER 7: Etcetera, etcetera! . . .
OLD BONES: We continued our journey. (*To 5 and 7*): We certainly had
    our share of troubles on our journey!
VILLAGER 5 and VILLAGER 7: Verily! Verily!
OLD BONES: And our hardships aren't over yet.
VILLAGER 5 and VILLAGER 7: Nay, verily!
OLD BONES: What are we suffering for?
VILLAGER 5 and VILLAGER 7: So we can continue our quest

for Hakamadare.

OLD BONES: And why do we quest for Hakamadare?

VILLAGER 5 and VILLAGER 7: So we can hasten the coming of the Hakamadarean Age!

OLD BONES: And what will the world be like after the coming of Hakamadare?

VILLAGER 7: We'll experience bliss like we've never known!

OLD BONES: What will it be like, this "bliss like we've never known"?

VILLAGER 5 (*gruffly*): How should we know?

VILLAGER 7: If we knew, it would be "bliss like we've known all along"!

VILLAGER 5: And if we'd seen it in a dream, it would be "bliss we'd seen before"!

OLD BONES: But is it possible not to wonder what it'd be like, not to dream of it at night?

VILLAGER 7: That depends on the person.

OLD BONES: How about you? If you dreamed a dream, it wouldn't hurt to share it with your fellows.

VILLAGER 7 (*chuckling*): I suppose not.

OLD BONES: Come on, tell us your dream.

VILLAGER 5: Tell us your dream.

VILLAGER 7: All right, then, this is my dream.

Old Bones and Villager 5 seat themselves upstage right. Music. (The pot and the bucket replace the drums used in nō.)

VILLAGER 7: First, I fall asleep. (*He pretends to sleep standing up.*) Like this. (*The following lines are spoken to no one in particular.*) Look! A scrumptious dumpling! (*He consumes it greedily.*) Look! A delicious fish! (*He gobbles it down.*) And look! Barrels of wine! (*He takes huge gulps.*) Look! Delicious. . . .

OLD BONES (*disgusted*): Is that all?

VILLAGER 7: No! There's more! Look! Delicious. . . .

OLD BONES: Don't you see anything but food?

VILLAGER 7: Money!

OLD BONES: Money?

VILLAGER 7 (*chuckling*): What should I do with all this money? I know! I'll buy a delicious. . . .

OLD BONES: Is food all you can think about? How about women?

VILLAGER 7 (*clapping his hands*): Women, right! Women would fix me all kinds of delicacies! Next time I'll have to dream about wo-men!

OLD BONES: Looks like "bliss" to you isn't anything special. It's my turn next.

VILLAGER 5 and VILLAGER 7: This should be good! This should be good!

OLD BONES (*chanting*): Men are creatures of desire and passion. . . .

VILLAGER 7: How's that different from what I said?

OLD BONES: Never mind! I'm giving you your cue!

OLD BONES, VILLAGER 5, and VILLAGER 7:

> Men are creatures of desire and passion.
> If others can dream,
> Then I will too,
> After my fashion!

Old Bones pretends to sleep.

OLD BONES: First, I sleep. All the worries of the day come flooding in: "I have to do this; I better do that." But before long, I slumber. All right, all you creatures who inhabit my dreams, appear!

WOMEN (*voices only*): At your command!

OLD BONES: Where are you?

WOMEN (*voices*): At your command!

Three Beauties appear.

OLD BONES: There you are!

BEAUTIES 1, 2, and 3: At your service, milord.

OLD BONES: You were quicker than I thought. Let me see what you look like!

The Beauties blush and cover their faces with their hands.

OLD BONES: Don't be shy!

The Beauties conceal their faces.

OLD BONES: Show me your faces! Now!

The Beauties raise their faces. They are wearing the masks of old hags. Old Bones recoils in shock.

OLD BONES: Ahhh! (*He tries to flee.*)

BEAUTY 1: Where do you think you're going?

BEAUTY 2: You said you wanted to see us.

BEAUTY 3: We're figments of your imagination!

BEAUTIES 1, 2, and 3: "Women! Give me women!" you said.

OLD BONES: But I didn't expect such shriveled. . . .

BEAUTIES 1, 2, and 3: Shriveled!? Look who's talking!

OLD BONES: But this is a dream! At least in my dreams. . . .

BEAUTIES 1, 2, and 3: All right, but only in your dreams.

OLD BONES: Agreed.

BEAUTIES 1, 2, and 3: All right, then.

The Beauties spin around and return wearing the masks of comely young women.

OLD BONES: That's more like it!

Old Bones tries to embrace them but is rebuffed and falls flat on his back. Villager 7 looks on with unconcealed mirth.

OLD BONES: Oh, my aching back! You'd think that in my dreams at least I'd be able to stand upright! Wait! I can! I can!

The Beauties and Old Bones dance. After a series of acrobatic gyrations, they coalesce in a tableau vivant.

VILLAGER 7: Now that's stretching things, dream or not!

Meanwhile, the Beauties and Old Bones continue.

BEAUTIES 1, 2, and 3: Darling, sweetie, lovey pie?

OLD BONES: Yes?

BEAUTY 1: This may be a dream . . .

OLD BONES: Yes?

BEAUTY 2: But don't you think three to one is excessive?

OLD BONES: Why?

BEAUTY 3: Even in the Age of Hakamadare, the ratio of women to men
. . .

OLD BONES: Will be the same? In other words, if I have three women, then two men will go without? That won't do. I'll settle for one.

BEAUTIES 1, 2, and 3 (*erotically*): Which one will you choose?

OLD BONES (*thinking*): Which shall I choose: the tall one, the plump one, the one who's petite? . . .

The Beauties dance in turn.

OLD BONES: I know!

BEAUTIES 1, 2, and 3: Have you made up your mind?

OLD BONES: Yes.

BEAUTIES 1, 2, and 3: Which one will it be?

OLD BONES: Here's what I've decided.

He selects a Beauty, let's say the tall one.

BEAUTIES 2 and 3: You old coot! (*They shove Old Bones, who spins around and lands on the ground.*) You make us so mad! You make us so mad! (*They exit.*)

The remaining Beauty (Beauty 1) nurses Old Bones.

OLD BONES (*happily*): Now it's just the two of us, alone at last!

BEAUTY 1: Now that we're man and wife, we have nothing to hide! (*She removes her mask and casts it aside.*)

OLD BONES (*seeing her face*): Help!

BEAUTY 1: Men! Men!

Old Bones is knocked to the ground again.

Villager 7 is beside himself with laughter.

BEAUTY 1: You make me so mad! You make me so mad! (*She exits.*)

OLD BONES (*massaging his rump*): Bliss isn't easy to imagine! Even with so many women, things just don't go right. I guess I've still got a lot to learn!

VILLAGER 7 (*to 5*): Now it's your turn, Gorōji.

OLD BONES: Get up!

Villager 5 has fallen asleep for real.

OLD BONES: Get up and tell us about your dream!

Villager 5 struggles to his feet, but he appears still to be sleeping. He glides downstage.

VILLAGER 5: All right, you barons, sheriffs! Appear!

VILLAGER 7: He's talking in his sleep!

OLD BONES: Let him be.

VILLAGER 5: Misers, show yourselves! I want to see the miserable swine who took the food from my mouth and rubbed my face in the dirt! I want to see all those who watched me suffer and pretended not to see. I want everyone who patted me on the back and told me that "the strong persevere," and to "render unto authority its due" to show your faces! I want to see every last one of you who told me, "I sympathize with you, but these things take time. Don't do anything rash." It's the Hakamadarean Age! The weak have inherited the earth. Now you'll get what's coming to you! Show your faces! Line up before me!

A herd of cows, horses, and other beasts appears. They wear hats and other accoutrements to indicate that they are the incarnations of landlords and sheriffs.

ANIMALS: As you command, my liege.
VILLAGER 5: Too slow! Do it again! (*He kicks them.*)
ANIMALS: As you command, my liege.
VILLAGER 5: Show more respect! (*He strikes them.*)
ANIMALS: As you command, my liege.
VILLAGER 5: You still haven't got it right! Take that, and that, and that!
   (*He beats them mercilessly.*)
Villager 7 and Old Bones try to restrain him.
VILLAGER 7: Take it easy, take it easy!
OLD BONES: Once you resort to violence, where's it going to end?
VILLAGER 5: Let me go! Let me go! (*He knocks Old Bones and Villager
   7 to the ground.*)
OLD BONES: Control yourself!
VILLAGER 7: I sympathize with you, but these things take time!
OLD BONES and VILLAGER 7: Don't do anything rash! (*Realizing what
   they are saying, they clap their hands over their mouths.*)
ANIMALS: Mercy! Have mercy!
VILLAGER 5: Mercy?! I'll show you mercy, the same mercy you showed
   us when we begged you on bended knees. I'll return it three-fold,
   seven-fold!
He goes berserk and finally collapses. The Animals exit.
After a few moments, he sits up.
OLD BONES and VILLAGER 7: You awake?
VILLAGER 5: Is it my turn already? All right, here's my dream. It goes
   like this. All of you, come out! It's the Hakamadarean Age!
*There is lively music. All the Villagers appear and dance. Villager 5
smiles broadly as the dancers swirl about him.*
SONG:

   Heave-to, heave-ho!
   We dance to and fro,
      For our dreams are not just exuberance.
   Mankind will awaken to the end of days,
   Heaven on earth, all mouths utter praise,
      For the one who will bring us deliverance.

The dance continues, and the interlude ends.

ACT 5
THERE'S SOMETHING SUSPICIOUS ABOUT THAT MAN

Scene 1
Several years later.
A valley deep in the mountains. It is late winter, almost spring.
Kogiku has grown into a young woman of sixteen. She sits combing
her hair as she sings.
KOGIKU:

> Shall I ask the hare,
> Bounding through the pass?
> Shall I ask the pheasant,
> Shrieking in the grass?
> Oh, tell me, do,
> Where my true love dwells.

> Shall I ask the crow,
> Cawing in the trees?
> Shall I ask the hawk,
> Sailing on the breeze?
> Oh, show me, do,
> Where my true love dwells.

A man has appeared unnoticed high on the stage. He is unshaved and
his hair is unkempt. A long sword hangs at his side. He stands motion-
less, watching Kogiku. He is thirty-five or six, perhaps younger.
MAN: Girl!
Kogiku notices him, but, ignorant of fear, only returns his stare.
MAN: You're beautiful. Do you live around here?
Kogiku shakes her head.
MAN (*smiling wryly*): Seems I look out of place here. Which means
   you're not. (*He sits down.*) A beautiful spot to call home, I'll say that.
   You follow the woodsmen's path along steep slopes deep into the
   bosom of the mountain. The path disappears, but I noticed some-
   thing: signs, almost imperceptible signs, that people—not animals—
   had passed this way. No ordinary man could follow those tracks.

Then all of a sudden, here I was. The sun is shining; there's water; there even appear to be fields ready for planting. But no houses and no people. Then I heard someone singing. (*He laughs.*) I thought it might be an apparition. For a while I just stood watching you, under your spell.

KOGIKU: You a sheriff?

MAN: Do I look like a sheriff?

Kogiku shakes her head.

MAN: Where are your parents?

Kogiku shakes her head furiously.

MAN: But surely you're not out here alone?

KOGIKU: I'm with my comrades.

MAN: Comrades? Is that so? And what sort of comrades are they?

KOGIKU: You'd be surprised if I told you.

MAN: That'd be a change! I'd like to be surprised. It would do me good. I'm still young. I think it's fair to say that. Then, why do I feel so weary? I suppose I only have myself to blame. But then again, perhaps there's more to it than that. Perhaps it's *because* I'm young. In any case, I sense something extraordinary is going to happen today. You really are beautiful, you know? It would seem I've been alone too long. I should have set out sooner. I should have revived my wandering long ago.

KOGIKU (*humming the song she sang earlier*): We're Hakamadare's band.

MAN: What!? Hakamadare?

KOGIKU (*pleased*): See, I told you you'd be surprised!

Man leaps down and grabs Kogiku. Kogiku lets out a choked scream.

MAN: Your scent is that of a woman. It appears you're no forest sprite trying to deceive me. All right then, what's this about Hakamadare?

KOGIKU: Le . . . let me go!

A stone streaks through the air and strikes Man, distracting him. Kogiku flees his grasp. Simultaneously, Villager 2 runs in from the opposite direction.

VILLAGER 2: Kogiku, you all right?

KOGIKU: Jirōta! (*She runs and hides behind him.*)

VILLAGER 2: Who are you?

MAN: You kin?

VILLAGER 2: No.

MAN: Lover?

VILLAGER 2: D . . . don't be stupid!

MAN: Take it easy! I'm sorry, girl, I just had to find out if you were flesh and blood. (*To 2*): You one of the "comrades" she was talking about?

VILLAGER 2: Where'd you come from?

MAN: She said you were Hakamadare's men.

Pause.

VILLAGER 2: What if we are?

MAN: I'd like to see him, this Hakamadare. Take me to him if he's here.

Villager 2 and Kogiku look at each other.

VILLAGER 2: You know him? You know Hakamadare?

MAN: You could say that. As a matter of fact, I know him rather well. Once upon a time, I was closer to him than any man alive.

KOGIKU: The real Hakamadare? Or. . . .

MAN: What do you mean, "or"? There's only one Hakamadare.

VILLAGER 2: Not so fast. The world is filled with imposters these days.

MAN: I just found that out. All sorts of things have happened while I was away. In any case, take me to your leader.

VILLAGER 2: Let me get this straight. The Hakamadare you know is the real Hakamadare?

MAN: Once upon a time, there wasn't a man in the capital who hadn't heard of Hakamadare. He was captured more than once, but no jail could hold him. Then he vanished without a trace. How many years has it been? Not a soul knows what became of Hakamadare after that. How could they? Except me, that is.

Villager 2 and Kogiku again exchange glances.

VILLAGER 2: It looks like. . . .

KOGIKU: Yes!

VILLAGER 2: We've finally found a clue! A clue to the real, the true Hakamadare!

Someone whistles, and Villager 5 appears high in one of the trees.

VILLAGER 2: You hear that?

VILLAGER 5: I heard.

Villager 2 signals.

A bird chatters. It is actually Villager 5 imitating the call on his flute.

The scene shifts. The mound in the center of the stage opens slowly, and inside is "the mountain fastness."

Scene 2

"Mountain fastness" may be an overstatement. It is more like a pit dug in the earth. Old Bones and the Villagers, including Kogiku, are seated in a ring. Man sits before them.

MAN (*impressed*): So even though you were only peasants, you wanted so much to be like Hakamadare that you. . . .

OLD BONES: That was seven years ago.

MAN: Seven years!

VILLAGER 1: But in all that time we never did anything to make Hakamadare ashamed.

VILLAGER 4: We've observed the rule to steal but never be cruel.

VILLAGER 3: We're sorry to have used Hakamadare's name, but we've done nothing to dishonor it.

VILLAGER 7: We're even sorrier to have told others to do the same thing.

VILLAGER 2: But it was the only way we knew to attract his attention!

VILLAGER 6: It's true! (*He weeps.*)

Pause.

VILLAGER 1: Now it's your turn. Tell us about Hakamadare!

VILLAGER 3: When was the last time you saw him? Where?

Man is lost in thought.

VILLAGER 6: When did you first meet him?

VILLAGER 7: And where?

Man is still absorbed in his own thoughts.

KOGIKU: What's wrong?

MAN: What? Oh, let me see. The last time I saw him was . . . how many years has it been? A year?

VILLAGER 1: A year?

MAN: Three years? . . .

VILLAGER 3: Three years?

MAN: No, longer than that. Five years, seven years. . . .

Pause.

VILLAGER 4: That can't be right.

The Villagers stir but do not speak.

OLD BONES: Quiet! Let him speak. (*To Man*): And what was Hakamadare doing in the capital at the time?

VILLAGER 1: What about his followers?

VILLAGER 2: Hakamadare's band?

MAN: Hakamadare's band was ... by that time, there was no band. It
had been destroyed by dissension.

VILLAGER 4: No band? How can that be?

VILLAGER 3: Destroyed by dissension, not Hakamadare's band!

VILLAGER 7: That's right! He's lying!

VILLAGERS: He's lying!

Pause.

MAN: You're right. Everything I said is lies.

There is commotion among the Villagers.

MAN: I never met anyone named Hakamadare. He may have earned
some fame in his time, but a thief's a thief. Just another scoundrel.

VILLAGER 2: What!

The Villagers jump to their feet.

OLD BONES: Sit down!

MAN: How can a thief who doesn't intend to steal *power* be anything
more than a thief? It's laughable! (*He smirks.*) I haven't eaten for
days. To tell the truth, all I wanted from you was a meal. I said
whatever I thought you wanted to hear. Sorry to disappoint you,
Hakamadare's band! (*He roars with laughter.*)

Pause.

OLD BONES: Kogiku, give our guest some food.

VILLAGER 2 and VILLAGER 4: Old Bones!

OLD BONES (*to Kogiku, who is hesitating*): Do as I say.

MAN: Some wine, too, please.

VILLAGER 7: Why, you! ...

VILLAGER 3 (*angry himself*): Don't forget the rules!

VILLAGER 1: The real Hakamadare treats everyone with respect.

KOGIKU: He serves them with a smile.

VILLAGER 1 and VILLAGER 3: That's right.

OLD BONES (*fondly*): You've learned your lessons well, Kogiku.

Kogiku prepares the food.

MAN: But I'll admit I'm impressed. Seven years! And you still expect to meet Hakamadare?

VILLAGER 1: We'll meet him.

VILLAGERS: Of course we will!

MAN: I see. Your faith ... it's almost obscene. (*He accepts the cup Kogiku offers.*)

Villager 7 takes the bottle of wine from Kogiku. He grins stupidly as he fills Man's cup.

MAN: What's so funny?

VILLAGER 7: Nothing. I'm serving you with a smile, that's all.

The remark breaks the tension, and the Villagers roar with laughter.

MAN (*to Old Bones*): You been here long?

OLD BONES: Five years. We hole up here for the winter and set out again each spring. When we return late in the fall, there's enough food in the fields to last us through the winter.

VILLAGER 6: We know some special tricks with fertilizer.

MAN: Hm, I've got to hand it to you. Will you be setting out again this year?

OLD BONES: Eventually.

VILLAGER 4: As usual, we'll find a few local misers before we do, and. . . . (*The Villagers look at him sternly and he stops.*)

MAN: Attack them like the wind? You people amaze me! (*He gulps the wine down and immediately extends the cup for more.*)

Blackout.

ACT 6
HAKAMADARE WOULD NEVER DO THAT!

Scene 1

Fields near the fastness.

SONG (*the Villagers sing*):

> Oh, the seeds we sow,
> Our food to grow!
> The seeds we sow!
> The seeds we sow!

Oh, the seeds you know,
Will grow and grow!
The seeds we sow!
The seeds we sow!

Oh, the food we grow,
'S from the seeds we sow!
The seeds we sow!
The seeds we sow!

The song repeats.

The Villagers are working in the fields. Man walks among them aloof to their labors.

Villager 2 approaches Old Bones. The Villagers should be walking back and forth, treading the wheat sprouts. Thus, Villager 2 approaches Old Bones and then passes him. Villagers 1 and 7 are in the same vicinity, and from the point of view of the audience they will appear to overlap and then disperse.

VILLAGER 2: Old Bones!

OLD BONES: Yes?

VILLAGER 2: How much longer is he going to hang around?

OLD BONES: He seems to like it here.

VILLAGER 2: He likes it too much, if you ask me. You think he's planning to come with us?

OLD BONES: I doubt it.

VILLAGER 2: You may doubt it, but . . . I think he's got his eye on Kogiku.

OLD BONES: Kogiku?

Villager 2 passes out of earshot and falls silent.

OLD BONES: What about Kogiku?

KOGIKU (*approaching*): Did you call me?

OLD BONES (*pretending not to understand and looking at Villager 2*): Did you say something, Kogiku?

KOGIKU (*looking at Villager 2 and then back to Old Bones*): Humph! (*She moves away.*)

VILLAGER 2 (*his work bringing him back toward Old Bones*): I said, I think he's after Kogiku!

OLD BONES: But she's only a child!

VILLAGER 2: Not any more.

OLD BONES: You think so?

VILLAGER 1 and VILLAGER 7 (*with certitude*): Not any more!

OLD BONES: I see. In other words, the fact that you're worried, Jirōta, means, . . .

VILLAGER 1 (*in a singsong*): Kogiku and Jirōta!

VILLAGER 7 (*similarly*): Jirōta and Kogiku!

OLD BONES: Is that it?

VILLAGER 2: D . . . don't be stupid! Kogiku'd never give me a second thought!

OLD BONES: Broke it off already, eh?

VILLAGER 2: Not exactly.

OLD BONES: Then what exactly?

VILLAGER 2: She's in love with someone else.

OLD BONES: You mean me?

VILLAGER 2: Hah!

Villagers 1 and 7 laugh also.

OLD BONES: What's so funny? Who then?

VILLAGER 2: Hakamadare. The real Hakamadare.

OLD BONES: Hakamadare? But she's never even seen him.

VILLAGER 2: All the more reason.

VILLAGER 1 and VILLAGER 7: Aye!

OLD BONES: Is that the way a young girl's mind works?

VILLAGER 2: She won't even look at another man till she meets Hakamadare.

VILLAGER 1 and VILLAGER 7: He's probably right.

OLD BONES: Well, I'll be!

VILLAGER 2: I want to look out for her until then.

VILLAGER 1 and VILLAGER 7: Aye!

OLD BONES: Well, I'll be!

At this point, the same bird call heard earlier resounds through the forest. If the planting song is still being sung, it ends now.

VILLAGER 7: Somebody's in the forest.

OLD BONES: But that signal means no serious threat.

VILLAGER 1: Maybe the woodcutters have lost their way again. We'll have to treat them to a meal and ask them to keep our secret.

The Sheriff who appeared in Act Three enters upstage. He is now dressed as an outlaw and is accompanied by three Henchmen. Two of the Henchmen appeared earlier, the third is new.

FORMER SHERIFF: Stay, churlish peasant knaves!

VILLAGERS: Yes, my liege! Good-day, my liege! (*They greet the intruder but whisper among themselves*): I've seen that face before! Me too! Isn't he? . . . That's right! (*Etcetera.*)

FORMER SHERIFF: What's all the commotion?

OLD BONES: A thousand apologies, my liege. (*To Villagers*): Show a little respect! (*To Former Sheriff*): We haven't seen your excellency in these parts before. Are you from around here?

FORMER SHERIFF: Ahem, I am none other than the illustrious Hakamadare!

Villagers wink at each other.

OLD BONES: So you're the famous Hakamadare! What does the world-famous Hakamadare want in these backwoods with churlish peasant knaves like us?

FORMER SHERIFF: Nothing in particular. I lost my way. I'm hungry and I felt like some wine. I see ye hast women too!

Kogiku hastily flees to Villager 2.

VILLAGER 2 (*to Kogiku*): Don't be afraid. That's right, you don't recognize him. You weren't with us yet!

FORMER SHERIFF: One doesn't see many damsels as fair these days. I could sell her or just keep her for myself.

VILLAGER 2: That's enough!

OLD BONES: Jirōta! (*He warns Villager 2 to keep quiet.*) Your excellency?

VILLAGER 1: Is Hakamadare really . . .

VILLAGER 3: Such a ruthless scoundrel?

VILLAGER 1: Of course, we wouldn't know, but. . . .

VILLAGER 4: What are you talking about? This vermin isn't Hakamadare! We ran into him a few years back. . . .

VILLAGERS (*silencing him*): We know!

Just then, Man looms up before Former Sheriff.

FORMER SHERIFF: Wha . . . what? . . .

The glistening blade of Man's sword slices through space like a serpent. Former Sheriff and two of his Henchmen fall down dead.

VILLAGERS (*shocked*): Ah!

With a shout, the frightened Villagers cluster together. The smaller

Villagers leap to the shoulders of their larger comrades and cling to them like locusts in a comic jumble of limbs.

Simultaneously, Henchman 3 curls himself into a ball and tries to roll away.

HENCHMAN 3: Mercy! Save me! (*He grinds his face into the earth.*)

MAN: You think you can get away! (*He raises his bloody sword to deal the final blow.*)

VILLAGERS (*still clustered together, sternly*): Don't! It's the rule!

MAN: Rule?

VILLAGERS (*in the same tone*): Hakamadare would never do that!

MAN (*laughing*): You fools! What are you afraid of?

The words are hardly out of Man's mouth when he realizes that the Villagers, who had seemed to be clustering together in fear, have actually arranged themselves in an ingenious system of defense. The Villager who occupies the uppermost position, for example, brandishes a sickle and is ready to pounce at any moment. In short, the Villagers have assumed the form of a giant with numberless hands and numberless weapons who looms menacingly overhead. What is more, there is the possibility that at any moment this titan will revert to its seven component parts (excluding Old Bones and Kogiku) and attack like a swarm of bees.

Even Man cannot help staggering back in surprise.

VILLAGERS: Hakamadare doesn't take life unnecessarily!

Henchman 3—actually a spy—grins.

HENCHMAN 3: Thank you! Oh, thank you!

Music.

Scene 2

The mountain fastness. The Villagers are honing their weapons. Man is seated in one corner. Kogiku is also present.

VILLAGER 1: Let's get down to business.

VILLAGERS: Aye!

VILLAGER 1: The snow has melted. The river's overflowing its banks, and the flowers are ready to burst into bloom. It's spring again.

VILLAGERS (*enthusiastically*): Spring!

VILLAGER 3: It's time for us to set out.

VILLAGERS (*enthusiastically*): Aye!

VILLAGER 4: This time comes every year, so I should be used to it, but. . . .

VILLAGER 2: I know. We go through the same thing every spring, so we shouldn't feel anything special, but. . . .

VILLAGER 7: But when it comes time to end our hibernation and look out of our hole. . . .

VILLAGER 6: It feels like, you know, it feels . . .

VILLAGERS: Good! (*They all laugh.*)

OLD BONES: You took the word right out of my mouth. All right, then, are we ready?

VILLAGERS: Aye!

VILLAGER 6: Don't worry about the fertilizer. (*He slaps his chest*): leave everything to me.

VILLAGER 7: And as for provisions, (*He slaps his chest*): leave them to me!

VILLAGER 1: Everything else is in order.

OLD BONES: Then we're ready . . .

VILLAGER 4 (*with bravado*): To teach the local landlords a lesson!

OLD BONES: How are the villages at the foot of the mountain doing?

VILLAGER 2: Aye, last year, we taught the local landlords a lesson, but. . . .

VILLAGER 7: We swept their coffers clean, but. . . .

VILLAGER 4: By this time they'll be filled with rice and gold.

VILLAGER 3: And the pain of the people will have increased to the same degree.

VILLAGER 2: Aye, we distributed gold among them, but they'll be reduced to poverty again by now.

VILLAGER 6: It was that way last year.

VILLAGER 4: And so it was the year before that.

VILLAGER 2 (*not particularly depressed at the prospect*): We're just going around in circles.

VILLAGERS (*similarly*): Around and around in circles.

Man bursts out laughing. The Villagers stare at him.

VILLAGER 2: What're you laughing at?

The others restrain Villager 2.

MAN: You people! So, what're you going to do?

Pause.

MAN: Where are you going to break the circle, that's what I want to know? (*He laughs.*) You're going to attack the landlords, but by next spring. . . .

VILLAGER 4: Next spring we'll attack them again.

MAN: And the year after that?

VILLAGER 4: We'll attack them again. (*To the other Villagers.*) Right?

The Villagers nod.

MAN (*his lips curling in a snide grin*): You're just going to go around in circles forever, is that it? I can see where you're going to end up.

OLD BONES: End up?

MAN: Nowhere.

VILLAGER 4: You don't know what you're talking about! The landlords stash away their gold, and we steal it. They stash and we steal. (*To the others*): He's dumber than I thought!

MAN: Old Bones!

OLD BONES: Yes?

MAN: Surely you must see? You're a wily old fox.

OLD BONES: See what?

MAN: Answer me! Where do you think you and your little band are going to end up?

Old Bones does not respond.

Everyone looks at Old Bones. Pause.

OLD BONES: We're not going around in circles.

MAN: No?

OLD BONES: It seems like we are, but in fact, (*he draws a spiral in the dirt with his cane*): we're moving in a spiral. We're going around and around, drawing closer and closer to the core. And there. . . . (*His cane stops at the center of the spiral.*)

VILLAGER 1: There?

VILLAGER 3: What's there?

OLD BONES (*sternly*): You know as well as I do! That's where we'll find Hakamadare! When we meet Hakamadare, that'll be the end of us as we have been, and we'll be born anew!

Man bursts out laughing. The Villagers stare at him resentfully.

OLD BONES (*calmly, as if Man does not disturb him in the least*): All right, let's get on with it. We start our raids tonight. Is everything ready?

VILLAGER 1: We plan to start with the east village.

VILLAGER 3: How're we going to break into the manor house?

VILLAGER 2: The guard's the weakest at the rear.

VILLAGER 5: But the servants and the women and children sleep near the rear.

VILLAGER 2: Then we'll have to go over the wall.

OLD BONES: Over the wall it is, then. Agreed?

VILLAGERS: Aye!

MAN (*bursting out*): Fools!

The Villagers stare at Man.

MAN (*spitting out the words in disgust*): There's only one way to attack, and that's where the guard is weakest. You're planning a night assault. You can't concern yourselves with women and children! You people! . . .

OLD BONES: Go ahead. Where do we set the fires?

VILLAGER 7: That's another problem. There are peasant huts built up alongside the manor house.

VILLAGER 6: We'll have to cover them with wet straw like we did before.

OLD BONES: Then that's what we'll do.

MAN (*in the same manner as before*): What difference do a few huts make? If you've got time to worry about that. . . .

VILLAGER 4: No!

VILLAGER 6: Hakamadare wouldn't do that!

MAN: How do you know?

Pause.

MAN (*standing*): Seriously: how can you believe so strongly in a man you've never met? What does this Hakamadare of yours look like? How old is he? Is he tall of short? What does his voice sound like?

Pause. The Villagers look at one another.

VILLAGER 1: You know, we used to spend a lot of time . . .

VILLAGER 3: Talking about what he'd look like . . .

VILLAGER 2: But then. . . .

VILLAGER 4: We stopped. It didn't seem to matter any more.

VILLAGER 7: I used to think he'd be a a big, strong man about forty, but these days . . . (*he looks out of the corner of his eye at Old Bones*): I

imagine him as a scrawny, long-legged old man with white hair. . . .
OLD BONES: Sounds like me!
VILLAGER 7: He'd be more refined than you, Old Bones.
The Villagers guffaw.
KOGIKU: I . . .
All eyes turn to Kogiku.
KOGIKU: I think he'd be tall as a cedar and. . . .
OLD BONES: We know what your Hakamadare'd be like: young and tan—like Jirōta, only more reliable.
Villagers laugh again.
VILLAGER 1: Old Bones, anytime you're ready.
OLD BONES: All right, let's go.
VILLAGERS: Aye!
Blackout. Music.

ACT 7
FORGIVE US, HAKAMADARE, WE DIDN'T RECOGNIZE YOU!

Near the fastness. Night. Kogiku is alone.
KOGIKU:

> Shall I ask the river,
> Through the valley flowing?
> Shall I ask the wind,
> Through the cedars blowing?
> Oh, tell me, do,
> Where my true love dwells.

Man appears in the moonlight.
KOGIKU (*sensing his presence*): Didn't you go with the others?
Man does not answer.
KOGIKU: I suppose not. Nobody asked you, did they?
Man still does not respond.
KOGIKU: If you ask me, the best thing'd be if you left. The sooner the better.

MAN: Why?

KOGIKU: There're rumors . . . that you've been going down into the villages, looting and raping. . . .

MAN: So what?

KOGIKU: Hakamadare would never. . . .

MAN: I wonder. After all, Hakamadare's human, too. Even the "real" Hakamadare you're always talking about. Granted, your comrades are also human, I suppose. (*He smiles.*) Although sometimes I wonder.

Kogiku starts to move away without speaking.

MAN: What's your hurry? Take last night, for example, when they were talking about the time they attacked the manor house to the east. Or better still, before that, that business about where to set the fires.

KOGIKU: They said there were peasant huts built right up against the manor house, so they'd cover them with wet straw.

MAN: You see! Because they took those foolish precautions, they almost got themselves caught last night. Old Bones was slow to escape, and the sheriff had him surrounded.

KOGIKU: So you slew all the sheriff's men. That's what you want to say, isn't it?

MAN: If I hadn't, they would have killed Old Bones.

KOGIKU (*laughing*): Not Old Bones! He'd have told them some story about how he came to watch the fire. They'd have let him go. Hah-hah-hah!

MAN: Maybe. But why take unnecessary chances? What does it get you?

KOGIKU (*defensively*): Otherwise, when we meet up with the real Hakamadare. . . .

MAN: Would you like to meet him, Kogiku?

Kogiku looks at him in surprise.

MAN: I'll introduce you.

KOGIKU: You can't fool me!

MAN: What good would it do to fool you? By all the stars in heaven, this alone is the truth. I swear it.

KOGIKU: You said you didn't know him.

MAN: Oh, I know him. Better than anyone. As a matter of fact, in all the world, I'm the only one who knows Hakamadare. It's time I helped you face the truth, Kogiku.

KOGIKU (*after a pause*): You're not going to tell me he's . . . dead?

MAN: No, he's alive. Right here.

KOGIKU: Here?

MAN: I'm Hakamadare.

Pause. The moonlight is white and cold.

Kogiku bursts out laughing.

MAN: You may not believe it. The truth is often difficult to accept. But sooner or later, you have to accept it, no matter how distasteful it may be. The sooner the better, I should think. If you like, there's a way to be sure. Find a sheriff from the capital, one who worked in the jail seven years ago. He's not likely to have forgotten a man who escaped so many times. Just draw a picture of me and show him. The city may be falling down, but if you put your mind to it, you won't have any trouble finding a sheriff who remembers me!

Kogiku is no longer smiling.

MAN: What did you expect? Hah-hah! Sorry if I disappointed you. I didn't mean to dash your dream. Or maybe I did. If part of me wanted to leave here quietly and let you preserve your precious dream, part of me was going crazy watching you good-hearted peasants play at being Hakamadare. That's the way I am, and always have been. Anyway, now I've chosen. I made my choice when I told you the truth. Starting today, I'm going back to being Hakamadare. Hakamadare! I'll kill and steal and rape as the spirit moves me! I'm the real Hakamadare!

KOGIKU: You're lying! It's all lies!

MAN: It appears the truth doesn't appeal to you, does it, Kogiku? But from now on, you'll have to place me beside the image of Hakamadare you've built out of dreams in your breast. Because, you see, the Hakamadare you imagine is the real imposter! He's a fabric of lies!

Kogiku tries to flee, but Man grabs her.

KOGIKU: Ah!

MAN: How does it feel to be held by a man whose arms are soaked to the elbow in blood?

KOGIKU: Le . . . let me go! The smell!

MAN (*still holding her*): The truth stinks, does it? The smell of a real man, not the gossamer Hakamadare you nurtured in your dreams. . . .

VILLAGER 2 (*bursting out of the trees*): Leave her alone! (*He pounces on Man.*)

Agilely, Man strikes him in the solar plexus with the scabbard of his sword. Villager 2 drops paralyzed to the ground.

KOGIKU: Jirōta!

She kneels at his side. Villager 2 groans but cannot move.

MAN (*into the surrounding forest*): The rest of you come out, too! I've known you were there all along. If you wanted my blood, you could have blown darts. Or were you afraid you'd hit the girl? Hah-hah! No, you were afraid you might kill me and break your precious rules. (*He roars with laughter.*) Show yourselves!

OLD BONES: All right.

Old Bones appears, followed by the other Villagers.

MAN: That's what I thought. All right, you all heard me, so there's no use repeating. Wait a minute! There's someone else!

OLD BONES: That can't be. Everyone's. . . .

MAN: I said, show yourself!

He looses a dagger, and a black shadow falls out of a tree. It is the spy (Henchman 3) who was saved in Act Six.

VILLAGER 1 (*running to the figure and looking at his face*): It's that fellow from the other day!

VILLAGER 5 (*pointing into the forest*): Look! Up there!

White smoke can be seen rising from one of the trees.

OLD BONES: It's a signal!

MAN (*examining the body*): He's one of the sheriff's men. I should have killed him when I had the chance. (*To the Villagers*): You see what your stupid sentimentality gets you? I hope you've learned your lesson!

Silence.

MAN: We don't have any choice now but to run. Get moving!

OLD BONES: Before we do. . . . (*He falls worshipfully to his knees.*) Please forgive us, Hakamadare, for not recognizing you! Please forgive our countless trespasses against you and your honorable name! (*To the Villagers*): You're standing before the real Hakamadare! The real Hakamadare we've waited so long for! Our seven years of hardship have been rewarded!

The Villagers still do not move.

OLD BONES: You heard what he said! The truth is the truth! Our laws were only valid until we met the real Hakamadare. (*Wringing the words out*): This is the end of our band! My role as your leader is over. From now on, you take your orders from Hakamadare. Do you understand?

One by one, the Villagers drop to the ground as if their knees have given way beneath them.

VILLAGER 4: I . . . I. . . .

Old Bones glares at him, and he also sits down.

MAN (*nodding*): All right. There are no objections to me taking over, are there?

OLD BONES: Of course not!

MAN: Then, let's get away from here. If we don't hurry, the sheriff. . . .

OLD BONES: There's no rush. It's only another sheriff. Before we leave, please share a few words with us. As you can see, the shock of your appearance has left everyone uncertain about the future.

MAN: I see. Fair enough. Here's what I have to say. Once we get off this mountain, our first order of business will be to find all those hiding in the countryside who claim to be Hakamadare. We have to let them know in every hamlet and backwater village that the real Hakamadare has appeared so they can assemble under my control. We'll build Hakamadare's band into an enormous . . . well, I'll explain all about that later.

OLD BONES: And your law? What about Hakamadare's true law?

MAN: Anyone who betrays Hakamadare's band will be put to death. Anyone who gets in our way will be killed. Within the band, anyone who opposes me will be executed on the spot. That's the only law. Beyond that, you're free to do as you like. You'll get as much gold as you can steal and as many women as you can rape. That's human nature. The more rules there are, the greater the possibility that they'll be broken. And broken rules will lead to the disintegration of the band. Of course, all I'm recommending is the law of the jungle. It will lead to competition between comrades for booty and women until everyone's at each other's throat. In that sense, I see some merit in your style. I can see how your integrity commands respect.

OLD BONES: Which means?

MAN: As the number of our comrades increases, we'll split into two groups. One will pillage and murder; the other will be chaste, distribute money to the poor, and honor life. Both groups will be Hakamadare; but one will be public and the other clandestine.

OLD BONES: I see. And we'll be the ones who distribute money and honor life?

MAN: No, from time to time we'll exchange roles. Everyone will participate in both groups, rotating on a monthly basis, let's say.

OLD BONES: But . . . but, no individual could. . . .

MAN: Do both? The same individual can't kill and love, is that what you want to say? Well, I think they can. Or rather, I think all human beings do both by turns; that's what it means to be human. It's in the nature of men that if you limit them, eventually they'll rebel. I'm convinced of that. That's why I'm concerned about how we are organized. (*He chuckles.*) For the time being, you'll be the ones who kill and pillage. It's high time you fulfilled the desires you've suppressed for the last seven years!

Without warning, an arrow lodges high in the trunk of a tree. Several more follow, apparently shot from a distance.

The war cries of attackers.

MAN: Damn! They arrived sooner than I thought!

OLD BONES: We'll take the back way! Come on!

MAN: Everyone, follow me!

As Man turns to flee, Old Bones runs into him from behind. In his hand he carries a dagger.

MAN: Ah! (*He staggers.*) You old! . . .

Man turns and unsheathes his sword. Villager 5 drives his dagger into Man's unprotected abdomen.

VILLAGER 5: Die!

Man groans. He staggers, brandishing his sword.

MAN: Fools! You damned peasant fools! With me dead, now what're you going to do? You're doomed! Mine is the only way! My. . . .

OLD BONES: We've heard enough!

The Villagers envelope Man like a wave. When they withdraw, Man is on his knees.

MAN (*laughing even as he strains for breath*): Hah-hah-hah! Now you've done it! You've killed me. Now you . . . you really *are* Hakamadare!

OLD BONES: What? What did you say?

MAN: Look at your hands! They're covered with blood! That's Hakama-dare! (*He dies.*)

Pause.

The moonlight, the approaching war cries, and arrows bristling in the trees.

OLD BONES (*weak and broken*): I don't . . . understand. What . . . what have I done?

VILLAGERS: Old Bones! Come on! The sheriff's almost here! Come on!

OLD BONES (*pulling himself together*): We meet at Devil's Rock! (*He slaps his chest with a practiced hand and gives the signal to disperse.*)

VILLAGERS (*softly*): Aye!

In an instant, the Villagers have vanished without a trace. Undoubtedly they have dived into a secret underground passage.

Old Bones remains behind to make sure that everyone is safe. As he prepares to follow them, an arrow transfixes his heart. He falls face down without a word.

More arrows fill the air.

ACT 8
THE QUEST CONTINUES

Morning. Thick fog.

Devil's Rock.

Villagers 4, 5, 6, 7, and Kogiku. They sit for a few moments in silence.

VILLAGER 4: They're not coming.

VILLAGER 7 (*shouting*): Hello!

An echo is the only response.

Silence.

VILLAGER 7: They're not coming.

Silence.

VILLAGER 4 (*to 6*): What's wrong? You're not crying.

VILLAGER 6: What do you mean?

VILLAGER 4: You always start bawling whenever something happens.

VILLAGER 6: But. . . .

VILLAGER 7: He's right. You're always sniveling.

VILLAGER 6: Maybe you're right. I guess I will. (*He tries.*)
Pause.

VILLAGER 6: I can't. I'm going crazy with grief, but I can't cry. I
wonder why?

VILLAGER 4: Never mind.

Pause. Kogiku is weeping quietly to herself.

VILLAGER 7: Kogiku's weeping for you.

VILLAGER 4: Don't cry, Kogiku.

VILLAGER 7: It's too bad Jirōta had to get killed, but. . . .

VILLAGER 4: But we're still here.

VILLAGER 6: That's right, we're still here. (*Realizing something*): I see!
When somebody cries, that gives everyone else the chance to con-
sole him or bawl him out. In other words, it was all right for me to
cry. But now I'm all cried out.

VILLAGER 5: I . . . (*Everyone looks at 5.*) I feel sorry for Kogiku, and I'm
sad if my friends got killed, but. . . .

VILLAGER 4: But what? Get to the point!

VILLAGER 5: I . . . I feel relieved somehow. I can't help it, but I do. Ever
since I killed the baron's son back in our village, I've felt like I was
carrying a heavy weight. But now. . . .

Villagers 4, 6, and 7 look at each other in dismay.

VILLAGER 5 (*shrinking back*): I'm sorry, really. I just. . . . Can't you
understand?

VILLAGERS 4, 6, and 7: No.

*Kogiku has gone to the edge of the cliff. Noticing her, the others react in
terror.*

VILLAGERS: Ko . . . Kogiku! What are you doing?

KOGIKU (*shouting*): Heave-to!

Her voice reverberates through the hills.

    Then faintly, among the echoes, the password is heard: "Heave-ho!"

VILLAGERS (*leaping to their feet*): You hear that? (*Shouting together*):
Heave-to!

VOICE: Heave-ho!

*The sound of many voices — a torrent of voices — responds to their call
and reverberates through the hills: "Heave-ho!"*

The scene changes.

During the scene change, there is a racket of noisemakers, preferably the same ones used during the Interlude.

When the lights come up, the Villagers are all assembled on a sunbathed mountain path. Kogiku is with them, of course. Old Bones and Villagers 1, 2, and 3 appear with arrows and broken spears protruding from their bodies. Doubtless, there is also blood flowing from their wounds.

VILLAGER 1 (*expansively*): It's a beautiful day again!

VILLAGER 2: Sure is! Walking like this in the warm sunshine . . .

VILLAGER 3: You get the feeling that . . .

VILLAGER 4 (*with conviction*): That today might be the day!

Just then, the bloody Phantom of Man looms up.

PHANTOM: Look at your hands! Your bloody hands! That's Hakamadare! (*The Phantom disappears.*)

The Villagers stand motionless.

As if they did not hear what was said — or perhaps they heard it perfectly well but have decided to do so anyway — they continue.

VILLAGER 5 (*responding to 4's last line*): The day we meet Hakamadare!

VILLAGER 6: The *real* Hakamadare!

VILLAGER 7: You get the feeling that today we'll meet him for sure!

KOGIKU: That's right! Isn't it, Old Bones?

OLD BONES: Absolutely!

The Phantom appears again.

PHANTOM: Look at your hands! Your bloody hands! That's Hakamadare!

The Villagers remain expressionless, but they look up triumphantly.

OLD BONES: Come on, everyone! Let's go!

They begin to walk. And continue walking.

SONG:

> We'll continue our journey,
> Our endless quest,
> We march 'cross the land,
> Seeking Hakamadare's band!

To weep is a sin,
Laugh through thick and thin,
Our lives in our hand,
We're Hakamadare's band!

No flag do we follow,
No one told us to go.
Wandering o'er the land,
We're Hakamadare's band!

Curtain.

KAISON THE PRIEST
OF HITACHI

Commentary

And in our day, when historical pressure no longer allows any escape, how can man tolerate the catastrophes and horrors of history—from collective deportations and massacres to atomic bombings—if beyond them he can glimpse no sign, no transhistorical meaning; if they are only the blind play of economic, social, or political forces, or, even worse, only the result of the "liberties" that a minority takes and exercises directly on the stage of universal history?

Mircea Eliade[1]

Kaison the Priest of Hitachi describes the fundamental existential situation that lies at the root of the post-shingeki movement. It is that in an age of "total war," when humanity is more vulnerable than ever before, vulnerable even to the threat of extinction, people need to be able to perceive some transhistorical meaning to their existence, to be able to sense some continuity in life that will transcend death. The problem is that many of the traditional immortalizing symbols in Japanese culture had become unavailable in the modernization process; and those like emperor-centered nationalism that had been fabricated to take their place had been discredited by the experience of defeat. As I indicated in my introduction to this anthology, this quest for immortalizing symbols in a world where traditional symbols had been discredited was a major preoccupation in Japanese culture in the 1960s.

Kaison stands at the beginning of the post-shingeki movement because with it Akimoto Matsuyo broke the taboo on evoking traditional symbols of immortality and showed how the Japanese continue to need and remain susceptible to archetypal figures like the venerable Kaison, who offer them an avenue of escape from the pressures of historical being. Her motives were not simple. She recognized that while they offer transhistorical meaning and the promise of immortality, assimilation to archetypes like Kaison means an abandonment of historical creativity and responsibility and surrender to the siren's call of endlessly repetitive, unchanging time. The only choice, she suggests, is to cease being Japanese, to flee Japan; but even this alternative is fraught with danger, for how can a Japanese imagine flight from his cultural identity except *as a Japanese*? What models does he have except those provided by his culture? And does this not mean that he will inevitably reconstruct his tradition wherever he goes? These questions fascinated other post-shingeki dramatists,[2] and to an important extent a concern with them defines the post-shingeki movement.

The Play

It is October 1944. Japan is losing the war. The Allies are bombing Japanese cities, and in response the Japanese have begun evacuating groups of school children to the countryside under the supervision of their teachers.[3] *Kaison the Priest of Hitachi* concerns the fate of one such child, Yasuda Keita, and his friend Itō Yutaka, who were evacuated to the Tōhoku (northeastern) region of Japan.

As the play begins, Keita and Yutaka have run away from the Kotobukiya Lodge where they are living with their classmates. They are desperately lonely. They meet Yukino, a beautiful young native of the area, who introduces them to the world of Kaison the Priest of Hitachi. It is a mysterious world where sex and death and the promise of eternal life are bound inextricably together. The boys are introduced to Kaison, the mummy worshiped in the small shrine operated by the Old Woman who is Yukino's only parent. The experience makes an overwhelming impression on the boys, and when their teacher arrives, he finds them in a state of stupefaction. Their souls, he is told, have been "spirited away by the gods of the mountain."

Time passes. It is now March 1945. The boys are immersed in a sea of death. Cut off from their families and living in a world of extreme sensory deprivation, they are continually terrorized with the idea that they are as good as dead: the war will last forever and their lives are already forfeit to the emperor. The defenseless children long for some means to conquer death, and the Old Woman and the Kaison cult provide it.[4]

The Old Woman lives in an ahistorical world. History and death have no hold on this world. It is possible for people from the twelfth and twentieth centuries to coexist and even have conjugal relations there. That is why it is possible for Toragoze and Shōshō, two local prostitutes, to claim truthfully to be the brides of the Soga brothers, heroic warriors who died in 1193, eight centuries ago.

Then the worst happens: Keita and Yutaka learn that their families have been killed in the massive bombing raid that destroyed much of downtown Tokyo on March 10.[5] They look to Kaison's ahistorical world for a means to conquer the reality of death, to annul their loss. Yutaka resists and flees, but Keita remains behind. The Old Woman conducts a seance, reuniting him with his mother; and Keita is trapped, dependent upon the Old Woman as his sole protection against the threat of death. The Old Woman uses Keita's dependency, grafting his soul to Yukino's will, exploiting him in order to guarantee the perpetuation of the matriarchal Kaison cult.

The war draws to a close and the Japanese gods are discredited. The Old Woman and her friends are the first victims of this turn of events. They are banished because, unlike the divine Emperor, who was protected by the Occupation, they are the weakest and most vulnerable deputies of the gods.[6] This is the first step in the repression of the gods that characterizes the postwar world. Rather than concede, the Old Woman considers following Kaison and becoming a mummy herself, but she decides instead to prepare Keita for his role in perpetuating the Kaison cult.

The war ends, and several of the evacuee children whose families had been killed are put up for adoption. Keita should be among them, but rather than face the reality of his parents' death, he flees to the Old Woman and Yukino, who promise eternal life.

Sixteen years pass. It is autumn 1961. Yutaka, now a white-collar worker in Tokyo, returns to the northeast, to the shrine where the Kaison cult has been installed. Yukino now presides over one of the most venerable shrines in Japan, and Yutaka finds Keita working there as a menial. Keita is a tortured wreck, teetering on the brink of insanity. Yutaka learns that Keita had helped make the Old Woman's mummy and that he had been imprisoned for abetting a suicide. The historical world had exacted a heavy price for Keita's participation in Kaison's realm.

Yutaka at first vehemently rejects Keita, but he is soon forced to admit that he shares Keita's attraction for Yukino and the whole ahistorical regimen she represents. He admits that given the opportunity, he too would be her slave. In a way Yutaka even envies Keita, for his life is tied into the great stream of Japanese culture. It is meaningful. By contrast, his own life is devoid of meaning; he is nothing but a cog in the giant apparatus of corporate Japan. He longs for the symbolic immortality the Kaison cult provides, whatever the cost.

Yutaka is brought to his senses by Hidemitsu, a young priest working at the shrine. Hidemitsu knows all too well Yukino's attraction, her irresistible siren's charm; but he knows equally well that it beckons men into a metahistorical kingdom from which none return. Hidemitsu realizes that the only way for a Japanese to resist the temptation of timelessness, the voluptuous invitation of tradition, is to leave Japan, to cease being Japanese. He grasps at a quirk in the complex of legends from which Kaison emerged, the tradition that Kaison's lord, Yoshitsune, had not died at Hiraizumi as history records but had fled across the straits to Mongolia, where he became Genghis Khan. This precedent provides sufficient justification for Hidemitsu to flee Japan.

With Yutaka and Hidemitsu gone, Keita is left alone. Faced with the choice of madness or death, he chooses neither. Instead, he takes refuge in the Kaison legend: he *becomes* Kaison. He abandons history completely and surrenders to the flow of fabulous time.

The lullaby Keita sings to Yukino's baby explains his transformation and the survival of Kaison for 750 years: "A cherry is still a cherry though but one blooms. A cherry is still a cherry though but two bloom." In other words, Kaison is still Kaison even though he is just Yasuda Keita. As Tsuno Kaitarō has put it, "In each age, the oppressed masses have bestowed upon Kaison not only their desolate misery, but also their emaciated flesh." This is the secret of the survival of Japanese culture through the ages: there have always been people who have lent their bodies to the culture, who have allowed the culture to incarnate itself through them. "Kaison . . . represents the hidden, changeless mechanism of Japanese history, the constant that makes Japanese history a unified, continuous process."[7]

Background

Hitachibō Kaison was a retainer of Minamoto-no-Yoshitsune (1159–1189), Japan's quintessential tragic hero.[8] Yoshitsune was the younger half-brother of Minamoto-no-Yoritomo, who led the Genji clan against the rival Heike and established the Kamakura Shogunate in 1185. For reasons that are not clear, but apparently in order to consolidate his rule and eliminate a potential rival, Yoritomo had Yoshitsune pursued and harassed into committing suicide.

Yoshitsune's romantic character, his brilliance as a warrior, his love for the beautiful courtesan Shizuka Gozen, and his untimely death combine to make him one of the most popular characters in Japanese history. Yoshitsune and his adventures have been the source of innumerable nō and kabuki plays, including *Yashima*, the nō play that Hidemitsu recites in the final act of Akimoto's work; and countless legends have grown up around him, including the one that maintains that he did not really die in 1189 but escaped to the continent where he continued his exploits as Genghis Khan (ca. 1167–1227).[9]

Kaison's crime was that he betrayed Yoshitsune. Instead of dying with his lord at Hiraizumi as duty required, he fled for his life. His punishment was to wander endlessly, recounting Yoshitsune's glory and his own cowardice. He became a *biwa hōshi*, one of the itinerant priests who, by reciting legends about the war between the Genji and the Heike to the accompaniment of the lute-like biwa,[10] transformed *The Tales of the Heike* (*Heike monogatari*) into the national saga it became.[11]

Kaison's apotheosis took place early and faith in his saving power continued into the eighteenth century, when he was worshiped as Awa daimyōjin in Hitachi (present-day Ibaraki prefecture). His fame and power spread, and at its zenith his cult reached as far as Edo (Tokyo).[12]

Akimoto's play takes place in the twentieth century, among the fortune-tellers, entertainers, and religious practitioners who continue to preserve the traditional practices of folk religion in the rural districts of Japan.[13] The Old Woman in the play is a shamaness (*itako*); and Kaison, whose mummy she preserves, is her tutelary deity. Tōsenbō Gentaku is a shaman (*yamabushi*) who practices in the mountains; he is the Old Woman's male equivalent. Shōshō and Toragoze are entertainers, who recite tales of the Soga brothers called *Soga-zaimon*.[14]

Mummification has been practiced in Japan since at least the eleventh century and as recently as 1903. Several mummies were newly discovered in Yamagata prefecture shortly before Akimoto wrote her play,[15] and this undoubtedly influenced her. The practice is related to Esoteric Buddhism and to millenarian beliefs in Miroku (Maitreya), the Buddha of the Future. According to these beliefs, Miroku will appear on earth 5,670,000,000 years after Sakyamuni's death (ca. 480 B.C.E.) to save all those still left unredeemed. Believers practice mummification in order to preserve themselves until Miroku's arrival so that they can aid the messiah in saving humanity.

Unlike Egyptian mummies, which were created through embalming, Japanese mummies are the result of a slow process of self-starvation that can take ten or more years. After death, the mummy is buried in a coffin for three years, after which it is exhumed and arranged, usually in an attitude of prayer. The mummy is then dried and dressed in priestly robes to be worshiped as a Buddha.[16]

Kaison and Elijah

Both Tsuno and the late Kogarimai Ken mention the legend of the wandering Jew in their discussions of *Kaison the Priest of Hitachi*.[17] Akimoto herself postulates an explicitly messianic dimension to the Kaison legend in her play through her references to mummification, which identify the Kaison cult with Miroku, the Buddhist messiah. A comparison between Kaison and Elijah, the herald of the Messiah in the Jewish tradition, is therefore appropriate in interpreting Akimoto's play.

When the English translation of *Kaison the Priest of Hitachi* was first published in *Concerned Theatre Japan* in 1973, it was accompanied by a very short story by Elie Wiesel entitled "An Evening Guest." The structure of Wiesel's story is simple. He describes how as a child he had pictured Elijah as a Yemenite Jew, "a prince ageless, rootless, fierce, turning up wherever he is awaited." Wiesel's image of the prophet is changed radically by his experience of the Holocaust. On the last Passover night he was to spend with his family, a beggar arrives and tries to warn the family of what lies in store. They ignore his warnings, and the beggar disappears; but Wiesel encounters him again on his way to Auschwitz:

> I saw our guest again a few weeks later. The first convoy was leaving the ghetto; he was in it. He seemed more at ease than his companions, as if he had already taken this route a thousand times. Men, women, and children, all of them carrying bundles on their backs, blankets, valises. He alone was empty-handed.
>
> Today I know what I did not know then: at the end of a long trip that was to last four days and three nights he got out in a small railway station, near a peaceful little town, somewhere in Silesia, where his fiery chariot was waiting to carry him up to the heavens: is that not proof enough that he was the prophet Elijah?[18]

Wiesel's Elijah is to the Jewish tradition what Akimoto's Kaison is to the Japanese: an avenue of escape from the terror of history and death into metahistory and immortality.

Why does Wiesel encounter Elijah on his way to Auschwitz? Elijah was an Israelite prophet active in the ninth century B.C.E. who became associated with images of immortality and salvation in the Jewish tradition. The Second Book of Kings (2:1–11) relates that Elijah did not die but was carried to heaven in a chariot of fire. Malachi established the connection between Elijah and the promise of Messianic redemption when he prophesied that God would send Elijah "before the coming of the great and terrible day of the Lord [to] turn the hearts of the fathers to the children and the hearts of the children to their fathers" (Mal. 3:23ff); and later, in the Talmud, Elijah was accorded the exclusive privilege of bringing about the resurrection of the dead (Sot. 9:15 end). The notion of Elijah and a Messiah hidden among the poorest and most oppressed of the Jews is also part of the Jewish tradition. According to the Talmud (Sanh. 98a), Elijah once told Rabbi Joshua bar

Levi that the Messiah was to be found among the beggars of Rome, ready to redeem the Children of Israel if they would only repent and obey God.[19]

Elijah's appearance at Auschwitz thus annuls death and transforms the meaning of annihilation. By having Elijah appear at Auschwitz, Wiesel transforms the crematoria into a chariot that will carry the Jews to eternal life; and he implies that the Jews' death was not meaningless but somehow heralded the coming of the Messiah.

Like Elijah, Kaison is a means to escape the horrors of history and achieve eternal life. Besides Keita, three different Kaisons appear in Akimoto's play. The first is the classical Kaison, the figure out of *The Tales of the Heike*, who betrayed his feudal lord. Kaison II is a man who fled into metahistory because of his experience in the Second World War. And the third is our contemporary, a forlorn metropolitan: "I fought for a livelihood in the dusty city," he chants, "but my efforts ended in utter defeat. Scarred and twisted, I was left without succor on the field of battle." Akimoto is saying that even today, the Japanese yet have need of their mendicant messiahs.[20]

Nevertheless, Kaison and Elijah are not identical. What distinguishes them is their relationship to history. Elijah, even though he provides an escape into metahistory, faces into the future and promises ultimate redemption *within historical time*.[21] With Elijah, the flight from history and responsibility is always temporary, reversible. Not so with Kaison. Kaison represents a flight into timelessness that is permanent. The salvation he offers is eternal surcease, the irreversible end of historical creativity and responsibility. It is probably this quality that Japanese critics have found so disquieting in *Kaison the Priest of Hitachi*, and it may disturb Western readers as well.[22]

Notes

1. *The Myth of the Eternal Return, Or, Cosmos and History*, tr. Willard R. Trask, Bollingen Series 46 (Princeton, NJ: Princeton University Press, 1971), p. 151.

2. For example, Satoh Makoto takes up precisely these questions in *Nezumi Kozō: The Rat*. See my translation and analysis of the play in *After Apocalypse: Four Japanese Plays of Hiroshima and Nagasaki* (New York: Columbia University Press, 1986), pp. 249–319.

3. Allied B29 Superfortress bombing of Japan began with the June 16, 1944, raid on the Yahata Steel Works. The Japanese began evacuating school children from Tokyo the following August. See Gordon Daniels, "The Great Tokyo Air Raid, 9–10 March 1945,"

in W. B. Beasley, ed. *Modern Japan: Aspects of History, Literature and Society* (Berkeley: University of California Press, 1977), p. 122.

4. The concept of "death immersion" was developed by Robert Jay Lifton in connection with survivors of Hiroshima. See Lifton's *Death in Life: Survivors of Hiroshima* (New York: Random House, 1967), pp. 19–33 and *passim*. See also Lifton, *The Broken Connection: On Death and the Continuity of Life* (New York: Simon and Schuster, 1979), p. 175 and *passim*.

5. For details, see Daniels, "The Great Tokyo Air Raid," pp. 113–131.

6. It is interesting to note that there was a widespread fear in Japan immediately following the surrender that the Emperor would also be banished. See, for example, Michihiko Hachiya, *Hiroshima Diary*, tr. Warner Wells (Chapel Hill: University of North Carolina Press, 1955), p. 138.

7. Tsuno Kaitarō, "The Tradition of Modern Theatre in Japan," tr. David G. Goodman, *The Canadian Theatre Review*, Fall 1978, pp. 14–16.

8. The best traditional account of Yoshitsune's career is *Yoshitsune: A Fifteenth Century Japanese Chronicle*, tr. Helen Craig McCullough (Tokyo: University of Tokyo Press, 1966).

9. Ivan Morris provides a superb analysis of the development of the Yoshitsune legend in *The Nobility of Failure* (New York: Holt, Rinehart and Winston, 1975), pp. 67–105.

10. The *biwa* and related instruments are found in Japan, China, and Korea. It is believed to have come to Japan in the eighth century from India by way of Korea. The biwa ordinarily has four strings, but some varieties have five. The body is pear-shaped, with a flat face, and measures 60 to 90 centimeters in length. In Japan, the biwa is played with a plectrum, but in Korea and China it is played with the fingernails. There are various kinds of biwas, but the biwa played by Kaison is known as the Heike biwa, a refinement of the *mōsō biwa* (literally "blind priest biwa") that had been played by itinerant blind priests since the ninth century to accompany the recitation of prayers and homilies.

11. Kenneth D. Butler describes the evolution of the *Heike* text and the contribution of the *biwa hōshi* in his article, "The Textual Evolution of the Heike Monogatari," *Harvard Journal of Asiatic Studies*, 26 (1966). There is an English translation of *The Tale of the Heike*, tr. Hiroshi Kitagawa and Bruce T. Tsuchida (Tokyo: University of Tokyo Press, 1975).

12. Kogarimai Ken, *Hyōi to kamen* (Serika shobō 1972), pp. 69–70.

13. The two best sources of information on this subject are Carmen Blacker, *The Catalpa Bow: A Study of Shamanistic Practices in Japan* (London: Allen and Unwin, 1975); and Ichirō Hori, *Folk Religion in Japan*, tr. Joseph M. Kitagawa and Alan L. Miller (Tokyo University Press, 1968). See also H. Byron Earhart, *A Religious Study of the Mount Haguro Sect of Shugendō: An Example of Japanese Mountain Religion* (Tokyo: Sophia University, 1970).

14. Hiroshi Kitagawa, tr., *The Tale of the Soga Brothers*, Study Series 7 (Shiga, Japan: Faculty of Economics, Shiga University, 1981).

15. Ichirō Hori, "Self-Mummified Buddhas in Japan: An Aspect of the Shugen-dō ('Mountain Asceticism') Sect," *History of Religions* (Winter 1966), I(2):223.

16. Sakurai Kiyohiko, "Miira," *Encyclopedia Japonica*, vol. 17 (Shōgakukan, 1971) p. 70. Andō Kōsei, "Miira," *Heibonsha's World Encyclopedia*, vol. 28 (Heibonsha, 1981) p. 289.

The early modern novelist Ueda Akinari (1734–1809) wrote a story entitled *Nisei no en*, in which he attempted to debunk the popular belief in mummies. The story has been translated as "The Destiny that Spanned Two Lifetimes" in Ueda Akinari, *Tales of the Spring Rain* , tr. Barry Jackman (Tokyo: The Japan Foundation, 1975), pp. 69–79.

17. Tsuno Kaitarō, "Biwa and Beatles: An Invitation to Modern Japanese Theatre," *Concerned Theatre Japan*, special introductory issue (October 1969), p. 19. Kogarimai, *Hyōi to kamen*, p. 71.

18. "An Evening Guest," *Legends of Our Time* (New York: Schocken Books, 1982), p. 30; *Concerned Theatre Japan*, II(3–4):260. *Legends of Our Time* was published by Tsuno's firm, Shōbunsha, in 1970 as *Shisha no uta*.

19. More about the image of Elijah may be found in the *Encyclopedia Judaica*, vol. 6, pp. 631–637, from which this account was taken.

20. Wiesel makes a similar suggestion with respect to the Jews in *A Beggar in Jerusalem*, tr. Elie Wiesel and Lily Edelman (New York: Avon Books, 1970), pp. 226–227.

21. Elijah is representative of the Jewish tradition in this respect. As Gershom Scholem has pointed out, "Judaism, in all its forms and manifestations, has always maintained a concept of redemption as *an event which takes place publicly, on the stage of history and within the community.* It is an occurrence which takes place in the visible world and which cannot be conceived apart from such a visible appearance. In contrast, Christianity conceives of redemption as an event in the spiritual and unseen realm, an event which is reflected in the soul, in the private world of each individual, and which effects an inner transformation which need not correspond to anything outside." (Gershom Scholem, *The Messianic Idea in Judaism* [New York: Schocken Books, 1971], p. 1. Emphasis added.)

22. Kogarimai, for instance, links Kaison directly to Japanese ultranationalism and the debacle of the Second World War: "Kaison suggests by his metamorphosis and the transmigration of his identity the location of 'madness' in our ethnos (nation and people), and he gives brilliant form to the source of the myth of the unbroken succession of emperors that has formed the basis of the *Kokutai* [national polity] ideology [of Japanese ultranationalism]." *Hyōi to kamen*, pp. 74–75.

See also, Hirosue Tamotsu, *Akubasho no hassō* (Sanseidō, 1970), pp. 37–58.

Kaison the Priest of Hitachi

A PLAY

by Akimoto Matsuyo

Kaison the Priest of Hitachi (*Hitachibō Kaison*) was originally published in 1965 in a limited private edition. The version used for this translation appears in *Kasabuta Shikibu-kō, Hitachibō Kaison* (Kawade shobō, 1969).

CAST OF CHARACTERS

Old Woman
Yukino
Tōsenbō Gentaku, a mountain priest
Teacher
Kotobukiya
Yasuda Keita, as a boy and as a man
Itō Yutaka, as a boy and as a man
Hidemitsu
Official
Fisherman
Housewife
Lumberman
Kaison I, II, III
Toragoze
Shōshō
Young Man 1–4
Man 1–2
Young Priestess
Tour Guide
Tourists
Masao
Yūichi

ACT 1

Scene 1

It is a pitch-black October night deep in the mountains. In the background the rising moon is hidden behind a stand of soaring pines, and the sounds of the wind and a mountain stream can be heard.

Voices are calling in the distance. It is hard to make out what they are saying as they echo through the mountains, but a search seems to be in progress.

Two diminutive black figures, like small animals, move in the underbrush.

The voices draw nearer. There appear to be two men calling, "Yasuda!" "Itō!"

One of the small, shadowy figures darts out of the brush and scampers into the trees. He is followed by the second figure, who also disappears in the darkness.

Two men enter. They are Teacher, attired in military cap and leggings, and Kotobukiya, whose flapping kimono skirts have been tucked up into his sash. They carry a flashlight and a lantern respectively.

TEACHER: Itō! Yasuda!

KOTOBUKIYA: Nobody's going to scold you! Come out of there!

TEACHER: Itō! Yasuda!

KOTOBUKIYA: Where could they have gotten to?

TEACHER: I swear, I just don't know what to do with these kids. More trouble than a pack of monkeys!

KOTOBUKIYA: I guess being a school teacher doesn't make this war any easier, does it?

TEACHER: You can say that again! I left my wife and children back in Tokyo when I came up here. I've got my family to worry about, and there hasn't been a word from Tokyo in over a month! . . . Oh! damn! (*His shoelace has broken.*) Give me a little light, there, will you?

KOTOBUKIYA: What happened?

TEACHER: Talk about living on a shoestring! Times are so bad even they're a luxury! (*He begins to tie the broken ends together.*)

KOTOBUKIYA: I hear Tokyo's getting a pretty bad beating.

TEACHER: I'd like a chance to go and take a look for myself. I heard the trains are running again.

KOTOBUKIYA: Couldn't say.

TEACHER: It's all because I lost my temper and hit that kid. . . . Why is that boy Yasuda always wetting his bed? Is that something for a fifth-grader to do?

KOTOBUKIYA: He's only a child, your honor. He'll grow out of it.

TEACHER: Even Itō's got to get into the act! I swear! . . . (*Finishing with his shoes*): Thanks.

KOTOBUKIYA: Be getting along then, will we?

TEACHER (*fed up*): Where does this path lead? I've got a weak heart, and these mountains aren't doing me any good.

KOTOBUKIYA: Not much farther now, your honor. Another eight miles and we'll be in Okusawa.

TEACHER: Eight miles! It's hard to believe they got that far. We've looked everywhere and still can't find them. Maybe they didn't run into the mountains after all.

KOTOBUKIYA: But we're responsible, your honor. Those kids were evacuated from Tokyo. You're their teacher, and they're staying at my lodge. We just have to look until we find them.

TEACHER (*screwing up his courage*): You're absolutely right. You've got a point there. Why, children today are one of Japan's most precious resources. If we just tell ourselves all this trouble is for the sake of our country. . . .

KOTOBUKIYA: Master Itō! Master Yasuda!

Both men exit. It is silent for a moment. Then a small figure crawls out of the forest. He seems to be planning to run in the direction opposite the one the search party has taken.

YUTAKA (*whispering*): Keita, come on. Hurry!

KEITA (*appears, crying*): I've got a tummyache!

YUTAKA: Quit bawling! Come on!

KEITA: I want to go back to Tokyo. I want my mommy!

YUTAKA: Cut it out, I said. Come on!

Bewildered, both boys remain crouched in the shadows. Keita sobs.

   Yukino, a girl of indeterminate age, looking ten at one moment, fourteen or fifteen the next, suddenly runs in from nowhere. She approaches the two fugitives stealthily.

YUKINO: Look like a couple of evacuee brats to me.

Keita and Yutaka stare at her in surprise.

YUKINO: Lost, ain't you? And hungry, too, I'll bet. (*She laughs.*) Then you'd best be calling on Lord Kaison. Go ahead, try it. Try it, I said! "Lord Kaison!!!" Like that.

KEITA and YUTAKA: Lord Kaison!

YUKINO (*laughing*): Good. Good. Now I'll bring you something to eat. Wait here. Just stay in the shadows and wait.

Keita and Yutaka crawl backward into the darkness.

YUKINO: That should do. Now just keep quiet and don't move! (*She exits, running.*)

The sounds of the mountain stream seem loud in the silence. The moon has risen higher in the sky. An owl cries, and, imitating it, their voices overlapping, Old Woman enters.

OLD WOMAN: Hooo! Hooo! Ho! Hooo! Hooo! Ho! Hooo! I could have sworn I heard somebody call Lord Kaison. Maybe I was just hearing things. Maybe it was that old owl. But there's Kaison's moon rising in the sky. Isn't any wonder the birds and beasts long for him. How it soars! How it soars! It's just as it was the night Lord Kaison first appeared to me.

Her tone changes as she begins to recite the legend of Kaison, Priest of Hitachi.

OLD WOMAN: "That day Benkei, Priest of Musashi, was attired in raven-braided armor marked with yellow crests and armed with a great halberd, which he gripped halfway down the shaft. In his service were seven warriors: Kataoka Hachirō, the two Suzuki brothers, Washio-no-Saburō, Mashio-no-Jurō, Ise-no-Saburō, and Hanshirō of Bizen. But eleven men, not the least of whom was Kaison, Priest of Hitachi, had abandoned His Lordship Yoshitsune. . . ."

TŌSENBŌ (*joining in, voice only*): "And from the estate in Hiraizumi, where His Lordship had taken refuge, fled headlong for their lives, fled headlong for their lives."

Tōsenbō appears out of the darkness.

TŌSENBŌ: It's been a long time, a long time since I heard your voice. I missed you.

OLD WOMAN (*shrewishly*): If you wanted to hear my voice so bad, you could've showed up when you were supposed to. Now you can take your ugly puss and mountain priest nonsense and be on your way. Spare me the sight!

TŌSENBŌ: Is that any way to greet me? I was up in the mountains and caught a cold. (*He coughs.*) That's why I'm late. Don't get so upset.

OLD WOMAN: Caught a cold, did you? Proof enough your heart's not in your prayers. It's a wonder you still have the nerve to call yourself a follower of Lord Kaison!

TŌSENBŌ: A man can't win with you. I may be late, but I ran all night to get here. You could at least pretend you're glad to see me.

OLD WOMAN: Where's my present? What did you bring me?

TŌSENBŌ: Now, now, you can wait till we get to the house, can't you? I wanted to buy you something nice, but money doesn't go far these days. Anyway, it's the thought that counts.

OLD WOMAN: The thought? Who needs it? No money, no bed.

TŌSENBŌ: With the war bad as it is, I hardly get any alms at all. Rice is rationed, wheat's regulated. Everywhere I go, people feed me potatoes.

OLD WOMAN: You must've eaten plenty, too—you even look like one! A lot of nerve you've got poking that potato-puss of yours around here. Get out of my sight!

TŌSENBŌ: You're going to hurt my feelings if you don't watch out. I thought we meant more to each other than that.

OLD WOMAN: You go down to the town and come back when you've got some money. Then I might reconsider. Hooo! It would have to cloud up just when we had such a beautiful moon. It's all because you showed up, you potato priest. Can't stand the sight! (*Exits.*)

TŌSENBŌ: Wait . . . (*whimpering*): you treat me like a stranger! What do you want me to do? (*He seats himself on a tree stump.*) Lord Kaison! Tell me what to do! Help me understand!

Something moves in the shadows of the trees. Tōsenbō turns and listens.

TŌSENBŌ: Who's there?

There is the sound of the two boys in flight. Tōsenbō leaps into the underbrush and drags the boys out by the scruff of the neck.

TŌSENBŌ: Now I've got you! Where are you two from? What're you doing wandering around here in the middle of the night? Let me have a look at you. (*He looks at each in turn.*) Well, what do you know! City kids, ain't you? I know a city brat when I see one. So that's it! There was a big commotion in the lodge at the foot of the mountain as I was passing through. Something about evacuee kids getting lost. You must be the ones they meant. No mistake about it. You're the ones, ain't you? Now there's an idea! Listen, I'll take you back where you belong. But mind you, I'm not doing it for the reward. Remember that. All right, let's go. Let's go.

YUTAKA: We don't want to go! We're waiting for Lord Kaison to come back.

KEITA: Lord Kaison!

TŌSENBŌ: You mean you met Lord Kaison?

Held by the scruff of the neck, the two boys manage to nod.

TŌSENBŌ: And what did this Lord Kaison look like? Out with it!

KEITA (*with difficulty*): It was a girl.

YUTAKA (*similarly*): A pretty girl.

TŌSENBŌ (*laughing*): That must have been Yukino. Waiting for Yukino, are you? (*Laughs.*) Then you'll be wanting to bring some money with you. (*He begins to walk, still gripping the boys firmly by the neck.*) That way you'll be able to meet her whenever your heart desires. Now come along with you. That's it, one foot after the other. *Blackout.*

Scene 2

Old Woman's house in the shade of the mountain. It is a dilapidated structure, unremarkable except for the Shinto altar that immediately catches the eye. Straw matting is spread in the yard, covered with nuts put out to dry. Persimmons and white radishes are also being dried. Crimson sunbeams from the late afternoon sky filter through the trees. Old woman stands under the eaves. In the yard are two Young Men, factory workers in military caps. Each carries a basket filled with mushrooms.

OLD WOMAN: What's that, the fortunes I tell are no good? And what's wrong with them, I'd like to know?

YOUNG MAN 1: They just don't come true, that's all. They're all wrong.

YOUNG MAN 2: Not one's hit the mark. You've got a lot of nerve, claiming you can communicate with the gods! You're just conning people out of their money.

YOUNG MAN 1: It's fraud. Fraud's all it is. We should've never gave you that money.

YOUNG MAN 2: We come to get it back. We figured, since the fortunes didn't come true. . . .

OLD WOMAN: Listen to that, will you? If you think money's all that matters, you've got another think coming. Fortune-telling's a delicate business. The medium and the believer have to be united heart and soul. Otherwise the gods won't deign to reveal the truth. If you want a fortune that'll come true, then come back when you're ready to address the gods sincerely. From the looks of things, all you're really after is a day off from the factory to go mushroom hunting.

The Young Men hide their baskets.

OLD WOMAN (*laughing*): What do you expect? You come to me in the right state of mind, and I'll see that you forget all the pain of this fleeting world. Whenever you're sad or in pain, just call on Lord Kaison. Then the world will turn to paradise. Now on your way with you. (*She shoulders a basket herself and exits.*)

YOUNG MAN 1: Never saw such a sly old bitch!

YOUNG MAN 2: We came out of our way to stop in here, and all for nothing.

YOUNG MAN 1: Let's go.

Yukino enters with a bag full of nuts over her shoulder. The Young Men stare at her with obvious interest.

YOUNG MAN 2: Hello there! Grown some, ain't you? How old would you be now? And by the way, where's your old man at?

YOUNG MAN 1: Leave off her. There's no point messing around with kidstuff.

YOUNG MAN 2: Kids get born and not a man in the house. Ain't it a wonder?

YOUNG MAN 1: Maybe that's why she acts like the gods' gift to the world.

Young Men exit, laughing. Paying them no attention, Yukino goes about spreading her harvest on the straw matting. Yutaka and Keita sneak around from behind the house and peer out at her.

YUTAKA (*under his breath*): Lord Kaison!

KEITA (*similarly*): Lord Kaison!

YUKINO: Who's there? Where're you at?

The boys show themselves.

YUKINO: Well, look at this! You're the evacuee kids from the other night. It's all right, you can come over here.

KEITA (*taking a small good-luck pouch from around his neck*): Here. It's for you.

YUKINO: What is it? (*She opens the pouch and removes a folded bill.*) Money! Ten whole yen! For me?

Keita nods.

YUKINO: Then you can stay here. (*To Yutaka*): You go home.

YUTAKA: Mine's sewn in here. (*He rips the lining from the cuff of his coat with his teeth.*)

YUKINO: Hurry, let me see!

YUTAKA (*removing a ten-yen bill*): See! This one's for you, too!

YUKINO: Today's my day! Ten yen each! Don't be asking for it back, now. It's mine, you hear?

KEITA: Please, Lord Kaison!

YUKINO: I'm not Lord Kaison. Lord Kaison's over there in the closet. You want to see him?

Both boys nod.

YUKINO: Then I'll show you. But don't tell the old woman. I'm doing this special for you. It's a secret. Come on.

Yukino enters the house. The two boys remove their sneakers and follow her.

YUKINO: Sit down over there. (*She opens the closet and removes a lustrous, black wooden box about three feet square.*) Remember, it's a secret. Just look, don't touch. Shhh! (*She removes the lid.*)

Seated inside the box is an almost simian mummy. The brown-black figure is attired in a gold-brocade cowl and habit. The boys look at the mummy in awe.

YUKINO: See? This is Lord Kaison. Take a good look. This is Lord Kaison's mummy.

Keita and Yutaka are speechless.

YUKINO (*replacing the lid*): I can't show him to you for long.

The boys exchange glances. In the distance Old Woman's voice can be heard calling Yukino's name.

YUKINO: Uh-oh! The old woman's coming! Help me put this back. (*She pushes the box back into the closet.*) Hurry up, get in here, quick! Hurry up! Hurry up!

Yukino and the two boys hide in the closet. A crow caws harshly.

Old Woman enters, swinging the basket she has filled with mushrooms.

OLD WOMAN: Yukino! Hm, looks like she ain't back yet. What could she be up to?

Tōsenbō enters with a basket of kindling on his back.

TŌSENBŌ: Please, I'm begging you! Don't be saying those awful things to me. I can't stand it when you say those things! Please!

OLD WOMAN: You still running off at the mouth? Never saw such a heap of mush call itself a man! If you still don't understand I'll tell you again: You're a good-for-nothing mountain priest and ever since you sailed in here you been keeping your big mouth open and stuffing my vittles in it!

TŌSENBŌ: I know! I know! But what can I do? It'll be winter soon. Sending me back out there now's the same as sending me out to die! Please! You know I can't forget your smooth, soft skin!

Old Woman cackles derisively.

TŌSENBŌ: I'm begging you! Please! As soon as spring comes I'll leave, I'll work. Just let me stay the winter!

OLD WOMAN: No. Yukino and I'd both starve trying to feed the likes of you. And if anything happened to us, who'd carry on for Lord Kaison? I'm his wife and Yukino's his grandchild. We can't be starving to death for you or anybody. If you want to stay here, there's only one way: become a mummy!

TŌSENBŌ: A mummy!

OLD WOMAN: That's right. Nothing to be surprised at. It was just about this time of year that Lord Kaison began himself. It was a lean year, that, without a decent harvest in these parts. Stayed warm all winter long, but it got cold enough when spring came. May came and we were still wearing our heavy jackets. June came and there was frost and sleet. July came and it rained like it would never stop. I thought the sky had caved in. Sixty-six days it fell. No one was surprised when the rice and wheat crops failed, but then even the millet wilted in the fields. Farmers sold their daughters to whorehouses in the town and tried to make ends meet that way. That's when Lord Kaison said he'd sacrifice himself, become a mummy for his people. He sat with his legs crossed facing west. And he chanted prayers in praise of the Buddha. And not so much as a drop of water passed his lips. And on the eighty-eighth day the process was complete: he became a mummy. (*She brings her hands together in an attitude of prayer.*) Isn't it time you made up your mind as well?

TŌSENBŌ: That's . . . that's asking too much!

OLD WOMAN: It ain't painful. All you have to do is stop eating. I'll help you. You can start right now.

TŌSENBŌ: Now?

OLD WOMAN: It's the best season. You don't dry properly in the spring or summer: you tend to rot. The finished product's no good at all. Fall's best: there's no moisture in the air, so you dry fast and turn out nice and crisp.

TŌSENBŌ: Stop . . . stop it! Stop it! Going back on the road's still better than becoming a mummy. At least there's a chance I'll survive. I'm going. Don't try to stop me. I'm going! (*He starts to leave.*) You're sure you won't be lonely without me? You'll be sleeping alone all winter.

OLD WOMAN: I guess it will be lonely without somebody around.

TŌSENBŌ: The snow'll come riding aback the north wind. Hew! Hew! The wind'll blow so hard through the cracks you'll have to hold down your freckles. It'll get colder and colder until you've got icicles on your eyelashes. It isn't a time you'll want to spend alone.

OLD WOMAN: Maybe, but . . . no. Duty first. I won't stop you. On your way with you! On your way!

TŌSENBŌ: You're a heartless beast, you are! A heartless beast!

OLD WOMAN (*rolling Tōsenbō's clothes into a ball and throwing them at him*): Here!

TŌSENBŌ (*weeping*): How many men have you made into mummies so far? I'm afraid to even think. But the memory of your warm, white flesh! Ah! It makes me hate you all the more! (*He exits, sobbing.*)

OLD WOMAN: Good riddance to bad rubbish! A lot of nerve! Can't forget my flesh, can he? (*She cackles scornfully.*) Let me see now, it's time we started supper. Where could that Yukino have gotten to?

Old Woman picks up the two pair of sneakers left in front of the house.

OLD WOMAN: Will you look at this now? Who's hiding in my house? Where are you? Come out of there before I tan your hides! (*She flings open the closet.*)

Yukino and the boys, hugging each other in fright, release a terrified squeal.

OLD WOMAN: Oh! It's quite a den of thieves I've uncovered, isn't it? You had me outsmarted for a while there. Now out with you!

The children crawl out timidly.

YUKINO: We didn't mean nothing by it.

OLD WOMAN: I'll take care of you later. Stand up straight there! Evacuee kids, eh? Let's hear your names then. Your names, I said!

YUTAKA: My name's Itō Yutaka.

OLD WOMAN: Hm. That's what we like to see, a little pluck. That's a man for you. What about you?

KEITA: My name is . . . (*He is unable to reply. His eyes remain downcast.*)

YUTAKA: He's Yasuda Keita.

OLD WOMAN: Hmmm. (*She gives the two a long, hard look.*)

YUKINO: They gave me money. See?

OLD WOMAN: What? Money? (*Angrily*): Yukino! You are Lord Kaison's granddaughter. It's all right to take money from men for a reason, but taking money for nothing's beggar's business. And we aren't beggars yet!

YUKINO: Then I'll give it back.

OLD WOMAN: Not so fast. I've got an idea. Now listen here, Master Yutaka, Master Keita, if you'll contribute this money to our shrine, I'll tell you the story of Lord Kaison. How'd that be?

The boys nod their assent.

OLD WOMAN: You agree, then?

The boys nod.

OLD WOMAN: That's a relief. Now everybody's happy. Good. Good. Get things ready, Yukino.

YUKINO: Yes, ma'am.

Old Woman pushes the boys backward and seats them against the wall. Yukino pulls the box from the closet, takes up a priest's staff, and sits down. Several brass rings hang from the top of the staff and jangle when the staff is shaken.

OLD WOMAN: As everything seems in order, we will begin our worship of Lord Kaison, Priest of Hitachi. (*She opens the casket.*)
Yukino shakes her staff, rattling the brass rings.
OLD WOMAN: Our Lord Kaison was a retainer of Kurō Hōgan Yoshitsune, illustrious general of the Minamoto clan. Kaison accompanied his master on the long journey from the capital to these provinces of the deep north. Yoshitsune had subdued the haughty warriors of the Heike clan, but evil detractors had planted false doubts in the mind of his brother, Yoritomo, who remained in the East at the seat of power. It was the spring of 1185. Disguised as mountain priests, Yoshitsune and his faithful retainer Benkei fled down the northern highway, enduring countless hardships on their way. Their aim was to reach Hiraizumi and receive the protection of Hidehira, noble patriarch of the Fujiwara clan. Among the retainers who followed Yoshitsune, Kaison, Priest of Hitachi, was to be found.
Yukino shakes her staff.
OLD WOMAN: Well? You understood all of that, didn't you? Let's see you bow.
The boys press their foreheads to the ground.
OLD WOMAN: Good! Good! (*She closes the box.*) You are among the few souls fortunate enough to have beheld Lord Kaison's saving grace. Whenever you are sad, whenever you are in pain, think of Lord Kaison and he will send his aid. I say so, so you can be sure it's true.
YUTAKA: But . . .
OLD WOMAN: What's that?
YUTAKA: But why do you have Lord Kaison's mummy in your house?
OLD WOMAN: Because Lord Kaison came and lived here before he passed away.
YUTAKA: But . . . but Yoshitsune lived a long time ago.
OLD WOMAN: A long, long time ago! More than 750 years ago. But what's so strange about that? Lord Kaison has survived for 750 years. He's conquered death. Yes, at least one man has conquered death. I saw him with these very eyes.
The light of dusk has vanished and it is night. The house is dark, and the moon is on the rise. An owl hoots.
OLD WOMAN: With these very eyes! Ah! It seems like yesterday! I was a girl of eighteen, light in body and light in soul, burning like a flame. It was a night bright with the moon and filled with

the sound of acorns dropping from the trees. The moonlight was so beautiful, I went out for a walk in the woods. All of a sudden, Lord Kaison appeared out of the darkness and stood before me.

A figure emerges from the darkness of Old Woman's yard. It is an old man carrying a biwa. He strikes a low chord.

KAISON (*with intensity*): Search though you may through the annals of the past, but often as you hear the word, seldom is courage found. (*He strikes a chord.*) Yet one man stands out from all the rest: the youngest son of Yoshitomo, Chief of the Imperial Stables of the Left, Kurō Yoshitsune. (*Biwa.*)

OLD WOMAN (*as a girl of eighteen*): Who are you, sir?

KAISON: My name? I am what is left of Kaison, Priest of Hitachi.

OLD WOMAN: Kaison? The famous Lord Kaison that everybody talks about?

KAISON: Then you know my name?

OLD WOMAN: Yes, I've heard it often in my mother's bedtime stories. But this is the first time I've seen your face.

KAISON: Well, well. . . . But no, I am not fit to stand before you. Please hear my story. I am Kaison, whose cowardice remains unmatched. At the battle of the Koromo River I turned my back on His Lordship Yoshitsune and fled for my life in the heat of battle! I was terrified of war! Terrified of dying! I betrayed my Lord Yoshitsune and ran!

OLD WOMAN: How terrible! Aren't you ashamed? How could you have been such a coward?

KAISON: I ran! I was a coward! Ah, I hate myself for what I did! I despise myself, but it doesn't change anything. My heart is as heavy with guilt as ever. Ever since I betrayed my master, I've wandered from village to village, town to town, doing penance for my crime. For 750 years I've shed tears of guilt for my irredeemable sin.

OLD WOMAN: Everyone is born in sin, they say, and no one can live without committing sins by the score.

KAISON: It's true! But the people of this world are crystal pure compared to me. I take every sin upon myself, to live as an example for others. Look at me! Even my eyes no longer see!

OLD WOMAN: How pitiful you are! Have you gone blind, too? They say that we must pay for our sins, but you have paid dearly indeed! How unhappy you must be!

KAISON: No, all is for my people. I pray only that they may have peace in this world and a better lot in the next. Now I must leave you. Farewell! (*He starts to leave.*)

OLD WOMAN: Please wait! Come to my house. There's only my mother and me. You can rest for a while. Please, Lord Kaison! I'll lead you by the hand.

KAISON: I'm much obliged, my child.

OLD WOMAN: This path is as bright as day. The moon is round as a ball in the sky! (*She laughs.*)

KAISON: That day Benkei, Priest of Musashi, was attired in raven-braided armor marked with yellow crests and was armed with a great halberd . . .

The two figures vanish in the darkness.

The interior of the house is dark. Not a sound is to be heard. Moonlight fills the yard. An owl is hooting.

Kotobukiya enters, holding a lantern aloft to light his way.

KOTOBUKIYA (*to someone behind him*): This way, your honor.

Teacher stumbles in. He carries a flashlight.

KOTOBUKIYA: This is the house I was telling you about.

TEACHER: It's so dark! Do you really think they're here?

KOTOBUKIYA: The old charcoal man said he saw them go in.

TEACHER: Place gives me the creeps!

KOTOBUKIYA: I'll give 'em a call. Anybody home? It's me, from the Kotobuki Lodge at the foot of the mountain. (*He moves closer and shines his light into the house.*)

Yukino is asleep in the corner of the room. Yutaka and Keita are lying face down on the floor.

KOTOBUKIYA: They're here, your honor! Both of them!

TEACHER (*bounding up to them*): Yasuda! Itō! Where's your sense of national spirit? What do you mean running off like this again? You're incorrigible! How often are you going to make me worry like this? Japan will never win the war with patriots like you! Get up! Get up, I said!

KOTOBUKIYA (*lifting the boys' heads and examining them carefully*): Now, now, your honor, come here and take a look at this. No doubt about it. Their souls have left their bodies.

TEACHER: What!

KOTOBUKIYA: Their eyes are wide open, but they don't recognize us.

They can't see a thing. If you try to call them back too fast, their souls will get mixed up and never find their way back.

TEACHER: That's the most unscientific! . . .

KOTOBUKIYA: No, your honor, this has happened four or five times to women and children from the village already. Just let their souls stay out of their bodies too long and see! They'll run into the mountains and won't come back for years. This isn't science, your honor. This is serious business.

TEACHER: I still think. . . .

KOTOBUKIYA: Let's just carry them back home quietly.

TEACHER: But this fortune-teller woman seems pretty suspicious to me, luring children into her den! I think we ought to inform the police.

KOTOBUKIYA: Oh, no, your honor! The old woman here is a blood relative of Lord Kaison. We couldn't do that. Anyway, we have to take these children home.

TEACHER: She's a blood relative of whose?

KOTOBUKIYA: I'll tell you as we're walking. (*He places one of the boys on Teacher's back.*)

TEACHER (*unsteadily*): Really . . . listen, I've got a weak heart, I tell you! This kind of thing isn't doing me any good at all.

KOTOBUKIYA (*hoisting the other child onto his own back*): It's a cruel world, that's for sure. (*Exits.*)

The moonlight is brighter than ever. Old Woman returns with long stalks of pampas grass over her shoulder.

OLD WOMAN: The mountains and valleys are bright as day. The light illumines unknown reaches of the soul, confounds and excites the mind. It's like a dream! (*She gazes at the moon and murmurs*): Lord Kaison!
Curtain.

ACT 2

Scene 1

It is a snowy, blustery night in March. The scene is the raised reception room just off the dirt-floored foyer of the Kotobuki Lodge.

There is a square fireplace in the center of the room where a pot has been set to boil over the charcoal fire. Kotobukiya is busy stirring the contents of the pot. Yutaka, Keita, and three other Boys are sitting with their backs to the wall, pensively listening to their Teacher.

TEACHER (*beginning to succumb to the contagious accent of the region*): Now then, we won't know the details until word comes from Tokyo, but one thing's for sure: today our country is at war, and nobody knows how long the war will last. Do you remember we talked about the Hundred Years' War? Well?

The boys nod.

TEACHER: What kind of answer is that? Let's see you show a little spirit!

BOYS (*together*): Yes, sir!

TEACHER: That's better. We must endure the unendurable! We must be loyal through thick and thin! We must be balls of fire to annihilate the Anglo-American devils! What did the Emperor Jimmu say?

BOYS (*in unison*): "Fight and die for glory! Fight and die for glory!"

TEACHER: That's right! That's the spirit of the loyal Japanese. Your homes have been destroyed by the enemy. Your school has burned down, too. But even if something has happened to your mothers and fathers, you should rejoice that they could lay down their lives for the greater glory of their country. That's the Japanese Spirit! You boys mustn't let a little bad news like this get you down! (*Reciting*): "From thoughts of self shall I be free/ My lord's poor shield for to be!" These petty desires to go home, to fill your stomachs with food, are pure selfishness! Your brothers, be they draftees or volunteers in the kamikaze corps, are fighting courageously on the land, on the sea, and in the sky! All is for His Highness the Emperor! All is for Imperial Japan! Let's sing together, then! (*He assumes the attitude of a conductor.*) "Were I to Fight."

BOYS (*chorally*):

Were I to fight on seas so high,
Then in their waters I would die!
And if I fought in mountains high,
Then in their grasses I would die!
My lord's great cause I'd ne'er forget,
I'd give my life and not regret!

TEACHER: This ends our talk for tonight.

BOYS (*loudly, in unison*): Long Live the Emperor! Long Live the Empress! Good night, Mother! Good night, Father! Pleasant dreams! (*They bow deeply to Teacher.*)

TEACHER: Good boys! Good boys!

KOTOBUKIYA: How would you boys like a cup of hot toddy? There's not enough to go around, so don't let the others see, you hear? (*He distributes cups.*) Careful, now, it's hot. I'll bet you're the one, aren't you? Snitched some dried fruit and ate it in the outhouse the other day. Careful there, don't drop it!

TEACHER: Take your cups into the corridor and drink it there. When you're finished, go upstairs to bed. And don't forget to go to the bathroom first, either.

The boys exit silently, cups in hand.

TEACHER (*grumbling*): Glad that's over! To tell the truth, these talks depress the hell out of me. "My lord's poor shield for to be"!

KOTOBUKIYA: Poor kids! Just think, wiped out! Not a single relative left alive!

TEACHER: Not so loud! (*He looks anxiously in the direction of the door.*) That's the way it looks.

KOTOBUKIYA: Really something, ain't it? Five kids losing their folks all at once. Really something! Tokyo must be in pretty bad shape.

TEACHER: No doubt about it. It's hard to tell how things are going to turn out.

KOTOBUKIYA (*proffering a cup of toddy*): But there's no chance we'll lose the war, is there?

TEACHER: Show a little faith, man, show a little faith! (*Sipping the contents of his cup*): Say, this is good! In any case, our school was right in the heart of Tokyo. Most of those kids' houses were in the main shopping area. The school and the houses must have gotten hit all at once.

KOTOBUKIYA: Are air raids bad as all that?

TEACHER: Yes, and now they've started what they call "saturation bombing." When we lost all contact with those kids' families, I began to fear the worst. But now there's no room for doubt. There's not a soul left alive.

KOTOBUKIYA: It makes your hair stand on end.

TEACHER: It was a relief for me, though: I evacuated my family to my wife's parents' house in the country during the New Year's holiday.

KOTOBUKIYA: But without folks, what's going to happen to them?

TEACHER: Hard to say. They should at least have an aunt or an uncle left to take care of them.

KOTOBUKIYA: I suppose. But city kids sure are strong, aren't they? You tell them we're not sure if their folks are dead or alive, and there's not a tear shed between them.

TEACHER: That's because of my firm hand and strict discipline. They're well prepared to accept these things. Besides, it's all so we can win the war. They should feel proud.

KOTOBUKIYA: I suppose. . . .

TEACHER: Really blowing out there again tonight, isn't it? How many months has it been snowing? Being holed up like this all winter long is hard on the nerves. It's hard on the nerves, let me tell you.

KOTOBUKIYA: For city folks, I suppose it is. But we've always lived this way.

TEACHER: Day after day the snow falls. Just when you think the wind's quieted down, it's sleet you've got to contend with.

KOTOBUKIYA: It won't be too much longer, your honor. We're over the worst of it. Spring's just around the corner.

TEACHER (*irritably*): I don't need you to tell me that! After winter comes spring; summer after spring; then fall, winter, spring, summer! Can't you think of anything more original to say?

KOTOBUKIYA: Of course. Looks like your honor's due for a breath of fresh air, though, doesn't it? In the snow country, trees that don't bend break.

TEACHER: What's that supposed to mean?

KOTOBUKIYA: Not too far from here you'll find the house of Toragoze.

TEACHER: Who?

KOTOBUKIYA: The wife of Jūrō Sukenari. She lives on the outskirts of the village with her sister Shōshō, the wife of Gorō Tokimune.

Teacher looks quizzically at Kotobukiya.

KOTOBUKIYA: Until a while back, they were living together with the boys' mother.

TEACHER: Wait a minute, wait a minute! What are you talking about? Those are the names of the Soga brothers.

KOTOBUKIYA: That's right.

TEACHER: What do you mean, "That's right"? The Soga brothers are dead! They died after they avenged the murder of their father. But that was 750 years ago! Look, I'm bored, I admit. But your ramblings are going to drive me nuts!

KOTOBUKIYA: But it's what they say themselves, your honor. It's not something we just made up.

TEACHER: And you . . . you people believe them? Seriously?

KOTOBUKIYA (*laconically*): It's what they say themselves.

TEACHER: Look, that's the same line you gave me about that priest, what's his name? Kaison. Boy, when you tell a story, you tell a good one!

Kotobukiya sips taciturnly from his cup.

TEACHER: How do you expect Japan to win the war when you're so damned unscientific!

Kotobukiya continues to take small sips from his cup, remaining utterly composed. Teacher's rantings do not affect him.

TEACHER (*irately*): Well, what about it? Say something! Don't just sit there! Talking to you's like talking to a brick wall!

KOTOBUKIYA (*unmoved*): It's what they say themselves, your honor.

TEACHER: Aaaa! How long do I have to live like this? Day in and day out the only faces I have to look at are the pitiful, hungry faces of those kids, and your ruddy, incomprehensible masks. And you keep up this insipid chatter, all the while sitting there with your shoulders rounded waiting for spring to come!

KOTOBUKIYA: Nothing else to do, is there? We've always lived this way.

TEACHER: It's a wonder you haven't lost your wits altogether! It's a wonder you don't all lose your minds! Aaaa! It's already 1945, can you believe it? (*Holding his head*): The snow blows. And then the sleet!

KOTOBUKIYA (*pulling a flask from the ashes*): It's warmed up just right, your honor. Why don't you have a nip before you go to bed?

TEACHER: Sake? Just what I needed. This is about the only pleasure left. (*Accepting the flask*): Well, I guess I'll be getting to bed. At least I can visit Tokyo in my dreams. Good night.

Exits.

KOTOBUKIYA: Good night.

Kotobukiya extinguishes the lights and exits, leaving behind him the sound of the storm. Snowblink and light from the embers dance across the walls.

Keita appears, crawling out of the darkness. He removes the lid from the pot on the fire, sticks his hand in and licks his fingers.

KEITA (*under his breath*): There's still some left!

Yutaka crawls in.

YUTAKA (*in a whisper*): There is?

KEITA: Yeah, come on. (*He pours the small amount of toddy remaining in the bottom of the pot into two cups.*)

YUTAKA (*eagle-eyed*): There's more in your cup!

KEITA: Okay! (*He pours some more into Yutaka's cup.*) That's all there is.

YUTAKA: Okay.

The boys drink.

YUTAKA: Sure is good!

KEITA: You can say that again! (*Licking his empty cup*): My mom's not dead, is she?

YUTAKA (*similarly*): Course not. It's all a big lie.

KEITA: Just a big lie, that's all.

YUTAKA: My mom's alive, too. So are my dad and my brother. They're all alive, I know it! (*He scrapes the ladle with his fingers.*)

KEITA: I don't have a brother, but I have a kid sister. (*He runs his fingers over the inner surface of the pot and licks them clean.*)

YUTAKA: Is she cute? (*He helps Keita clean out the pot.*)

KEITA: I guess so.

YUTAKA: How cute? Cute as Yukino?

KEITA: Not that cute.

YUTAKA: I wish she'd come play with us. Yukino, I mean.

KEITA: She won't come here. Not to a place like this.

YUTAKA: Let's go visit her. (*He giggles.*)

KEITA: It's a secret from the others. (*He also giggles.*)

Kotobukiya enters stealthily.

KOTOBUKIYA: Who's there? Who's doing all this giggling and carrying on?

Keita and Yutaka scream in terror and flee to a corner of the room.

KOTOBUKIYA (*turning on the light*): Raiding the pantry again, are you?

All right, who is it? Let me have a look at you. I'll see your teacher hears about this! Ah, so it's you!

Both boys are paralyzed with fear.

KOTOBUKIYA: Well, I guess you didn't mean no harm. If there was enough food around, I'd feed you so you wouldn't have to be running about in the middle of the night like this. But I've got fifteen of you kids to look after, and I might as well be closed for all the other customers I get. Put yourselves in my shoes, eh? Just be glad I found you and not your teacher. He'd have beat you again for sure.

Yutaka sobs.

KEITA (*screaming*): Lord Kaison!

KOTOBUKIYA: What's that?

KEITA: Kaison! Kaison! Kaison! Kaison! Kaison! Mommy!!! (*He throws himself on the floor and bursts into tears.*)

Kotobukiya is at a complete loss. Teacher enters to find out what is happening. He is drunk and reeling.

TEACHER: Hey! You kids! Hey! Stand up! I'll teach you crybabies to behave like men! Stand up, I said!

KOTOBUKIYA: Now, now, your honor, they're only children. They can't help it. Everything's all right. Now come on, you two, up to bed with you. Come one, stand up. (*He exits, taking the boys with him.*)

TEACHER: Give 'em an inch and they take a mile! (*To himself*): What's wrong with those kids, anyway? What've they got to cry about? I'm doing the best I can. I'm the one who's hard up! Kids have it easy! At least they can bawl all they like. (*Singing softly*): "It's only when you understand/ That all of life's for nought/ That you understand its pathos." (*He stares at the embers in the fireplace.*)

Outside, the snowstorm continues to howl. You can almost hear a woman's voice mixed with the sound of the wind, beckoning, "Evening, milord! Evening, milord!"

Teacher shivers violently. "Evening, milord! Evening, milord!" the voice continues, blown by the storm.

TEACHER: Ko . . . Kotobukiya! Kotobukiya!

Kotobukiya enters.

KOTOBUKIYA: What is it? What's wrong?

TEACHER: Out . . . outside . . . there's, there's a woman outside.

Kotobukiya fails to understand immediately.

TEACHER: Listen. See? You can hear her. Somebody's saying something. There's a woman out there.

KOTOBUKIYA: I can't hear anything. . . .

TEACHER: Go out and look! Please! She's knocking on the door! I'm sure of it! Listen!

Kotobukiya steps down into the dirt foyer and takes a straw rain cape and hat from pegs on the wall. He brings them with a pair of straw snow boots to Teacher.

KOTOBUKIYA (*handing him the boots*): Put these on, your honor.

TEACHER: What . . . what for?

KOTOBUKIYA: Never mind, just do as I say.

Teacher puts on the boots.

KOTOBUKIYA: Now put these on, too, and out you go.

TEACHER: Where . . . where am I going?

KOTOBUKIYA: Like it or not you've become one of us. That's the snow talking. The snowflakes have tongues.

Teacher stands stunned and confused.

KOTOBUKIYA: Can you still hear them?

TEACHER: Where should I go? What should I do?

KOTOBUKIYA: I wouldn't be surprised if Toragoze and Shōshō are lonely too on a night like this. Pay them a call.

TEACHER (*his head drooping despondently*): Where do I go to meet them?

KOTOBUKIYA: Straight down the road. You won't get lost. Go straight along to the foot of the mountain. There's a shrine there. You remember! You look to the side of the shrine and you'll see where to go. There'll be a house with a bit of light in the window. It's the only one.

TEACHER (*submissively*): What do I say?

KOTOBUKIYA: Say you're Jūrō Sukenari. If the door doesn't open, say it's Gorō Tokimune. It it still doesn't open, you'll have to try again tomorrow. But I wouldn't worry. No, not on a snowy night like this.

Kotobukiya open a small hatch in the wooden shutters that protect the doorway. Snow rushes in with a roar. Teacher shields his face beneath the straw hat and slips through the opening in silence.

Kotobukiya closes the hatch behind him, turns off the light, and exits. The sound of the snow lashing the lodge is mixed with a voice

that seems to be calling, "Evening, milord! Evening, milord!"
Blackout.

Scene 2

A room in Old Woman's house. It is a May afternoon, and the house is enveloped by plum, peach, and cherry trees all blooming at once. The swollen stream rushes down the mountainside, and birds cry sharply in the sky. Yutaka and Keita are sitting in a stiff, formal posture in one corner of the room. Both are quiet, their eyes fixed on the floor.
YUTAKA (*softly*): Keita?
KEITA: What?
YUTAKA: Your mother and mine died in the air raids. They were both killed when our houses burned down.
KEITA: I told you, she's alive! My mother's alive! I met her!
YUTAKA: When? Where did you meet her?
KEITA: Here! She comes to meet me when I'm here.
YUTAKA: Liar!
KEITA: Go ahead and call me a liar. You'll see!
Both boys revert to their former silence and fix their eyes on the floor. Birds cry raucously.
Old Woman enters with Yukino, carrying a basket filled with mountain herbs.
YUKINO: Hey, what do you think you're doing sitting in our house?
OLD WOMAN: Keita, is that you? Where've you been? I was worried you caught a cold or something.
KEITA: Yutaka called me a liar. My mother's not dead, is she? She's alive, right?
OLD WOMAN: Of course she's alive! Of course she is! (*She begins to sort her harvest.*)
KEITA (*to Yutaka*): See! My mom'll live for a hundred years, a thousand years. Yukino knows it, too!
YUKINO: Keita's seen his ma lots of times.
YUTAKA: Really?
KEITA: Yes, really! But it's a secret just between the three of us.
YUTAKA: You can't fool me! (*He gets up to leave.*) Everybody's dead! Our teacher and Kotobukiya and the man from the county seat said

so. Nobody comes to see us. We don't even get letters anymore! (*He is on the brink of tears.*) You liar, Keita! Stop lying! You can keep your old secret! Who needs it? (*He exits in a mixture of dejection and rage.*)

KEITA: Yutaka! Try for yourself and see! You can see your mom, honest!

OLD WOMAN (*sorting the herbs*): Just smell this, will you? Have you ever smelled anything so heavenly? It was worth waiting out the winter for.

YUKINO: And look, the cherries are in bloom. It makes me want to go someplace, someplace far, far away.

OLD WOMAN: With that wayward heart of yours, I hate to think where you'd wind up.

YUKINO: But I'm tired of this place! There must be much better places in the world. If only I could go and see them!

OLD WOMAN: That's enough of your selfishness. This land's been blessed by Lord Kaison. It's here that you belong and it's here you'll stay. Now take Keita and gather some more of these herbs.

YUKINO: I'd rather go alone.

OLD WOMAN: You heard me.

YUKINO (*complying sullenly*): Oh, all right. Come on! (*She strides briskly away.*)

OLD WOMAN (*to Keita*): You be friends with Yukino, now. Don't be getting into any scraps.

KEITA: Yes, ma'am. Afterward will you let me see my mom?

OLD WOMAN: All right, all right. Whatever my boy Keita wants.

Keita exits, taking a basket with him.

KEITA (*watching him go*): Nothing like having a man around the house! Yukino and Keita: could have done worse, I suppose. Could have done worse. (*She disappears behind the house.*)

Yutaka creeps cautiously out of the underbrush and gazes in the direction Keita has gone.

Toragoze and Shōshō enter. They are dressed for travel. Strapped to the bundles on their back are the shamisen and lute with which they have entertained many a male guest.

TORAGOZE: Well, look who's here! One of the evacuee kids, ain't you?

Yutaka turns with a start.

TORAGOZE: I thought so. How's your teacher these days?

YUTAKA: Teacher? Our teacher's gone. He went to Tokyo, and he's not back yet.

TORAGOZE: But he will come back, won't he?

YUTAKA: Who cares! (*He exits, running.*)

TORAGOZE (*tears filling her eyes*): He's forgotten me, Shōshō! I just know he has! I wanted to see him one more time. I wanted to see him. . . .

SHŌSHŌ: Have you still got that man on your mind? Look, everything in life's preordained. If you're meant to see him again, you'll see him, so stop worrying.

TORAGOZE: I know . . . I just love him so!

SHŌSHŌ: Love! We've got enough troubles without love! (*Calling into the house*): Anybody home? It's Tora and Shōshō from town! *Old Woman hurries out from behind the house.*

OLD WOMAN: Well, look what the wind blew in! It's been a long time! Good to see you! You're both looking well.

TORAGOZE: Yes, we're healthy enough. Looks like you survived the winter all right yourself.

SHŌSHŌ: You seem to get younger all the time. I'll bet you've got some secret potion you're not telling us about.

OLD WOMAN (*laughing*): From what I hear you've been doing well enough without it. But now that you're here it really feels like spring! I hope you're planning to stay a few days.

SHŌSHŌ: I'm afraid we can't. We have to be over the south ridge by sundown.

OLD WOMAN: What's your hurry? I was looking forward to hearing you chant your requiem for the Soga brothers tonight. Now that you mention it, though, you are loaded down for a long journey. What's wrong?

TORAGOZE: We're fugitives from the law! Can you believe it? They may be after us this very minute. We had to close up our house and run for our lives.

OLD WOMAN: You mean you've closed up the House of Soga? You're forsaking your heritage?

TORAGOZE: What else can we do?

OLD WOMAN: Now your ma and I were friends for years. I'm not letting you go anyplace until I get to the bottom of this. Let's hear the whole story. There had better be a good reason for this, or I won't stand for it!

SHŌSHŌ: Tora, she hasn't heard. (*To Old Woman*): The police and the county seat are out to get us. Not just Tora and me, everybody! Even the fortune-tellers. They gave us a lecture like you never heard before.

OLD WOMAN: But why? What did you do wrong?

SHŌSHŌ: We never did understand exactly, but they said that women like us and fortune-tellers and the like were "undesirable elements" and good for nothing. And they said if we didn't change our ways they'd run us out of town!

TORAGOZE: We told them again and again that we were the wives of Sukenari and Tokimune and that we weren't doing nothing wrong, but they wouldn't listen. They kept on yelling at us and yelling at us until we just couldn't stay around there anymore.

OLD WOMAN: It's a cruel world for sure! Never heard anything so terrible in all my days. How come we're "undesirable elements"?

TORAGOZE: They said it's because we make our living by stirring people up and leading them astray.

OLD WOMAN: It's them politicians and coppers that don't know which end is up! Without you two, what's to become of all the Sukenaris and Tokimunes in these parts?

TORAGOZE: That's what we said!

OLD WOMAN: It'll be terrible to behold.

SHŌSHŌ: I'm glad we won't be around to see it.

OLD WOMAN: They'll pine away. They'll lose their minds thinking about you! Then you'll see people getting stirred up, believe me!

Toragoze sobs.

OLD WOMAN: It's the end for sure! I never thought I'd live to see the day!

Tōsenbō runs in, panting loudly.

TŌSENBŌ: There's news! News! You've never heard anything like it! It's the biggest news since Creation!

OLD WOMAN: Quiet! Still breathing, eh? Where've you been holed up all winter? Here it is spring and no word from you. I figured you'd dropped dead.

TŌSENBŌ: Heaven forbid! But wait, I'll explain everything later. I've brought news. (*Noticing Toragoze and Shōshō*: Oh, you're here, too! How'd you get out of town? The county seat's after you, you know.

TORAGOZE: That's it! They really are after us!

SHŌSHŌ: Tora, if they catch us it'll be the end of everything. Let's get going while the going's still good.

TŌSENBŌ: You're right there! (*Helping them with their bundles*): It's a fine turn things have taken, a fine turn indeed. If they weren't after me, too, I'd see you on your way, but . . .

SHŌSHŌ: Thanks but no thanks! With friends like you seeing us off, we wouldn't need any enemies! (*She laughs.*)

TORAGOZE (*to Old Woman*): We'll be on our way, then. Take care of yourself.

OLD WOMAN: Same to you.

TORAGOZE: We'll be all right.

SHŌSHŌ: We'll be back soon as the war's over. If we don't find rich husbands first! (*She laughs.*) Good-bye, then.

TŌSENBŌ: Take care of yourselves!

Toragoze and Shōshō exit.

OLD WOMAN (*calling after them*): Times are really bad when girls like you go without a place to lay your heads!

TŌSENBŌ: Take care of yourselves! . . . It makes even me sad to see them go. (*Trying to get Old Woman's attention*): I . . . Look at me for a minute, will you?

OLD WOMAN: What is it now, you whining potato priest? I'll bet you're figuring to come rolling in on me again.

TŌSENBŌ: You've got me all wrong! I've only come to tell you the news. You'll be telling no more fortunes in these parts. It's been prohibited by law! Mountain priests and fortune-tellers distract and confuse the people, and we're not supposed to cast spells or say prayers anymore. Otherwise they'll send us to work in the munitions factory. It's a harsh order they've issued this time, that's for sure.

OLD WOMAN: Munitions factory, eh? Why don't you go? The pay can't be that bad.

TŌSENBŌ: Not me. Not me! They work you till you drop in those places.

OLD WOMAN: Then you're out of luck, aren't you? There are two kinds of men I won't have nothing to do with—those without money and those without brains!

TŌSENBŌ: Then what are you going to do? You can't be a fortune-teller anymore; you haven't the land to be a farmer; and there's no money to start a business. There's nothing left for you to do but become a mummy!

OLD WOMAN: A mummy?

TŌSENBŌ: It's a question of life or death. The munitions factory for me and mummification for you. (*He chuckles.*)

OLD WOMAN: What's so funny? I'm ready to become a mummy any time. I'm wife to Lord Kaison. An end to my divinations is an end to my life. So be it. It's mummification for me.

TŌSENBŌ: Wait, I didn't mean. . . .

OLD WOMAN: There's Yukino's future to worry about, but that can't be helped. My mind's made up!

TŌSENBŌ: Wait . . . wait a minute, not so fast. All I meant was. . . .

OLD WOMAN: It's too late. Don't try to stop me. You can do me one favor, though. I'll teach you how to make my mummy. It's the secret method handed down from Lord Kaison himself, so bow down and heed me well!

Tōsenbō throws himself on the ground.

OLD WOMAN: Thirty days without cereals of any kind. Thirty days without the fruits of trees or the roots of plants. And twenty-eight days without water. Eighty-eight days and I should have breathed my last. When you're certain the last trace of life has left my body, carry my corpse to the river and bathe and purify me for three days and three nights without rest. When you've performed this task, carry me back here and hang me from the eaves in a spot where the breeze blows well, about there should be as good a place as any, and let me dry in the shadows seven days and seven nights.

TŌSENBŌ: But! . . .

OLD WOMAN: Then my mummy will be finished. It's what I've always wanted. I'll sit next to Lord Kaison. He'll be my king. I'll be his queen! I'm counting on you, now. See that you do as I say and make no mistakes!

TŌSENBŌ (*shuddering uncontrollably*): Please, I'll do anything, but not that! You'd have to cast your most powerful spell over me before I could do what you ask. Please, I beg you, reconsider. Please! (*He crawls to her.*) You're too young! Your skin is still soft and warm. Please! For me!

OLD WOMAN (*pushing him away*): A wretch of a priest you are! I'm not going to ask you twice. I'll just have to depend on Yukino, that's all. Now where could she have gotten to? (*She steps down from the house into the garden.*)

TŌSENBŌ: Then you won't change your mind?

Young Man 3 and Young Man 4, factory workers by the look of them, enter with rucksacks on their backs. They appear to be on their way to the black market.

YOUNG MAN 3: Will you look at that! The old witch is still here. Hey, you old bat, it's a wonder the cops haven't thrown you in the clink and thrown away the key!

YOUNG MAN 4: You've been predicting that the war'll be over soon, haven't you? The cops really blew their stacks at that one!

OLD WOMAN: Well you can tell them for me you can all go to hell! I only repeated what the gods revealed. The war will be over in August, by the end of the month at the latest.

TŌSENBŌ: Come off it! You're only going to make things worse for yourself.

YOUNG MAN 3: Lies and more lies! She can't help herself!

YOUNG MAN 4: You can't really blame her. Her mind's not quite right, you know!

YOUNG MAN 3: If you're so smart, tell us who's going to win. Japan? America? What do the gods have to say about that?

YOUNG MAN 4: Come on, give it a whirl. We'll pay you twice the usual amount. How about it?

YOUNG MAN 3: Who'll it be, them or us?

YOUNG MAN 4: Them or us?

OLD WOMAN: I could tell you, it'd be easy enough, but what's in those packs you're carrying? From the look of it, I'd say you were taking off from work to visit the black market. How do you expect me to tell an accurate fortune when your money comes from lying and deceit? Away with you! I don't want to look at you another second!

YOUNG MAN 3: You're the stubbornest old bitch I've ever seen! We'll see that the cops hear about you, just wait!

YOUNG MAN 4: You can bet your life on that. You'll rot from the mouth for spreading lies like this!

The Young Men exit, taunting, "Them or us? Them or us?"

TŌSENBŌ (*to Young Men*): You'll be sorry you said that! (*To Old Woman*): Can't you be more careful? These are bad times. Try to get along with people.

OLD WOMAN: Tōsenbō!

TŌSENBŌ: What?

OLD WOMAN: I've changed my mind. I'll not become a mummy after all.

TŌSENBŌ: Then you've reconsidered? That's wonderful!

OLD WOMAN: My life doesn't matter, but there's someone who comes to me, someone I've grown too fond of.

TŌSENBŌ: What! Who is it? Another man?

Old Woman cackles.

TŌSENBŌ (*excitedly*): How old is he? What does he look like?

OLD WOMAN: He's still young. And good looking, too. If I became a mummy now, Keita would pine away for sure. I can't become a mummy for thinking of him. (*She strolls smiling among the blossoming shrubs.*)

TŌSENBŌ: It's a lie! You're the cruelest woman! You're trying to drive me mad with jealousy! Does this upstart mean that much to you?

OLD WOMAN: Yes, indeed. If I don't see Keita once every three days, my world seems empty.

TŌSENBŌ: You're too cruel! (*Tears well up in his eyes.*) I can't bear it!

OLD WOMAN: You'll just have to resign yourself. A woman in love's got no control over her heart.

TŌSENBŌ: So be it! I'm a man, too. I'll not be hanging around here knowing you don't care for me no more. I'll leave and I won't come back. But I have one thing to say before I go. Any man who falls into your clutches will never be the same again. I'm living proof. All I did was come near you, and I broke my vows and abandoned my everlasting soul! This Keita of yours will end up like me: a wasted, useless hulk. (*He weeps.*) You made a mummy of me as I lived and breathed! It's the curse of Lord Kaison! It's a curse! (*He exits, wailing.*)

OLD WOMAN: Humph! That takes care of that runny-nosed good-for-nothing! That's one troublemaker cut in chunks and thrown to the dogs! (*She laughs.*) I won't allow Lord Kaison's lineage to be broken.

It's too early to become a mummy yet.

Keita and Yukino return. Keita's face is streaming with tears.

OLD WOMAN: So you're back. Come over here, then.

YUKINO: I hate Keita! He's such a crybaby! The least little thing and he starts bawling.

OLD WOMAN (*to Keita*): What's wrong? Have you got a tummyache? *Keita shakes his head.*

OLD WOMAN: Look sharp, then. Act like a man or Yukino won't like you anymore.

KEITA: I want my mommy! Let me see my mommy! Let me see her right now!

OLD WOMAN: All right, all right. You can see your mommy whenever you like. People never die, you know that. Yukino, get things ready.

YUKINO: Yes, ma'am.

Yukino carefully lays out a long rosary and a set of bells attached to a hand-held implement. She opens the box containing Kaison's mummy.

OLD WOMAN (*to Keita*): You have to be quiet now and put your mind at ease. If your mind's in turmoil, the gods won't deign to visit. Do you understand?

KEITA: Yes, ma'am.

OLD WOMAN: Good. Now pray. (*She presses her palms together.*)

Keita follows Old Woman's example.

OLD WOMAN: Yukino, is everything ready?

YUKINO: Yes, ma'am. (*She takes the bells in hand and improvises an incantation.*) We realize we're not supposed to reveal your mysteries to kids, but the old woman's decided that Keita believes with all his heart, so she's going to lend him a hand. (*To Keita*): And don't you forget it! (*She gives the bells a violent shake.*)

OLD WOMAN: Keita, who is it you call when you're sad and in pain? Let me hear you say his name.

KEITA (*softly*): Lord Kaison, Lord Kaison, Lord Kaison.

OLD WOMAN: That's right. You do just as I say and call his name from the bottom of your heart. Yukino!

Yukino again shakes the bells.

OLD WOMAN (*fingering the rosary*): Lord Kaison, Lord Kaison, Lord Kaison! We beseech you to send forth the mother of our friend,

Yasuda Keita. Bestow your mercy on those in need. Lend your strength to those bereft. If it please you, send forth Keita's mother! (*She repeats this incantation.*)
Yukino rings the bells again violently.
Old Woman utters a cry and falls prostrate on the floor.
Yukino rings the bells slowly, deliberately, then silences them.
Old Woman rises slowly to an upright position.

OLD WOMAN: Keita, it's Mommy. I'm glad you came to see me. Mommy wanted to see you very badly, too. I really wanted to see you. Come, now, come close to your Mommy.

KEITA: Mommy!

OLD WOMAN: Ah, ah, that's my baby. You haven't changed a bit since we were together in Tokyo. I can't tell you how happy I am. Let's always meet like this.

KEITA: Mommy, I want to go home.

OLD WOMAN: No, Keita, that won't do. Mommy wants you to come home, too, but now American soldiers are coming with guns to capture the city. There's no telling what might happen to you if you came home now. I know you're lonesome, but stay where you are. You understand what Mommy is telling you, don't you?

KEITA: All right, I'll do as you say.

OLD WOMAN: That's Mommy's good boy. Remember, I'm always thinking of you. Take good care of yourself, listen to what your teacher tells you, and grow up to be big and strong.

KEITA (*with tears in his voice*): Yes, Mommy. But what about our house? Has Daddy come home yet?

OLD WOMAN: No, Keita, Daddy hasn't come home yet, and our house burned down. But you mustn't get discouraged. Nothing's going to happen to Daddy. He'll be back to see you soon. And even though the house burned down, you can always rebuild it when you get older. Because only appearances change. Everything else remains the same. Nothing will be lost. Nothing forsaken. All right, Keita? Do you understand?

KEITA: Yes, ma'am.

OLD WOMAN: Whenever you want to see me, you just tell the old woman. She'll love you in Mommy's place. Remember, you must never leave her, not ever.

KEITA: I'll remember.

OLD WOMAN: Then I'll come and see you again. You be patient and wait like a good boy. All right?

KEITA: Mommy! Stay with me a little longer. Please!

OLD WOMAN: Mommy has lots of things to do. Don't you be chasing after me now like a baby. Stay well then, Keita.

KEITA: Mommy! (*He collapses in tears.*)

Old Woman utters another cry and falls prostrate on the floor. Yukino rings the bells violently, then silences them.

YUKINO: The seance is over. Keita's mother has gone back where she came from. The old woman has fainted, and you better be quiet! Shhh! (*She puts down the bells.*) Well, that's that.

KEITA: I feel much better.

YUKINO: Of course you do. I'll bet you were glad to see your ma.

KEITA: Yutaka was stupid to go home. Next time I'll bring him along.

YUKINO: It's time for you to go, too. The old woman's fainted, so you just go quietly. Be seeing you. (*She picks up her basket to leave.*)

KEITA: Where you going?

YUKINO: To see the cherry blossoms on top of the mountain. You can't come.

KEITA: Why not!

YUKINO: Because I don't want you to. I'd rather play alone. (*Exits.*)

KEITA: I'll come again soon, okay? (*Keita exits, looking back over his shoulder as he goes.*)

Yutaka creeps out of the underbrush. He is speechless with fear and amazement. He notices Old Woman move and scurries backward into the bushes.

Drained, Old Woman rises slowly, takes a deep breath, and gazes dreamily at the peach blossoms in the garden.

OLD WOMAN (*gazing at the thin, upper branches of the tree*): Lord Kaison! There hasn't been a man here, you know, and I was beginning to wonder what was to become of us. But thanks to you, things are looking up. I've taken a liking to this boy, Keita. He's just what we need: a man who'll do exactly as I say. I'll start preparing him right now, and he'll look after you when I'm gone. Please help me make this plan a success. (*She presses her hands together in prayer.*) Lord Kaison, in every generation the world has need of you. You

must survive! You must live on until the paradise of the Pure Land is realized in this world! (*She continues to pray in silence.*)
Blackout.

Scene 3

The reception room of the Kotobuki Lodge. It is a cloudy morning in October. The deliberate pounding of a festival drum, apparently beaten by children, can be heard in the distance.

Three boys—Yutaka, Masao, and Yūichi—sit huddled together in frightened silence on the edge of the raised floor. They wear school caps and tennis shoes and seem ready for an imminent departure. Behind each boy is a large bundle of bedding, a wicker suitcase, a small handbag, and a school briefcase.

OFFICIAL (*speaking as he enters from the next room*): Kotobukiya should be back any time now. Sorry to keep you folks waiting like this.

Housewife, Lumberman, and Fisherman follow Official into the room.

OFFICIAL: He went looking for the other boy. Couldn't have gone too far. You kids ready? Haven't forgotten anything, have you?

The boys shake their heads.

FISHERMAN: I don't know about these city kids. Look at them—a strong wind'd blow 'em apart at the seams.

HOUSEWIFE: But see how intelligent they look! You can't beat city kids for brains.

LUMBERMAN: Yeah, but you get 'em too smart and they're no use to anybody.

FISHERMAN: That's what I say. Now, which one of you's coming with me? Is it you? Or you?

HOUSEWIFE: That one's promised to me.

LUMBERMAN: Now nobody's decided who gets which yet. Don't be trying to have everything your own way all the time. A lumberjack's life ain't easy. I need a kid who can take it.

HOUSEWIFE: Well that's just fine, but we're farmers, and my old man told me to pick out a kid we can depend on.

FISHERMAN: You people don't know what you're talking about. I'm figuring to raise my kid as a fisherman. This one here's coming with me.

HOUSEWIFE: No! I just told you that one's mine!

LUMBERMAN: That's a woman for you! Won't listen to a word anybody says.

OFFICIAL: Now, now. Why don't you just leave this up to me. Anyway, as I'm the representative of the county seat; these kids are my responsibility. We've all been able to agree on the terms of adoption so far, but if we keep up these arguments, we'll be right back where we started from.

LUMBERMAN: He's right.

OFFICIAL: Think of all the trouble we've gone to down at the county seat. These kids are a heavy responsibility, not merchandise up for sale.

HOUSEWIFE: Yeah, and they eat like horses, too. What's in it for us, that's what I want to know.

OFFICIAL: During the war we had our hands full taking care of all the evacuees from the cities. Now, thank goodness, the war's over. But still, nobody's come to claim these kids. We can't just leave them here with Kotobukiya, can we?

HOUSEWIFE: I suppose not.

OFFICIAL: And that's not the half of it. These kids' teacher went off to restore contact with Tokyo, but we haven't seen hide nor hair of him since. Nobody knows where he ran off to.

LUMBERMAN: The coward couldn't see his kids through to the end, could he?

HOUSEWIFE: He probably had problems of his own.

LUMBERMAN: Yeah, problems but no responsibilities.

FISHERMAN: He figured he was irresponsible and he was right! (*He laughs.*) Just like Japan. Unconditional surrender! We didn't let our enemies impose a single condition on us! That's not easy. Anybody can lose a war, but it takes a bit of doing to lose it unconditionally!

OFFICIAL: Let me see, how far did we get in our discussions? Oh, yes. Ahem. After serious deliberations and numerous discussions, we at the county seat have decided to ask you gentlemen . . . and ladies . . . to take these kids in. Allow me to express our sincerest thanks. I'm sure that fate has destined you to look after these children, and I know you will love them as if they were your own. Thank you. (*He bows deeply.*)

FISHERMAN: The agreement was that I'd get two. Now listen, you kids, you come with me and you'll get as much fish as you can eat. We'll go out in boats and catch 'em by the net-full. When you grow up, I'll see you get a pretty little woman to look after you, too. How about it? (*He laughs.*)

OFFICIAL: Sounds good, doesn't it? This man over here is in the lumber business, and that lady lives on a farm. What's wrong? Can't you even say hello?

The boys huddle closer together, their eyes riveted to the ground.

OFFICIAL: What kind of a way is that to act? And you call yourselves sixth graders?

Yūichi begins to cry.

OFFICIAL: Stop that! (*He laughs nervously.*) They're just shy, that's all. They're very grateful, really. They just don't know how to express it. I can see through their tears, though, can't you?

LUMBERMAN: City kids don't have what it takes.

HOUSEWIFE: Poor things! I mean, even if their parents are dead, there should be at least an aunt or an uncle to care for them. (*She weeps.*)

LUMBERMAN: City folks don't have no feelings. They probably forgot these kids even existed.

FISHERMAN: Wouldn't be surprised.

OFFICIAL: Isn't it the truth? We've had our hands full, let me tell you. There are 250 of these kids in this prefecture alone, you know.

HOUSEWIFE: I have to be getting home early or my old man will really let me have it. And the weather's changing, too. I wish you'd decide this business and get it over with.

LUMBERMAN: We could draw straws. That'd be fair. How about it?

FISHERMAN: Okay with me. You watch, I'll draw those two just like I said. (*He laughs.*)

HOUSEWIFE: Count me out! You know I always get the dregs.

OFFICIAL: Now, now, no need to get excited.

HOUSEWIFE: There must be other people who'd take these kids. We're not all that excited about having another mouth to feed. You came begging, so we figured we'd lend a hand, but. . . .

FISHERMAN: We thought we'd do a good turn, too. We don't have to take in these evacuee brats, you know. There're plenty of youngsters looking for work. You kids just get yourselves adopted by a farmer—you'll spend half your time babysitting and the rest wading around in the paddies covered with dung. You might get enough to eat, but you'll never see a trace of hard cash. Take my word for it.

HOUSEWIFE: Look who's talking! I pity the kids who end up with a slavemaster like you! (*To the children*): Nothing but lickings morning till night. You'll be lucky to come out alive!

LUMBERMAN: That's enough, you two! If you're going to make such a fuss, you can count me out, too!

OFFICIAL (*fidgeting uncomfortably*): Well, how about some refreshments. In the other room. They should be ready by now. If you'll just come this way, we can discuss the final details. . . .

FISHERMAN: I heard that democracy meant a lot of dillydallying around, but I wish I knew what the dillydallying was for!

LUMBERMAN: You've got me.

OFFICIAL (*to the children*): You sure you don't know where that boy Keita is?

The boys all shake their heads.

OFFICIAL: I can't understand where he could have gotten to.

The adults exit.

MASAO: Quit bawling!

YŪICHI: I don't want to live with any old fisherman! (*Cries.*)

YUTAKA: Stupid! Nobody's decided that yet. You heard them, they're going to draw straws for us.

MASAO: Keita really pulled one off, didn't he?

YUTAKA: He ran away.

MASAO: Yeah!

YŪICHI: Maybe he's in Tokyo!

YUTAKA: Don't be silly. Tokyo's far away.

Kotobukiya enters from outdoors. Sleet glistens on his head and shoulders.

KOTOBUKIYA: You kids still here? (*He shakes off the sleet.*) Looks like the snow's going to start early this year.

YUTAKA: Did you find Keita?

KOTOBUKIYA: No, couldn't find him anywhere. Nobody seems to know where he went. I went as far as the old woman's house on the mountain, but, there wasn't a soul about. Nobody lives there anymore.

YUTAKA: How come?

KOTOBUKIYA: Couldn't say. Maybe they went on a trip.

YUTAKA: Yukino too?

KOTOBUKIYA: Yukino? Oh, you mean the girl? She wasn't there either. Looks like Keita's been spirited away by the gods of the mountain. Yutaka, Masao, Yūichi, you kids do just as the man from the county seat says, now, and get yourselves adopted. It's better than winding up like Keita, a lot better, believe me. You kids are sixth graders. From now on you have to earn your own keep. All right?

The boys sit perfectly still, their faces downcast.

KOTOBUKIYA: I'd like to keep you here, but you're not my kids, and well, you understand. Things will look up, you'll see. (*He starts to go inside.*)

YUTAKA: Lord Kaison! (*Bursts into tears.*)

MASAO: Lord Kaison! (*Burst into tears.*)

YŪICHI: Lord Kaison! (*Burst into tears.*)

Kotobukiya stops in his tracks but says nothing. The outer door opens and a middle-aged man enters. He is dressed in an odd combination of civilian and military clothes. He wears U.S. army boots and gives the overall impression of a black marketeer. A weathered biwa hangs from his neck.

KAISON II: By your leave, my friends, by your leave. You have called my name, and though ashamed to appear before you, I have ventured to answer. Wretched beggar, I am Kaison, Priest of Hitachi. Once I was a soldier who followed the great general Yoshitsune. I was one of those who accompanied him from Kyoto to these northern provinces. (*He strikes a chord on his biwa.*) Though we fought the Americans like a hundred million balls of fire, we met with defeat, unmitigated defeat. (*Biwa.*) With Yoshitsune in the lead, our armies conquered Guam, Saipan, China, and Manchuria, but all was for nought. Our forces were routed and our valorous soldiers killed. (*Biwa.*) The man you see before you betrayed Yoshitsune. I turned my back on helpless women and children and fled to save my own life! I am a traitor and a coward! How could I have done such a thing?

How could I have been so cruel? My days and nights are hell for me, but even the flames of hell cannot cleanse me of my shame. (*Biwa.*) I bathe my aching heart in tears, but it is not enough. In penance I wander from town to town. And so it has been these 750 years. But the longer I wander, the longer I repent, the more grievous my sin becomes. Listen to me, please!

Kaison rakes the plectrum over the strings of his biwa, releasing a torrent of sound. Snow falls from the overcast sky with a brittle whisper. The boys and Kotobukiya listen in motionless silence.
Curtain.

ACT 3

Scene 1

It is a clear autumn afternoon in 1961. The scene is the inner garden of a Shinto shrine set on a spit of land jutting out into the sea.

The garden has an air of antiquity that suggests a long and proud heritage. The shrine consists of two buildings, a main sanctuary and a smaller hall for the performance of ritual dances. An open-air corridor runs between them. A lighthouse, white and large enough to be of major importance, is visible in the background. The hoary strains of ritual music can be heard.

As the music ends, Hidemitsu, a novice, enters. He is followed, although not immediately, by a group of Tourists. They troop behind a Guide, who carries a small flag to identify herself as leader of the group. The tour is an ad hoc assembly of white-collar workers, shopkeepers, and housewives from the Tokyo area. Every one of them carries a camera around his neck, but their lugubrious movements suggest that this visit has been less than inspirational.

Hidemitsu is an ingenuous, serious-looking young man of twenty-four or twenty-five.

GUIDE: This way, everybody! Be careful not to trip over the roots of these trees.

HIDEMITSU: We are now in the inner garden. This shrine dates from the same period as the Chūsōnji Buddhist temple in Hiraizumi. Because of its unique style of Shinto architecture, the government has designated this shrine as one of the most important cultural sites in the region north of Sendai. While historians generally agree that the great Yoshitsune took his own life after the battle of the Koromo River, legend has it that he survived and that in 1190, the fifth year of the Bunji period, he succeeded in fleeing from this spit of land to Ezo, the land we today know as Hokkaido. Historical documents, pottery, and sculpture designated by the government as important cultural treasures are on display in the main sanctuary and in the inner shrine. Those wishing to view these objects are welcome to do so.

GUIDE (*by rote*): How time flies! It has already been five days since our departure from Tokyo, ladies and gentlemen, and now we stand at the northern extremity of Japan's main island. Tomorrow we return to Tokyo, our hearts brimming with memories. Some of you may wish to spend the last hours of our tour of northeastern Japan recalling the story of that tragic hero Yoshitsune; others may prefer to immerse yourselves in the natural beauty of this scenic land. Whichever the case may be, please savor these last few poignant moments of our tour.

It is impossible to tell if the Tourists are listening. They remain expressionless, gathering in knots of conversation, tuning their transistor radios.

GUIDE: Please follow me, then, to the main sanctuary. Try not to become separated from the group.

The Tourists exit in disorder, following Hidemitsu and Guide.

Garbed in robes for the ritual dance, Yukino appears, gliding gracefully along the corridor. As if attracted by an irresistible force, Keita approaches the low railing that borders the runway. He is dressed as a menial and drags a rake behind him. He stares up at Yukino as he trails along at her feet. His gaze is that of a man possessed.

YUKINO (*icily*): Finish cleaning the garden.

Keita is silent.

YUKINO: We're having visitors.

KEITA: Please. . . . (*He touches the hem of Yukino's robe.*)

YUKINO: What?

KEITA: I. . . .

As if swatting a fly, Yukino strikes Keita's hand sharply with her fan, then continues her stately exit. Keita stares idiotically at the stricken limb.

A Young Priestess enters with Itō Yutaka. Yutaka carries a small valise and has the air of an earnest though unexceptional company employee.

PRIESTESS: I think that's him over there.

YUTAKA (*incredulous*): His name is Yasuda?

PRIESTESS: I'm afraid I couldn't say. We just call him Keita. I don't know what his family name is.

YUTAKA: I see.

PRIESTESS: You can ask him yourself if you like.

YUTAKA: Yes, thank you for your trouble.

PRIESTESS (*giggling*): But I'm not sure he knows himself. (*Exits.*)

Yutaka takes two or three steps forward but stops, overwhelmed by an inexplicable sense of foreboding. Keita continues to stare at his hand. Without warning, as if enraged, he bites it viciously; then exits with an anguished cry. Yutaka watches him in utter amazement, then goes after him.

Led by Guide, the Tourists straggle back.

GUIDE: Our next stop will be Lighthouse Point. Please board the bus, everyone. Move along, please. Everyone on the bus. Time is running short. Please move along. Be careful not to trip over the roots of these trees. Please make sure that everyone's here. Look again to see that you haven't lost or forgotten anything.

The Tourists exit, talking quietly among themselves.

Keita stolidly returns. Yutaka follows him.

YUTAKA: I can't believe you'd forget. It's me, Itō. Itō Yutaka. We spent the fifth grade together as evacuees in the Kotobuki Lodge in Yunosawa. You must remember me! Look, when we were in Tokyo, our houses were back-to-back: your house was the tailor's on the main street, and mine was the electrician's behind it. Have I really changed that much? I guess I didn't realize. . . .

KEITA: I remember you.

YUTAKA: Of course you do! How could you forget?

KEITA: You caught me by surprise. What do you want?

YUTAKA: Please, don't misunderstand. I don't want anything in particular. Your memory's stayed with me all these years, that's all. I thought I'd like to see you again if I could.

KEITA: Oh.

YUTAKA: Would anybody mind if I sat down here?

KEITA: Go ahead.

Both men find seats. Keita is absolutely expressionless.
Yutaka's expectations have been disappointed, and he sits in bewilderment.

YUTAKA: Of course it all happened so long ago. This place is quite far from Yunosawa, isn't it?

KEITA: Yes. How did you find me?

YUTAKA: Kotobukiya told me. I got sent up here on company business. I don't often get sent out on company business. I've been waiting for a chance like this. I just went a little out of my way and dropped in at Yunosawa. Kotobukiya's fit as a fiddle. He seemed really glad to see me.

KEITA: Oh.

YUTAKA: I'm working for a small company in Tokyo.

Keita does not respond.

YUTAKA: After you ran away I was adopted by a farmer and his wife, but about a year later a distant relative remembered me and took me back to Tokyo.

KEITA: Oh.

YUTAKA: Have you been here all along?

KEITA: No.

Yutaka does not know how to interpret this answer, and the conversation comes to a standstill. Hidemitsu passes. Yutaka stands and offers him his card.

YUTAKA: I'm a friend of Mr. Yasuda's from primary school. I'd like to talk with him for a while.

HIDEMITSU: Of course, please. Have you come all the way from Tokyo?

YUTAKA: That's right.

HIDEMITSU: Well, this is an honor. Keita, why don't you take your friend into the guest room. This is no place to entertain a visitor.

YUTAKA: Thank you, but I'm quite comfortable here.

HIDEMITSU: But . . . well, at least stay the night. The guest room is available. It's the least we can do after you've come all this way.

YUTAKA: Thank you.

HIDEMITSU: Keita, see that Mr. Itō is properly taken care of.

KEITA: Yes, sir.

HIDEMITSU: I'm afraid our guest quarters are not the most luxurious, but please make yourself at home.

YUTAKA: Thank you very much. I think I will accept your invitation at that.

HIDEMITSU: Wonderful. Well, excuse me. (*Leaving*): Tell me, is Keita originally from Tokyo, then?

YUTAKA: That's right.

Hidemitsu exits, surprised at this revelation.

YUTAKA: You don't mind if I spend the night, do you?

KEITA: No.

YUTAKA: I wasn't really planning to, but. . . . This certainly is a nice, quiet place. This shrine must be pretty old?

KEITA: Yes.

YASUDA (*looking around*): I guess it must be important, too. Afterward I'd like to take a look around. Does it have something to do with the Yoshitsune legend, too?

KEITA: I guess so.

YUTAKA (*laughing*): We have our own memories of Kurō Hōgan Yoshitsune, don't we? It's funny, but I can't get that Kaison story out of my mind. It springs into my head at the strangest times, when I'm working in the office or about to eat a meal. I wonder who makes up these stories?

KEITA: The winters are long in the north country. . . .

YUTAKA: Yes, they are.

KEITA: People talk about a lot of things while they're cooped up inside, sitting around the fire.

YUTAKA: Yes.

KEITA: Strange ideas come to roost. 'Cause people while away the whole winter whispering, whispering.

YUTAKA: Yes, maybe that's it. By the way, whatever happened to that old woman? Do you know?

Keita is silent.

YUTAKA: You remember, the one who held a seance for you.

KEITA: Didn't Kotobukiya tell you?

YUTAKA: What?

KEITA: She's dead.

YUTAKA: I see. Keita, they told us you were spirited away by the gods of the mountain, but you ran away to that old woman, didn't you?

KEITA: Yes. But it's the same thing.

YUTAKA: The same thing? Then it's just as I thought. I always thought you went to that old woman's place. I've spent a lot of time thinking about her myself, as a matter of fact. She's stayed with me all these years, too.

Keita remains silent.

YUTAKA: Tell me, what do you mean it was the same as being spirited away by the gods of the mountain? You say some strange things, don't you?

Keita does not respond.

YUTAKA: Then you think that old woman. . . . (*He does not complete his sentence.*)

Keita slowly raises his head and looks at Yutaka, who shrinks from Keita's gaze.

KEITA: I have to. . . . What time is it now?

YUTAKA: Three o'clock, a little after three.

KEITA: I'll be back. I have to give the baby its milk.

YUTAKA: Baby?

KEITA: Yukino's baby.

YUTAKA: Yukino's. . . . You don't mean that Yukino?

KEITA: Yes.

YUTAKA: Then you've been with Yukino all along. Is that right? Ever since you disappeared?

KEITA: Together.

YUTAKA: Why that's. . . . (*He is beset by contradictory emotions.*) And now you've had this baby. That's wonderful! I can hardly believe. . . . Oh, I'm sorry, that's not what I meant at all. I'm glad everything's turned out so well for you. Well, I'll be!

KEITA: Will you be seeing Yukino?

YUTAKA: She's here, isn't she?

KEITA: Yes.

YUTAKA: Then of course I'd like to see her. I'd like you to introduce me to your wife. She probably doesn't remember me anymore, but. . . .

KEITA (*looking at Yutaka with dark, cavernous eyes*): She's coming this way now.

Keita begins moving stupidly away. Yukino traverses the corridor with light, gliding steps.

YUKINO: Keita, what are you doing? The baby wants its milk. Hurry.

Keita exits submissively.

YUKINO (*smiling alluringly*): Welcome. Please don't pay any attention to that half-wit. I would be glad to tell you anything you'd like to know about the garden myself. Please forgive me for not coming to help you sooner.

YUTAKA: Not at all.

YUKINO (*flirtatiously*): Have you seen our sanctuary?

YUTAKA: No, not yet.

YUKINO: Then please do. This shrine is affiliated with the holy shrine of Mt. Haguro and has a long and rich history. The gods will surely reward those who pray here in faith. Follow me, please.

YUTAKA: I. . . . (*He looks away as if from a dazzling light.*) I didn't come as a tourist. I'm here to see Mr. Yasuda.

YUKINO: See Keita?

YUTAKA: Your husband, yes.

YUKINO: Husband? (*She laughs.*)

YUTAKA: Your husband and I are old friends.

YUKINO: I can't imagine what Keita's told you . . . (*laughter*): but I am unmarried. I have no husband now, nor have I any intention of taking a husband in the future. I prefer to remain alone.

YUTAKA: Perhaps I misunderstood. Mr. Yasuda is not your? . . .

YUKINO: He serves me.

YUTAKA: Serves you?

YUKINO: That's correct.

YUTAKA: Stop trying to confuse me! He told me you had a child. He said it was yours.

YUKINO: How very droll you are! I gave birth to the child, but Keita is not the father. You seem to have jumped to conclusions, haven't you? (*She laughs.*)

YUTAKA: Yukino. . . .

YUKINO: You know my name. Have we met before? I'm afraid I don't remember. (*She laughs. Her laughter is erotic and seductive.*) Tell me your name.

YUTAKA: Itō, Itō Yutaka.

YUKINO: Really? (*She does not remove her eyes from him.*)

YUTAKA: That's all right. It doesn't matter if you don't remember me. I haven't the least desire to be remembered by you. That's not what I came for.

YUKINO: I understand. Please don't get so excited. You are a most unusual gentleman! (*She laughs to herself.*)

YUTAKA (*confused by his own emotions*): Yes. I'm sure you find me strange. Of course. I wanted to know, that's all. I wanted to know what became of my friend Keita after he was spirited away by the gods of the mountain. I have no idea why I wanted to know so badly. But for some reason the same question has haunted me for years. That's why I came.

YUKINO (*watching Yutaka with predatory pleasure*): What do you do in Tokyo? Do you work for a company?

YUTAKA: Yes, that's right. I live in a mixed-up part of the city, one of the livelier sections you might say, but clean enough and orderly. I leave my lodgings at 7:45 and arrive at my company fifty-five minutes later. I'm head of the records department, so I spend my whole day surrounded by adding machines, files, invoices, and receipts. I get enough exercise, though, during my break: twelve minutes.

YUKINO (*laughing*): And then?

YUTAKA: I repeat the process in reverse. I spend another fifty-five minutes on the train to get home. It takes eight minutes to walk from the station. You turn left at the corner before the candy store, and it's the sixth or seventh house down.

Yukino is all but doubled up with amusement.

YUTAKA: I don't always talk like this. (*He knits his brow.*)

YUKINO: You said your name was Yutaka. Well, come with me to the sanctuary, Yutaka. (*She draws near him.*) I'm sure you'd like to see our relics. We have some most interesting specimens.

YUTAKA (*backing away*): Yes, I remember. I remember!

YUKINO: Then you'll want to see them again. Rest assured: your prayers will be answered. We don't ordinarily display our relics to the public, but I think we can make an exception in your case.

Yutaka hesitates.

YUKINO: Are you afraid?

YUTAKA: No . . . I've seen your "relics" before. Once is enough.

YUKINO: We've added a second mummy, you know.

YUTAKA: A second?

YUKINO: The old woman's mummy. Now there's a male mummy and a female mummy.

YUTAKA (*gasping for breath*): Why show them to me?

YUKINO: You didn't come to see Keita. You came to see me. Can you

deny it? (*She smiles.*) You came to see me, didn't you?
Yutaka is dumbstruck.
YUKINO: Come to the sanctuary later. I'll be waiting.
YUTAKA: Whe . . . when?
YUKINO: When I've finished the ritual dance. (*She smiles at him and exits along the runway.*)
Yutaka watches her with hypnotic fascination.
Hidemitsu has been standing hidden in the shadows. He now wails an anguished entreaty, unable to restrain himself a moment longer.
HIDEMITSU: Hail! Hail, Bodhisattva Kongō Zaō! I beseech you: show me a place free from suffering! I wish to flee there! This depraved world is too much for me. It is a world of filth, a living hell of demons and vagrant souls, outrage piled upon outrage! I beg you! Savior! Lead me unto salvation! (*He falls prostrate on the ground.*)
YUTAKA: Are you all right? Why, you're. . . .
HIDEMITSU: I'm a novice here. My name's Hidemitsu.
YUTAKA: But what happened to you all of a sudden?
HIDEMITSU: You hardly need me to tell you. That Yukino is no woman but a fiend from hell! And I'm no man but a soul sunk to the depths of damnation!
YUTAKA: Then you're the father of Yukino's child?
HIDEMITSU: No, it wasn't me. (*Rearranging his robes*): I'm sorry you had to see me this way. Please forget this ever happened. I'm terribly ashamed.
YUTAKA: I can hardly believe what I'm seeing! What's come over you people around here?
HIDEMITSU: I've known for a long time what kind of woman Yukino is, but I haven't had the strength to leave her. I'm desperate. Keita is too.
YUTAKA: And you felt that justified eavesdropping on our conversation, is that it?
Hidemitsu covers his face and sobs. Yutaka looks at him with a combination of anger and contempt.
Music for the Kagura ritual dance filters from the main sanctuary. Transmitted from the deepest recesses of the shrine, the deliberate strains of the music disturb the soul.
HIDEMITSU: Ah! Yukino is dancing. Yukino! (*He wails.*)
YUTAKA (*murmuring*): She's right. I came to see her. I came because

deep down I, too, want to be spirited away by the gods of the mountain.

HIDEMITSU: Stop! Stop while you still can! (*He writhes in anguish.*)

YUTAKA: You can sob and wail, you can writhe and call on all the bodhisattvas you like, but I'm going to meet Yukino. As soon as the dance ends. Now get out of here and back to your prayers.

HIDEMITSU: So be it. (*He continues to shiver.*) I know very well I can't stop you. I'm a man, too, and I understand. Go ahead! See Yukino dance! She is dancing before the mummies. She is the most gorgeous woman on the face of this earth. And yet, merciful Buddha, she is a five-headed serpent of lust and temptation!

YUTAKA: Yes. You're probably right. But I don't want to hear any more.

HIDEMITSU: Before long you'll be just like Keita and me. Who do you think made the old woman's mummy?

YUTAKA: What?

HIDEMITSU: You have a pretty good idea already, don't you?

YUTAKA (*paling*): You don't mean . . . Keita?

HIDEMITSU: Keita.

Yutaka is speechless.

HIDEMITSU: Next I'll make Keita's mummy. I may be contemptible, I may be corrupt, but lord help me, not that!

Yutaka looks at him in utter astonishment.

Two young men enter the garden. Both are dressed head to foot in black rain gear. They carry an unlit lantern.

MAN 1 (*whispering*): Hidemitsu! Hurry up!

HIDEMITSU: Right away.

MAN 2 (*similarly*): We're going to miss the tide!

HIDEMITSU: All right.

MAN 1: The tide's perfect. If we miss it tonight, you'll change your mind again for sure.

MAN 2: This is the last time we're going to wait around for you.

HIDEMITSU: I said all right! Go to my room. Everything's ready.

MAN 2: You're sure this time?

MAN 1: You'd better be or we'll go without you. We'll give you thirty minutes.

MAN 2: If you don't show up, fine. We'll go alone.

HIDEMITSU: Don't worry. I'll be there.

The two Men exit.

HIDEMITSU: Tonight I set out from Lighthouse Point and sail for Russia.

YUTAKA: What?

HIDEMITSU: You're the only one besides us who knows.

YUTAKA: To Russia?

HIDEMITSU: Yes. Of course we'll have to smuggle ourselves into the country, but we won't be the first Japanese to make for foreign shores from this spit of land.

YUTAKA: You'll never make it! What'll you do if you get caught? Why do you have to go? Because of Yukino?

HIDEMITSU: Yes. As long as I'm in Japan, no matter what I do, someday I'll have to see her. My soul's been spirited away by the gods of the mountain. This is the only way I can break their spell. Look, the men who were just here are taking me with them. They're fleeing because they couldn't break the spell any other way either.

YUTAKA: But the seas are so rough in the straits.

HIDEMITSU: And the wind is strong and gusty. Of ten boats, seven or eight capsize before reaching land. There are already ice floes in the offing, too, so . . . but we've got a better chance now than at any other time of year.

YUTAKA: Are you sure you'll be all right?

HIDEMITSU: It was just about this time of year that His Lordship Yoshitsune crossed the straits. (*He chants and dances.*)

> Waves toward battlefield roll and
> Helmets in the tide with moonlight swords,
> Torrents of cloud, even the sky seas roar,
> Urging me on, urging me on.

> For like a piece of mirror broken,
> A blossom severed from its branch,
> Perchance I go now, returning never,
> But better death than honor soiled.

Farewell.

YUTAKA: Be careful.

HIDEMITSU: Thanks.

Keita appears on the runway. He walks slowly and carries a baby in his arms. He stares at Yutaka and Hidemitsu, his eyes red with fury.

KEITA: Yutaka . . . Yutaka . . . you had better stay away from her! You had better stay away!

YUTAKA: I won't go near her. I'm not going anywhere near her! Never!

KEITA: Hidemitsu?

HIDEMITSU: Never again! I'm not going ever again!

KEITA: Are there any other male visitors?

HIDEMITSU: No. Just us.

KEITA: All right, then. Everyone's safe.

HIDEMITSU: Farewell. (*He bows silently and exits.*)

Keita descends into the garden. He watches Yutaka as he rocks the baby to sleep. He murmurs a lullaby.

KEITA:

A cherry is still a cherry though but one blooms.
A cherry is still a cherry though but two bloom.
A cherry is still a cherry though but three bloom.

YUTAKA (*exploding*): Keita!

Keita looks at him.

YUTAKA: I'm leaving. I've seen you. . . . I've done what I came for. I'm going back to Tokyo.

KEITA: I thought you were going to spend the night?

YUTAKA: That's right, but now that I think about it, I really don't have the time. There's a lot of work waiting for me back at the office.

KEITA: Will you come again?

YUTAKA: It's hard to tell. It doesn't seem likely. A man can't be taking many trips on my salary. And besides, you're so far from Tokyo here,
. . .

KEITA: Oh.

YUTAKA: Well, take care of yourself. Give my regards to Yukino.

KEITA: Yutaka!

YUTAKA: Yes?

KEITA: Yutaka, I'm . . . really, I'm . . .

YUTAKA: Really you're what?

KEITA (*tears streaking his face*): I'm glad you came. It was a nice surprise.

YUTAKA: Yes. Well. . . .

KEITA: I'm glad to see you, but now I'll be lonely.

YUTAKA: That's enough now. I feel the same way.

KEITA: Yutaka, they . . . they put me in prison!

YUTAKA: Prison?

KEITA: I was eighteen. I didn't do anything bad. Before the old woman died she told me. She said not to bury her. She said not to burn her or bury her. She said I should do certain other things instead. Then she died. You've seen the other one.

YUTAKA: No! I haven't seen anything!

KEITA: I did just like the old woman said. But then they put me on trial. And they put me in prison! (*He sobs.*)

YUTAKA: How could you have? . . . (*His suppressed anger erupting*): I never want to see you as long as I live! You . . . how could you have done such a thing? You're grotesque! You make me want to puke! I . . . I'm surprised you aren't completely mad! I'm amazed you haven't killed yourself!

KEITA: It's because I'm mad that I stay alive. I'm near Yukino and at her mercy. Totally. I hate that woman with all my heart and soul. Fires consume me! I sleep on a bed of nails!

YUTAKA: What do you expect from me? Sympathy? You're nothing but a wild animal! You chose the flames! You chose the bed of nails! Pain and suffering are all you deserve!

KEITA: Yes! Yes! (*He is wailing.*)

YUTAKA: I'm beginning to understand. Why the old woman made you do such a thing, her motive. (*Anger turning to terror*): It was so she could control you, control you from the grave! She made you Yukino's slave. You made a mummy of the old woman's body, but she made a mummy of your soul! She robbed you of your soul and grafted it to Yukino's will!

KEITA: Yes! Yes!

YUTAKA: All the more reason for you to lie down and die! You're nothing but a worm and deserve to be crushed like one!

KEITA: I want to die! I'd be better off dead!

YUTAKA: Yes, you would be. But worms don't have the guts for suicide. You make me sick to my stomach! Whatever possessed me to come and see you? What am I doing here? From now on, every time I think of you I'll want to puke!

KEITA: I knew you'd come, someday. I knew you'd come.

YUTAKA: How could you know that? (*More attentively*): Why?

KEITA: You and I, we're all alone in this world. Our roots were cut; we lost everything. We're lost souls, evacuated, forgotten, abandoned. If we were ordinary lost children, our folks would call and weep for us. But we've got no folks. The world forgot us.

Yutaka is silent.

KEITA: If things were different, I'd have gone to visit you. I wanted to see you, too, but I was too ashamed. . . .

YUTAKA: I'm sorry, Keita. I understand. I don't think you're bad.

KEITA: You don't?

YUTAKA: No. I'm sorry I said all those things.

KEITA: I. . . . (*He weeps.*)

YUTAKA: I wonder what happened to the others? Masao was adopted by a lumberman, and Yūichi wound up with a fisherman on the Shimokita Peninsula.

KEITA: But you're happy. That's important.

YUTAKA: Do I look happy? I feel as if I were seventy years old. I'm all tired out.

All at once, Keita emits a low cry and stands up with a look of intense anxiety.

KEITA: Hurry!

YUTAKA: What's wrong?

KEITA: Get out of here! (*Terrified*): Yutaka, promise me! Promise me you won't see Yukino! Promise me, please!

Yukino enters, gliding along the runway. She stares at Yutaka and Keita with hatred and contempt. Yutaka gazes back at her with a voiceless cry.

KEITA: Yukino. . . . (*Imploringly*): Yukino!

YUKINO: Keita! Give me the baby. You're not to touch it ever again!

KEITA: Yukino!

YUKINO: Now!

Keita timidly relinquishes the child.

YUKINO: I know you've been blocking Yutaka's path to me. I know, and I'll see that you rot for it!

KEITA: Mercy! Have mercy! It wasn't me. I didn't do it!

YUKINO: You're a cur, Keita. You're not even fit to be a slave. Mr. Itō, you'd best be on your way. My tastes don't run to cowards. See that you never come back here again!

YUTAKA: My. . . . (*He chokes on the words.*) My tastes have their limits, too. Hidemitsu was right, you're a five-headed serpent of lust and temptation. I'm not going to be your slave. I don't want to be your slave!

YUKINO (*laughing*): Get out of my sight! Go back to Tokyo and think of me. Think about why you came to see me. Then you can rail against me—if you're able! (*Rocking the baby*):

> A cherry is still a cherry though but one blooms.
> A cherry is still a cherry though but two bloom.

Mesmerized, Yutaka goes to the runway and reaches to touch Yukino's feet. Yukino treads on his hand, grinding it into the polished woodwork first with one foot and then with the other.

YUKINO:

> A cherry is still a cherry though but three bloom.
> A cherry is still a cherry though but four bloom.

Yutaka stares up at Yukino. He has lost all will to resist.

YUKINO:

> A cherry is still a cherry though but five bloom.
> A cherry is still a cherry though but six bloom.

Keita throws himself on the ground.

KEITA: Kaison! Kaison! Kaison!

Keita writhes on the ground. He tears at his breast as he continues to call on Kaison, Priest of Hitachi. Yutaka stares at Keita in shocked amazement.

Yukino watches the two men with amusement. Her sensuous, carefree laughter continues.

Blackout.

Scene 3

The same garden a short time later. It is dusk. Keita is alone on the

stage. He is lying on the ground and looks as if he had died in
excruciating pain.
The beam from the lighthouse traverses the scene.
Kaison's voice is heard in the distance, accompanied by a biwa. The
voice draws nearer: ". . . the youngest son of Yoshitomo, Chief of the
Imperial Stables of the Left, Kurō Yoshitsune. . . ."
Keita jumps to his feet.
An old man enters. He is walking very slowly. He wears a worn
business suit. He is bare-headed and has hair streaked with grey. He
gives the impression of a man who has been forcibly retired from his
job. Both his hands are raised to his chest, as if embracing a biwa.
KAISON III: I am what has become of Kaison, Priest of Hitachi, who
traveled here from distant Kyoto. (*He strikes a chord on the biwa.*) I
fought for a livelihood in the dusty city, but my efforts ended in utter
defeat. Scarred and twisted, I was left without succor on the field of
battle, and call though I might for aid from my allies, they flowed
from me like the tide. (*Biwa.*) At each passing moment I am remind-
ed anew that these are the wages earned by betraying His Lordship
Yoshitsune. And so I tread this northern highway in search of those
who, in compassion, will hear me. (*Biwa.*)
Keita crawls to Kaison.
KAISON III: Ah, what have we here?
KEITA: Lord Kaison, please, take me as your disciple. I have committed
terrible crimes. Let me follow you. I am more lowly than a worm!
(*He weeps.*)
KAISON III: I pity you, but Kaison admits no disciples, and so it has
always been.
KEITA: Then what shall I do? Tell me how I can be saved! Rotting as I
live, my life is a living death! Have mercy! Lord Kaison, I have no
one else but you!
KAISON III (*looking at Keita with new understanding*): Perhaps . . .
perhaps you're a Kaison, too. So it would seem. So it would seem.
Come! Come and stand!
KEITA (*writhing on the ground*): I . . . I can't, I can't stand up. The
earth sucks me down. It's pulling me down. Help me! Help me!
KAISON III: I know. I was just like you. I look at you and see myself. I
can hardly bear the sight. What are you afraid of? There isn't a
villain or devil in this world as ridden with sin as you. Stand! (*He

strikes his biwa with force, releasing an explosion of sound.)
Keita climbs unsteadily to his feet.
KAISON III: You see! It's just as I thought. There is a biwa in your
breast! (*He bows reverently.*) Strike your biwa. Go ahead. See how it
sounds.
KEITA: Where? Where?
KAISON III: You novices can't do anything for yourselves, can you?
See? This is how you play it. Now try for yourself. Strike a chord!
KEITA (*raising both hands to his breast and strumming, his biwa
reverberates*): Ah! It made a sound! It made a sound! (*He strikes it
repeatedly.*)
KAISON III: Good, good, a fine sound, too! A really fine sound!
KEITA: Ah! (*Sadly*): I had no idea I was Kaison. But who will hear a man
like me? Where can I go?
KAISON III: There are lots of people who await you. But never forget
that you have set out to atone for every sin, to wipe out every trace
of guilt. Lord Kaison, peace be with you!
KEITA: Yes, and peace be with you.
*The men bow reverentially, turn back to back, and then, striking their
biwas, begin to walk away.*
KAISON III and KAISON IV (*in unison*): People of the world! Compared
to Kaison, your hearts are as pure as new-fallen snow. I take upon
myself all the sins of this world and stand as a lesson to those who
would err. Thus have I wandered these 750 years, bathing my guilty
flesh in tears of repentance, trying to atone for my sins. (*Biwa.*) I
have come in the terror of my guilt. Hear me! Hear me!
*The two Kaisons exit. The sound of their biwas is still audible as they
retreat into the distance.*
The beam from the lighthouse traverses the scene.
Curtain.

MY BEATLES

Commentary

Beatles fans were not so much hysterical as spellbound. The Beatles' music was a form of sympathetic magic, and the Beatles were local divinities who could change the mood and look of their times by a song, a style, a word. "We're more popular than Jesus," Lennon wisecracked; but at first the Beatles didn't understand either their healing power or their shamanistic role. "It seemed that we were just surrounded by cripples and blind people all the time," Lennon recalled. "And when we would go through the corridors, they would be touching us."

John Lahr (1981)[1]

Find Hakamadare! had revealed the wizened puppeteer who animated the automaton of historical materialism and had shown how profound theological and eschatological questions would have to be confronted before an alternative to the Old Left political and cultural movement could be found. *Kaison the Priest of Hitachi* showed those questions would necessarily involve the Japanese gods, who remained alive and influential in the Japanese imagination. Satoh Makoto's *My Beatles* continued this process. The play reveals how the twenty-three-year-old playwright arrived at the unexpected and unwelcome conclusion that hoary cultural archetypes in modern dress continue to shape Japanese political attitudes and reflexes.

The Komatsugawa Incident

My Beatles deals with the 1958 murder of a teenage girl on the roof of Komatsugawa High School in Tokyo. The crime was committed by Li Jin-wu (Japanese: Ri Chin'u), a Japanese-born Korean enrolled in the night division of the school. The affair left a deep and lasting impression on Satoh and his generation. "For us, the Komatsugawa Incident is a living wound that will never heal."[2]

Li Jin-wu was born on February 28, 1940, the second of seven children. His family lived in a predominantly Korean slum in Kami-Shinozaki-chō, Edogawa-ku, Tokyo. They were desperately poor. Li's father was a day laborer whose income was inadequate to sustain his large family; and his mother, twenty years her husband's junior, had a severe hearing and speech impediment that rendered her a functional deafmute.[3]

Despite his difficult home life, Li was a youth of intellectual promise. He had been a member of his student government in elementary school and had served on his junior high school student council every year of his enrollment, including several terms as council president. Li was unable to attend regular high school because he had to help support his family, but he attended the night division of Komatsugawa High School, where he went by the Japanese name Kaneko Shizuo. Neither his teachers nor his fellow students were aware that he was Korean. Li's night school teachers thought him a normal, relaxed, mature youth with an interest in literature and expressed disbelief when they learned of his arrest.

Li began to experience anti-Korean prejudice when he sought employment with large corporations like Hitachi and Seiko. He was told that because of his Korean nationality he need not apply. He later testified that he found this rejection deeply humiliating. He was eventually hired as a factory worker by several smaller concerns, but he quit each job after only a few months.

Li Jin-wu was arrested on September 1, 1958, and accused of the murder of Ōta Yoshie, a sixteen-year-old girl who attended Komatsugawa High School during the day. According to the indictment, at approximately 6:00 p.m. on August 17, 1958, Li went to Komatsugawa High School and proceeded to the roof, where he found Ōta reading a book. Li threatened Ōta with a knife and forced her to accompany him to the vicinity of the clock tower on the roof. When Ōta screamed for help, Li choked her until she was unconscious, raped her, then strangled her to death.[4] After his arrest, Li also admitted having killed Tanaka Setsuko, twenty-three, the previous April 20. He was tried and convicted of both murders and sentenced to death by hanging. The Tokyo District Appeals Court denied his petition for leniency on December 28, 1959, and he was executed at Miyagi Prison on November 16, 1962. He was twenty-two years old.

What gripped Satoh about the Komatsugawa Incident was the way Li's crime seemed to distill in his own generation the legacy of Japanese imperialism and Japanese exploitation of the Korean people. Satoh perceived Li's crime as a desperate protest against decades of injustice. Japan had annexed Korea in 1910. Until Korean independence was restored in 1945, the Japanese expropriated vast areas of Korean land, pressed hundreds of thousands of Korean laborers into service in Japanese industry, and conscripted Korean men into service in the Imperial Armed Forces. In 1944, there were 1,936,843 Koreans living in Japan.[5] Approximately 1.5 million were repatriated to Korea after the war. Today the number of ethnic Koreans in Japan is usually put at between 600,000 and 700,000.[6]

Exploitation, squalid living conditions, systematic discrimination at both the popular and governmental levels, and even murder have characterized the Japanese treatment of Koreans both before and since the war.[7] Conscientious Japanese view the record of Japanese-Korean relations as a deplorable history of discrimination.[8] Tsuno Kaitarō belongs to this group, and his view of Li's offense is representative.

The first "modern men" annihilated the American Indians, pillaged East India, and hunted down the Africans. In this way, it is said, they forwarded the accumulation of primitive capital. Japan's modernization progressed according to the same formula: by robbing the Koreans of their labor and sacrificing them upon the altar of progress. [Li Jin-wu's] crime would fit perfectly into the worlds of Aimé Césaire, Sartre, Genet, Leroi Jones, and Peter Weiss. . . . [Li's crime] was the crime of a Korean—no, actually the crime of one who had been deprived of his national identity at birth. His parents, like hundreds of thousands of other Koreans, had been brought to Japan during the thirty-odd years before World War II. They had been stripped of their language and given new Japanized names. This youth, who first began to learn Korean while in prison and who shouted during his trial, "A language is its country's breath!" had committed the crime of a Korean born in Japan, a Korean who knew no language but Japanese, a Korean who had been taught to despise his own national origins. To borrow the vocabulary of Frantz Fanon's analysis of the French-acculturized blacks of Martinique, this was the crime of a Korean *évolué*.[9]

Satoh has said that he identified with Li and his crime; he saw it as a justified protest and Li as a symbol of resistance against Japanese imperialism.[10] The thing that riveted Satoh to the Komatsugawa Incident, however, was the fact that he ultimately found that it would not allow this identification. As Tsuno continues,

> We see [Li's] crime, but we are denied participation. We belong to those who placed the rope around his neck; we find within ourselves the nation Japan that called his act a crime and killed him for it. Along with the murdered girl, we had to be taught that we are not innocents who arrived on the scene at the end of our fathers' and grandfathers' careers as proud invaders of the Korean Peninsula, that we were born very much in the midst of those careers and that we remain in their midst today.[11]

Tragedy and Escape

My Beatles is not a play about the Komatsugawa Incident, but a play about the irreconcilable attempts of two young people to deal with it and the history of exploitation it represents.

The action takes place in the small apartment of a young couple. It is late at night, and they are rehearsing a play. Judging from their names, the husband is Korean and his wife Japanese. The play they are rehearsing has a very simple plot: a Japanese girl is raped and murdered by a Korean, who in turn is killed in revenge by the Japanese masses. It is, in short, a reenactment of the Komatsugawa Incident. The question is, why are they rehearsing such a play? What purpose does it serve? The play has been conceived by the young husband, Chong, but it becomes increasingly clear as the action progresses that Chong is actually a Japanese and that his name, like that of all the characters in *My Beatles*, is the name of his *persona* in the play-within-a-play. Like

Satoh himself, Chong is a Japanese youth racked by feelings of guilt over the Japanese treatment of Koreans. The play is a literal-minded attempt to identify with the oppressed and thereby achieve atonement.

Chong's play is a tragedy: through identification with the tragic hero, catharsis is to be achieved. Chong's evil self is to be consumed by the tragic fire, and he is to be resurrected out of the ashes pure and absolved of guilt.

> You'll bury me in a hole and cover me over with sand so that no trace remains. You'll bury the wretched Korean who's raped Katsura and strangled her to death. Then I'll return to life! Glorious revenge, my blood's atonement! I'll die and thus gain new life.

For Chong, this drama of catharsis has more than personal significance, however. It is part of a larger vision. That vision is revealed in the verses of the song he sings at various points in the play:

> All men will be equal
> On an even plane.
>
> Mountains will be leveled,
> Seas their waters drained.
>
> All the world will be afire,
> Turned to flame and heat.

It is an apocalyptic vision of tragic catharsis on a global scale. Chong's individual tragic drama is a mere microcosm, adumbrating the world-enveloping holocaust that will usher in the millennium.[12]

Chong is having considerable difficulty acting out this play, however. Somehow the mechanism of tragedy is not functioning as it should. The problem stems from the fact that Katsura, his leading lady, has a rather different conception of the play and what it is intended to achieve. Katsura does not share Chong's tragic vision. For her, the play is a means to act out her fantasy that the Beatles are on their way to fetch her and spirit her away across the sea.

We can reconstruct Katsura's identity from the various comments made by and about her throughout the play. She is a Korean born and raised in Japan. Her father had been brought from Korea before the war as a conscript laborer to work in Japan's coal mines. Crippled in a mining accident, however, he had lost his job, which forced Katsura's mother into prostitution and led her to eventually abandoned her family. Despite these hardships, Katsura's brother had done very well in school and had been accepted by a university. Unable to bear the schizophrenic existence of a Korean eternally trying "to pass" as a Japanese, though, he had taken his own life.

With his wife gone and his son dead, Katsura's father returned to Korea to live out his remaining days in his homeland. Left alone and frustrated, Katsura immersed herself in the drug culture. She met Chong in a coffee shop called Chester frequented by drug users. Chong needed someone to help him act out his tragic vision, and judging from her background, Katsura seemed ideal.

Contrary to Chong's expectations, however, Katsura did not identify with him and his tragic scheme. Instead, she dreams of traveling by ship in the company of the Beatles home to Korea, a utopia she idealizes as "The Emerald Peninsula."

It is the incongruence of Chong and Katsura's relationship to the historical incident they are portraying that constitutes the basic conflict of My Beatles. Chong seeks to deal with the Komatsugawa Incident by identifying with Li Jin-wu, dying in his guise, and thus achieving absolution from his intense feelings of guilt. Katsura, who like Li is a Japanese-born Korean, only seeks to escape from the terror of her existence.

Between Chong and Katsura stands a third character, The Japanese. He plays the part of the Japanese masses, avenging the death of Katsura by killing Chong. Like Katsura, however, there is a gap between his real motives for participating in Chong's play and those Chong ascribes to him.

The Japanese' real motive for participating in Chong's play is his interest in Katsura. He has apparently been working for some time to develop a relationship with her behind Chong's back, and he steals kisses whenever the opportunity arises. As the polarization of the young couple progresses, The Japanese takes advantage of the situation to consummate his desire for Katsura.

Then, in a rapid series of events, Chong is killed. It is not immediately apparent who killed Chong, but the reason for his death is clear. Far from atoning for the Japanese exploitation of Korea and the Korean people, Chong's actions had extended and renewed that exploitation. In order to assuage his guilty conscience, to purge his sense of complicity, Chong had sought to appropriate the unique death of a Korean who had committed murder in a last desperate protest against submersion in Japanese culture. By presuming that he as a Japanese could comprehend that crime and identify with it, acting it out as his own, Chong had shown that he had missed the point of the youth's act entirely. Rather than respect its inimitability, Chong had desecrated the young Korean's gory demise, reconfirming his identity as a Japanese, mindlessly exploiting the Korean people. At the end of the play, The Japanese covers Chong's corpse with a Japanese flag, driving home the point.

But Chong had gone beyond this symbolic insult. He had also applied his conception of Japanese-Korean relations to Katsura, herself a Japanese-born Korean struggling with severe self-alienation. Casting her in a part that robbed her of her autonomy, Chong had raped her in a very elemental way. He had failed to comprehend her situation and had forced her to conform to his Japanese preconceptions. It is for this crime of ethnocentrism compounded by gross personal insensitivity that Chong dies. Satoh's rejection of the healing power of tragedy could hardly be more explicit. His rejection of Katsura's fantasy of escape as a means to deal with the Komatsugawa Incident and the problem of Japanese-Korean relations is equally unequivocal.

The Beatles

The most important thing to note about the Quartet who appear claiming that they are the Beatles is that from the standpoint of the story they are completely superfluous. Nothing substantial would change without them. The Quartet do not create the tensions that obtain in the situation but only exacerbate them and expedite their ultimate resolution.

The Quartet resemble characters who appear in many of Satoh's plays.[13] They are amoral beings, movers, facilitators who make the inevitable happen. They participate in Katsura's fantasy and bring her conflict with Chong out in the open. This does not mean that they are sympathetic with Katsura. In fact, they ultimately betray her and bring the walls of her fantasy crashing down around her.

Immediately upon their arrival, Katsura identifies the Quartet as the Beatles and agrees to perform the play for them over Chong's objections. With their participation, the play gradually swerves out of control. Chong is forced to compete with the Quartet for Katsura's loyalty, and slowly the play falls completely into the hands of the four interlopers, who abet Katsura in acting out her fantasy. As they do so, the incompatibility of that fantasy and Chong's tragic expectations becomes increasingly obvious, until The Japanese steps in and the play veers toward its ultimate denouement.

My Beatles plays deftly on the disparity between the actual, historical Beatles; the personal Beatles nurtured in the imagination of Katsura; and the communal fantasy of the Beatles shared by fans at large.

The title of the play derives from this disparity. The Quartet claim that they are the Beatles. This alarms Chong and The Japanese, who misunderstand the Quartet to be claiming that they are the actual, historical Beatles. Katsura also misunderstands but in a different, idiosyncratic way: she believes naively that they are *her* Beatles, the Fab Four who will spirit her away to the Emerald Peninsula.

The Quartet's claim that they are the Beatles is true only in the third sense, however. As a communal fantasy, the Beatles had no objective reality but existed solely in the minds of the millions of fans who invested portions of their lives in them. Since the Beatles as a communal fantasy owed their existence solely to those who identified with them, those who identified with them *were* the Beatles. That is why Lennon is correct when he says in the play, "There's no reason we can't be the Beatles and movers at the same time. The fact of the matter is we're both."

Within the space of the play, the Quartet exist simultaneously and unconditionally as the historical, personal, and communal Beatles. The language of the play is absolutely neutral, giving no more weight or credence to one dimension than another. This gives the dialogue a madrigal-like quality. To a large extent, the interaction that takes place between Chong, Katsura, and The Japanese is determined by their relationship to the historical, personal, and communal dimensions of the Beatles.

The net result of the Quartet's appearance is to exacerbate the tensions inherent in the *ménage à trois*. They are not responsible for creating those tensions, and without them nothing substantial would change. They merely act as a catalyst, accelerating the action and expediting the climax.

Gods, Birds, and Red High Heels

The Quartet may be superfluous from the standpoint of the story, but they are essential to the dialectic that governs the action of *My Beatles*.

In the introductory sequence, the words "bird" and "God" appear frequently. The words are printed in English or are accompanied by phonetic transcriptions (*furigana*) of the English terms, so there can be no mistake about Satoh's meaning. There is a distinct theological dimension to this play.

As the play begins, the Quartet are performing some sort of ritual and intoning a strange incantation. They are banishing God and replacing Him with a bird. The image of the bird is repeated in several of Satoh's plays.[14] All that is apparent here, however, is that "bird" is a synecdoche for a metaphysical regimen other than God's. The ritual the Quartet are performing, which is described as a funeral, has the dual function of bidding farewell to God and invoking a bird or birds in His stead.

Judging from the introductory sequence, there is something distinctly supernatural about the Quartet. They live above Chong and Katsura, not just literally, but also in a more ethereal sense. They seem to be deeply concerned about what is going on below them, particularly about Katsura, despite the fact that they have never met. And when, to communicate that concern, they drop a red high-heeled shoe through the ceiling, it becomes clear that they have the superhuman power to dematerialize objects and pass them through walls.

The unique behavior of the Quartet can best be explained by noting their similarity to the *marebito* (or *marōdo*), the "unexpected visitors" who stand at the intersection of Japanese religion and the performing arts. According to Origuchi Shinobu, all the Japanese performing arts first developed as religious rituals performed within the context of the household. The *sine qua non* of these rituals was the appearance of a god, who would arrive from afar accompanied by a number of attendant divinities. This god was known as the *marebito* or "unexpected visitor."[15] According to Origuchi the *marebito* and his attendants were actually members of the community who had lived apart from it for a period so they could "come from afar" at the appointed time. The people of the community would "not know" the *marebito* because they would return in the guise of gods from across the sea.[16]

The *marebito* would perform a dance and deliver a message in poetry or song to the household. Their performance had two complementary aspects: an incantatory aspect (*henbai*) intended to suppress unwanted spirits or gods, and an invocative aspect (*chinkon*) intended to attract and invest desirable spirits in the household. These songs and dances eventually became secularized and evolved into the Japanese performing arts.[17]

It is worth noting that the master of the household also danced on these occasions, and that, in Origuchi's opinion, the performance by the master of the house or by his representative (*maibito* or *maihime*) probably preceded that of the unexpected guest.[18]

The Quartet bears a striking resemblance to the *marebito*. Like the *marebito*, the Quartet belong to the same community but live separately from the household they visit. Chong and Katsura are aware of them as neighbors, but they do not recognize them when they arrive because they appear in the guise of the Beatles, godlike figures from across the sea. The Quartet have been performing a ritual with two complementary aspects, an incantatory aspect intended to suppress God and an invocative aspect intended to call forth "birds." Once inside Chong and Katsura's apartment, they first ask their hosts to perform for them, and then they begin to perform themselves. The modern interpretation of the *marebito*'s appearance is a moralistic one,[19] and this is the net effect of the Quartet's intervention, to force events to their proper conclusion.

Viewing the Quartet in this way helps to explain their invasion of Chong and Katsura's household and the ultimate result of that invasion: Chong's death and Katsura's rape.

A special relationship exists between Katsura and the Quartet. The sign of this special relationship is the red high heel Starr drops through the ceiling into Chong and Katsura's apartment. As we learn subsequently, the red high heel has special significance for Katsura because it was the keepsake left her by her mother when she abandoned her family. But what is the meaning of this legacy?

The red high-heel represents Katsura's fantasy of escape. The symbol derives from a popular children's song written by Noguchi Ujō in the early 1920s entitled *Akai kutsu* (Red Shoes). The song is sung by a young girl and describes her fantasy of being taken abroad by a foreigner. The girl in the song is wearing red shoes. She takes a ship from Yokohama and goes abroad with a foreigner. By this time, the song speculates, she must have been completely transformed in the foreigner's country and even have blue eyes!

In short, the red high heel represents the fantasy of escape that is the legacy of Katsura's mother. The Beatles are the foreigners who Katsura dreams will take her away. And the Quartet are the neighbors who appear in the guise of the Beatles just as neighbors would appear as gods from across the sea in the Japanese *marebito* tradition.

Who Killed Chong?

If the Quartet resemble *marebito*, Katsura resembles a *miko*, the shamanic medium who summons gods like them. Katsura longs for the Beatles. She dreams of having sexual intercourse with them one by one on board the ship that will take her to the Emerald Peninsula. In effect, she uses her sexuality to attract the Beatles exactly as female shamans have allured their tutelary deities throughout Japanese history: with sex. One need only recall Yukino in *Kaison the Priest of Hitachi*. The Quartet enter Chong and Katsura's apartment because in a very real sense they have been summoned.

Just as the sexually aroused female spirit is capable of summoning gods, enraged it is also capable of murder. The homicidal capacity of the aroused female spirit is enshrined in Japanese literature as early as *The Tale of Genji*. Umehara Takeshi enumerates "two murders, one attempted murder, and one incitement to rape" committed by Lady Rokujō's enraged spirit in Murasaki's novel.[20]

Katsura is thus the prime suspect in Chong's murder. When the lights come up revealing Chong's lifeless form, "Katsura is beside

Chong. The Quartet and Japanese stand around them." Her motive is to redress the insult Chong's Procrustean drama inflicted on her, and her interaction with the Quartet is in essence the steady arousal of her spirit to the point where it is prepared to answer the insult she has suffered.

Drama as Discovery

Satoh did not read Origuchi Shinobu or take particular interest in Japanese religious traditions until he wrote *Nezumi Kozō: The Rat* in 1969, two years after *My Beatles*. That is, he did not begin with a detailed knowledge of Japanese mythology and proceed to write *My Beatles*. On the contrary: he set out to write a play about the Komatsugawa Incident and the legacy of Japanese imperialism and in the process arrived at forms that were congruent with the most basic archetypes of Japanese culture. Satoh's subsequent work, particularly *Nezumi Kozō*, can be understood as his attempt to present in a more self-conscious manner the powerful forces he had conjured up in *My Beatles*.

Notes

1. John Lahr, "The Beatles Considered," *The New Republic*, December 2, 1981, p. 22.

2. Tsuno Kaitarō, "Biwa and Beatles," *Concerned Theatre Japan*, special introductory issue (October 1969):25.

The Komatsugawa Incident is also the subject of Ōshima Nagisa's 1968 film *Death by Hanging (Kōshikei)*. Joan Mellen has written a succinct synopsis of the film. See *The Waves at Genji's Door: Japan Through Its Cinema* (New York: Pantheon, 1976), pp. 419–425.

3. Details concerning the Komatsugawa Incident are taken from Pak Su-nam (Japanese: Boku Junan), *Tsumi to ai to shi to* (San'ichi shobō, 1963), pp. 249–270.

Satoh suggests the use of slides to familiarize the audience with the historical background of the play. Satoh Makoto, *Atashi no Beatles* (Shōbunsha, 1970), p. 51.

4. Li denied the rape charge, and the autopsy revealed no evidence of sexual intercourse.

5. Changsoo Lee and George De Vos, *Koreans in Japan: Ethnic Conflict and Accommodation* (Berkeley: University of California Press, 1981), p. 37.

6. Lee and De Vos, *Koreans in Japan*, p. ix.

7. See Lee and De Vos, *Koreans in Japan*, for a detailed description of the history and modern consequences of anti-Korean discrimination in Japan. Of particular interest in the present context are the essays contained in "Part Three: The Ethnic Experi-

ence," especially chapter 13, "Problems of Self-Identity Among Korean Youth in Japan"; and chapter 14, "Negative Self-Identity in a Delinquent Korean Youth": pp. 304–353.

8. See for example Fujimoto Kazuko, "Discrimination and the Perception of Difference," *Concerned Theatre Japan* (Spring 1973), II(3–4):136–151; and Morisaki Kazue, "Two Languages, Two Souls," tr. David G. Goodman, *Bulletin of Concerned Asian Scholars* (July-September 1978), 10(3):12–18.

9. Tsuno, "Biwa and Beatles," pp. 25–26.

10. Conversation with Satoh, November 16, 1980.

11. Tsuno, "Biwa and Beatles," p. 26.

12. It is no coincidence that Chong's tragic drama is to be played out on a Sunday. Throughout Satoh's work, Sunday is identified, not simply as the weekly sabbath, but as the Sabbath of History. Satoh probably derived his concept of an eternal Sabbath ushered in on the seventh day from Saint Augustine, whom he had read and hoped to study in college. In the final lines of *The City of God*, Augustine wrote, "Suffice it to say that [it] shall be our Sabbath, which shall be brought to a close, not by an evening, but by the Lord's day, as an eighth and eternal day, consecrated by the resurrection of Christ, and prefiguring the eternal repose not only of the spirit, but also of the body. There we shall rest and see, see and love, love and praise. This is what shall be in the end without end. For what other end do we propose to ourselves than to attain to the kingdom of where there is no end." (*The City of God*, tr. Marcus Dods [New York: Random House, 1950], p. 867.)

I analyze Satoh's symbolic use of Sunday in my "Satoh Makoto and the Post-Shingeki Movement in Japanese Contemporary Theatre" (Ph.D. diss., Cornell University, 1982), pp. 178–181.

13. For example, Heh-heh, So-so, and Bo-bo in *Nezumi Kozō: The Rat*. See David G. Goodman, ed. and tr., *After Apocalypse: Four Japanese Plays of Hiroshima and Nagasaki* (New York: Columbia University Press, 1986), pp. 269–319.

14. See, for example, *The Dance of Angels Who Burn Their Own Wings* below. In *Yoru to yoru no yoru* (Night of Night's Night, Shōbunsha 1981), the gods appear as chickens, birds who cannot fly.

15. Origuchi Shinobu, *Nihon geinō-shi rokkō*, *Origuchi Shinobu zenshū*, vol. 18 (Chūō kōronsha, 1976), pp. 341–343.

16. Origuchi, pp. 346–347. See also, Carmen Blacker, *The Catalpa Bow: A Study of Shamanistic Practices in Japan* (London: George Allen and Unwin, 1975), pp. 74–75; and Teigo Yoshida, "The Stranger as God: The Place of the Outsider in Japanese Folk Religion," *Ethnology* (1981), 20(2):87–99.

17. Origuchi, pp. 355–361.

18. Origuchi, p. 344.

19. Origuchi, p. 347.

20. Umehara Takeshi, *Jigoku no shisō* (Chūō kōronsha, 1967), pp. 110–114. Mishima Yukio treated the homicidal assault by the jealous spirit of Lady Rokujō upon Genji's wife Aoi in his modern nō play *The Lady Aoi*. Yukio Mishima, *Five Modern Nō Plays*, tr. Donald Keene (New York: Knopf, 1957; Vintage edition, 1973), pp. 143–171.

My Beatles

A PLAY IN ONE ACT

by Satoh Makoto

The text of *My Beatles* (*Atashi no Beatles*) appears in *Atashi no Beatles* (Shōbunsha, 1970). The play was first performed by *Jiyū gekijō* (The Freedom Theatre), directed by the playwright, in 1967.

CAST OF CHARACTERS

Three Young People:
Chong: young husband; plays the guitar
Katsura: young wife
The Japanese: dressed in black and carries a pistol, an onion, and something resembling a bomb

The Quartet:
Sundown Lennon: soft-spoken, intense leader of the group; dresses formally and has long hair
McCartney the Stripe: wears a knit shirt and small square sunglasses
Side-Street Harrison: bearded and wears a "Make Love Not War" button
Twinkle Starr: smokes a pipe and wears flowered slacks with a man's white shirt

A room the size and description of a cheap flat, the home that Chong and Katsura call their castle. There is one door and one window, both carelessly painted green. A naked light bulb swings just above the floor on a cord that is much too long. There is a record player and a stack of records, but otherwise the room is bare. The ceiling is low and the floor slopes gently. The overall impression is less of a room than the inside of a large crate.

It is one o'clock in the morning.

It is dark. The voices of several young people can be heard: "Bird!" "God!" "My Bird!" "My God!" The alternating voices of men and women repeat: "Oh my bird!"

The strains of a Beatles' song are also audible.

The naked light bulb brightens slowly. Katsura is seated in the center of the room. Chong pokes his head in through the window from outside. Beneath the light bulb a record revolves on a cheap phonograph.

CHONG: Bird?

Katsura shakes her head.

CHONG: But it seemed as if. . . .

Katsura nods. A woman's voice is heard. It is Twinkle Starr. Half stoned, she sounds like a child.

STARR (*voice only*): Maybe I should throw it away.

CHONG: It was a bird, I'm sure of it.

Katsura shakes her head again.

LENNON (*voice only*): Why are you crying?

HARRISON (*voice only*): Dear Lord, we beseech you to accept these, your humble servants, and grant eternal rest. We. . . .

Suddenly the Quartet breaks into raucous laughter. Katsura slowly gets to her feet.

CHONG: It was a bird. What are you getting up for? Sit down. (*He notices the commotion and looks up.*)

Katsura smiles briefly to herself.

LENNON (*voice only*): Answer my question. Why are you crying?

STARR (*voice only*): None of your business.

HARRISON (*voice only*): Oh, lay off her. She doesn't have to have a reason. Hail Mary. . . .

LENNON (*voice only*): That's no answer. There's got to be a reason.

STARR (*voice only*): I guess I will throw it away.

MC CARTNEY (*voice only, simply*): All right.

A red high-heeled shoe falls into the room from above.

KATSURA: Whirling around. A bird?

CHONG: No.

STARR (*voice only, discordantly*): Our Father who art in Heaven. . . .

MC CARTNEY (*voice only*): Like Elvis, man!

HARRISON (*voice only*): It is our fervent hope that you will judge our departed. . . .

STARR (*voice only*): Our departed and deceased!

CHONG: Sit down, will you? You're reading a book. Just as we rehearsed it. All right?

Katsura seats herself lethargically on the floor with both legs folded to one side and pretends to read.

CHONG: There's only one light on the roof. It's the lamp over the emergency exit. It's very dim, so you've pasted yourself to the wall, trying to get enough light to read by. The last light of evening fades. All of a sudden the chimney that soars up before you seems somehow different. You don't look up, but you notice the change all the same. Until a few minutes ago it was dusk—until a few minutes ago the sky was orange and the chimney stood bold and inorganic before you. But now it is night. Against the darkened sky, the chimney's silhouette begins to expand; its contours diffuse into the darkness.

KATSURA: That's not the way it was at all.

CHONG: As a matter of fact you don't notice the end of evening. You're too engrossed in your book. But you notice the change in the chimney all the same.

KATSURA: No, there was no chimney. You couldn't see any chimney from that roof.

CHONG: Listen, it's a factory district. There have to be chimneys in a factory district. Now look, Katsura, you're still not doing as I said. The light on the roof is dim. You'd never be able to read like that.

Katsura moves to the wall opposite the window and presses herself up against it. She continues to pore over her imaginary book.

CHONG: That's better.

KATSURA: There was no chimney. But a river was flowing nearby, a thick, lazy river, a river like a swamp.

CHONG: You must mean the canal. Yes, I suppose there could have been a canal there.

KATSURA: I named the river "Stupid Street."

CHONG (*trying to capture Katsura's mood*): Shhh . . . don't you feel a little cold?

KATSURA: Yes, a little.

CHONG: It's autumn. But there's nothing more interesting to do now than there was in the summer.

KATSURA: Maybe it was autumn, but I thought it might be winter.

CHONG: You're wearing your school uniform—a middy blouse and a thin cotton skirt—and you're reading a book on the roof. It has to be autumn.

KATSURA: Wouldn't you like to take a break for tea or something?

CHONG: Keep going.

KATSURA: It was a river.

CHONG: All right, a river! We'll make it a river. "Stupid Street," right? It was flowing.

KATSURA: Without moving. From here to there. Quietly. Almost as if it weren't moving at all.

CHONG: You can see it, then, can't you?

Katsura shakes her head.

CHONG: Can you hear it? Smell it?

Wordlessly, Katsura indicates that the answer to both questions is no.

CHONG: Then. . . .

KATSURA: I remember: There was a river and I was asleep. "Stupid Street," broad as the sea. And no one passed by, not a soul.

CHONG: All right. If you don't like the idea of a chimney, then a river will do just as well. The important thing is that you can see it from here, whatever it is. The sun sets. The landscape slowly fades into darkness—and yet, strangely, there is something that becomes more and more clear to you. You can feel it. If it's that river you remember, fine, of course. You can see it, and. . . .

KATSURA: You mean from here?

CHONG: We're on the roof, remember?

KATSURA (*vaguely*): Oh.

CHONG: Can you see it?

KATSURA: No. I can't smell it or hear it either.

CHONG: No, no, that's all wrong! You can see it. Look hard. Don't let your mind wander. I don't know how many times I've told you this already, but it's the beginning that's important. If you don't do your part right, we're going to blow the whole thing. Look, all of a sudden the river begins to rise. It's dark, so you can't see it, and besides you're reading a book. But at a certain point you sense it; you begin to feel the river rising, slowly. Like a sleeping beast awakening to its power, the river is changing direction. It rises up and starts flowing toward the sky. The wide canal opens its eyes in the gloom. It shivers almost imperceptibly. All right?

KATSURA: "Stupid Street." Maybe it wasn't such a good name after all.

CHONG: In the yellow afternoon haze of the factories, the canal was flat and empty. "Stupid Street" was probably a perfect name. Dull and lazy, it matched the long, tired five o'clock siren to a T. "Stupid Street" was probably a perfect name for it.

KATSURA: Rivers don't change, though.

CHONG: You continue to read your book. The river rises, hesitantly, as if it were being forced against its will. Unsteadily, fearfully, feeling its way it faces the sky. You're reading; you're completely absorbed in your book. All right, go!

KATSURA (*reading her imaginary book*): "I suppose I'm the type that thinks with her tummy. Both my mind and my spirit are embedded in its soft, white flesh. I while away the long day, thinking of the roar of a distant sea in its gentle reaches, rocking back and forth in my rocking chair."

CHONG: The lamp is red. The pages of your book are bathed in red light. Okay, a little more softly now.

KATSURA (*continuing to read, turning the pages of her book*): "The ideas conceived in my tummy are gentle and calm. They reek of its raw fragrance. It seems to me that my way of thinking must be awfully like a horse. Most horses do their thinking as they walk. Of course, horses don't take quiet strolls through the countryside; so thinking as they walk means thinking as they work. Horses contemplate the world hitched to a wagon, to its simple, sad rhythms.

CHONG: Good. Don't rush things. Concentrate on what you're doing. The direction of the river has changed. It's almost perpendicular now. The canal flows toward the sky.

KATSURA (*reading*): "I was waiting for the ship."

CHONG (*sharply*): No!

KATSURA: "I was waiting for the ship."

CHONG: Katsura, that's all wrong! There's nothing about a ship written there.

KATSURA (*not too insistently*): I'm reading my diary. There are bound to be things in it Chong doesn't know.

CHONG: Listen, I made up this play! . . .

KATSURA: You decided that I should be reading, that I should be engrossed in a book. (*She touches the wall of the room.*) This is a concrete wall on the roof. There's an emergency exit lamp attached to it. The lamp is red. That's right, isn't it?

CHONG: Yes, that's right.

KATSURA: I'm just part of the setting. I'm leaning against the wall and reading. But I only need to pretend I'm reading. The play has only just begun; nothing really happens until Chong appears on the roof.

CHONG: You just don't understand!

KATSURA (*paying no attention, reading*): "I was waiting for the ship." If you don't like it we'll forget the whole thing.

CHONG: All right, have it your way. Keep reading. I just won't listen, that's all.

KATSURA (*reading*): "I was waiting for the ship. I have a bicycle, but a bicycle won't do. I can't go by bicycle. The Beatles are on the ship. I will board the ship and set off. Two of the Beatles will carry me on board, while the other two load my bicycle and rocking chair: the bicycle on the deck, the rocking chair in my cabin. I'll ask them to help me. And when they're finished, I'll thank them one by one. I'll let them feel my smooth, even tummy."

CHONG (*interrupting*): The canal flowing into the night sky symbolizes Katsura's presentiment, the presentiment that a sinister change is taking place in the vicinity of the river, a change that terrifies her. And yet her presentiment is mistaken, for the danger lurks in an entirely different direction. . . . (*Shouting unexpectedly*): Who's there?

Unnoticed, The Japanese has arrived and is standing in the doorway.

JAPANESE: It's me, "The Japanese." Just go ahead with what you were doing.

The record ends.

CHONG: You see, this is what always happens—we never get to the end! *Katsura no longer pretends to read but remains sitting on her haunches.*

KATSURA: Are we going on, Chong?

CHONG (*to Japanese*): Come on in. (*Chong also enters the room through the window.*) Which direction was the canal? *Katsura is silent but points toward the audience.*

CHONG: Over there? Then Chong would approach from the direction of The Japanese. (*He sits down and picks up his guitar.*)

KATSURA: I wind up as usual, don't I, just reading my book and waiting?

JAPANESE (*still standing in the doorway*): It's the same old story, isn't it? The same old story.

KATSURA: I wonder if things would go as you say?

CHONG (*strumming his guitar*): What do you mean?

KATSURA: If we got any farther.

CHONG: There's no way to tell. There's always the chance we'll flop.

JAPANESE: Don't worry. Things will go just fine. They have to.

CHONG: Listen, you're not even supposed to be here yet! And anyway, how do you know? We'll just have to try and see what happens.

JAPANESE: Things had better go well. Otherwise I'm the odd man out.

CHONG: Then the first thing to do is avoid arriving so damned early! You show up prematurely and I have to quit right in the middle of everything. Every night it's the same way. I never get far enough to see how things will turn out. How can you stand there and tell me not to worry?

JAPANESE: I just haven't been able to find a good way to kill the time, that's all.

CHONG: Sure.

JAPANESE: But I know everything will go fine.

CHONG: Do you think Chong will show up, though? Will he really appear there, in your place?

JAPANESE: Will he show up? You mean, will you show up? Yes, you'll show up. You have to.

KATSURA: Let's have something to drink. It looks like we've gotten as far as we're going to tonight, anyway.

CHONG: All right.

JAPANESE: I'd just like a glass of water. I'm hot.

KATSURA: Okay, I'll be right back.

Katsura exits. Japanese enters the room and sits with his back to the wall like Chong.

CHONG: You're always so easy-going. I can count on you, can't I? Are you certain you can handle your part?

JAPANESE: That depends entirely on you. I'm ready whenever you are. I've made all the necessary preparations, and starting tomorrow I'll make it a point to plan the time of my arrival more precisely. What I'm most afraid of is that you'll lose your nerve.

CHONG: If we could just get through it once, I'm sure there'd be nothing to it. We were doing pretty well tonight, too, as a matter of fact. Did you hear the part about the canal?

JAPANESE: Just half. (*He takes an onion from his bag and begins to eat it without peeling it, as if it were an apple.*)

CHONG (*singing half to himself*):

> All men will be equal,
> On an even plane.

JAPANESE: Do you have everything you need?

CHONG: What do you mean?

JAPANESE: Weapons and such. I was just wondering how you expect to go about it.

CHONG: I don't need anything. I'll just have my hands in the pockets of my trench coat.

JAPANESE: And then?

CHONG: "Hey!" I'll yell, but I won't look at her. This first "Hey!" will be more to reassure myself than anything else. "Hey!" I'll be practicing, see? I'll be asking myself if I can really take her, take her properly, like a man.

JAPANESE: "Hey"?

CHONG: I'll be tired—being tired's good, don't you think? It's appropriate for a man performing his duty to be tired. A weary man in a trench coat, dispensing justice.

JAPANESE: Justice . . . interesting.

CHONG (*again singing half to himself*):

> Mountains will be leveled,
> Seas their waters drained.

I'll appear before her without saying a word. I won't say a word, but I'll grab the book she's reading. She'll look up at me . . . or perhaps she won't. If she does, I'll smile at her with as much affection as I can. If she just looks at the ground, I'll say, "It's not good for a man to smile alone," and then I'll ask her if she'd like an apple. How does that sound?

JAPANESE: I suppose it will do. There's no reason you have to force yourself on her right away. Just so you don't miss your chance. It's probably as good a way as any.

CHONG: She'll probably refuse the apple and ask for her book back.

JAPANESE: Perhaps.

CHONG: Why not?

JAPANESE: I don't think she'll say anything. She'll be silent. She won't respond to your question or ask for her book back.

CHONG: She won't say anything?

JAPANESE: Much better that way, I should think. More realistic. You're the one who does the talking. The only thing that matters about her is that she's there. She'll just remain passive until you've finished your part in the play.

CHONG: Yes, when you show up I'll probably act the same way. I'll just be passive until you've finished your part in the play. I can understand that. My role is very much like hers. You're the assailant and I'm your victim. But Katsura and I have to be more than that. We have to be more like accomplices. She talks to me, just a bit. We need that moment of intimacy, of warmth, before anything else happens.

JAPANESE: I was only offering my opinion. I didn't mean you have to follow my advice.

Katsura returns. She carries two cups and a glass on a tray.

KATSURA (*handing the glass to Japanese*): You were just kidding about feeling hot. You don't really want water, do you?

CHONG: Just then she says, "I don't care for an apple. Please return my book."

Chong is absorbed in his own thoughts. Japanese and Katsura take advantage of their moment of privacy to kiss quickly on the lips.

KATSURA (*handing Chong his cup*): I would like an apple, thank you. In return you can keep the book!

Japanese chuckles, drinks his water, and eats his onion.

CHONG (*annoyed*): "You can't have it. You'll catch cold from eating apples."

KATSURA: Chong is ashamed because his apple is so small. Men with small apples hate themselves.

Japanese laughs again.

CHONG (*to Japanese*): Are you going to kill me with a knife? I don't think I could take a poisoned apple.

JAPANESE: Are you kidding?

KATSURA (*interrupting, her imagination sparked*): Death by hanging, of course!

JAPANESE (*ignoring her*): The trouble with a knife is that the chances of failure are so great. It requires a certain amount of skill, don't you think?

CHONG: But that's the way it's supposed to happen, isn't it? I'll do everything I can to cooperate. I'll only start writhing and struggling once I'm drenched in my own blood, tottering on the brink of death.

JAPANESE: I suppose a knife isn't entirely out of the question.

KATSURA: Poison would be pretty awful, too, wouldn't it?

CHONG: Of course, but there's no blood.

KATSURA: There must be a little bleeding from the nose.

CHONG: I don't want a bloody nose, I want to bleed!

KATSURA: Of course you do, dear.

CHONG: Bleed, you hear! (*To Japanese*): Right?

JAPANESE: I suppose. Here, look what I made. (*He removes a bomb from his pocket. It is small, round, and black.*) I don't know whether it'll do the job or not.

CHONG: How does it work?

JAPANESE: There's really nothing to it. You just light this fuse and in five seconds, bang! I tested it on a mouse—blew the beast to smithereens!

CHONG: Smithereens. . . .

KATSURA: Did you throw it?

JAPANESE: No. I had the mouse trapped in a box back in the woods. The bomb made quite a noise when it went off; even sent up a column of flame in the air.

KATSURA: Sounds terrific!

CHONG: Isn't it overdoing things a bit?

JAPANESE: Don't you like the idea of using explosives?

CHONG: No, explosives are all right, I suppose.

JAPANESE (*relieved*): Well, I'm glad to hear that! (*He returns the bomb to his pocket.*)

KATSURA: This is really going to be fun!

CHONG: You think so?

KATSURA: Is there anything wrong with that?

CHONG: No, I'm glad it makes you happy. It's just that I had no idea he'd use a bomb, that's all. I always assumed he'd use a knife. You know: the dark of night, a narrow alley, a knife in the back. With a bomb an alley's out of the question, and daylight would be better, too. A major thoroughfare in broad daylight, that's it.

JAPANESE: Right: broad daylight, a beautiful, wide boulevard. I'll blow you to kingdom come!

CHONG: I'm beginning to see what you mean!

JAPANESE: I'll wait for you to climb the stairs out of the subway. You'll squint as you emerge into the daylight, and that will be my signal. The bomb will land exactly six inches in front of you. I'll have dropped it from the roof of a building.

CHONG: Have you given it a run-through already?

JAPANESE: No, I'm still in the planning stages.

KATSURA: Don't you think we ought to give it a trial, though? It would be awfully embarrassing to fail.

JAPANESE: Yes, there always is that possibility.

CHONG (*singing*):

> All the world will be afire,
> Turned to flame and heat.

KATSURA: Failure would mean Chong would be the sole survivor.

CHONG: When I come out of the subway, I could walk real slowly. I could even stand still. You just can't count on "The Japanese": they might spoil the whole thing. If I'm not dead when this is over, it will all have been for nothing.

KATSURA: You could lose a leg and still survive, you know. That's what happened to my father.

JAPANESE (*chanting*): Smithereens . . . smithereens . . . smi-ther-eens!

CHONG: That's right. Just like the mouse in your experiment. I'm counting on you. Blow me to bits!

JAPANESE: Leave it to me. One fine day you can be sure you'll be blown as high as the clear, blue sky. A cloudless Sunday would be ideal.

CHONG: Sunday.

KATSURA: The day after tomorrow!

CHONG: I wonder if it'll clear up by then.

JAPANESE (*noticing something*): Did somebody just come in? (*He looks at the door.*)

KATSURA: Did you hear something?

JAPANESE: I thought so.

Katsura stands up, goes to the door, opens it, and looks out.

KATSURA: Nobody there now.

JAPANESE (*deliberately*): The Beatles. (*He begins to laugh.*)

CHONG: Nonsense! (*To Katsura*): Right?

KATSURA: Sure. (*Laughing, she closes the door and returns to her place.*)

CHONG: Listen, the Beatles aren't coming. The whole idea's ridiculous.

KATSURA: Maybe they won't come. Then again, maybe they will. Either way it's too early to tell.

CHONG: They're not coming, I said.

KATSURA: Yes, they will! They'll come to take me back to the Emerald Peninsula, where the air is fresh and the grass is green.

JAPANESE: They'll come by ship . . . won't they?

KATSURA: A fabulous yacht!

CHONG: It's a lie! I've told you a hundred times—all this talk about the Emerald Peninsula is a pack of lies. It isn't green and it isn't fresh. It's a land of wasted soil and mountains stripped of foliage. It's a parched land, and the only time the wind isn't filled with dust is when it's whipping the snow into drifts.

KATSURA: My father told me there are gentle, rolling hills, and pastures where herds of horses graze.

CHONG (*sarcastically*): And where's your father now?

KATSURA: He's gone. He went back.

JAPANESE: Back? (*Making a ditty of the words.*) He went back. He went back. He went back-a-back-a-back!

CHONG: He went back all right. He headed back to the Emerald Peninsula as fast as he could go. But he didn't go by yacht. He took the rusty, mottled ferry that came for him.

KATSURA (*urgently*): You don't understand!

CHONG: And did you get letters from the pastures and the hills? Did your father write you about the blue sky and the fresh air?

KATSURA: The letters came from a tiny shanty built in the shadow of a forest of chimneys. My father wrote that he would walk around the corner with his crutch under his arm and hear a baby crying.

CHONG: Even so, he's pretty damn happy, isn't he? He dishes hot vittles onto a tin plate and it's enough to make him weep with joy. If you ask me, I think your old man crossed the straits all right, but when he got to the other side he didn't find what he expected. He was rotten with years, and he filled your head with a pack of fairy tales and lies.

JAPANESE: Who knows? Maybe he never made it after all.

CHONG: Katsura's old man got where he was going, all right. But it wasn't green. I know. I've known for a long time. Katsura shouldn't waste her time dreaming about the Beatles and their peninsula. There isn't a chance in a million we'll ever get there.

KATSURA: You're not going. The Beatles are coming for me alone.

CHONG: We'll see how things go when and if the Beatles get here. Until then. . . . Listen, you haven't been good for anything around here lately. You couldn't even read with enthusiasm. It's half your fault I never get anywhere.

KATSURA: I read just as I was told. Maybe I'm just sick and tired of play-acting. Sometimes I think I am. But who cares? Either way. . . .

CHONG: You have no choice but to be here, to go on being here, to go on play-acting with me.

Pause.

STARR (*voice only*): Bye-bye, my God!

MC CARTNEY (*voice only*): Like Elvis Presley!

STARR (*voice only*): God? Bird?

JAPANESE (*looking up*): What's all the noise about?

CHONG: Somebody's grandmother died. They must be having a wake.

JAPANESE: Grandmother?

CHONG: Used to live up there. I never met her, though. Seems like they're going a little overboard, doesn't it?

JAPANESE: For a wake, yes.

KATSURA: Under her breath. "Bye-bye, my God." . . .

CHONG: What?

KATSURA: Nothing. What sort of people are they?

CHONG: You mean upstairs? Let me see. They're a strange bunch, certainly not ordinary. There are four of them.

KATSURA: Four?

CHONG: Yes.

Pause.

CHONG: Well, what shall we do? Is tonight going to be like all the others?

JAPANESE: We don't have much choice, do we?

KATSURA: The nights certainly are long, though.

JAPANESE: Yes.

CHONG: If you'd like to go home. . . .

JAPANESE: No, there's nothing to do at home but sleep and mess around. But if you'd like me to. . . .

CHONG: No, it doesn't matter. In fact, I'd rather have you here. The nights are so damn long, sometimes I wonder if I'll last till morning. I thought maybe we were keeping you, that's all.

JAPANESE: Don't worry about me. I'm all right.

KATSURA: There's no part in the play for you at this point anyway. But your name, "The Japanese," don't you think it's funny?

JAPANESE: Not particularly. The avenging Japanese, that's my role, after all. I take the necessary reprisals for what Chong does.

CHONG: You'll bury me in a hole and cover me over with sand so that no trace remains. You'll bury the wretched Korean who's raped Katsura and strangled her to death. Then I'll return to life! Glorious revenge, my blood's atonement! I'll die and thus gain new life. You see, I'll be murdered by "The Japanese," by their rage, and so I'll be able to die smiling and satisfied. I'll die proud that I could be murdered in just revenge. That will be my resurrection. "The Japanese" will see me through my resurrection and then quietly bury my remains.

JAPANESE: I understand. Perfectly. I'll do just as you say. You don't have to worry.

CHONG: Tomorrow we're going to run through the whole thing. And then on Sunday. . . .

JAPANESE: Yes.

KATSURA: Tomorrow? Really?

CHONG: Yes, tomorrow. We'll play this thing out to the very end.

KATSURA: The Beatles won't make it, will they?

CHONG: Not a chance. Okay, you'd better get back to rehearsing.

Katsura stands, walks over to the window, takes out her imaginary book, and begins to read aloud. Japanese takes out his pistol and polishes it. Chong is strumming his guitar.

KATSURA *(reading):* "My father was lame. He had a pair of red high heels. I wanted to try them on. I wanted to try them on for the longest time. Father was generally grumpy, and I was afraid of him, but once I told my brother. We were standing up on top of this mountain of cinders, and I screwed up the courage to tell him that I wanted to try on Father's red high heels. He laughed, and as he laughed he hit me. He hit me again and again; he hit me until my cheeks were red and swollen. But all the time, even as he was hitting me, I couldn't think of anything but the red high heels placed so carefully on that dark shelf in our house. My brother's fist hurt me terribly, and I could have cursed him, but for some reason I didn't cry. He hit me for a long time and then suddenly left me alone on the mountain of cinders. As I watched him disappear into the darkness at the foot of the cinder mountain I was struck by how grown-up he seemed. It was just a year later that he hanged himself. We found a letter of acceptance from a university somewhere in his pocket. Afterward Father and I took the red high heels and the letter out back to the garbage dump and burned them. Somehow it seemed like a terrible waste to burn those things, but I was afraid of what Father might do if I said anything, so I kept quiet. I helped him carry books and newspapers and our battered old desk out of the house to feed the fire. Somehow, though, our kindling wouldn't burn, and for a long time it sputtered and smoked without catching fire. Eventually we burned everything in the house. Then Father boarded the ship and left."

While Katsura is speaking the door opens and Lennon and Harrison look in. Katsura, Chong, and Japanese do not notice them. Lennon and Harrison examine the room carefully, then look at each other and nod.

LENNON (*deliberately, oppressively, just as Katsura finishes speaking*): Guitar. . . .

Chong notices the intruders and swings around. Katsura and Japanese also notice.

LENNON (*continuing*): . . . girl, pistol. Three people in all. No mistake, this is the place.

Chong, Katsura, and Japanese are silent.

LENNON (*looking around the room*): The room is swaying. Maybe it's the wind.

HARRISON (*sniffing*): Smells like sweat and cum in here.

JAPANESE: What do you want? Who are you?

LENNON: We're movers. Officially, that is.

JAPANESE: Movers?

LENNON: We have a truck, a tarpaulin, ropes, and all the necessary gear. Moving, packing, transport, that's our line. "You groove it, we'll move it!"

Harrison enters and approaches Katsura.

HARRISON (*turning to Lennon*): Nice piece, eh?

JAPANESE (*to Lennon*): What business do movers have here at this time of night?

LENNON: We've brought some packages for you.

JAPANESE: Well why didn't you say so? Bring them in and be on your way. (*Worrying about Harrison*): There's no need to barge in here like this.

HARRISON: Button up, buddy. (*Indicating the pistol*): And let's have a look at that six-shooter.

JAPANESE: What right do you have to make demands? This is my pistol. There's no reason I should hand it over to you. If you're movers, then you should act like movers and be about your business.

LENNON: It may not seem like it, but we're acting as much like movers as we can. It'd just be better if you'd hand the gun over, that's all. In order to avoid any unpleasantness. You see what I mean?

JAPANESE: Unpleasantness? Listen, you force your way in here. . . .

LENNON: I told you, we've brought something for you.

JAPANESE: Then for heaven's sake hurry up with it!

HARRISON: In our own sweet time, baby. We don't need you to tell us how to do our job. Just keep your trap shut and hand over the gun.

JAPANESE: No.

LENNON: It would be best if you'd obey orders. Nothing's going to happen to you. We'll give it back as soon as we're finished.

JAPANESE: There's no reason I should take orders from you.

CHONG: Let them have it.

JAPANESE: You know them?

CHONG: They're the ones from upstairs. They said they wouldn't do anything.

JAPANESE: But. . . .

Harrison, seeing his chance, grabs the pistol from Japanese. Japanese, in turn, moves to attack Harrison, but he is subdued by Lennon, who pins him with more than amateur dexterity.

LENNON: All right, now relax! Just take it easy. We aren't going to be the first to resort to violence, but we do reserve the right to defend ourselves.

JAPANESE: Let me go!

HARRISON: Hey, the bastard's carrying a bomb!

LENNON (*to Harrison*): Never mind about that. It's only the pistol that's an immediate danger. Put it away so it won't get broken.

HARRISON: Right. (*He turns it over two or three times in the palm of his hand and then puts it in his pocket.*)

LENNON (*to Japanese*): You're not going to cause any more trouble, now, are you?

HARRISON: It's loaded, isn't it? (*He places his hand menacingly over his pocket.*)

Lennon releases Japanese, who sits smoldering.

KATSURA: Uh. . . .

LENNON: Yes?

KATSURA: Are there only two of you?

LENNON: No, four. The other two'll be here in a minute —McCartney the Stripe and Twinkle Starr.

HARRISON: I'm Side-Street Harrison and this is Sundown Lennon. Glad to meet you.

KATSURA: You're a quartet, then?

McCartney and Starr enter. Starr walks uncertainly and is supported by McCartney.

MC CARTNEY: Good evening.

LENNON: We're the Beatles.

STARR: Bea-tles! Don't you guys have any music around here?

Harrison quickly spies the record player and puts on a record. This, too, is a Beatles number.

KATSURA: The Beatles!

JAPANESE: You said you were movers.

LENNON: There's no reason we can't be the Beatles and movers at the same time. The fact of the matter is we're both!

HARRISON: We were having a wake. Couldn't you hear us? "Our Father who art in heaven." . . .

STARR: Departed and deceased! (*She dances to the music.*)

CHONG: Did somebody die?

LENNON: Good thinking! The fact that we were having a wake means that somebody died!

CHONG: Your grandmother?

LENNON: That's one way of putting it.

Harrison guffaws.

LENNON (*to Harrison*): It was my grandmother!

HARRISON: Yes, yes. Your grandmother. Your grandmother, of course.

MC CARTNEY (*to Lennon*): Come on, let's ask them.

LENNON: Oh, yeah! Listen, we seem to have started off on the wrong foot, but we've got a favor to ask.

CHONG: A favor?

LENNON: Yes, we were wondering if you wouldn't do it for us.

HARRISON: We're bored.

STARR: Just like Elvis Presley!

MC CARTNEY: Shut up, stupid!

CHONG: Do it for you? You mean our play?

MC CARTNEY: That's right. We've come all the way down here now. You wouldn't mind, would you?

CHONG: No, it's out of the question.

LENNON: Plays require an audience. That's the way it works.

CHONG: It's not that kind of play—it's not a play to be shown to anyone.

It's . . . it's a play for the acting out.

HARRISON: We're not going to do anything. We'll just sit here quietly and watch, that's all.

LENNON: Of course you're still rehearsing, but that doesn't matter. We realize it's not finished yet.

CHONG: Please leave.

KATSURA: Let's do it! Come on, Chong!

HARRISON: Chong?

STARR: What's a "chong"?

LENNON: It's his name, I guess.

HARRISON (*looking at Chong*): Ah, a Korean. A diarrhean Korean.

CHONG: Katsura!

KATSURA: It won't make any difference. We were just rehearsing, anyway. (*To Lennon*): We'll be glad to do the play for you.

CHONG: Katsura!

STARR: Hurray! (*She claps her hands gleefully.*)

CHONG: Katsura!

KATSURA: Please come and sit over here, will you? (*To Japanese*): You, too. (*She arranges the Quartet and Japanese against the wall near the window.*)

JAPANESE (*changing his tone, unusually familiar.*) Are we really going through with it?

HARRISON: You bet! And you're going to sit with us right here and watch.

CHONG: Not me!

KATSURA: If you don't like it you can just stand there and be quiet. I want the Beatles to see our play.

CHONG: Katsura, these aren't the Beatles! The Beatles you're waiting for. . . .

LENNON: We're the Beatles all right. There's no mistake.

KATSURA (*to the Quartet*): The play begins. We're on the roof. It's winter. (*She looks at Chong, but he remains expressionless.*) Or perhaps it's autumn, I don't remember exactly. I'm wearing a middy blouse and a thin cotton skirt. It's been two hours since the siren from the factories signaled the end of the day. I'm alone on the roof of the school, reading. (*She goes to the wall opposite the Quartet, leans against it and pretends to read.*) "Do

you know the lollipop song?"
Starr, who is embracing McCartney as she watches, suddenly breaks into song.
MC CARTNEY: Shhh!
STARR (*singing*):

Lollipop, lollipop, beautiful lollipop.
Lollipop ponies pink and marching
Lollipop stops and lollipop starting
Pop a lolli pill, pop a lolli Polly.

LENNON (*interested in Starr's song, but turning back to Katsura*): And then?
KATSURA (*reading*): "Do you know the lollipop song? . . . I loved that basement room. There was always a party going on down there, where everyone danced and bodies touched one another. The place was called Chester, and every evening I spent three hours there, doing nothing but feeling alive. Everyone in the place was unsure, unsure of something. Hardly anyone could afford a cup of coffee; everyone seemed weary somehow; and everyone carried with him a lonely secret. . . . After everyone had politely shaken hands, we formed a circle and sang the lollipop song at the top of our lungs. We passed the multicolored capsules around the circle, popping one, two, three, then sank slowly into our rainbow lollipop whirlpool." (*No longer reading but explaining the play*): All of a sudden he is standing in front of me. . . .
HARRISON: Who?
Katsura indicates Chong.
HARRISON: Hey, you're on, buster!
KATSURA: He speaks to me, gently.
MC CARTNEY (*to Chong*): Come on, be a sport. Look how hard she's trying.
Chong moves toward Katsura almost unconsciously. Perhaps he was intending to stop the play.
LENNON (*forcefully*): Speak to her!
CHONG (*unenthusiastically*): Hey. (*Apparently resigned, he goes through the motions of taking Katsura's book away from her.*)

Tsuno Kaitarō directing
Their Very Own and Golden City, 1968.
Photo by David G. Goodman

Their Very Own and Golden City, as
performed by the June Theatre, 1968.
Photo by David G. Goodman

Kaison the Priest of Hitachi
Act One, Scene Two: Kaison I.
Photo courtesy of Akimoto Matsuyo

Kaison the Priest of Hitachi
Act Two, Scene Two: The seance.
Photo courtesy of Akimoto Matsuyo

John Silver: The Beggar of Love
Kara Jūrō as "Chinese" Chichi
Photo © Mikoshiba Shigeru

John Silver: The Beggar of Love
Act Three: The pirates struggle over the gold teeth.
Photo © Mikoshiba Shigeru

John Silver: The Beggar of Love
Ri Reisen as Orchid Flower
Photo © Mikoshiba Shigeru

The Dance of Angels Who Burn Their Own Wings
The Birds dance before their King.
Photo © Mikoshiba Shigeru

The Dance of Angels Who Burn Their Own Wings
Scene Seven: Angel Red is restrained by the Birds.
Photo © Mikoshiba Shigeru

The Dance of Angels Who Burn Their Own Wings
Scene Six: Red Wind 2 embraces Red Wind 6.
Photo © Mikoshiba Shigeru

The Dance of Angels Who Burn Their Own Wings
Scene Eight: Red Wind 1 ravaged by disease.
Photo © Mikoshiba Shigeru

Katsura looks up and smiles. Chong tries to smile back, but his face assumes a cramped, unhappy expression instead. He looks at Lennon, who returns the look with a friendly wink.

MC CARTNEY: Not bad, not bad!

CHONG: Here's an apple.

STARR: That's the spirit!

KATSURA: Please return my book.

CHONG: It's green and hard and sour. . . . The two of us used to take apples out of a paper bag and eat them in this room. It hasn't been such a long time since we started doing that and came to live together.

HARRISON: I'll return your book. I'm sorry I took it. If you don't mind, though, I'd like to talk to you.

LENNON (*to Harrison*): The audience seems to know the lines better than the actors.

KATSURA (*to both Chong and Harrison*): Who are you?

CHONG: I'm. . . .

HARRISON: Katsura, forgive me, I'm. . . .

KATSURA: How do you know my name?

HARRISON: I've been admiring you from afar for some time. I'm sure you've noticed.

CHONG: I've been watching you, you and your friends, sitting there nearly every day at the back of the coffee shop, mixing cheap whisky, sleeping pills, barbies and bennies. I've seen your faces contorted in the shadow of a grin. I've looked at you and wondered if your wandering eyes had pierced the white walls to gaze at some distant landscape.

HARRISON: Why do you run from me? Yesterday it was like this, and the day before.

CHONG: Come with me, and let's perform a little play I have in mind. I've been looking for someone to work with, and you seem perfect for the part.

LENNON (*to Japanese*): You have a smoke?

Japanese silently hands him a cigarette and lights one for himself.

MC CARTNEY: I know where you live. It's the brick house with the little garden. It's at the top of the hill. Every night I stand in front of your house and look up at the window on the second floor. The window facing the road is yours, isn't it?

CHONG: If you're waiting for the Beatles, that's all right. Come with me and we'll wait together. We can even have an apple as we wait.

HARRISON: Last Sunday you went out, didn't you? Do you remember? I didn't recognize you at first. You were wearing makeup and a pair of red high heels.

CHONG: Your mother had already left by the time your father got home. You'd cried yourself to sleep and were lying in the middle of the room, rolled into a little ball. On the table were a cardboard box and a letter. Inside the box was a pair of high-heeled shoes. They were the keepsake your mother had left for you.

MC CARTNEY: You didn't notice me. Clutching your handbag, your nose in the air, you walked down the hill. I watched you until you disappeared into the distance.

CHONG (to Katsura): I'll work hard and buy you everything you want. Our room will be our castle, and our castle will be our reason for living. No matter how hard the day has been, your smile will make it all worthwhile.

HARRISON: Please say something. Your silence makes me feel as if I were doing something wrong.

KATSURA: I want to go home. Please . . . let me go home.

CHONG: Home? Where is that?

KATSURA: Home. . . .

CHONG: What are you talking about? This is your home. This is our castle. You have no place else.

KATSURA: Mother will be worried. It's late, and. . . .

CHONG: Your mother ran away. You don't remember her, and you never want to see her. You said so yourself.

HARRISON: I'll see you home, and I'll explain to your mother, so stay just a few minutes more.

KATSURA: Home is neither here nor at the top of the hill. It's somewhere else, somewhere far away.

CHONG: Somewhere else?

KATSURA: You've been very kind to me. You're one of the nicest people I've ever met. But I can't go on. I don't understand what you want me to do. I have to wait for the Beatles. I'm tired. I want to sleep. Suddenly I feel very cold.

HARRISON: I've captured you at last. I'll never let you go. Come with me to the. . . .

CHONG (*almost simultaneously*): Come with me. . . .

KATSURA: Thank you. Thank you very much, but I can't. I. . . .

MC CARTNEY (*changing his attitude*): You feel cold because it's going to snow. But don't worry. It won't be much longer. You can close your eyes. It'll be all right. Soon you'll be where the wind never blows.

KATSURA: I'm afraid. You're so . . . I'm going home. I can find my way alone. Good-bye. Please, don't follow me. She starts to get up.

MC CARTNEY: Wait!

CHONG: Wait!

Katsura attempts to move toward the door, but Harrison shoves her in McCartney's direction. McCartney wraps his arms roughly around her.

Harrison attacks Chong. Grabbing him in a double arm-lock, he forces him into a corner of the room opposite Katsura and her captor.

LENNON (*to Chong*): It's a play, that's all, just a play. You understand.

CHONG: Katsura! (*He tries desperately to resist, but Harrison is much too strong for him. To Japanese*): Do something!

HARRISON: I wouldn't count on him if I were you. What good do you think he'll be?

CHONG: Hurry up! Help Katsura!

Japanese remains immobile. Inhaling his cigarette, he calmly observes the two struggling groups of people. Before long both McCartney and Harrison have their adversaries helplessly pinned to the ground.

CHONG: Cut it out! Please! What are you trying to do? This is our castle. Get out! The play is over. Get out of here! Get out!

LENNON: No, the play's not over yet. We'll see it through to the end.

HARRISON: What are you so afraid of? We aren't going to do anything. We're just trying to lend a hand, that's all. (*To Japanese*): That's right, isn't it?

Japanese puts out his cigarette, drinks his water, and eats his onion. Ignoring Harrison and Chong, Starr approaches McCartney and speaks softly to Katsura.

STARR: There's a song about a whorehouse in New Orleans called the House of the Rising Sun. Unless I'm mistaken, the name of your house on the hill was the Hotel Fuji. You remember, don't you? But of course, that was no brothel, was it? It was just an ordinary hotel. Everyone knew that. There was a maid in the Hotel Fuji. Her name was O'Tsune and she used to climb into bed wearing a pair of red high heels. She was small, dark, and a little scrawny. Did the rising sun shine on the Hotel Fuji? It was high on a hill, so the sun must have shone through its windows. Please don't struggle.

McCartney removes Katsura's blouse and throws it to Harrison.

STARR: O'Tsune used to say she'd become a maid at the Hotel Fuji after she ran away from a one-legged coal miner. Of course you can't believe what women like that tell you. She also claimed that she had two children. You remember, don't you? Now you see? That wasn't your house. You just felt like it was, that's all. The Hotel Fuji seemed more like a mansion to you than a house of ill repute. To tell the truth, I have no idea where you belong.

HARRISON (*to Chong*): Boy, do you guys stink! What is that smell?

STARR: I can't understand it. I can't understand why you have to run away. O'Tsune never tried to run away.

MC CARTNEY: During the summer I worked part time for the iceman. I pulled a heavy wagon loaded with ice.

JAPANESE: A white short-sleeved blouse and white socks. (*Abstractly, to Chong*): Do you really think it'll clear up by Sunday? Do you think everything will go all right?

MC CARTNEY: The minute I saw you my summer seemed long and hot. Let me tell you about my long, hot summer.

JAPANESE: Will you really appear out of the subway as we planned?

CHONG (*to McCartney*): Please, leave her alone! Leave us both in peace! You're spoiling everything!

LENNON (*to Chong*): Do you really understand what we're doing? How about being a bit quieter?

MC CARTNEY: I saved my money. I read books. I had hopes for my summer. It was easy to live from one day to the next.

LENNON: You're the one who was supposed to act this out. Instead, look at the mess you made of it. You couldn't even speak your lines properly. We're here to finish what you've begun. Believe me, we're doing this out of the goodness of our hearts.

CHONG: It's all wrong. We were trying to do something different. We. . . .

HARRISON: Then why don't you do it? (*Indicating McCartney*): It's not much, but at least he's trying. If you think you can do better, go ahead. Nobody's stopping you.

STARR: Suddenly I felt as if an icy wind had blown through my heart. I thought at first that I'd been out in the sun too long.

JAPANESE (*to Chong*): My bomb is perfect. You're the one I'm worried about.

CHONG: I thought we agreed to run through the whole thing tomorrow night. You said so yourself!

HARRISON: What's wrong with tonight?

CHONG: Who asked you anyway? We're the ones who have to do it.

LENNON: That's right, you are.

STARR: Suddenly my summer seemed hot and oppressive. I had never given much thought to my empty stomach, but suddenly it began to bother me. I came to curse the piercing rays of the sun.

MC CARTNEY: You glanced in my direction. I was halfway up the hill and had put down the handle of the wagon to wipe the sweat off my forehead. You remember, don't you?

CHONG: Of course she doesn't remember. That nonsense has nothing to do with our play.

HARRISON: If you're so damned smart, get up and do it yourself!

JAPANESE: Yeah, go ahead.

CHONG: Fuck off!

HARRISON: As you like. You couldn't do it anyway. Just keep your trap shut, that's all.

JAPANESE: You're not going to chicken out on me, are you?

Chong remains silent with eyes downcast.

JAPANESE: That's what I was afraid of. You're the one who came up with this idea. We knew the story, but the story had no ending. You said you'd go give it one. You're the one who suggested the whole thing. Now I've gone and made this bomb and everything. What do you expect me to do?

CHONG: It's all Katsura's. . . .

LENNON: She'll do whatever you say. Isn't that the way it's always been?

CHONG: She's waiting for the Beatles. She didn't really want to go through with this in the first place.

All of a sudden Japanese begins to participate in the play. Roughly, almost violently, he covers Katsura's body with his own and begins to speak as if he were Chong.

JAPANESE: Listen. This is a play. From now on you have to play your part in it. Okay, now look at me. I'm Chong. Chong. Chong. Chong. Chong. Chong! A Korean. And you're Katsura. You are a Japanese girl named Katsura. I'm Korean and you're Japanese. That's why your father isn't going back to the peninsula. Why should he? He's having a nice cup of hot tea with your mother and waiting for you to come home. But your old man's in for a surprise, because Chong's going to murder you. Rape you and then murder you. Next Chong will be murdered by the Japanese. That's the play. We have to act it out. We have to see it through. Yes, we have to act the play out to the end. We have to be faithful to its pattern until the curtain falls and the house lights come up.

STARR: You passed me by. You didn't even know I existed. Yes, perhaps that's the way it happened. You didn't see that as I watched you walk down that narrow, dusty road I imagined myself jumping you from behind.

HARRISON: You hate me, don't you? You hate me! You hate me, I can tell. But maybe that's why. Maybe I try so hard to hold you because you try so hard to get away. Maybe someone else might have done as well, someone else who pretended I didn't exist.

STARR: Hate me! It doesn't matter. Hate me! I'm going to kill you. Struggle! Try to run away. Try as if your life depended upon it!

JAPANESE: She ran away. My mother and the others tried to run away. But your old man . . . your old man! He sits smoking his pipe in that big house on the hill. He's waiting for his daughter to come home, and he's beginning to get worried because it's late. That's your old man today. But in the yellow distance of an all but forgotten past, it was your old man who dragged my mother by the hair from her hut and did just what I'm doing! (*He fondles Katsura's thighs, and his tone changes suddenly.*) Is that the way it was, Katsura? Can you believe it? Can you perform a play like this and really believe it? Don't you think it's ridiculous? Chong? The very idea that he could

ever be a Korean! Katsura, you understand, don't you? You've understood for a long time. He failed. Failed! He brought you here and
tried to make you play opposite his imitation Korean. But as luck
would have it . . . (*he laughs convulsively.*) . . . as luck would have it,
your father, bless his soul, your father really was a Korean! (*His
laughter grows louder.*) That really threw him for a loop. Like some
idiot he tried to reconcile his fantasies with the facts. His little play
got all caught up in itself! What a mess! Can you believe it? Fantas-
tic! Katsura, can you believe it?

*Japanese goes on laughing. He buries his face in Katsura's crotch, his
whole body shaking with laughter. His hands move spasmodically over
Katsura's body. Katsura groans quietly, pleasurably, her body responding to the stimulation, increasingly . . .*

JAPANESE (*lifting his head, in a small voice*): Katsura, keep your eyes
closed. There's nothing to see. There's no such person as Chong. It
was only make-believe. Stupid play-acting. A common . . . ordinary
. . . KATSURA!!!

Katsura draws a sudden, deep breath. It sounds like a cry of anguish.

KATSURA: Beatles! I've been waiting so long! Finally . . . finally! . . .

CHONG: Katsura! . . .

KATSURA: I knew it. I just knew that someday I'd have a wonderful
dinner with John, George, Paul, and Ringo in the dining room of the
ship, with freshly caught fish and sweet wine. That was all I wanted.
I'd sleep with you in turn and have your children one by one. But by
that time you'd be gone. I'd be satisfied with just one dinner and a
night on the high seas, sleeping with one of you and then another.
Then smiling, wearing a long, white dress, I'd take our four children
out for a stroll. I'd be proud of my soft, gentle, tummy, and I'd sing
the song I made in it.

Katsura greedily embraces Japanese.

JAPANESE (*to Chong*): It was on the beach. You never knew. The two of
us looked far out to sea for a long time. "It's a yacht. It may arrive
here any minute," she said and invited me to join her.

STARR (*disappointed*): You're not going to try to escape after all! You're
not going to hate me, are you!

LENNON (*to Chong*): You strangle Katsura.

MC CARTNEY: I murder you.

HARRISON: Let me at the son of a bitch!

STARR: Get him!

JAPANESE: Please understand. I really don't care what happens to you. The reason I've worked so hard to help you with this play has had nothing to do with the little crime you hoped to mimic.

LENNON (*laughing*): Crime? The murder of a schoolgirl? Chickenshit!

CHONG: Katsura! You've been after Katsura from the first!

HARRISON: Big deal!

The Quartet moves away from Katsura, apparently having lost interest in her.

KATSURA: Hold me, Paul. Hold me, John. Hold me, George and Ringo!

JAPANESE: I touched her tummy. You're listening, aren't you? Her tummy taught me how to make my bomb. I'm afraid it won't do for you to be stabbed to death. It wouldn't do for you to die peacefully, reassured by the blood flowing from your body. You have to be blown limb from limb. Because it's all your fault!

CHONG: Yes, the bomb . . . the bomb will be fine. Now!

JAPANESE: I knew from the first. I knew you wouldn't be able to go through with it. You couldn't even take Katsura. Do you deny it? You've never even held her!

KATSURA (*murmuring*): Come to me . . . come . . . come to me, everyone. Touch my tummy . . . listen to its song.

CHONG: Katsura. . . .

Chong leaps at Japanese. Japanese, however, is unresisting; he gives Katsura up without a struggle.

JAPANESE: Too late, my friend. Much, much too late.

Chong straddles Katsura. McCartney, Harrison, Lennon, and Starr once again turn their attention to the play.

KATSURA: Who is it? Who are you?

CHONG: It's me.

KATSURA: Chong?

CHONG: Yes, it's me.

LENNON (*coolly*): You have to do things in order. You mustn't kill her yet.

HARRISON: First you have to rape her.

CHONG: This is my revenge for what your father. . . .

JAPANESE (*scornfully*): Her feet are cold inside her white bobby-socks.

STARR (*angrily*): I was bored beyond words. I want my summer back!

CHONG (*suppressing his emotions as much as possible*): I've been cold every summer of my life.

KATSURA: I wrote in my diary. . . .

LENNON: Invisible diary. . . nonexistent diary. Say it! Say you hate me! I'm a Korean!

QUARTET: Diarrhean Korean smells like shit! Not worth a penny or his weight in spit!

KATSURA: I mustn't wear the red high heels. I mustn't wait for the Beatles, either. That's what you said. You made an awful face. Every night I read my old diary and try not to sing the lollipop song. I'm just a simple girl with a wandering glance and a soft tummy. . . a girl like any other, that's all. But I knew. I knew, because I'm the type who thinks with her tummy, that you'd never be able to touch me. The Japanese bit my shoulder. It hurt terribly, but that's his way of being kind. He tries hard to set me afire with his flickering flame. That's his way of being kind. But you're different. You have no flame of your own. You're lame. You came limping to me out of loneliness. You spoke to me self-consciously of a murder I'd heard about long ago. Before I knew it you had things arranged so that on a certain Sunday, you and the Japanese and I would march out of the subway, arms locked and whistling, onto a broad avenue. And a bomb would come floating down almost like a joke and land in front of us. . . . But it's too late. You didn't make it. This is where our paths part. They have to. The Beatles are coming for me!

CHONG: The velocity of the falling bomb . . . a back alley. . . a knife . . . the peninsula . . . noise, laughing voices. . . .

The stage goes black for an instant. Out of the darkness Starr's voice, "Departed and deceased!" A Beatles song begins, and then the lights come up again.

Chong lies with a knife in his chest. He is dead. Katsura is beside Chong. The Quartet and Japanese stand around them.

KATSURA: Reading an imaginary book. "'Chong' leaves on a lonely journey. 'Chong' doesn't ride a bicycle or take a boat. He turns his back on the others and walks toward a kindness of his own at the speed of clotting blood."

The Quartet claps enthusiastically.

LENNON: Wonderful! Really marvelous!

HARRISON (*mimicking*): "This is where our paths part. They have to. The Beatles are coming for me." Ha-ha-ha-ha!

LENNON (*to Japanese*): Looks like you've lost your part.

HARRISON: You don't have to take revenge anymore.

KATSURA: Take me with you.

LENNON: Where?

KATSURA: To Liverpool, my Liverpool, to the Emerald Peninsula.

HARRISON: Sorry. We're the Beatles, all right, but I'm afraid we're not your Beatles. (*Realizing*): That's right, I almost forgot!

Harrison looks over his shoulder at Lennon, who nods.

HARRISON: We'll introduce you to your Beatles. We'll introduce you right away. Wait one second.

Lennon and Harrison exit.

JAPANESE (*to Chong's lifeless form*): "The Japanese." It seems the time has come to return your role. You were "The Japanese" all along. It would have been better if you'd played your own part from the first. (*He produces a flag, red sun on white field, and carefully covers the corpse. Pointing*): He looks like a hero, dying like this.

KATSURA: Yes.

JAPANESE: You must be tired. You'd better rest.

KATSURA: They weren't the ones, were they?

JAPANESE: It doesn't look like it.

McCartney and Starr start to hum a funeral march. Picking up the tune, Lennon and Harrison enter carrying four white coffins.

KATSURA: Are . . . are those the Beatles?

HARRISON: I'm afraid they're no longer with us.

JAPANESE: Don't believe them, Katsura. They're lying. Those coffins are empty.

Japanese approaches the coffins and is about to open their lids.

KATSURA (*firmly*): Don't!

JAPANESE: But. . . .

KATSURA: Please, just leave them as they are.

HARRISON: Now you see, we're movers. Are you satisfied? We've brought these four parcels, just as we said.

KATSURA: You've come at last. But you're dead! Why? Why? (*She bursts into tears over the coffins.*)

HARRISON (*staring at Katsura*): What's she bawling about? Maybe it's that onion.

KATSURA: Why did they have to die?

LENNON: It's hard to say, actually. It was a cold night. All four of them went at once.

JAPANESE: That's ridiculous! You're back to playing games.

KATSURA: They were my Beatles. I'd waited for them so long!

HARRISON: Of course.

KATSURA: They came from the peninsula, didn't they?

LENNON: Couldn't be sure, actually. Perhaps.

KATSURA: Was the peninsula emerald-colored?

LENNON: Perhaps.

KATSURA: Were there open pastures at the foot of rolling hills?

LENNON: Perhaps.

KATSURA: And horses grazing?

LENNON: Perhaps.

KATSURA: Grass with flowers?

LENNON: Perhaps!! (*The Quartet exchange glances and burst out laughing.*)

KATSURA: Oh.

STARR (*still laughing*): Come on, everybody, let's have a funeral, a double funeral for Chong and the Beatles, how about it?

McCartney puts on a record.

STARR: Let's dance!

LENNON: That's the ticket! (*To Japanese*): Come on, you too! (*To Katsura*): You, too! We'll have a wild funeral for our departed friends!

KATSURA (*softly*): Wait.

Everyone looks at Katsura.

KATSURA: Just now . . . there was something there. It looked like a bird.

Everyone stares at Katsura for a moment, then goes back to dancing. The song is "A Hard Day's Night" by the Beatles.

Curtain.

JOHN SILVER:
THE BEGGAR OF LOVE

Commentary

Japan is the Truth of the World, Foundation of Human Salvation, and the Finality of the World.

Tanaka Chigaku (1861–1939)[1]

The door to the toilet stall swings open. There stands Long John Silver, the noonday sea roaring at his back. Silver beckons the haggard urbanites who await him beyond, to Manchuria and the promise of salvation. In *My Beatles*, Satoh Makoto had discovered the influence of the Japanese gods in recent political events. In *John Silver: The Beggar of Love*, Kara Jūrō describes the continuing attraction of those gods in Tokyo's urban jungle and warns that their promise of immortality may yet have political implications.

Anomaly and Contradiction

The post-shingeki movement rejected both the West and Western drama as a model. This rejection derived not only from the new movement's disaffection with orthodox shingeki, which had idealized European drama, but also from the experience of 1960 and the desire to affirm an autonomous Japanese culture. Cultural autonomy was a logical corollary to the political autonomy that the New Left had sought for Japan by opposing the Mutual Security pact and Japan's *de facto* alliance with the United States.

Post-shingeki troupes denied shingeki's implicit acceptance of the notion of Western universalism and Japanese particularity, the concept that the West somehow constitutes the mainstream of world history and Japan, if not exactly an aberration, little more than a special case. Kara Jūrō made the point explicitly when he blasphemed, "What have we to learn from Europe? All they have to show us is their women, and they bleed 30 days a month!"[2]

The post-shingeki movement's rejection of the West as a model and ideal was accompanied by a new insistence on the legitimacy of particularity and the value of being an anomaly. Saeki Ryūkō expressed this new attitude when he described his meeting with French critic Jean-Marie Domenach.

> The reason for my frustration was that, while I was developing one version of the ideas behind our black tent [theatre], I was doing so in the spirit of our movement—the point of which is not to achieve universality and wide understanding. Regardless of how much countervailing power they seek to amass, movements that seek universality are universal by virtue of that very fact. To us the problem is rather how to dismantle "the will to universality" as a mandatory structure of interaction that rears its ugly head in words and signs every time an attempt at communication is made. The problem is to maintain the traces left by our objections to systematized theatre, our movement, in a constant state of jeopardy even as we intone them. This is the perpetual motion mechanism of contradiction. . . . In our terminology, that which embodies the perpetual motion mechanism of contradiction is an anomaly. . . . What Domenach was unable to comprehend was that he was encountering an anomalous structure that made radical use of universal terms for the express purpose of destroying universal language.[3]

This reaffirmation of the legitimacy of particularity and the aggressive embrace of anomaly and contradiction is characteristic of the entire post-shingeki movement. It has served an essential function: to allow the movement, and its playwrights in particular, to treat all those irrational, anomalous, particularistic aspects of life and thought that modern drama had either refused or been unable to explore.

The Situation Theatre

If the Youth Art Theatre provided the transition from orthodox shingeki to the post-shingeki movement, Kara Jūrō and his Situation Theatre (*Jōkyō gekijō*) did more than anyone else to initiate the movement itself.[4] Kara had joined the Youth Art Theatre in 1962, the year he graduated from Meiji University, but he resigned a year later, disillusioned with the hierarchy of the troupe and uncertain of his prospects in it.[5] With a group of friends, he immediately founded the Situation Theatre.

As the name implies, Kara has been deeply influenced by the existentialist thought of Jean-Paul Sartre.[6] Indeed the troupe's first production was the French playwright's *Respectful Prostitute*. Kara's career has been characterized by the skillful creation and manipulation of situations; and his "theory of privileged entities" (*tokkenteki nikutairon*), Kara's fundamental theory of theatre, also reveals his existentialist disposition. "If there is such a thing as 'dramatic imagination,'" Kara writes,

> it may be the dramatic force active inside each actor, each playwright, before expression begins that urges toward *a negation of reality*. When, through the activities of those involved in creation upon the stage, this force takes form and proliferates, it manifests itself as the privileged entityship of the actor or of the stage itself.[7]

A devotee of surrealism who experienced André Breton's *Nadja* as "divine revelation,"[8] Kara founded his theatre on the proposition that "reality" is nothing more than an arbitrary social construction that can be challenged and altered by art.

In 1967, the Situation Theatre mounted its first performance in the red tent that has since become its symbol. The tent was Kara's way of negating reality. By embedding it as an anomaly in the sinews of the city, Kara sought to manipulate the prevailing situation and create a new one.

Punctuated today by the spires of skyscrapers, Shinjuku in 1967 was just beginning to emerge as the symbol of the Japanese megalopolis. In direct opposition to the manifest aspirations of the urban environment, Kara's troupe pitched its tent in the precincts of the traditional Hanazono Shrine and performed *Koshimaki O-Sen: giri-ninjō irohanihoetohen* (Petticoat O-Sen: A Rhapsody of Love and Duty), a lewd, chaotic drama reminiscent of kabuki plays of yore.[9] It was an incendiary act that enflamed the tempers of city officials and warmed the hearts of the younger generation.[10]

John Silver: The Beggar of Love

John Silver: The Beggar of Love embodies and articulates Kara's situational, existential approach to the theatre. The play takes place in a public toilet. At least that is the popular construction placed on the site. According to Kara, however, there is no reason why it could not be construed equally well as a library or a cabaret. According to Kara, the social construction of reality is merely arbitrary and may be discarded or altered at will.

While no less arbitrary, the reinterpretation of the public lavatory as the Korean Cabaret Pu-shee[11] is not without rhyme or reason. It corresponds to the needs of its present inhabitants, a motley crew of nondescripts barely eking out a living in the urban jungle. Miss Safety, the Guardian, Taguchi and the others are all figures for whom the pressures and loneliness of urban life are as crushing as the pressures of war were for Yasuda Keita in *Kaison the Priest of Hitachi*. They long to be saved from their sense of purposelessness, their superfluity; they dream of a time when men were men and their possibilities were unlimited.

That time was the heyday of Japanese imperialism in Asia. Miss Safety reveals that he is in fact the former buccaneer Amazō of the S.S. Brilliant, and the W.C. becomes a trapdoor in time. Like Alice slipping through the rabbit hole, Amazō and his compatriots return through the toilet stall to the magical land of Pu-shee, their idealized vision of Manchuria, where they relive their days of adventure, extracting gold treasure from the mouths of their victims.

When the scene shifts back to the present, the reunited buccaneers display their treasure, the proof of their piracy in the twenty-five years since the war. All they have to show for their peacetime piracy, however, are children's shoes and overdue parking tickets, symbols of their pathetic quest for love and recognition in the postwar world. There is nothing inherently wrong with their treasure: it represents years of toil and dedication and is valuable as such to its owner. But, as Umada says, they've lost their common treasure, the shared values and sense of common purpose that once bound them together and made them feel truly alive. "We only move farther and father apart, we drifting pirates of the present," Umada laments.

Amazō refuses to acquiesce so easily. "Just as you can become Silver by the way you make your entrance," he says, "so you can become

Silver by the way you leave the stage." All is not lost, in other words. One can make a bid for immortality in death as well as in life. Amazō dies in a last, desperate attempt to return to Manchuria and the promise of eternal life it offered.

Long John Silver of Pu-shee

Like Kaison, Kara's Long John Silver is an immortal hero who wanders endlessly through time begging for love and forgiveness. He is a god, an archetype of survival. By "becoming Silver," by assimilating himself to his transhistorical mode of being, a man can transcend his death and achieve immortality. But, as in Kaison's case, assimilation to mythic time is not without its cost.

The Beggar of Love is one of Kara's "Manchuria plays" and one in a series in which John Silver appears.[12] It may seem incongruous at first for Robert Louis Stevenson's hero of *Treasure Island* to show up in Manchuria, but Silver had a knack for survival, after all; and if Minamoto-no-Yoshitsune could be reborn on the continent as Genghis Khan, what is to prevent Silver from appearing there in the 1930s?

John Silver is modeled after the Japanese "soldiers of fortune" (*tairiku rōnin*, literally "masterless samurai of the continent") who had migrated to the Asian continent around the turn of the twentieth century. Silver is an extrapolation from men like Uchida Ryōhei (1874–1937), a founder of the right-wing Amur River Society (*Kokuryūkai*). Uchida had traveled to Korea in 1894 in search of adventure and had gone on to help lay the groundwork for Japan's annexation of Korea and the creation of the puppet kingdom of Manchukuo.

Kara could not simply condemn this history of imperialism, for he understood all too well its allure. His father had been fascinated by the romance of the Manchurian "new frontier";[13] his maternal grandfather had worked for the South Manchurian Railroad; and his mother, whom Kara describes as "the pampered daughter of Japanese imperialism," had been raised in Manchuria and Korea.[14] Moreover, Japan's acquisition of Manchuria was motivated by more than a simple quest for *Lebensraum*. It had a definite soteriological dimension. According to Ishiwara Kanji, its leading ideologist, Japanese imperialism in Manchuria would lead not only to the salvation of Japan, but to the redemption of all mankind.[15] "Japan must be victorious," he wrote, "not for the sake of her own national interest, but for the salvation of the world."[16] Japanese imperialism was justified because, by making Japan the dominant power in Asia, it would "mean the end of centuries of strife and the establishment of universal peace."[17]

Manchuria was the linchpin in Ishiwara's ideology. "It is only by bringing about Japanese-Manchurian cooperation and Japanese-Chinese friendship," he wrote, "that the Japanese people can become rulers of Asia and be prepared to wage the final and decisive war against the various white races."[18] This "final war" would usher in the millennium:

> The last war in human history is approaching—Nichiren's "titanic world conflict, unprecedented in human history"—which will be the gateway to a golden age of human culture, a synthesis of East and West, the last and highest stage of human civilization.[19]

In short, the immortality John Silver offers is the ultimate immortality of the messianic age, when "a new world, free from old age, death, decomposition and corruption, living eternally, increasing eternally, when the dead shall rise, when immortality shall come to the living, when the world shall be perfectly renewed" will be realized.[20] It is an immortality not unlike that promised by another contemporary ideology, Nazism. Satoh Makoto has compared Ishiwara Kanji to Joseph Goebbels and the eschatology of Ishiwara's "final war" to the Nazis' "final solution."[21] The gold teeth in *The Beggar of Love* evoke the image of the gold teeth extracted from gassing victims at Auschwitz; and the Kara's "pirates," for all their humanity, are not unlike former Nazis reminiscing about "the good old days."

Kara is fully aware of these implications. The power of his work derives from its aggressive moral ambiguity, from Kara's willingness to accept imperialism and even mass murder at face value, as conceivable and tested methods for achieving salvation and defying death.[22] The question then becomes, can Long John Silver, the Manchurian messiah, redeem those who await him? Can assimilation to the Silver archetype, a recrudescence of chiliastic imperialism, save contemporary Japanese from meaningless and anomie in the urban jungle?

The answer Kara gives is ambiguous. At the end of Act Two, the one-legged MP who is the manifestation of Silver in the play appears, but he is stabbed to death by Umada, Ōtani, and Amazō. When the curtain rises on Act Three, however, it is the lonely Guardian who lies dead on the ground, a knife protruding from his side. Today Long John Silver is the superfluous man, a pathetic failure unable to save himself much less anyone else.

In the final moments of the play, however, the one-legged MP appears again, continuing his eternal quest for Orchid Flower, his one true love. He is immortal, an authentic transhistorical figure kept alive by the dreams, longing, and despair of the Japanese people. Kara is saying that even though Silver can no longer save, he will nonetheless continue to wander eternally, begging for love, because people like Taguchi of Asahi Life or the lone passerby who enters the lavatory at the end of the play need to dream. Chiliastic Japanese imperialism, piracy on a grand scale, may be dormant in contemporary Japan, but it is not extinct. That is the message of Kara's play.

What Became of Kara Jūrō?

Not long after he completed *The Beggar of Love*, Kara abandoned the Long John Silver and Manchuria motifs and began to write works intended for production abroad. Unlike Terayama Shūji, however, who had become the darling of the European avant-garde and was making annual trips to Europe at this time, Kara and his troupe chose the Third World and traveled to Korea (1972), Bangladesh (1973), and Palestinian refugee camps in Lebanon and Syria (1974). Kara had come to understand the limitations of the salvific myths of the ultranationalist right, and he was looking for people and places where vivifying myths of national salvation still fired people's minds.

After his trip to the Middle East, however, Kara's drama changed again. It became more realistic and nostalgic, depicting the world of Kara's childhood in downtown Tokyo. And, while continuing to use moral ambiguity as a weapon, describing homosexuality in Shitaya Mannen-chō and cannibalism in Paris, for example, his work also was reduced drastically in scale.[23] Kara had found in the Palestinian camps a world where salvific national myth and real politics were inextricably and uncritically linked. He found in the Palestinians an ideology of national salvation like the one he had described in his plays, a vivifying myth that justified every act, including international piracy (terrorism) and murder. Whatever his feelings about the political situation in the Middle East, he was repelled by the experience of a situation he could not negate, a reality that manipulated him, a world the theatre

234 JOHN SILVER: THE BEGGAR OF LOVE

could not alter. Given the choice between submitting to "reality" as the Palestinians construed it and making his theatre a vehicle of anti-Zionist propaganda, or preserving the independent, countervailing power of the theatre, Kara chose the latter.

Notes

1. Tanaka Chigaku was highly influential in shaping the thought of Ishiwara Kanji, architect and ideologist of Manchukuo. Mark R. Peattie, *Ishiwara Kanji and Japan's Confrontation with the West* (Princeton: Princeton University Press, 1975), p. 42.
2. Quoted in Tsuno Kaitarō, "The Tradition of Modern Theatre in Japan," *Canadian Theatre Review* (Autumn 1978), p. 8.
3. Saeki Ryūkō, *Ika suru jikan* (Shōbunsha, 1973), pp. 136–137; "On Understanding and Not Understanding," *Concerned Theatre Japan*, II(3–4):6.
4. Terayama Shūji and his *Tenjō sajiki* troupe were also highly influential. Terayama did not share the post-shingeki movement's fascination with millenarianism, however, and he remained outside of and antagonistic toward the movement.
   The particular animosity between Terayama and Kara reached a climax on December 12, 1969, when members of Terayama's troupe delivered a funeral wreath to the Situation Theatre, which was performing near their theatre. After the performance ended, Kara and his actors marched on Terayama's theatre and a scuffle ensued. Seven members of the Situation Theatre, including Kara, and two members of Tenjō sajiki, including Terayama, were arrested. They were released on December 14. For more details on Terayama and his relationship to the post-shingeki movement, see my article in *Theatre Companies of the World*, ed. William C. Young and Colby H. Kullman (Westport, CT: Greenwood Press, 1986). See also Carol Jay Sorgenfrei, "Shuji Terayama: Avant Garde Dramatist of Japan" (Ph.D. diss., University of California-Santa Barbara, 1978).
5. Senda Akihiko, *Gekiteki runessansu* (Libroport, 1983), pp. 220–223.
6. Kara has denied that he is an existentialist. See Thomas R. H. Havens, *Artist and Patron in Postwar Japan: Dance, Music, and the Visual Arts, 1955–1980* (Princeton: Princeton University Press, 1982), p. 167. Kara may not consider himself a member of any particular philosophical school, but the fundamentally existentialist nature of his thought and activities seems to me undeniable.
   For Sartre's thinking on "situation theatre" see Jean-Paul Sartre, *Sartre on Theater*, ed. Michel Contat and Michel Rybalka, tr. Frank Jellinek (New York: Pantheon, 1976).
7. Kara Jūrō, *Koshimaki O-Sen* (Gendai shichōsha, 1968), pp. 33–34. Emphasis added.
8. Senda, *Gekiteki runessansu*, p. 231.
9. Kara delighted in identifying himself with Edo period kabuki actors, who had been treated as pariahs (*kawara kojiki*) by the state and society. Ōshima Nagisa's 1968 film *Diary of a Shinjuku Thief* (*Shinjuku dorobō nikki*) vividly captures the ambiance of Shinjuku in the late sixties and Kara's iconoclastic relationship to it.
10. Kara's subversion did not stop here. On January 3, 1969, Kara pitched the red tent in the park at the west entrance to Shinjuku station and was promptly arrested for

trespassing and using public land without a permit. The incident demonstrated the provocative effect of Kara's strategy and enhanced his status among the young.

11. Pu-shee is the way I have rendered *Zumanko*. *Zumanko* is a popular misreading of *Tomankō*, the Japanese pronunciation of the name of the third-largest river in Korea, the Tuman'gang. The text is filled with puns on the name, since *manko* is a vulgar Japanese term for the female genitals equivalent to the English "pussy." Hence my translation.

12. The first John Silver play was titled simply *John Silver* and was written in 1965. Kara's "Manchurian period" extends from *Shōjo kamen* (Virgin Mask, 1969) to *Are kara no John Silver* (What Became of John Silver, 1973), the last John Silver play.

13. Yamaguchi Takeshi, *Dōjidaijin to shite no Kara Jūrō* (San'ichi shobō, 1980), p. 50.

14. Senda, *Gekiteki runessansu*, p. 210.

15. No one was more influential in the creation of Manchukuo than Ishiwara Kanji. "The motivation, the planning, and the conduct of Ishiwara Kanji were central to the conquest of Manchuria," writes Mark Peattie. (*Ishiwara Kanji*, p. 133.)

16. Peattie, *Ishiwara Kanji*, p. 57.

17. Peattie, *Ishiwara Kanji*, p. 56.

18. Peattie, *Ishiwara Kanji*, p. 166.

19. Peattie, *Ishiwara Kanji*, pp. 57–58.

20. Mircea Eliade, *The Myth of the Eternal Return or, Cosmos and History*, Willard R. Trask, tr. Bollingen Series 46 (Princeton: Princeton University Press, 1971), p. 124.

21. Satoh Makoto, *Kinema to kaijin* (Shōbunsha, 1976), pp. 182–184.

22. Lucy L. Dawidowicz observes, "'The Final Solution of the Jewish Question' in the National Socialist conception was not just another anti-Semitic undertaking, but a metahistorical program devised with an eschatological perspective. It was part of a salvational ideology that envisaged the attainment of Heaven by bringing Hell on earth." (*The War Against the Jews, 1933–1945* [New York: Bantam Books, 1976], p. xxii.)

Robert Lifton elaborates on this by saying, "One of Hitler's greatest rhetorical talents was to evoke in the German people a sense of perpetual life-or-death crisis. Always at stake was the spirit, the essence, vitality, and the purity—that is, the life-power—of the German people. And the threatening force was the Jew, by his very existence." (Robert Jay Lifton, *The Broken Connection* [New York: Simon and Schuster, 1979], p. 317.)

Thus, for the Nazis, mass murder of the Jews was a life-enhancing, life-preserving, therapeutic undertaking. Lifton undertakes a detailed analysis of this phenomenon in *The Nazi Doctors* (New York: Basic Books, 1986).

23. Respectively, *Shitaya Mannen-chō monogatari* (Parco, 1981) and *Sagawa-kun kara no tegami* (Kawade shobō shinsha, 1983), the novel for which Kara was awarded the 88th Akutagawa Prize.

John Silver:
The Beggar of Love

A PLAY

by Kara Jūrō

John Silver: The Beggar of Love (*John Silver: Ai no kojiki*) was first performed in Tokyo on August 1, 1970, beside Shibuya's Kitaya Inari Shrine. The play was performed simultaneously in Naha, Okinawa, by a second contingent of the Situation Theatre. Both productions were directed by Kara Jūrō. The text of the play appears in *Kara Jūrō zensakuhin-shū*, vol. 2 (Tōjusha, 1979). First published in the magazine *Umi* (March 1970), it is also included in two other collections of Kara's plays: *Renmujutsu* (Chūō kōronsha, 1971) and *Kyūketsuki* (Kadokawa shoten, 1975).

CAST OF CHARACTERS

Miss Safety (in reality, the former pirate Amazō)
Taguchi, a salesman for Asahi Life Insurance
Police Inspector 1 (former pirate Umada)
Police Inspector 2 (former pirate Ōtani)
Chichi the Gimp
Orchid Flower, a maiden
The Guardian
Demobilized Soldier 1
Demobilized Soldier 2
Barmaid
Patrolman 1
Patrolman 2
One-Legged MP

ACT 1
THE CABARET PU-SHEE

The scene is a dilapidated public toilet facility somewhere in the city.
The toilet stands in the shadow of tall buildings, amid a snowdrift of
litter. Only the the sound of water flushing is violent, energetic; other-
wise all is quiet. Grass sprouts from cracks in the urinal, and flies
teem in the doorway to the toilet stall at the right. A street light comes
on prematurely as late afternoon sunlight still streams through the
toilet's high window. The sound of a hurdy-gurdy drifts in from a
merry-go-round on the roof of a nearby department store.
  Miss Safety is squatting before the urinal and retching. Taguchi is
rubbing Miss Safety's back.

SAFETY: Thank you, laddy.

TAGUCHI: Is that enough?

SAFETY: Yes, that's enough, laddy.

TAGUCHI: Are you feeling better now?

SAFETY: Just leave me alone, laddy.

TAGUCHI: You really are feeling better, aren't you?

SAFETY: Hey, how come you're paying so much attention to me?

TAGUCHI: Does it annoy you?

SAFETY: I can take care of myself. I never rubbed my wife's back. How
  come you rubbed mine?

TAGUCHI: Because you didn't seem to be feeling well.

SAFETY: There's nothing wrong with me.

TAGUCHI: But you're white as a sheet.

SAFETY: Tired, that's all. Just tired. I'll bet you get exhausted when
  you're tired, too.

TAGUCHI: I suppose I do. Well, I guess I'll be getting home now.

SAFETY: Wait a minute. The portal of youth remains ajar.

TAGUCHI: What?

SAFETY: Your zipper.

TAGUCHI: Oh, I can take care of this with a snap.

SAFETY: You going home?

TAGUCHI: Yes.

SAFETY: Come on, rub my back some more.

TAGUCHI: Okay.

SAFETY: Rub my back, and I'll give you a treat.

TAGUCHI: I don't want anything.

SAFETY: As you like, but come closer.

TAGUCHI: I've really got to be going.

SAFETY: Somebody waiting for you? A woman maybe?

TAGUCHI: A woman? Insurance salesmen like me can't afford to keep women waiting.

SAFETY: Women are best kept waiting.

TAGUCHI: I live alone.

SAFETY: You must be lonely. Let me guess. The bed's never made; there are cigarette ashes all over the floor; and no woman's ever set foot in the place. You've led a serious life. Am I right?

TAGUCHI: I'm a washout!

SAFETY: What do you mean, a washout?

TAGUCHI: There's nothing special about me. I'm just average. I've been average ever since junior high school. I'm a common man who grows older and older in his little nook.

SAFETY: Nobody grows older at your age.

TAGUCHI: Yes, but the appointment book in my apartment does. The years go by and I haven't got anything to write in it.

SAFETY: Why don't you buy a new one?

TAGUCHI: But I haven't got anything to write in it.

SAFETY: You're just a late bloomer. You've got talent. You're just too cautious.

TAGUCHI: You really think so?

SAFETY: Indeed I do.

TAGUCHI: Well, I'll be going then. I have to go to the bath.

SAFETY: Which bath are you going to?

TAGUCHI: Iris Vapors across the street.

SAFETY: All the baths are closed today. It's the sixteenth, a holiday. The baths are always closed on the second Monday of the month.

TAGUCHI: The baths are closed? That's awful!

SAFETY: Awful?

TAGUCHI: I haven't got anything else to do.

SAFETY: Come hither.

TAGUCHI: Huh?

SAFETY: Come hither and rub my back.

TAGUCHI: Are you still feeling ill?

SAFETY: I want someone to pamper me.

TAGUCHI: Pamper you?

SAFETY: Look, I'm just about the sweetest man in the world. I stand out there in the withering heat dolled up like this, keeping my vigil for traffic safety. I pour my heart into my work, and for what? A measly 350 yen a day.

TAGUCHI: I understand.

SAFETY: Ah, yes, but not everyone understands like you. They think I'm some kind of cricket in winter.

TAGUCHI: Makes my teeth chatter.

SAFETY: Something wrong with your teeth?

TAGUCHI: No, you were saying you were a cricket in winter, and . . .

SAFETY: A prodigal son who's over the hill, that's what they think. Come on, rub my back. The sun's almost set, but I'm so . . . I'm still warm, see?

TAGUCHI (*touching him*): Yes.

SAFETY: I retain heat. When the sun goes down, I feel like I'm going to burn up.

TAGUCHI: You're pretty warm all right. You think you're breaking out?

SAFETY: Yes! In a rash of love!

TAGUCHI: Love!?

SAFETY: You think it's funny?

TAGUCHI: No. I just never heard a man use the word so *distinctly* before.

SAFETY: Embarrassed?

TAGUCHI: Sort of.

SAFETY: Alas, I fear I might perish from this rash of love.

Taguchi is at a loss.

SAFETY: Come hither and rub my back.

TAGUCHI: Yes, but the bath. . . .

SAFETY: If you don't mind a shower, you can take one here.

TAGUCHI: A shower of piss? No thanks!

SAFETY: I'm surprised at you! I'd never suggest anything so vulgar. We'll collect water from the tap in that funnel, and I'll splash it on you through the window.

TAGUCHI: But this is a public toilet!

SAFETY: Don't worry, nobody'll come. I arranged with the city government to make this my study after six. Make yourself at home. Ah,
that year, that summer, just you and me and the Sea of Japan!
Benbow, Benbow!

TAGUCHI: Huh?

SAFETY: Benbow, Binbow!

TAGUCHI: What?

SAFETY: Binbow, Binbow!

TAGUCHI: What's "Binbow, Binbow!"?

SAFETY: Oh, darling, listen to the sound of the waves! This is our
Fortress Binbow!

TAGUCHI: You changed your tone so *drastically*!

SAFETY: I can't help it. My poor heart is all a-flutter!

TAGUCHI: See! There you go again with that "heart" business.

SAFETY: Don't you like things to be a little drastic?

TAGUCHI: When they have to be, I suppose.

SAFETY: So you prefer the inevitable to be drastic?

TAGUCHI: When the inevitable is rooted in necessity, yes.

SAFETY: And yet, I am as rootless as a leaf in the wind! (*He sings*):

> O Flint of Fortress Binbow,
> His tail was cold or was it hot?
> Did he stand or did he not?
> Take a word from me.
>
> O screams to rend the ocean waves
> Across the sea, the vast Black Sea,
> What was it like, what did you see?
> Flint of Fortress Binbow.
>
> O scenes so terrible, hard to believe,
> Over the lull, black motionless lull,
> What did you hear, what could you cull,
> Flint laid low with fear?
>
> O Flint of Fortress Binbow,
> His tail was cold or was it hot?

Did he stand or did he not?
Take a word from me.

TAGUCHI: I was sure you were going to sing some silly ditty after that
"Binbow" business, but the song's better than I expected!
SAFETY: How about rubbing my back some more?
TAGUCHI: Have you considered using a vibrator?
SAFETY: It's better by hand.
TAGUCHI: But it's tiring.
SAFETY: Tiring? What's that got to do with it? Why, I'm always rub-
bing him down.
TAGUCHI: Huh?
SAFETY: The wall.
TAGUCHI: You mean you give the wall rubdowns?
SAFETY: It just stands there all day, and at night it complains about
feeling run down. Look, even the toilet bowl is yawning. So I give
them a rubdown, a massage. It's the only decent thing to do.
*A Man in his fifties enters to relieve himself. He stands before the
urinal, shifting his weight from one leg to the other. This intrusion
does not escape Safety, who sneaks up behind him.*
SAFETY (*at the top of his lungs*): Waaaa!!!!
OLD MAN: Aaaaa!!!! What, what?
SAFETY: Who said you could piss in the sink?
OLD MAN: What?
SAFETY: You heard me.
OLD MAN: This is a public toilet.
SAFETY: It's me house.
OLD MAN: You house?
SAFETY: I lives here. It's where I makes me living.
OLD MAN: Here?
SAFETY: You're pissing in the kitchen sink!
OLD MAN: You must be kidding! I was here yesterday. In fact, I've been
peeing here for years!
SAFETY: But this be me house after six, starting today.
OLD MAN: Come, come, my friend, it's not as if the war just ended.
There's no reason why people have to live in public toilets.
SAFETY: You've got a lot of nerve, standing up and saying that. What

makes you think you know what "the postwar period" meant—to yourself much less to me? I'm living here, now—that's who I am; it's my identity. Somebody's probably written it down someplace: "What is man without flowers?" That . . . that's the point!

OLD MAN: You keep this up and I'll see that the police hear about you!

SAFETY: I'm not doing anything the cops would want to know.

OLD MAN: You are!

SAFETY: Am not!

OLD MAN: Are!

SAFETY: Am not, was not, have not!

OLD MAN: Ah, so you're studying grammar!

SAFETY: What's wrong with that?

OLD MAN: You're not taking this seriously. You just want to make a fool of me because I'm a security guard—one of *The Guardians*.

SAFETY: But ever since *The Guardians* came on TV, security guards have been the biggest celebrities in the city!

OLD MAN: That's what everybody thinks, but we're really just a bunch of errand boys. When *The Guardians* first came on, everybody in my family saw me as you do. But then they caught on that I wasn't like them. I didn't think it was gonna last. I mean, I don't wear such good suits. After a while, they stopped watching so often. They watched less and less. They stopped watching altogether. One look at me and they'd start making faces. You think they hate me? How about it, does everybody hate me? Whenever I pick up a pair of chopsticks; whenever I hold my briefcase; whenever I put on my shoes; whenever I open the front door; whenever I take off my hat; whenever I get ready for bed, everybody's thinking: "Ah, the Guardians were never like that!" (*He is sobbing.*)

SAFETY: Don't you think you're overreacting?

OLD MAN: Overreacting! My wife says she doesn't care if I ever came home, Sakiko the bastard! "Just try stacking yourself up against the Guardians!" she says. And Ichirō, the little fart, he laughs at me, "Go on, get on the tube and see!" he says.

SAFETY: Better just ignore her.

OLD MAN: I can't ignore her! She says I shouldn't come home any more!

SAFETY: You think she's serious?

OLD MAN: Sure she's serious! I tried going home once and she threw my briefcase out in the rain! Sakiko the bastard!

SAFETY: Seems to have a mean streak, doesn't she?

OLD MAN: Hey, you understand things pretty good! After that—the night I had my briefcase thrown out in the rain—I went down to the TV studio.

SAFETY: What for?

OLD MAN: I read in *TV Guide* that they were doing *The Guardians* live. So I ran straight through the lobby and into the studio. Sure enough, they'd already started. Just at the end there's this place where the music goes, "Da-da-da-dang!" and the head Guardian says, "Society is to blame!" right? Well, this is where I come in, I thought, and I ran out, screaming, "The family is to blame!"—but before I could stack myself up against the Guardians, I ran smack into this camera panning in from the side.

SAFETY: But you got on the tube, right?

OLD MAN: Just my hand.

SAFETY: Oh.

OLD MAN: That's not the half of it. The camera fell over, and now I have to be on *The Guardians* till I die in order to pay for it. Sakiko the bastard, she won't even give me money for cigarettes!

SAFETY: Aah!

OLD MAN: You sighed!

SAFETY: Huh?

OLD MAN: Fink! You're getting fed up with me, aren't you. You think I'm ludicrous! (*He feverishly tries to hide his face.*) Ah! I should never have confided in you! How could I have been such a fool? Stop it! Stop it! Don't look at me that way!!!

SAFETY: Hey, take it easy!

OLD MAN (*in the tone and manner of a sportscaster*): Ah! He's raising his voice. Before you know it he'll be raising his fist to strike!

SAFETY: Fool!

OLD MAN (*hand to his head*): Listen to that, ladies and gentlemen! Such malicious abuse! He belches it forth without regard to truth or falsehood! The man's completely out of control!

SAFETY: Look who's talking.

TAGUCHI (*standing apart from the others*): You'd better leave him alone.

SAFETY: You've got a point.

OLD MAN (*glaring at Taguchi suspiciously out of the corner of his eye*): There are two of them, ladies and gentlemen. They're conspiring against me!

SAFETY: Shut up, will you!

OLD MAN: See! Two against one! They're threatening my life! Now, ladies and gentlemen, that's what I call teamwork!

A young girl in a sailor-suit enters.

GIRL: I'm home!

SAFETY: Orchid Flower!

OLD MAN: My goodness, ladies and gentlemen, a most attractive young girl has just come home to this dreadful place. What could it mean? What should I do? Let's switch down to the batter's box!

GIRL (*to Safety*): Who's he?

Old Man stares at Safety and Girl.

SAFETY: He's a one-man TV station.

OLD MAN (*as if taking up the microphone again*): Well now, batter's box, did you hear that? Yes, yes, we heard it.

GIRL: Oh, by the way, there's someone here to see you. I brought him with me.

SAFETY: Who is it, Orchid Flower?

The face of one of the Guardians appears in the entrance.

OLD MAN: Oh my God! It's him!

Chichi the Gimp enters. He rolls himself in on a low wagon. He is wearing a Guardian mask cut from the cover of a weekly magazine.

CHICHI (*removing his mask and speaking with a heavy accent*): Good evening, chentlemen, my tear. Maybe it too late for introduction, but time is money, no? I am wanderer, Chichi the Gimp.

GIRL: My name is Orchid Flower.

TAGUCHI: I'm Taguchi of Asahi Life.

CHICHI (*to Old Man*): And you, my friend?

SAFETY: He's a superfluous Guardian.

ALL: Superfluous, eh?

OLD MAN (*reeling*): What solidarity! A veritable flood of vituperation!

Oh, Sakiko, why must I be made a fool of by these scum in this stinky hole?

SAFETY: Oh, go back to Sakiko, Mr. Guardian.

OLD MAN: Listen, I'll get you for this! From now on I'm Guardian the Avenger! Oh! Now I'm making a fool of myself!

Old Man exits leaving four people on the stage. Beyond the window it is night. All are silent.

SAFETY: Orchid Flower, you'd better get ready to open up.

GIRL: Yes, sir. (*She takes off her sailor-suit and begins to don a Korean costume in a corner to the right.*)

Chichi and Safety look on in silence.

TAGUCHI (*approaching Girl*): He said something about opening up. What are you going to open?

GIRL (*as she is changing*): Huh?

SAFETY: Orchid Flower, give Mr. Taguchi a drink.

GIRL: Yes, sir. (*She fills a glass from a bottle on the shelf and flings it at Taguchi.*)

TAGUCHI: Listen, you're in junior high school, aren't you?

GIRL: Yes, sir—eighth grade, middle course, Peers Junior High School.

TAGUCHI: And evenings you "open up" here, is that right?

GIRL: Yes, sir.

TAGUCHI: And what exactly do you open?

GIRL: A Korean cabaret.

TAGUCHI: A Korean cabaret!?

GIRL: Beginning tonight, this is the Korean cabaret Pu-shee. (*She sings*):

> Just twixt China and Korea
> You'll find the lands of Pu-shee.
> Lesser Pu-shee and Greater Pu-shee
> As deep as deep can be.

She does not even glance at Taguchi.

> You'll find not a drop of water
> There in the Lesser Pu-shee;

But it'll drown a man in minutes,
Be he six or five-foot three.

Go strike it rich in Pu-shee: sell life insurance to the drowning men of
Pu-shee. (*She hangs the paper lantern of the Cabaret Pu-shee over
the entrance to the public toilet. The flickering light of the candle
dances over her face. Staring at it she sings*):

With each spring I remember
The flower that fell in Pu-shee.
Engulfed as she bloomed, she mastered
All forty-eight ways to please.
Then her desolate flesh washed ashore,
Beneath the rainbow that followed the storm.

(*Abruptly, to Taguchi*): Don't just stand there, go out and do the
shopping—we've got nothing to serve with the drinks.
TAGUCHI: Shopping?
GIRL: I noticed on my way home from school. They're having a special
on popcorn on the Candy Cane Lane.
CHICHI: Coincidence, coincidence! I bought some on my way over.
Catch! (*He takes a bag of popcorn out of his wagon and tosses it to
Girl.*)
GIRL: How nice of you, Mr. Chichi the Gimp. (*To Taguchi*): All right,
then go find a swallow's nest for the soup.
TAGUCHI: Where?
GIRL: Up the smokestack in Kita-Senju.
TAGUCHI: You've got to be kidding!
GIRL: Climb it and tell them Orchid Flower sent you.
CHICHI: Pardon me, but I brought nest, too. Here! (*He tosses the nest to
Orchid Flower.*)
GIRL: But you're a cripple, Mr. Chichi the Gimp. How did you climb the
chimney?
CHICHI: Didn't have to. Nest blessing of urban sun.
GIRL: A blessing, huh?
TAGUCHI: Much obliged, Mr. Chichi the Gimp.
CHICHI: Don't mention it, Asahi Life.

GIRL (*to Taguchi*): Go and get some french-fried fireflies then.
TAGUCHI: Is the sight of me so distasteful?
GIRL: What's that?
TAGUCHI: My presence, it offends you, doesn't it?
GIRL: Young men depress me.
TAGUCHI: I'm not in your way, am I?
GIRL: Isn't it time you got back to your office?
TAGUCHI: I never thought I'd hear you say that!
GIRL: I'm not woman enough, is that it?
TAGUCHI: Just be quiet now.
GIRL: If I'm quiet, the first thing you'll say is "Talk to me!"
CHICHI: Now, now, Orchid Flower, no quarreling before you even open the Pu-shee.
GIRL: All right, Mr. Chichi the Gimp. (*To Taguchi*): Just don't be hanging around me, that's all.
Girl goes and stands beneath the lantern at the entrance. She leans languorously against the wall and dangles a cigarette from her lips.
  Taguchi remains rigidly erect. Behind him there is the roar of water flushing in the toilet stall.
  Chichi rolls himself over to Safety.
SAFETY: Didn't take you long to find me, did it, Chichi?
CHICHI: It took some searching.
SAFETY: Didn't think you were still alive.
CHICHI: You happy?
SAFETY: Are you?
CHICHI: Nothing make Chichi happy anymore. But I figure I meet up with you again someday.
SAFETY: What happened to your legs?
CHICHI: Lost legs running after daily bread. Sure picked great spot for your place, though, didn't you?
SAFETY: Yeah, close to the harbor, too.
CHICHI: Harbor?
SAFETY: Just behind here.
CHICHI: Superhighway commission building's behind here.
SAFETY: To all outward appearances. But look, Chichi, you can smell the salt breezes!
CHICHI: You trying to remind me of ships again?

SAFETY: Chichi, this is the unforgettable Pu-shee!

CHICHI: What you make me do this time?

SAFETY: Come on, what did I ever make you do? I'm not such a big deal.

CHICHI: You our old saber wound.

SAFETY: Wound?

CHICHI: Our horrible old wound.

SAFETY: What is this, twenty questions?

CHICHI (*suddenly losing his accent*): I always used to think that as a man grew older, so would his wounds. But a man's history's like his old lady's box. The flesh gets fatter in its own sweet way, but the wound stays open, wreaking of the sea.

SAFETY: Just take a look at me, Chichi the Gimp. About all Miss Safety's good for is taking carnations from the children. The thing is, Chichi, the minute I take a bright red carnation in my hand, the color fades and the flower turns white. And that's not all. I'll absorb anything red—it'd give you the creeps. The best thing that could happen would be if one of these days, while I was waving the children across the street, a car would run me over like a puppy.

CHICHI: Hey, I haven't seen you in years! What's all this talk about dying?

SAFETY: Ah, Taguchi, come hither.

TAGUCHI: Sure.

SAFETY: Be much obliged if you'd rub my back.

TAGUCHI: You feeling poorly again?

SAFETY: It's me old affliction. See, there's a hump already forming on my back.

TAGUCHI (*rubbing*): You mean here?

SAFETY: Everywhere. What do you think is stored inside? Blood, that's what. Not mine. The blood of strangers!

CHICHI (*his accent returning*): Blood of Pu-shee! And my legs they dangle in Pu-shee.

SAFETY: Not bad, Taguchi, not bad at all. (*Breaking into song*):

> O Flint of Fortress Binbow
> His tail was cold or was it hot?
> Did he stand or did he not?
> Take a word from me.

O screams to rend the ocean waves,

. . . .

(*He turns suddenly to the entrance and bellows*): A man with one
leg, Orchid Flower . . . You're looking for a man with one leg!
GIRL (*languorously*): Sure, sure. (*She draws deeply on her cigarette.*)
CHICHI: And don't let nobody know who you're after.
GIRL: Gotcha.
SAFETY (*as Taguchi rubs his back*): Listen, how come you went to
work for Asahi Life?
TAGUCHI: I did it for my family.
SAFETY: For his family? You hear that, Chichi the Gimp?
CHICHI: Yeah—it's been a long time, too.
TAGUCHI: My father died, and my mother began taking in work at
home. Being an only child, I had to go to work early.
SAFETY: What kind of work did your ma take in?
TAGUCHI: She made artificial flowers.
SAFETY: Artificial flowers?
TAGUCHI: Yes, she dyed artificial flowers. In order to earn enough for
us to eat, she'd have to work straight through the night.
SAFETY: Your mother? You mean she dyed artificial flowers?
TAGUCHI: Yes, that's why I said she dyed artificial flowers.
SAFETY: And the flowers turned red and blue? Is that right?
TAGUCHI: It was so pretty. I'd peek out from under the covers and
watch her as she worked all night long beneath that single, dim bare
bulb.
Safety sobs.
CHICHI (*similarly*): Mmmmm.
TAGUCHI: Is something the matter?
SAFETY: You're so sweet! Everything you do is so . . . meticulous!
(*Abruptly changing his tone*): What's wrong with you? You
should've gotten a job sooner! How come you didn't help her? Idiot!
TAGUCHI: But I had years of compulsory education. . . .
SAFETY: That nonsense? You should've quit! Imbecile!
TAGUCHI: But society wouldn't . . .
SAFETY: Stand for it? Well, screw society! Why the hell should you
stand for society?

TAGUCHI: But I'm only one man. If I protested too much it would only cause my mother greater pain.

SAFETY: You mean to tell me there's no way both you and your mother could be happy?

TAGUCHI: Go ahead, laugh at my impotence!

SAFETY: Will it help if I laugh?

TAGUCHI: No.

SAFETY: Then who the fuck's gonna laugh, you goddamn idiot!

Taguchi stops rubbing Safety's back.

SAFETY: See! The minute I get angry you quit rubbing my back! That's the pity of it all! When I was your age, I asked the great buckwagon in the sky whether or not I should go to Manchuria, what would be best for my parents, for myself.

TAGUCHI: And that's when you had your first taste of Pu-shee?

SAFETY: Wait a minute! When I first met you, you said you lived alone. What happened to your mother? Where'd you stash her!

Taguchi continues to rub Safety's back.

SAFETY: What happened to your mother and the artificial flowers?

TAGUCHI: She died.

SAFETY: What?

TAGUCHI: She died during that cold winter last year.

Safety is silent.

TAGUCHI: I asked her to please stop taking in work since I'd found a job, but she just went on dying those artificial flowers. That was in February; it was bitter cold. One morning I woke up and found her face down in a field of blue artificial flowers. It was as if she'd fallen asleep in a mountain glen. There were so many, flowers swirling around her, overflowing, it could have been the sea.

SAFETY: The sea!?

TAGUCHI: Yes.

SAFETY: What was your mother's name?

TAGUCHI: They called her Sunshine!

Safety is silent.

Chichi the Gimp, struggling to control his feelings, rises from his box. He has legs! He makes for the urinal and pretends to relieve himself in an effort to conceal his emotions.

SAFETY: But tell me, why do you speak of her romantically, the way you do?

TAGUCHI: She always seems so distant, I. . . .

GIRL (*singing*):

> With each spring I remember
> The flower that fell in Pu-shee.
> Engulfed as she bloomed, she mastered
> All forty-eight ways to please.
>
> Then her desolate flesh washed ashore,
> Beneath the rainbow that followed the storm.

Police Inspector 1 appears suddenly in the entrance and grabs Girl by the arm.

INSPECTOR 1: Caught you in the act! Ah-hah, still young, aren't you!

Old Man and Police Inspector 2 appear next. Chichi leaps back into his wagon.

OLD MAN: They're the ones, officer, it's them I want arrested!

INSPECTOR 2: All right, all right! (*He looks around inside the lavatory.*) What are you guys doing in here?

SAFETY: Huh?

INSPECTOR 2: I'm asking you what the hell you think you're doing in here! This is a public toilet for public use. When you've taken care of your business, you get your ass out, and quick!.

All are silent.

INSPECTOR 2: People who rendezvous in public toilets are viewed as perverts. Doesn't that mean anything to you? Hey, what are you being so goddamn quiet about! Come on! Just exactly what are you doing here?

SAFETY: Huh?

INSPECTOR 2: What a bunch of suspicious characters! Don't you guys understand what I've been telling you?

SAFETY: No.

INSPECTOR 2: You don't understand?

SAFETY: No.

INSPECTOR 2: Now look, I'm asking you what the fuck you're up to in here.

SAFETY: You suddenly barge into our little establishment and demand to know what we're doing here? Would you mind telling me what this is all about?

INSPECTOR 2: What's that?

OLD MAN: You see, this is the way they talk! Didn't I tell you?

SAFETY: Do you make it a practice of running into department stores and coffee shops and screaming at the crowds, "What the fuck do you guys think you're doing in here!"?

OLD MAN: You see, this is the way they talk! Didn't I tell you?

INSPECTOR 2: Now just hold on, hold on! (*To Safety*): I'm not sure I understand what you're getting at.

SAFETY: I don't understand you very well either.

INSPECTOR 2: You talk about this place the same way you'd talk about a department store or a coffee shop. But this is a fundamentally different sort of place from a department store or a coffee shop, see? This is a public lavatory. "Public," not in the sense that here is a place for the masses to mingle, but "public" in the sense that here is a place for the execution of formal business. Ordinarily, in public facilities of this nature, a person will take approximately two minutes to answer nature's call. He will pass water and not words with his fellows. Sad as it may seem, they part without speaking. Whoever heard of doing your homework, holding a song fest, or drinking yourself under the table in a public toilet?! Who! You, nonetheless, have mingled here for hours and have conducted friendly relations, have you not! And are you not, in fact, occupying this facility before my very eyes? A public lavatory must not be occupied. It is a temple where a man comes to relieve himself in solitude, his head bowed in prayerful meditation—this is the commonly held image of a public toilet. Nevertheless, you have profaned these hallowed precincts by hanging a paper lantern at the entrance and you are conducting business of a somewhat dubious nature. Now, what the hell do you think this is?!

SAFETY: It's a cabaret, your honor.

INSPECTOR 2: A cabaret!?

SAFETY: A Korean cabaret where we serve a few drinks, sing a song or two, and put our patrons on a ship to wherever they want to go.

INSPECTOR 2: Who gave you permission! This area is zoned for scenery. Who gave you permission?

SAFETY: Superiors.

OLD MAN: You see, this is the way they talk! Didn't I tell you?

INSPECTOR 2: Superiors? What do you mean "superiors"?

SAFETY: My superiors.

INSPECTOR 2: What kind of superiors? Make some sense, will you!

SAFETY: My superiors above me.

INSPECTOR 2: Where above you?

SAFETY: In the sky.

OLD MAN: See, this is the way they talk!.

INSPECTOR 2: They're in the sky, are they, these superiors of yours?

SAFETY: Yes, their buckboard. . . . (*Without warning, he rushes forward, strikes Police Inspector 1, and rescues Girl from his grasp.*)

INSPECTOR 2: You . . . what do you think you're doing!

INSPECTOR 1: Resisting arrest, eh?

Police Inspector 1 grabs Safety. Safety's hat flies off, and for the first time his sword-scarred face appears in the light.

INSPECTOR 2: Ah!

Police Inspectors 1 and 2 stop in their tracks.

SAFETY: Ōtani! Umada! Where the hell do you think you are? This be the Cabaret Pu-shee!

UMADA (*Inspector 2*): It's . . . it's Amazō, Amazō of the S.S. Brilliant!

OLD MAN: Just one coincidence after another!

UMADA: You doing the Miss Safety routine?

AMAZŌ (*Safety*): Yeah. You fuzz?

ŌTANI: (*Inspector 1*): We're on the force, all right, but that needn't stand between us, Amazō.

AMAZŌ: Come inside! This be me place.

CHICHI (*from the recesses of the lavatory*): Been long time. Ōtani, Umada. It's me!

UMADA: It's. . . .

CHICHI: "Chinese" Chichi, the river pilot.

UMADA: Ah, Chichi with the long pole!

ŌTANI: Now I remember! You was always up on deck working your pole!

CHICHI: Those were my three-legged days. Now only the middle one's left.

UMADA: Some things never change. You never let go of your pole! *Amazō laughs and everyone joins him.*

OLD MAN (*nervously scurrying about*): Officer, I . . . what should I do?

UMADA: Why not become the bouncer at this club?

OLD MAN: Ah! Now the police are making a fool of me! Will the world never cease ridiculing me? The lost Guardian, where will he find a reason to live? Well, down in the batter's box, I'm turning the mike back to you. (*He exits meekly.*)

AMAZŌ: Well then, the Cabaret Pu-shee's doors are open, and the guests are assembled, righto, Flint?

UMADA: Hey, quit it, Amazō.

AMAZŌ: Hear that, Flint? He wants me to quit it.

CHICHI (*imitating Flint the Parrot's voice*): A bottle of rum! A bottle of rum!

ŌTANI: Chichi, cut it out!

AMAZŌ: You that worried about him, you pirate police?

UMADA and ŌTANI: Worried? Us?

GIRL (*interrupting*): I want to know what you blockheads are going to do about this bruise on my arm?

ŌTANI: Sorry, young lady.

UMADA: Who is this kid anyway?

AMAZŌ: Forget it, Orchid Flower. They're not much, but they're still customers. (*To Umada and Ōtani*): I'll introduce you. This here's the only survivor of that little escapade. . . .

UMADA: You mean somebody survived?

ŌTANI: There was one—the fourteenth Korean.

AMAZŌ: She's that Korean.

UMADA: How long's it been?

ŌTANI: Forty years! You trying to tell us this kid is? . . .

UMADA and ŌTANI (*they stare at Girl in wonderment*): Well preserved!

ŌTANI: How about this one over here?

AMAZŌ: That's Asahi Life.

UMADA and ŌTANI: Asahi Life!?

UMADA: What's Asahi Life doing in with a bunch of buccaneers?

AMAZŌ: Data processing, me hardies!

CHICHI (*mimicking Flint*): Though he cared nothing for it, he had his

life insured! Squawk! Had his life insured! Squawk!
GIRL: That's an imitation of Cap'n Flint.
(*She sings*):

> O Flint of Fortress Binbow
> His tail was cold or was it hot?
> Did he stand or did he not?
> Take a word from me.
>
> O screams to rend the ocean waves,
> Across the sea, the vast Black Sea,

ALL:

> What was it like, what did you see?
> Flint of Fortress Binbow.

GIRL:

> O scenes so terrible, hard to believe,
> Over the lull, black motionless lull,

ALL:

> What did you hear, what could you cull,
> Flint laid low with fear?

There is the sound of a peg-legged man approaching.
  Everyone freezes.
GIRL: What's wrong?
AMAZŌ: Sh!
UMADA: It's him. That's his crutch.
ŌTANI: They say he died in the Patriotic Manchurian Development
  Corps after twelve years at hard labor in the mines.
ALL: Who the hell are you talking about?
AMAZŌ: John Silver—Long John Silver of Pu-shee.
A song can be heard in the distance:

> Seventy-four men on the dead man's chest—
> Yo-ho-ho, and a bottle of rum!

Drink and the devil had done for the rest!
Yo-ho-ho, and a bottle of rum!

CHICHI: That's his song.
UMADA: What the hell does he have to come back for in this day and age?
AMAZŌ: It ain't us Silver's coming to meet.
ALL: Then who?
AMAZŌ: Orchid Flower. You were his woman, weren't you?
GIRL: When?
AMAZŌ: During the twenties, Orchid Flower, when you were still young.
GIRL: Wait. I've grown so old, I don't quite recall.
The sound of the crutch stops. The door to the toilet stall flies open with a bang. Beyond it is the sea, radiant and sparkling in the sunlight. A peg-legged shadow slowly seems to enter.
GIRL (*facing the shadow*): Oh, it's you!
Blackout.

ACT 2

Scene 1
Red Lilacs of Pu-shee

The curtain opens onto what might as well be a harbor in Manchuria. There is the sound of a ship's bell. In the background, the darkened bar, its patrons like motionless shadow puppets. Downstage, a wharf illuminated by a dim electric light. The sound of the ship's bell.
A Demobilized Soldier, shouldering his pack, and a Korean woman (none other than Orchid Flower) appear, their arms around each other. They stumble and fall.
DEMOBILIZED SOLDIER 1 (*shaking Girl*): Look, Lil, the harbor lights!
LIL: Yes, dearest, and that's the sound of the ship's bell!
SOLDIER: We made it, Lil! You've been swell!
LIL: You've been swell, too. Now you'll be able to return to Japan.
SOLDIER: Yes! And when we get back, we'll open a public bath!
LIL: But what of your wife back home? I'll only be a burden to you. Soon you'll grow to hate me, I know it!
SOLDIER: I'll split up with my wife, you'll see. Just trust me!

LIL: But I'm a foreigner. If you take me back to your country, you'll only be treated with suspicion and contempt!

SOLDIER: Don't worry! Times like these can't last forever!

LIL: If only that were true! If only that were. . . . (*She coughs convulsively and cannot continue.*)

SOLDIER: Lil! What's wrong?

LIL: It's nothing. Dearest, am I going to die?

SOLDIER: Of course not! Don't be silly!

LIL: Dearest, you go ahead without me.

SOLDIER: After all we've been through! Come on, Lil, let's board the ship.

A one-legged soldier appears. He uses a crutch and resembles Umada.

MAN: Ship's full.

SOLDIER: But the Ogura unit, "A" company, second division hasn't embarked yet!

MAN: The Ogura unit left this morning.

SOLDIER: That can't be! Who are you anyway?

MAN: I's from Silver's platoon.

SOLDIER: Okay, then take us with you.

MAN: You think you'd blend in?

SOLDIER: Please!

MAN: I'll see what I can do. Whatchoo got?

SOLDIER: Huh?

MAN: You got any caramels?

SOLDIER: No, I haven't got any caramels.

MAN: I loves 'em.

LIL: Offer him your gold teeth, dearest. You haven't any choice.

SOLDIER: I haven't got any left. We traded them for your medicine, remember?

LIL: That's right!

SOLDIER: Please! I'll do anything. Use me as you would a beast of burden, please!

MAN: Ain't your foreign wife got no gold teeth?

SOLDIER (*shielding the woman*): No!

MAN: Looks like she might.

SOLDIER: I said she hasn't!

LIL (*coughing suddenly*): Dearest, go on alone! I'm done for! When you get back, wave to me in my grave from the Island of Sado.

SOLDIER: Lil!!

MAN: Your wife, she's sick, ain't she?

SOLDIER: Lil, hang on! I'll get some water!

LIL: The ship will sail! Hurry and get on board!

SOLDIER: Lil! I'll be right back! (*He runs off in search of water.*)

The One-Legged Man and Lil are alone. Lil is coughing violently.

MAN (*cramming his mouth with caramels*): I ask you, Madam, what is health?

LIL: What?!

MAN: We have comprehensive medical care, and what good does it do? Men still die. Consider yourself lucky, madam. You were able to fall ill of your own accord.

LIL: What are you talking about?

MAN: Madam, is this your first marriage?

LIL: What do you? . . .

MAN: I married my wife in her twilight years. Madam, be ye chaste?

LIL: Please, take care of my man.

MAN: Of course.

LIL: Will he be able to sail on your ship?

MAN: I'll see that he gets where he's going.

LIL: What?

MAN: I mean, I'll take him on a nice romantic cruise. Madam, your cheeks are so warm! (*He touches her.*) You're not going to die! See how the the furnace of your body roars against the cold! Now, madam, I'll have those teeth! (*He looms over her.*)

LIL: Aaargh! What are you doing?! Help, somebody! . . .

MAN: Try to restrain yourself, madam, future proprietress of a public bath! (*His hands close about her neck.*)

The bell of the departing ship clangs violently, and the stage grows dark. Having strangled Lil, Man rises and leaves.

Soldier 1 appears carrying a cup of water.

SOLDIER: Here's some water, Lil!

Lil does not answer.

SOLDIER: Lil! (*He realizes she is not breathing and recoils in terror.*) Who did it? Lil! Who did it!

The fog horn sounds, and a song is heard in the distance. It grows dark.

A bridge was built across the plain
Of broad Manchuria,
A thousand miles of track were lain
To be a courier.

Now o'er the fields of Asia
The Manchurian Railroad sails
To carry Co-Prosperity
Across the silver rails!

Our platoon aboard to guard its passage,
A holy mission, a sacred message.

The lights come up. Demobilized Soldier 2 and Goobers enter. He is supporting her. This Korean woman also bears a striking resemblance to Orchid Flower.

DEMOBILIZED SOLDIER 2 (*shaking the Girl*): Look, Goobers, the harbor lights!

GOOBERS: Yes, dearest, and that's the sound of the ship's bell!

SOLDIER: We made it, Goobers! You've been swell!

GOOBERS: You've been swell, too. Now you'll be able to return to Japan.

SOLDIER: Yes! And when we get back, we'll open a luggage store!

GOOBERS: But what of your wife back home? I'll only be a burden to you. Soon you'll grow to hate me, I know it!

SOLDIER: I'll split up with my wife, you'll see! Just trust me!

GOOBERS: But I'm a foreigner. If you take me back to your country, you'll be treated with suspicion and contempt!

SOLDIER: Don't worry! Times like these can't last forever!

GOOBERS: If only that were true! If only that were. . . . (*She coughs convulsively and cannot continue.*)

SOLDIER: Goobers! What's wrong?

GOOBERS: It's nothing. Dearest, am I going to die?

SOLDIER: Of course not! Don't be silly!

GOOBERS: Dearest, you go ahead without me.

SOLDIER: After all we've been through! Come on, Goobers, let's board the ship.

A one-legged soldier appears. It is Ōtani in disguise.

MAN: Ship's full.

SOLDIER: But the Taguchi unit, "A" company, second division hasn't embarked yet!

MAN: The Taguchi unit left this morning.

SOLDIER: That can't be! Who are you anyway?

MAN: I's from Silver's platoon.

SOLDIER: Okay, then let us go with you.

MAN: You think you'd blend in?

SOLDIER: Please!

MAN: I'll see what I can do. Whatchoo got?

SOLDIER: Huh?

MAN: You got any caramels?

SOLDIER: No, I haven't got any caramels.

MAN: I loves 'em.

GOOBERS: Offer him your gold teeth, dearest. You haven't got any choice.

SOLDIER: I haven't got any left. We traded them for your medicine, remember?

GOOBERS: That's right!

SOLDIER: Please! I'll do anything. Use me as you would a beast of burden, please!

MAN: Ain't your foreign wife got no gold teeth?

SOLDIER (*shielding the woman*): No!

MAN: Looks like she might.

SOLDIER: I said she hasn't!

GOOBERS (*coughing suddenly*): Dearest, go on alone! I'm done for! When you get back, wave to me in my grave from the Island of Sado.

SOLDIER: Goobers!!

MAN: Your wife, she's sick, ain't she?

SOLDIER: Goobers, hang on! I'll go get some water!

GOOBERS: The ship will sail! Hurry and get on board!

SOLDIER: Goobers! I'll be right back! (*He runs off in search of water.*) *The One-Legged Man and Goobers are alone. Goobers is coughing violently.*

MAN: Madam, I ask you, what is health?

GOOBERS: What?!

MAN: We have comprehensive medical care, and what good does it do? Men still die. Consider yourself lucky, madam. You were able to fall ill of your own accord.

GOOBERS: What are you talking about?

MAN: Madam, is this your first marriage?

GOOBERS: What do you? . . .

MAN: I married my wife in her twilight years. Madam, be ye chaste?

GOOBERS: Please, take care of my man.

MAN: Of course.

GOOBERS: Will he be able to sail on your ship?

MAN: I'll see that he gets where he's going.

GOOBERS: What?

MAN: I mean, I'll take him on a nice romantic cruise. Madam, your cheeks are so warm! (*He touches her.*) You're not going to die! See how the furnace of your body roars against the cold! Madam, I'll have those gold teeth! (*He looms over her.*)

GOOBERS: Aaargh! What are you doing! Help, somebody! . . . .

MAN: Try to restrain yourself, madam, future proprietress of a luggage store! Let's tan a little hide! (*His hands close about her neck.*)

The bell of a departing ship clangs violently, and the stage darkens. Having strangled the woman, Man rises and leaves. Soldier 2 appears carrying a cup of water.

SOLDIER: Here's some water, Goobers!

Goobers does not answer.

SOLDIER: Goobers! (*He realizes she is not breathing and recoils in terror.*) Who did it? Goobers! Who did it!

The bell rings, and a song is heard in the distance, a song of Manchuria.

All at once, the bar in the background springs to life. Threadbare soldiers are singing "The Song of the Southern Manchurian Railroad." Beyond the open toilet stall, the nocturnal Sea of China can be seen.

The Bartender is "Chinese" Chichi. A man with only one leg appears at the entrance to the bar. It is Umada. He seats himself at a table to the left and shouts his order.

UMADA: Sake! Bartender, bring me sake!

BARTENDER: Not on life! Your bill already long as arm!

UMADA: I'll pay you! Just bring on the booze!

BARTENDER: What you pay with, huh?

UMADA: How 'bout these? (*He produces a fistful of gold teeth from his pocket.*)

BARTENDER: You dentist?

UMADA: At home I am. I'm head of the Quick Silver Clinic.

BARTENDER: You big shot?

UMADA: Sake! Sake, I said! And I'll have my regular caramels to go with it.

BARTENDER: You big shot?

UMADA: What?

BARTENDER: You big shot?

UMADA: I ride roughshod over Pu-shee, I do!

BARTENDER: Maybe you make as much water in bed as in all Pu-shee?

UMADA: Swine!

A barmaid approaches. She is transfixed by the gold teeth.

BARMAID: Baby, let me sing you a song:

> A girl, an only child,
> And her little sister with her,
> Burned alive and died
> In a dried up river.
>
> A blindman found them.
> A cripple brought them up.
> A deaf-mute reported that
> A cripple brought them up!

The one-legged man played by Ōtani appears at the door. He enters and sits at Umada's table. Without a word, he pulls a handful of gold teeth from his pocket and piles them next to Umada's.

Bartender eyes the teeth avariciously. Barmaid follows the proceedings out of the corner of her eye as she continues her song.

BARMAID:

> A girl, an only child,
> And her little sister with her. . . .

Yet another peg-legged man, played by Amazō, appears at the entrance. He joins Umada and Ōtani at their table. He too takes gold teeth from his pocket and piles them in a mound.

BARTENDER (*his eyes wide with amazement*): Three dentists piling gold teeth on table! What is this, convention?

AMAZŌ:

> Thirteen men on the dead man's chest—
> Yo-ho-ho, and thirty gold teeth!

UMADA, ŌTANI, and AMAZŌ: Yo-ho-ho! Yo-ho-ho!

BARMAID: How about a gold tooth for me, big boy?

UMADA: Whore! You want to get that paw bit?

AMAZŌ (*to Barmaid*): Baby, now we can back to Japan!

BARMAID: Japan?

AMAZŌ: When we get back, what kind of business you want to open? (*He draws her to him.*) I'll tell you what—we'll open a little restaurant.

BARMAID: Hey, what are you doing!

AMAZŌ: We'll open a little restaurant, and you'll be the main course— Marinated Continental Clap!

BARTENDER (*approaching, he separates Amazō and Barmaid*): Please not to handle merchandise.

AMAZŌ: She that important to you?

BARTENDER: She only one I got. Women scarce these days.

AMAZŌ: Getting killed off, they are.

UMADA: This be a treacherous port if ever there was one. (*To Bartender*): Hey, open that hand!

BARTENDER: Hand? What hand?

UMADA: I knew something was up when you came to the aid of a damsel in distress. Chivalry doesn't become you! Let's see what you got in that hand!

BARTENDER: Nothing!

UMADA: Come on! You pinched our gold teeth!

BARTENDER: I not pinch teeth!

ŌTANI: Oh yeah? (*He forces open Bartender's fist.*)

BARTENDER (*looking at the gold teeth in his hand*): Now when could they have fallen out? Do you know? You don't know? Knowing is the beginning of knowledge. Thus do I beat a hasty retreat! (*He tries to escape.*)

AMAZŌ: You bastard! (*He starts after him.*)

BARTENDER: Ah! I'm going to . . . I'm going to . . . fall! (*He collapses, but no sooner has he hit the ground than he springs to his feet and strikes a karate pose.*) Taaa-ooooo! Ke-ke-ke-ke!

The customers ignore Bartender and help themselves to more drinks. Umada, Ōtani, and Amazō also ignore him and husband their gold teeth. Bartender stands alone, ready to take on all comers.

A Flower Girl (Orchid Flower) appears at the door. She surveys the room and, spying the men at the table to the left, makes straight for them.

GIRL: Buy a flower. Please, sir.

AMAZŌ: What kind of flowers be they now, me pretty?

GIRL: Orchid flowers.

AMAZŌ: Then give one to me.

BARTENDER: Hang on to your molars, girl!

Girl gives Amazō one flower. He gives her a few coins, and returns to assaying his teeth with the others.

Girl does not move.

AMAZŌ: That'll be all for now.

GIRL: Um, it's er . . . about the money.

AMAZŌ: I paid you.

GIRL: Yes, but it wasn't enough.

AMAZŌ: Not enough?

GIRL: Not by a long shot.

AMAZŌ: How much do you want?

GIRL: Those gold teeth, all of them.

The three men stare at Girl.

AMAZŌ: All of them?

GIRL: Don't you recognize me?

AMAZŌ, UMADA, and ŌTANI: Mm?

GIRL: Have all three of you forgotten me? I'm the fourteenth woman you attacked at the harbor!

AMAZŌ, UMADA, and ŌTANI: Who? Us?

AMAZŌ: I don't know what you're talking about, but . . . didn't you just say you were the fourteenth one attacked? I heard there were only thirteen.

GIRL: No, I was the fourteenth. My name is Orchid Flower. The charm my mother gave me protected me and restored breath to my body.

AMAZŌ: Maiden of a faraway land, you must be dreaming. The cold must have gotten to you. You only imagined you were being strangled. It was just the Manchurian Gale blowing down from the north.

GIRL: But the man had a crutch and was full of sweet-talk just like you. The only difference was he had a parrot on his shoulder who kept saying, "A flower! A flower!" What did you do to the parrot? You didn't eat him, did you? Now that I take a better look, you resemble the parrot more than him.

AMAZŌ: Watch your tongue, me pretty.

GIRL: You bastards got a lot of nerve! Those gold teeth are ours—mine and my sisters! You're not taking them anyplace!

AMAZŌ: You seem to be confused. These are the assets of our dental clinic. Did you personally have any gold teeth stolen?

GIRL: Now what's a girl like me going to be doing with a mouthful of gold teeth? All I've got is cavities.

AMAZŌ: Then how come you figure these belong to the women who got attacked?

GIRL: I just know, that's all.

AMAZŌ: How?

GIRL: You're one-legged, you're Japanese, and you call yourselves Silver. That's all I need to know.

AMAZŌ: Who's one-legged?

GIRL: Don't try to deny it!

AMAZŌ: Who's one-legged? (*He stands and walks with his crutch on his shoulder.*)

Umada and Ōtani also rise and walk clapping their hands.

AMAZŌ: We're not one-legged.

AMAZŌ, UMADA and ŌTANI (*circling Girl*):

> Thirteen men on the dead man's chest—
> Yo-ho-ho, and thirty gold teeth!
> Yo-ho-ho! Yo-ho-ho!

GIRL: It can't be!

BARTENDER: Then why do you carry crutches?

AMAZŌ: We do a little bone work on the side.

BARMAID (*laughing loudly and singing*):

> A blindman found them.
> A cripple brought them up.
> A deaf-mute reported that
> A cripple brought them up.

AMAZŌ: You couldn't have been the fourteenth one attacked. Maybe you heard it from the deaf-mute.

GIRL: No! He put his hands around my neck and said, "Cold, isn't it, me lovely?"

AMAZŌ: And then?

GIRL: He loomed up and started to choke me. "Cold, isn't it, me lovely," he said, and his hot breath poured over me. Maybe if I'd looked into his eyes. . . . Maybe he wasn't trying to kill me. His breath was so warm . . . Maybe he wasn't trying to strangle me. . . .

AMAZŌ: See, it was only a dream. You were dreaming. There were only thirteen women attacked.

GIRL: And you're the ones who attacked them! (*So saying, she grabs the gold teeth on the table and flees.*)

UMADA: Why, you! . . .

ŌTANI: I was afraid of that!

BARTENDER: Damn! She beat me to it! (*Clucking his tongue in disgust*): Call the MPs! Call the MPs!

AMAZŌ: Not the MPs!

BARTENDER: Call the MPs!

Girl makes for the door but collides with an MP who is on his way in.

GIRL (*looking up at the MP*): Ah!

MP slips around Girl and enters the bar. He walks slowly, and low and behold! He only has one leg! He moves laboriously to the center of the bar. All eyes are upon him.

GIRL (*to the One-Legged MP*): You always show up at the last minute!

Blackout.

Bartender Chichi the Gimp moves to center stage.

Scene 2

The Manchurian Gale of Love

BARTENDER (*singing*):

Piss from the Great Wall of China,
And a rainbow domes the Gobi.

(*Without an accent*): On April 23, 1923. A ship captained by the Russian Mikhailovich Khimelzo was attacked by pirates off Nicolayevsk. The crew of four Chinese, eight Russians, and a Korean fell into the hell swirl of the northern sea, but only after their blood had begun to corrode the weapons of their assailants. The pirates got away with 183 kegs of salted salmon, forty-four barrels of whale oil, 120 drums of petrol, three engines, and 3,000 salted salmon as yet unpacked. In 1924, the ringleader of the gang, Silver by name, was captured with his henchmen Umada and Ōtani at their hideout in Chiba prefecture, east of Tokyo. Silver was sentenced to twelve years in prison; Ōtani got seven years, and Umada five. But Silver was released after three years, and Ōtani and Umada served only one. They crossed over to Manchuria. If memory serves, it was called the Affair of the S.S. Brilliant. (*His accent returning*): Then night after night, women of my country attacked in harbors by one-legged soldier. People call it Silver Rush. Many women confuse with gold rush and lose lives and more. Lots of one-legged men come to my place, but not a good one in the lot. But me, I don't know Silver. Nobody know Silver. Oh, plenty who pass for Silver, but no one know real McCoy. Not even Umada nor Ōtani. Plenty rumors around. Say Silver got hit by truck and died in Manchurian Development Corps. That's what they say. Japanese pirates dirty rats. Murder you for gold teeth. But we knew: "Silver not steal gold teeth—Silver after maidens' hearts." If you ask me, he sometimes make mistake and steal old lady's bellybutton. Wait a minute! Who I'm talking to? Ah, here's Orchid Flower! Very well! All you eyeballs fixed on me, *Hasta la vista!*
It is broad daylight in the tavern. The tables and so forth are just as they were.

GIRL (*to Bartender*): Hide me, will you, mister?

BARTENDER: My pale Orchid Flower, what seem to be trouble?

GIRL: They're out to get me. They say they're going to maim me!

BARTENDER: Maim you? What you mean, Orchid Flower?

GIRL: They say they're going to fix me good!

BARTENDER: A young virgin like you?

GIRL: The three of them, they're waiting for me with razors!

BARTENDER: They shave you?

GIRL: Then I'd only be ashamed to go to the bath. No! They're out to kill me!

BARTENDER: I hide you, you give me something, maybe?

GIRL: I'll give you all the gold teeth I stole the other day!

BARTENDER: You give me those? But if you hide here, Orchid Flower, they find you in no time.

GIRL: I know. Two or three days will be enough.

BARTENDER: You have someplace to go?

GIRL: I'll roam down south to look for that man.

BARTENDER: "That man"?

GIRL: The one-legged MP.

BARTENDER: Orchid Flower, when you realize? Only good one-legged man, dead one-legged man. You want love, best to look for three-legged one.

GIRL: To a Manchurian orphan like me, there's no such thing as bad love. Like my dead mother, I'll spend my days buffeted by the waves of life, the orchid flower of the man I love.

BARTENDER: You talk like that, you done for for sure. I won't waste breath on you. You going to be used and forgotten.

GIRL: I don't care if I'm forgotten. I don't care if I'm murdered. I just want to hear him say, "Cold, isn't it, my lovely?" Then he can kill me and to hell with the gold teeth.

BARTENDER: Then you ready to die for love!

GIRL: I thought his parrot said, "A gold tooth! A gold tooth!" but that's not what he was saying at all! He was saying, "A flower! A flower!" What did he need with a flower out on that frozen wharf? I'll tell you what: his heart had been parched by the Manchurian Gale. I wronged him! He put his hands around my neck, and I thought he wanted to kill me, but maybe he was just staring at my mother's charm. "Cold, isn't it?" His voice, that faltering voice! I want to hear it once more!

BARTENDER: Okay, but I just like to know why virgins always talk like this and still outlive everybody else.

GIRL: Maybe that MP will even take me back to Japan with him!

BARTENDER: His betrothed will be waiting for him over there.

GIRL: I'd become his mistress. I wouldn't mind.

BARTENDER: Become what you like, but before you do, hand over the teeth!

GIRL (*handing him the bag*): How many have you accumulated so far?

BARTENDER: Still short. Few more and family gets mouth paved with gold. (*He exits.*)

Left alone, Girl sits on a table and dangles her legs. She tries to recall Silver's song and sing it to herself.

GIRL: Thirteen men on the dead man's chest . . . and then . . . and then . . . how did it go? . . . Thirteen men on the dead man's chest . . . and then? . . .

Suddenly, the door to the toilet stall flies open and a lone, one-legged man appears, the bright noonday sea at his back. A parrot is perched on his shoulder.

MP (*magisterially*): A bottle of rum, bartender, a bottle of rum!

Girl jumps to her feet, eyeing the newcomer.

The MP supports his weight on his crutch. Lighted from behind, he is a black silhouette.

MP: A bottle of rum, bartender!

GIRL: He's in the back room.

MP: Then you bring me a bottle of rum, my lovely.

PARROT: A flower . . . a flower.

MP: Shut up, Flint!

Girl runs and gets a bottle of rum. She timidly passes it to the MP, who takes a long, hard swig from the bottle.

PARROT: Shut up, Flint! Shut up, Flint!

GIRL: Do you remember me, Mr. MP?

PARROT: Watch it, Silver!

MP: Give me a hint.

GIRL: That night, you were so close, you brought your face so very close to mine. I'm Orchid Flower.

PARROT: A flower! A flower!

MP: Orchid Flower?

GIRL: Come on, remember! Or don't you want to? Why are men always like this?

MP: I remember now.

GIRL: You've known who I was all along, haven't you? You knew the minute you walked in the door.

MP: No. You see, I'm blind.

GIRL: Blind?!

MP: Yes, it happened quite a while ago. I got what I deserved and lost my sight.

GIRL: But . . . you approached me . . . that night.

MP: That cold night. You said your name was Orchid Flower. Flint here led me to you, that's all. I couldn't see your face, Orchid Flower.

GIRL: You were looking at the charm around my neck!

MP: Were you wearing a charm?

GIRL: Yes!

MP: I'm sure it's lovely.

GIRL: Then what were you looking at with those eyes?

MP: What eyes?

GIRL: I don't know, they looked . . . possessed!

MP: My eyes burn. They're filled with blood. I'm blind—to beauty and everything else.

PARROT: A flower . . . a flower.

MP: You find a flower, Flint?

PARROT: A flower.

MP: A Manchurian beauty fair as a flower.

GIRL: I . . . I wanted to go with you!

MP takes a long swig from his bottle.

GIRL: You heard what I said: I want to go with you!

MP: I'm not going anyplace.

GIRL: You mean you're ready to settle down?

MP: I'd like to show you what the world looks like through my eyes.

GIRL: I can see it all now!

MP: You can't see it. Where I'm bound there's only vertigo and the stench of blood.

GIRL: And my blood's not good enough for you, is that it?

MP: Are the seas running high, Flint?

PARROT: Gwaa . . . gwaa . . . .

GIRL: See, he's telling you to listen to me.

MP: All right then, you answer me. Are the seas running high?

GIRL: Feel for yourself.

MP is silent.

GIRL: Tell me, what did you want that night? You and I, we came this close to each other. You put your hands around my neck and said, "Cold, isn't it, my lovely?" You're blind, you say, but what about that hollow voice, those bloodshot eyes?

MP: I was going to kill you.

GIRL: You don't have it in you.

MP: Yes, I do. Like this. (*He caresses her neck.*) You smell so sweet, your breath's so soft! I was going to put an end to that once and for all.

GIRL: What did I ever do to you?

MP is silent.

GIRL: What did I ever do to make you want to kill me? I don't even know you! That night was our first brief encounter! What grudge do you bear me, Mr. MP? Mr. One-legged MP?

MP: I bear no grudges and have no regrets.

GIRL: Then why? Why these hands?

MP: Do my hands frighten you, my lovely?

GIRL: You always want your hands to do your talking for you.

MP: These are iron hands.

GIRL: They're plastic hands, Mr. MP. Aaargh! You're choking me!

MP: Say, "I'm home!" Orchid Flower!

GIRL: Do I say that to you or to your hands?

MP: Say, "I'm home!"

GIRL: I don't know how far your hands will go, and I'm supposed to say, "I'm home!"?

MP: Say it! Flint, are the seas running high?

The Parrot does not speak.

GIRL: You're . . . hurting . . . me! (*She lurches forward.*)

MP (*forcing her up against the lavatory wall, still throttling her*): Starboard rudder, Flint! Starboard rudder!! Where the hell does she

think this is?! An iron starboard rudder! This is the blood-slicked
northern sea!

PARROT: Gwaa! Sunshine! Sunshine!

*MP clutches at the air. Three men with knives have stabbed him in the
back. He lurches forward and falls. The three men move forward on
crutches. They are Umada, Ōtani, and Amazō, the three false Silvers.*

AMAZŌ *(kicking Silver)*: Hundreds of miles from home.

UMADA: A dilapidated tavern in the Manchurian Gale.

ŌTANI: In the cultural upheaval of Asian Co-Prosperity.

AMAZŌ: Even immortals die.

UMADA: And we are . . .

ŌTANI: The Antidental Gold Tooth Union . . .

AMAZŌ, UMADA, and ŌTANI: Of wet Pu-shee!

*Bartender Chichi the Gimp appears upstage left and coldly surveys
the scene. He laughs maniacally.*

Curtain.

ACT 3
A GHOST SHIP OF FLOWERS

*When the lights come up, the scene has returned to the inimitable
public toilet of Act One. Chichi the Gimp's laughter reverberates
through the room, as if spilling over from the previous scene.*

*The door to the toilet stall to the right is open, and Girl and Guard-
ian are lying face to face on the ground. The bright sea is visible beyond
them. A knife protrudes from Guardian's side.*

*Amazō, Ōtani, and Umada stand downstage, confronting the audi-
ence in the same manner as their predecessors in the last act.*

*There is the sound of water running in the toilets. The sound of peg-
legged men walking can no longer be heard. Plaintive, flamenco-style
music plays in the background.*

CHICHI: Heh-heh-heh-heh!

AMAZŌ: Everything's the same as it was that day. I hear the changeless
roar of the sea, and brothers, I think to myself: Only fools die. Only
fools get themselves killed. I can't say it makes much sense to live
ashamed, but if this be shame, then the color of the sea and the sun

too be shame itself.

UMADA: But brother, was that really Silver?

ŌTANI: What's that?

UMADA: Was that MP really Silver?

AMAZŌ: Was there ever anyone named Silver?

UMADA: Eh?

AMAZŌ: Anyone we get our hands on could be called Silver. Anybody can be Silver—it just depends on how he makes his entrance. The Guardian . . . or you . . .

UMADA (*to Ōtani*): Or you . . .

ŌTANI (*to Amazō*): Or you too.

AMAZŌ: The guy the world singles out . . . no, the one we single out— he's Silver. Hey, twirp, where do you think you're going?

TAGUCHI (*about to flee through the door*): I was just about to flee through the door.

AMAZŌ: And where might you be going?

TAGUCHI: To the bath. The bath's going to close soon, so . . .

AMAZŌ: I told you I'd take care of the bath for you, didn't I?

UMADA and ŌTANI: Yeah, we'll take care of it for you too, Asahi Life.

TAGUCHI: Yes, but I'm supposed to meet my wife in front of the bath. . . .

AMAZŌ: Listen, in the first act you said you lived alone in a boarding house.

TAGUCHI: Sometimes I do.

AMAZŌ: Never mind! Just come over here and rub my back.

UMADA: And mine.

ŌTANI: And mine, too.

AMAZŌ: When the girl wakes up, we've got to board ship. Chichi! Hurry up and get rid of that Guardian.

CHICHI: Goddamit! How come you always pick on cripple?

AMAZŌ: Quit talking Chinese!

CHICHI: What you say?

AMAZŌ: I said, cut the crazy lingo!

CHICHI: I not speak Chinese. I not speak Japanese and not Chinese. I speak language without a country. In first place, no such country as China at moment anyway.

AMAZŌ: Just get rid of the Guardian and be quick about it.

CHICHI: You keep saying get rid of him . . . but where?
AMAZŌ: In the river.
CHICHI: There no river around here.
AMAZŌ: The river of neon signs.
CHICHI: Now how I get rid of him in river of neon signs? (*Nevertheless, he rises out of his box, hefts Guardian over his shoulder, and exits.*)
Amazō, Ōtani, and Umada sit at the table to the left. Taguchi massages their backs in turn. In the toilet stall, Girl sleeps on alone. Amazo takes a bottle of rum from the shelf and fills three glasses to the brim. The Man from Asahi Life massages their backs in silence.
AMAZŌ: Cheers!
UMADA and ŌTANI: Cheers!
The three men raise their glasses in a toast and, shouting, "Yo-ho-ho!" down the liquid.
AMAZŌ, ŌTANI, and UMADA (*singing "The Pirates' Song"*):

It's a long, hard road we've traveled
Since those glory days:
Forty years at the pirate's trade.
Red blood on the white mast sprays.

Thirteen victims each passing year,
And thirty golden teeth.
The setting sun, mackerel,
Like condoms to the sea float we.

If forty years have come and gone,
Then gold teeth forty fold!
How very long we've waited for
Our story to be told!

Now to introduce ourselves,
Pirates of love are we:
The Antidental Gold Tooth Union,
Pains in the ass all three!

AMAZŌ: Well then, brothers, let's see the fruit, as it were, of forty years of sweat and blood? To start with, it is my great pleasure to be able to produce the the harvest reaped by the former bartender of Pushee, now the cripple of Senju, which I have in my possession. (*He empties the contents of a bag on the table, and gold teeth cascade noisily into a mound.*) Hands to yourself, mates! Listen, keep your hands! . . . Keep your fucking hands to yourself! From hands unkempt all evil flows! Watch it, you sticky fingered ape!

ŌTANI: Ouch!

UMADA: Take it easy, brother.

AMAZŌ: You see, my passionate, avaricious brothers, Chichi is tough. Thirteen gold teeth a year—forty years without missing a day, and here you have 520 gold teeth. First of all we'll divide 'em evenly. Asahi Life, what's 520 divided by four?

TAGUCHI: One hundred and thirty.

AMAZŌ: No mistake, then. Each of us takes 130 to begin with. I'll just divide this mound roughly into four piles. (*He divides the mound of gold teeth unevenly.*)

UMADA: Hey, there's only two in Chichi's pile!

AMAZŌ: The rest must have fallen under the table.

Ōtani looks under the table but finds nothing.

UMADA: Amazō, you bilge-brain, you're dividing them up without counting.

ŌTANI: He is?

AMAZŌ: I counted them!

UMADA: Then how come there's so many in your pile?

AMAZŌ: Some large ones must have gotten clustered together. There are bound to be big ones and little ones, you know.

UMADA: Then why don't we divide them by weight instead of number?

ŌTANI: You bastard, you want them all for yourself!

AMAZŌ: Settle down, brothers! You're wasting calories!

ŌTANI: Who's talking about nutrition!

UMADA: It's a problem of numbers!

AMAZŌ: All right! All right! Here's your share and here's yours. (*He gives Ōtani and Umada each equal amounts.*) Now we'll have no more petty bickering over numbers. I'm beat!

UMADA: We ain't complaining, but what about Chichi? What's he gonna say?

ŌTANI: Two out of 130: not much of a return on his investment.

AMAZŌ: Never mind about Chichi. We've disposed of the first portion of our take; now, my brothers, let's have the rest!

UMADA: Shall we?

ŌTANI (*looking at Umada*): It's all right with me.

AMAZŌ: Come on, let's have the proof of your piracy.

Umada picks up his briefcase and glances at Ōtani.

AMAZŌ: That's a mighty fancy satchel you got there!

ŌTANI (*glancing at Umada as he picks up his briefcase*): You go first.

UMADA: I don't mind, but I've got to piss. (*He gets up and loiters before the urinal.*)

AMAZŌ (*to Ōtani*): Come on, let's see what you got.

ŌTANI: Um, the lock seems to be broken.

AMAZŌ: What are you idiots going on about! You haven't opened savings accounts, have you? Let me see that bag! (*He snatches it away.*)

ŌTANI: If you're going to open my bag, then you ought to open Umada's too.

AMAZŌ: Fair enough. (*He grabs Umada's case as well.*)

UMADA (*returning*): Keep your hands off my stuff!

AMAZŌ: What!?

UMADA: Amazō, before you open that bag, I want you to keep in mind our forty years of hardship and suffering.

AMAZŌ: Not even the sharks can stomach a pirate's complaints!

Amazō opens one bag and then the other. Umada and Ōtani avert their eyes. Amazō takes something from their cases.

AMAZŌ: What's this?

ŌTANI and UMADA: Evidence.

AMAZŌ: Of what?

UMADA: Petty larceny.

ŌTANI: Traffic violations.

AMAZŌ: You mean to tell me all you've got to show for yourselves is evidence of petty larceny and traffic violations?

UMADA: Amazō try to understand—we've been a couple of two-bit coppers, that's all!

ŌTANI: The postwar wind was cruel!

AMAZŌ: And this is all you've got to show for booty?

UMADA and ŌTANI (*hesitantly*): Yes.

AMAZŌ (*throwing the slips of paper into the air*): Don't make me laugh, you buccaneers of democracy! This is all you brought, but that didn't stop you from helping yourselves to them gold teeth!

UMADA: Get off your high horse, Amazō. Evidence, scraps of paper, you say, but we can still arrest you and write you out a slip of paper reading "vagrancy." We may not have treasure, but we still have power.

AMAZŌ: You saying you're going to take me in?

ŌTANI: That depends on you.

AMAZŌ: The power you use to intimidate me's the same power's got you by the balls, you goddamn pirates. . . .

TAGUCHI (*who has been massaging their shoulders*): Please don't fight.

AMAZŌ: Shut up, Asahi Life!

Taguchi flees to a corner.

UMADA: Amazō, you been swaggering around here, telling us our booty's no good, but you haven't shown us yours yet, have you?

ŌTANI: You got some terrific treasure, that'll knock us on our ass, I'll bet. An anti-establishment hippie-type like you must really have his hands into something that'll make us all rich quick. Let's have a look!

AMAZŌ: My turn, then, is it?

UMADA: Hats-off if your treasure's any good.

AMAZŌ: I'm a pirate of love.

UMADA: So what!

AMAZŌ: I've been standing at intersections at lunchtime. . . .

ŌTANI: Working in broad daylight, eh? That's like you, Amazō.

UMADA: And your prey?

AMAZŌ: Children.

UMADA and ŌTANI: Kids! From some high-class joint like the Peers School, no doubt. Listen, you're not the child molester we've been after, are you?

AMAZŌ: If I saw them just once more, I'd give them everything back.

UMADA: The treasure?

ŌTANI: Let's have a look at it first, Amazō.

Ōtani and Umada pounce on Amazō and thrust their hands into the pockets of his green Miss Safety outfit. Ōtani bursts out laughing as he produces children's shoes, rulers, lunchboxes, and the like.

ŌTANI: You call this treasure?! Umada, this here's treasure you don't lay your eyes on every day!

AMAZŌ: I've been thinking that if I could only see those children one more time, I'd return all that stuff.

Umada bursts out laughing.

ŌTANI: (*returning the shoes and the like*): Tee-hee-hee-hee! . . . A pirate pederast! Ha-ha-ha-ha-ha!

Suddenly, a knife rips into Ōtani's belly.

ŌTANI: Gaaaaa!!! You done it! You son-of-a . . . .

Ōtani clutches at the air and falls.

AMAZŌ (*removing his knife*): The cock-sucker laughed at my treasure— the blood and sweat of my piracy of love!

UMADA: Amazō, this is how we've ended up. Thirteen victims and thirty gold teeth a year, that's the way it was when the rhythm of the times beat with violence. It's been twenty-five years. Pirates of democracy like us, who sail on tranquil seas: it ain't us that's changed, it's the booty. Amazō, a piece of evidence or a pair of sneakers were grand treasure for us. But we've lost our common treasures, see. We only move farther and farther apart, us drifting pirates of the present. What do you say we enjoy this night in the Cabaret Pu-shee, split the remaining gold teeth between us, and go our separate ways?

AMAZŌ: I ain't falling for your sweet talk, Umada. Your theory of limited piracy makes sense enough, but you've been too long on the force: you've lost sight of the sea. I leave tonight. My ship'll be here any minute—I'm off to Manchuria again.

UMADA: You can't see how the wind blows in the world anymore, can you Amazō? There is no Manchuria anymore, and no boat's on its way.

AMAZŌ: Maybe this time I will get screwed by this world of yours, who knows. But let me tell you one thing, Umada. Just as you can become Silver by the way you make your entrance, so you can become Silver by the way you leave the stage. My ship will come, I know it.

UMADA: The only ship coming for you is the ship of death. You've gone senile; you're blind!

AMAZŌ: I can see all right, the Northern Sea. . . .

UMADA: There is no Northern Sea, no Manchuria. You've even forgotten the Manchurian waterways.

AMAZŌ: That girl will open her eyes any minute. She'll be my guide, that Orchid Flower.

UMADA: That lost child of time? All right, but I'll just keep these gold teeth to make the payments on your pension.

AMAZŌ: Keep your hands off them teeth or you'll answer to this knife!

UMADA: You've forgotten my trade, you bastard! Can't you see this pistol in my hand?

AMAZŌ: I just want to know which has priority, Manchuria or my pension.

With the mound of gold teeth between them, the two men continue their silent tug of war. The Man from Asahi Life watches them from his corner. Suddenly, Amazō and Umada lunge at each other across the table and begin grappling. There is a shout and the report of a pistol. Amazō has been shot through the forehead. The knife is lodged in Umada's chest. The two men fall, and the mound of gold teeth slides from the table with a hiss.

The roar of the sea can be heard. The steam whistle of a ship, too, is approaching. Girl, who has been lying on the floor of the toilet stall, comes back to life and slowly gets to her feet.

GIRL (*finding Taguchi huddled in the darkness*): Who is it? Who's there?

Taguchi is trembling with fear.

GIRL: Are you the MP? Are you the one-legged MP?

TAGUCHI: Where do you think this is?

GIRL: Pu-shee, isn't it?

TAGUCHI: It's a public toilet. It's a public toilet and there's just been a murder here.

GIRL: In Pu-shee, murder's an everyday affair. We're right in the middle of the Manchurian Incident, after all.

TAGUCHI: What was a pirates daily routine like, I wonder?

GIRL: Pirates have no routine.

TAGUCHI: Eh?

GIRL: Their days are filled with love and gore; they don't have time to stand around and gossip. What are you, anyway, a bell-hop or a dumpling salesman, maybe?

TAGUCHI: I'm a salesman for Asahi Life.

GIRL: That must have been a long time ago. But excuse me, I've got to board ship with him.

TAGUCHI: With the man who strangled you?

GIRL: He didn't mean it. He was just trying to recall something, I'm sure. Good-bye, Mr. Insurance Salesman. I'll be his crutch and guide him through uncharted waters. I'll steal him away from your country.

There is the violent sound of waves pounding the shore. Through the toilet stall, a ghost ship appears.

GIRL: Look! Our ship of love! It's come!

Girl runs toward the ship. She is about to exit, but two Patrolmen insert themselves between the toilet stall and the picture of the ship. They apprehend her.

PATROLMAN 1: You'll have to come to the station with us. We're holding you as a material witness to murder and the attempted disposal of the body.

GIRL: What?!

PATROLMAN 2 (*leading the handcuffed Chichi the Gimp*): This idiot tried to dispose of a corpse in the middle of Ginza last night.

CHICHI: Throwing him in neon river, I was.

PATROLMAN 2: Probably an escapee from the nut house.

PATROLMAN 1 (*to Girl*): Okay, come along.

GIRL: I'll miss the ship! His ship is waiting!

PATROLMAN 1: Ship? What are you talking about? Looks like she's not all there either. (*He leads Girl off and exits.*)

GIRL (*from off-stage*): I've got to get on that ship! I'm leaving on Silver's ship! Let me go! Let me go, I said! Japanese pig! Japanese swine!

Taguchi is alone on stage with Patrolman 2, who still leads the handcuffed Chichi. The Patrolman discovers three more corpses and recoils in surprise.

PATROLMAN 2 (*to Taguchi*): You saw the whole thing, didn't you?

TAGUCHI: I didn't see anything.

PATROLMAN 2: Liar!

CHICHI (*spying the gold teeth*): My teeth! My gold teeth!

PATROLMAN 2: Shut up, you idiot! (*He beats Chichi.*)

TAGUCHI (*to PATROLMAN 2*): I'm a pirate! A pirate, you hear! The pirate of Asahi Life! I've come to get you—all of you! I'm the pirate of Asahi Life!

PATROLMAN 2: Shown your real colors, eh? All right, you're under arrest, too!

Patrolman 2 leads Chichi and the struggling Taguchi off the stage. Momentarily, both Patrolmen return and carry Amazō, Ōtani, and Umada off on a stretcher.

Pause.

The public toilet stands just as it did at the outset. The door to the toilet stall is closed. The lively sounds of a cabaret can be heard nearby. A lone Passerby enters hurriedly to relieve himself. He stands before the urinal. Suddenly, the door to the toilet stall flies open. The roar of the sea is heard, and the Peg-Legged MP looms in the aperture. Passerby chokes with horror.

MP: Orchid Flower! Where are you, Orchid Flower!!

PARROT: A flower! A flower!

MP: Orchid Flower!!

The band of pirates behind him sing.

PIRATES:

> Thirteen men on the dead man's chest—
> Yo-ho-ho, and thirty gold teeth!
> Yo-ho-ho! Yo-ho-ho!

> Drink and the devil had done for the rest—
> Yo-ho-ho, and a bottle of rum!
> Yo-ho-ho! Yo-ho-ho!

> With one man of her crew alive,
> What put to sea with seventy-five.
> Yo-ho-ho! Yo-ho-ho!

The pirates' procession passes through the audience.
The sea roars so violently, it seems about to engulf the world.
Curtain.

THE DANCE OF
ANGELS WHO BURN
THEIR OWN WINGS

Commentary

I believe Beckett is also saying, again consciously or unconsciously, that God's destiny is flesh and blood with ours, and so, far from conceiving of a God who sits in judgment and allows souls, lost souls, to leave purgatory and be reborn again, there is the greater agony of God at the mercy of man's fate, God determined by man's efforts, man who has free will and can no longer exercise it and God therefore in bondage to the result of man's efforts.

Norman Mailer, "A Public Notice on
Waiting for Godot" (1956)[1]

The Beggar of Love reveals the danger inherent in millenarianism: that the vivifying promise of ultimate redemption and eternal life may serve to justify the most heinous crimes. *The Dance of Angels Who Burn Their Own Wings* expands upon this theme, exclaiming, "We'll be all right if we don't dream!"

Even as it radically questions the wisdom of humanity's quest for ultimate liberation, however, the play reaffirms that quest. It places the idea of political revolution back in its theological context and defines revolution as a manifestation of the divine promise of deliverance. The play redefines the relationship between Man and God, however. In Norman Mailer's words, it sees God as being "at the mercy of man's fate . . . determined by man's efforts." In this play, perhaps the ultimate post-shingeki work, humanity is no longer the passive slave to an absolute historical dialectic or an omnipotent Being's incontestable will, but an equal and empowered partner with God in the continuing quest for mutual salvation.

Marat/Sade

The Dance of Angels Who Burn Their Own Wings was written by Satoh Makoto in collaboration with three other playwrights affiliated with Theatre Centre 68/70:[2] Yamamoto Kiyokazu (1939-), Saitō Ren (1940-), and Katō Tadashi (1942-).[3] It is a critical response to Peter Weiss's 1964 play, *The Persecution and Assassination of Jean Paul Marat by the Inmates of the Asylum of Charenton Under the Direction of the Marquis de Sade (Marat/Sade)*.[4]

As we learn in a 1969 interview with Satoh, *The Dance of Angels* stands in a rather special relationship with *Marat/Sade*.

> The impression I got when I first read *Marat/Sade* is going to be the fundamental motif in our production. I don't want to do a faithful production of Weiss's play, but rather a dramatic reconstruction of my impression of that play.[5]

Satoh preferred not to stage *Marat/Sade* as Weiss had written it for a specific reason:

> In the end Weiss wasn't able to push his ideas to the limits of their implications. What interests me is how to make theatre out of the inability to make straightforward statements about those things to which straightforward statements are inappropriate. In the case of Peter Brook [who directed the original English-language production and film version of the play] or anybody else for that matter, in each production so far, a degree of certainty has been imposed on those things about which Weiss himself was uncertain, by emphasizing certain ideas over others. For example, when the play as a whole is performed within the framework of madness, that is, when tension is created between madness and sanity, Marat's peculiar indecisiveness is explained. Or, if the Four Singers (who Weiss claims represent the masses) are made totally awakened beings, everything else in the play falls into place. I don't want to make everything so nice and tidy. While having everything develop in parallel, I also want our uncertainties, Weiss's uncertainties, to remain alive and to actually appear on stage.[6]

Satoh objected to *Marat/Sade* primarily because he felt that it forced the subject with which Weiss was dealing, the revolutionary idea in Western civilization since the French Revolution, into a Procrustean bed for the sake of clarity.

The first step Satoh and his co-authors took in reworking *Marat/ Sade* was, consequently, to remove those devices Weiss had employed to give his play a coherent structure. The most significant of these was the setting, the asylum of Charenton, where the Marquis de Sade was actually incarcerated between 1801 and 1814. Aware that Sade had staged dramas at Charenton, Weiss imagined that in 1808 he had reenacted Charlotte Corday's Saturday, July 13, 1793, assassination of Jean Paul Marat with the inmates of the asylum as his actors.[7]

Satoh objected to placing the action in an asylum because he felt that madness could be invoked to dispense with all those problems unsolvable within the given scheme of ideas. Any inconsistency, such as Marat's "peculiar indecisiveness," could be dismissed as a mad aberration. The clairvoyance of the Four Singers, unbound by their own historical particularity, could also be put down to the insight of the insane. In both cases, madness made it possible to avoid addressing the really difficult problems Weiss's play raised: the character of the revolutionary idea, its origin and articulation, and the identity of "the masses."

Unlike *Marat/Sade*, therefore, *The Dance of Angels* does not take place in an asylum, and no reference or appeal to madness is made. Removing the action of Weiss's play from the asylum of Charenton deprives it of its major premise, however. The consequences of this can best be understood in the difference in the historical structure of the two plays. Weiss's play has a very straightforward historical structure. We the audience are in the present, watching a play being produced at Charenton in 1808, which concerns events that took place in 1793. Removing the action of the play from Charenton denies this structure.

The decision to remove the action of *Marat/Sade* from the asylum of Charenton also brought into question the very intelligence that would conceive of history in such terms. What is this intelligence? Satoh understood it as the reifying tendency of petit bourgeois class consciousness, and he perceived Peter Weiss as a petit bourgeois intellectual looking back into history and believing that everything could be comprehended in his own static terms.[8]

Satoh, on the other hand, wanted

> to combine Weiss's play with an analysis of the *process* of class conscious-ness. . . . I get the distinct impression that analyses of class consciousness have, up until now, only been carried out bathed in the light of a future when all class consciousness will, supposedly, have vanished, and, on the other hand, in terms of a totally pervasive bourgeois society, the extension of bourgeois society as it first appeared. But to force bourgeois conscious-ness and proletarian consciousness off to opposite extremities of history like that is to presuppose salvation through a historical dialectic. At present, the class consciousness of the petit bourgeoisie is being ignored because it is assumed to be disappearing. When I talk about class con-sciousness, though, I try to choose a given point in the flow of petit bourgeois consciousness and examine the physicalizations of that con-sciousness that emanate from there. That was the case in my play about the Beatles and the one about Nezumi Kozō. And that will also be the case as I examine the fragmentation of the class consciousness of one petit bourgeois intellectual, Peter Weiss.[9]

According to Satoh, then, what we are watching in *The Dance of Angels* is "the fragmentation of bourgeois class consciousness" and its understanding of history. It is a trenchant critique of the Hegelian-Marxist historical model[10] and an attempt to describe in a dynamic fashion the subliminal workings of the contemporary mind that had occupied Satoh in *My Beatles* and *Nezumi Kozō: The Rat.*

A Dream Within a Dream Within a Dream

In contrast to the linear historical structure of *Marat/Sade*, *The Dance of Angels Who Burn Their Own Wings* is structured concentrically, as "a dream within a dream within a dream." The first dream is the dream of revolution dreamt by Jean Paul Marat and the Marquis de Sade. In Weiss's conception, both Marat and Sade accepted the possi-bility of revolution, albeit in distinct ways. That is, they shared the same dream: "Sade knew the Revolution to be necessary; his works are one single attack on a corrupt ruling class. He flinched, however, from the violent methods of the progressives." Marat, on the other hand, "was one of those who were building the socialist image"; and "his ideas lead in a direct line to Marxism."[11]

In *The Dance of Angels*, the Marat-Sade dichotomy is preserved, but the emphasis changes significantly. Where Weiss had stressed the conflict between Marat and Sade, Satoh and his coauthors stress their common fascination with the revolutionary dream. They are saying, in effect, that the common acceptance of the dream of revolution by both Marat and Sade is far more significant than any differences that may have existed between them.

Marat and Sade are therefore depersonalized in *The Dance of Angels* and appear as members of two interacting ensembles of actors, the Grey Wind and the Red Wind. Marat and Sade are called Grey Wind I and Red Wind I, respectively. The Winds occupy the circular stage with movable, pie-shaped segments called the Lunatic Landau (*kichigai basha*) that stands at one end of the tent theatre. (See illustration.) In other words, the Grey and Red Winds, of which Marat and Sade are merely a leading part, occupy a distinct temporal and spatial dimension: they exist in the *historical* dimension of the play, the French Revolution.

This historical dimension has very limited objective reality, however. The Grey and Red Winds and their dream of revolution are nothing more than a figment of the imagination of the Angels, another ensemble of actors. These Angels are a motorcycle gang questing for redemption,[12] and their dream of revolution has two conflicting tendencies: a political tendency represented by the Grey Wind, which moves ineluctably toward totalitarian violence; and an individualistic tendency represented by the Red Wind, which moves ineluctably in the direction of unrestrained hedonism. In *The Dance of Angels*, the momentous events of the French Revolution take place within the Angels' imagination. Just as the Beatles were the communal fantasy of contemporary youth, the Winds are the Angels' communal fantasy of the French revolution.

Since they belong to the present, the Angels occupy center stage, the floor of the tent. The history of the French Revolution and the reenactment of Marat's assassination are mediated by their consciousness; they are "a dream within a dream."

The Angels are themselves a dream, however. They are a dream

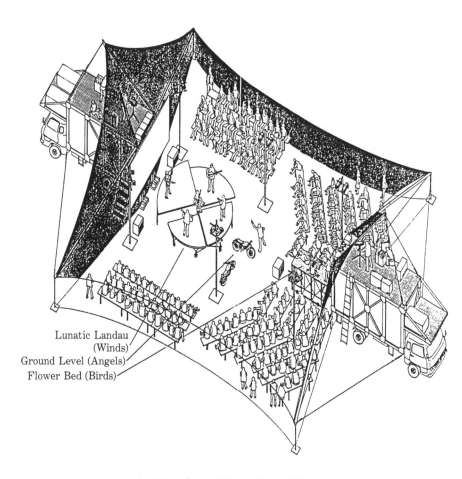

Lunatic Landau
(Winds)
Ground Level (Angels)
Flower Bed (Birds)

The Dance of Angels Who Burn Their Own Wings
The Black Tent Theatre as it was arranged for the 1970 production.

being dreamt by the third ensemble of actors in the play, the Birds, and specifically by their ruler, the King of the Birds. The unique spatial dimension occupied by the Birds is the Flower Bed (*hana no shindai*), the highest of the three performance areas called for by the script. The Flower Bed is set up at the opposite end of the tent from the Lunatic Landau and looks down over the Angels and the Winds. Temporally, the Birds occupy neither the historical past nor the present, but the *metahistorical* dimension of the play. I will return to this idea in a moment.

In contrast to the straightforward, linear historical structure of *Marat/Sade*, therefore, *The Dance of Angels Who Burn Their Own Wings* incorporates a multidimensional, concentric time structure like that of *Nezumi Kozō: The Rat.*[13]

The "dream-within-a-dream-within-a-dream" structure is Satoh's way of representing "bourgeois class consciousness" fragmented into historical, present, and metahistorical dimensions. Like *Nezumi Kozō*, which described the idea of revolution in Japan, it is a dynamic model of the revolutionary imagination, this time set in the West. It is a theatrical reproduction of the subliminal processes of consciousness that underlie the Western concept of revolution.

Revolution Discredited

By defining it as "a dream," *The Dance of Angels* brings the entire concept of revolution into question. The first thing that happens in the play is the projection of a slide reading, "This is a dream." Then the Angels sing "The Ballad of Fallen Birds." Let's be honest about the history of revolution since 1789, the song and play are saying. Much blood has been let, but has anything really changed? Once the last assassination ended, once the last reprisal had been carried out, what happened? From that point on, what happened? Did the French really come closer to a state of grace? Did the Russians enter the Millennium? Were the Chinese redeemed? No, the human condition has remained unchanged. Since that is the case, dreaming of revolution, of redemption, of fundamental alterations in the human condition is not only a waste of time but extremely dangerous. Perhaps one is better off not hoping for a better world. "We'll be all right if we don't dream!" Instead of Peter Weiss's question, "Marat or Sade?" the question raised by Satoh and his coauthors is, "If not Marat-Sade, then what?" If revolution conceived along the lines of the French model cannot be accepted, then how is revolution to be conceived? Is it really a possibility? This is the problem posed by *The Dance of Angels Who Burn Their Own Wings.*

One of the things that made *The Dance of Angels* an intense theatrical experience, bringing thousands of people out into the bitter cold of winter nights to sit for nearly four hours in an unheated tent, was the way this general philosophical theme was taken up as an urgent issue for the theatre.[14]

The slides that flashed on the screen as the Angels sang "The Ballad of Fallen Birds" revealed this sense of urgency.

THEATRE MUST BE REVOLUTIONARY.

MORAL: IN A CRIMINAL SOCIETY ONE
HAS NO CHOICE BUT TO BE CRIMINAL.

IT IS IMPOSSIBLE FOR THE THEATRE TO BE REVOLUTIONARY.

THE FIRST REVOLUTION: REVOLUTION WITHIN
THE REVOLUTION.

TO TURN ONESELF FROM THE INSIDE OUT.

The first proposition is that the theatre must work to further the realization of the revolution, that is, a total, once-and-for-all amelioration of the human condition. The moral to be drawn from this is the terrorist's credo, to wit, that since the structure of society as it is presently constituted is criminally inequitable, actions that society defines as "criminal" are justified in order to destroy it. If this is what it means for the theatre to be revolutionary, however, then "it is impossible for the theatre to be revolutionary." The concept of revolution itself must therefore be revolutionized. An attempt must be made to "turn oneself inside out," or, in Susan Sontag's phrase, "to step over one's own feet."[15] "Theatre must be of the first revolution," therefore. It must facilitate this act of self-transcendence by helping to reformulate the concept of revolution.

The first step in this process is to reject received ideas of revolution. The theatre must not agitate uncritically for discredited ideas of revolution, as Satoh and his coauthors believed Weiss had done. When Marat and Sade first meet, therefore, Sade is homosexually penetrated by Marat in Marat's bath as Sade eulogizes the revolutionary hero. The Red Winds ridicule every word. The simplistic juxtaposition of Marat and Sade presented by Peter Weiss is thus rejected with a stream of profane invective and an image of anal sex.

In this context, what is the meaning of Charlotte Corday's assassination of Marat, the centerpiece of Weiss's play? It is "the embodiment of murder in the name of abstract laws." Corday is an example of the individual revolutionary whose terroristic act is intended to once and for all end tyranny and liberate humanity. Corday is the liberating heroine who seeks to redeem humanity by her personal selflessness. But as she, with the combined voices of the Winds and the Birds, demands that the King of the Birds arm her to carry out her holy mission, the Angels ridicule the notion that her act of revolutionary violence can transcend the inherent poverty of the idea of revolution it seeks to realize. The knife she demands is "worthless."

Corday (Red Wind 6) eventually finds a knife stuck in the back of a mannequin. Her act is not original, the play states; she is only continuing the tradition of revolutionary violence. As she withdraws the knife from the back of the last victim to die for the good of the revolution, she asks the fateful question: "What will this cost me?"

True to history, Charlotte Corday assassinates Marat in his bath on her third visit to his home. But by the time this happens at the end of the play, the futility of her act is painfully clear. In an age of mass murder, of the Holocaust and Hiroshima, revolution modeled on acts of individual terrorism, conceived as an extension of individual murder and death, is meaningless at best. At the end of the play, as Corday approaches her victim for the third and final time, the Winds lie about her, ravaged by a terrible disease. Judging from their disfigured corpses, they are the victims of atomic radiation. The play is asking what possible significance such an act can have in our post-Hiroshima age. And yet, "Today's age . . . is not an age of revolution; it is an age of assassination."

Revolution and Redemption

The Angels' dream begins late one night on a beach, where they have ridden to meet a mysterious figure described as "the Weatherman Rabbit." The Angels believe that the Weatherman Rabbit, a figure straight out of the revolutionary Wonderland, will tell them "which way the wind is blowing," thus enabling them to overcome their sense of paralysis, of death, and empowering to move, to act.

Instead of finding a white rabbit in a waistcoat, the Angels come face-to-face with the decrepit incarnation of revolution in our time. They encounter Angel Red, a diseased, wounded, and bedraggled figure who is both the physical embodiment of the legions of proletarians who have perished in the pursuit of revolution and the manifestation of the dilapidated idea of revolution itself.

Angel Red provides the bridge between the time of the present in which the Angels exist and the historical time of the Winds. He rises and leads them on a grand tour of the idea of revolution since 1793. Far from offering the Angels an easy, magical way out of their dilemma, Angel Red reveals the multitudinous contradictions in the convoluted career of the revolutionary idea.[16] He explains to the Angels and to the audience the origins of the *cul-de-sac* in which they find themselves.

And it is here that the metahistorical dimension comes into play. "A strong shaft of light falls on the Flower Bed, revealing the prostrate King of the Birds and his four subjects."

Unlike the Winds, who appear in rags and tatters, or the Angels, who wear jeans and beads, the Birds are dressed in pure white. They have large white wings sprouting from their back that augment their stately appearance. And of all the dreamers in the play, only the King of the Birds is in bed. The fact is, the action of the play is the King's dream projected onto the stage from the Flower Bed. The Winds' dream of revolution and the Angels' dream of the Winds exist solely within the dream of the King of the Birds.

Throughout the play, the King of the Birds continually insists that it is morning and demands tea. He is catered to obsequiously by *both* the Angels and the Birds, who are equally his servants. But morning does not come.

As the dream of the King of the Birds progresses, he becomes increasingly distraught. Apparently what he is seeing distresses him, and morning refuses to dawn and release him. And then there is the terrible discovery. In response to the question, "Who is that behind you?" the refrain of a song that accompanies the Japanese equivalent of Blindman's Bluff, the King of the Birds wails, "It's me . . . behind me, looking at my back . . . it's me." The dream of the King of the Birds is his own creation. He is seeing himself projected before his eyes. It is as if he had been chasing someone around a tree only to discover upon grabbing him that his hand had fallen on his own shoulder.

The King of the Birds is God. Whenever birds appear in Satoh Makoto's plays, they represent the gods. *My Beatles* is a good example. But if birds represent local divinities in Satoh's plays, then the *King* of the birds can only be the supreme divinity, that is, God Almighty.

The Dance of Angels differs most decisively from *Marat/Sade* because it acknowledges the theological foundations of Western revolutionary thought. It dares to ask what is behind humanity's struggle for revolution, for release from the human condition, for redemption. It recognizes that the Western imagination tacitly posits a transcendent intelligence beyond man's and beyond history that dictates that mankind shall struggle, generation after generation, to be free. Humanity (represented by the Angels) and its dream of revolution (the Winds) is a dream dreamt by this superior intelligence: by God, the King of the Birds.

It is hard not to conclude that this is what Satoh meant when he said that Peter Weiss had not pushed his ideas to their logical conclusions. *The Dance of Angels Who Burn Their Own Wings* attempts to reformulate the Western idea of revolution within its appropriate monotheistic theological context and thereby to escape the dualism of Marat-Sade. The play argues that implicit in the Western concept of revolution is the notion that mankind struggles for revolution and redemption because it is subject to the dictates of God. The struggle for revolution, redemption, is *a revealed necessity.* It is an existential imperative that exists *a priori* in the way people in the West conceive of the relationship between Man and God. Humanity struggles toward ultimate liberation because of the nature of its relationship with God, because in a real sense God has ordered them to do so. Why has He done so? The play suggests that it is because He experiences Creation as a nightmare. He is not viewing something outside Himself but, like a true dream, a phantasm of His own making.

Human history is therefore a projection of the dream of God onto the stage of the world. God dispatches His creatures on missions of escalating violence in order to jolt himself out of his reverie. These revolutionary missions dictated by God in His attempts to wake Himself from the nightmare of Creation constitute human history.

Revolution Reformulated

The Dance of Angels Who Burn Their Own Wings accepts this reformulation of the revolutionary idea. It asserts a certain equality, a parity between humanity and the Godhead. It dares to suggest a degree of Divine culpability for the unredeemed state of human history, and it enfranchises Man and God as co-equal partners in the process of history, struggling, sometimes together, sometimes at cross purposes, toward final release. This is the way the play and its authors seek to transcend what they perceive as the critical limitations of the idea of revolution as it is currently conceived in the West and as it was presented in Peter Weiss's *Marat/Sade.*

The Dance of Angels accepts the notion of human freedom. At the end of Scene Seven, the Angels revolt. They are once again on the beach with Angel Red. Suddenly, Angel Red lunges toward the King of the Birds, his knife at the ready.

Angel Red's act is attempted deicide. Since human history is a nightmare in the mind of God, killing God would end history and achieve redemption, true revolution. That is why Angel Red rushes at the King of the Birds, but the King's guards restrain him, and the attempt to end the dream by killing the dreamer concludes in failure.

With this failure, nothing remains to prevent the repetition of Marat's tragedy. His assassination is reenacted as a redundant affirmation of man's inability to achieve redemption, to end history. It has no message as it did in Weiss's play; it has lost its provocative power.

Marat's death is simply a nightmare recapitulated time and again before God.

But then something unexpected happens:

> One entire side of the tent suddenly opens onto the outside world. The Angels come roaring out of the distance on their motorcycles. and drive into the tent in a cloud of exhaust smoke and dust. They are "White Angels" with white wings sprouting from their back. They dance and sing.

The Angels sing an unabashed paean to youthful optimism. Then, "Angel 1 picks up the knife Angel Red has dropped," and he and his compatriots set off once again in pursuit of the Weatherman Rabbit.

The drama is beginning all over again. The knife is passed on; the tragic cycle of revolution-assassination-betrayal is about to be repeated and nothing will change. Or will it? There is always the possibility that *this* time the Angels will succeed. The fact that the Angels are dressed in pure white, with wings sprouting from their backs, is significant. In addition to being motorcycle angels, they are *real* angels, children of God, empowered to act in meaningful ways. Like all the other gods who appear in post-shingeki dramas, this apotheosis reveals that the angels who may ultimately save humanity are none other than the human beings awaiting salvation themselves.

The "wings" of the title of the play have two functions: they identify the Angels with the King of the Birds and His creatures, and they are "the wings of imagination." The relationship between the two functions is made clear in a speech by Grey Wind 2:

> You the damned! You who throw yourselves against the prison walls! You who try to soar high into the skies on the wings of imagination! You shall be tortured, treated with contempt, and finally thrown helplessly aside.[17]

What identifies the Angels as angels is their wings, the wings of imagination, which have been granted them by the King of the Birds to allow them to attempt in new, imaginative ways to find the Weatherman Rabbit and discover a way to transcend the dream, the nightmare of the human condition. God has granted the Angels wings; He has given humanity imagination because He needs it to achieve revolution.

Revolution means, therefore, not only the redemption of Man but also of God. Only through revolution, a definitive end to history, will God be able to wake from His terrifying dream. Just as the necessity to struggle for redemption and revolution is a revelation of God to humankind, so are humanity's continuing attempts to achieve redemption revelations of humankind to God. They are co-equal and mutually dependent partners fated to struggle together toward an end to history.

Within the image of "angels who burn their own wings," therefore, is concentrated the image of revolution that is expressed in this play. True revolution, an end to human history and the entry into redeemed time, implies the extinction of imagination. Revolution implies an end to dreaming; redemption implies a burning of wings. Wings (imagination), the very means by which revolution/redemption is to be achieved, become useless appendages once that goal is reached.

The Dance of Angels ends on an ambiguous note. The Angels set off again, this time to end the dream of redemption by assassinating the Weatherman Rabbit, its prophet. Because of the nature of its relationship with God, humanity is doomed out of ontological necessity to repeat endlessly the Sisyphean cycle of revolution and betrayal. At the same time, however, humanity has been reenfranchised, reendowed with the potency to create, alter, and potentially end history. There is the possibility that *this time*, against all odds, the revolution will succeed, that, in Walter Benjamin's words, *this* moment might be "the strait gate through which the Messiah might enter."[18]

The play's final song is thus a reiteration of the notion of revolution-as-immanence articulated in *Nezumi Kozō: The Rat.*[19] It is simultaneously an affirmation of the power and potential of the imagination to achieve revolution and a recognition of the fact that once revolution is achieved, imagination will no longer be necessary. Man perishes as man. As Buddhism teaches, imagination ultimately exists as a hindrance to enlightenment.

Notes

1. Norman Mailer, *Advertisements for Myself* (New York: Putnam, 1959), p. 302.
2. Presently known as the Black Tent Theatre 68/71 (*Kuro tento roku-hachi-nana-ichi*).
3. Satoh's was the determining influence, however, and I will treat the play as

basically the product of his imagination. Satoh worked out the basic plan for the play with Yamamoto, authored three of its eight scenes as well as the finale, and rewrote the entire play in its final form. Satoh also directed the play in production. See *Gendai nihon gikyoku taikei*, vol. 8 (San'ichi shobō, 1972), p. 227.

4. Peter Weiss, *The Persecution and Assassination of Jean Paul Marat by the Inmates of the Asylum of Charenton Under the Direction of the Marquis de Sade*, tr. Geoffrey Skelton and Adrian Mitchell (New York: Atheneum, 1976).

5. Satoh Makoto, "Interview," *Concerned Theatre Japan* (Autumn 1970), I(3):21.

6. Satoh, "Interview," p. 21.

7. *Marat/Sade*, pp. 105–106.

8. This is the heart of the debate that took place between Weiss and Hans Magnus Enzensberger as well. See Fujimoto Kazuko, "Discrimination and the Perception of Difference," *Concerned Theatre Japan* (Spring 1973), II(3–4):121–122.

9. Satoh, "Interview," pp. 21–22.

10. See the final chapter of this volume for a discussion of the significance of this critique in the context of the post-shingeki movement.

11. *Marat/Sade*, pp. 106–108.

12. The Angels are, of course, the Hell's Angels. Satoh first used the Hell's Angels in his 1969 play *Onna-goroshi abura no jigoku* (Murder in Oil Hell). For a discussion of this play, see my "Satoh Makoto and the Post-Shingeki Movement in Japanese Contemporary Theatre" (Ph.D. diss., Cornell University, 1982), pp. 165–200.

13. For an analysis of this time structure in *Nezumi Kozō: The Rat*, see my introduction to the play in *After Apocalypse: Four Japanese Plays of Hiroshima and Nagasaki* (New York: Columbia University Press, 1986), pp. 251–267.

14. First-hand accounts of the production appear in *Concerned Theatre Japan* (Winter-Spring 1971), I(4):28–52.

15. Susan Sontag, *Trip to Hanoi* (New York: Farrar, Straus and Giroux, 1968), pp. 88–89.

16. The play is replete with references to Western revolutionary literature as well as to Weiss's *Marat/Sade*. For the most part I have not attempted to render allusions faithfully, but have let the logic of the action govern my translation. No citations are given in the original text, but I have indicated some of the sources in notes to the play.

17. This is basically the same speech delivered by Roux in *Marat/Sade*, pp. 69–70. Here, however, the warning is delivered to all the Winds, not just to Marat alone.

18. Walter Benjamin, "Theses on the Philosophy of History," *Illuminations*, ed. Hannah Arendt, tr. Harry Zohn (New York: Schocken Books, 1969), p. 264. Satoh is familiar with Benjamin's work and has quoted it frequently in epigraphs to his plays. See *Abe Sada no inu* (Abe Sada's Dogs; Shōbunsha, 1976), *Kinema to kaijin* (The Phantom of the Cinema; Shōbunsha, 1976), and *Blanqui-goroshi shanhai no haru* (The Killing of Blanqui, Spring in Shanghai; Shōbunsha, 1979).

19. I explain this idea in *After Apocalypse*, pp. 266–267.

The Dance of Angels Who Burn Their Own Wings

A PLAY

by Satoh Makoto, Yamamoto Kiyokazu,
Katō Tadashi, and Saitō Ren

The translation of *The Dance of Angels Who Burn Their Own Wings* (*Tsubasa o moyasu tenshi-tachi no butō*) is based on the original, unpublished script and my personal observations of the 1970–71 production. The closest published version of the text appears in *Dōjidai engeki* (1970), I:3. Yet another version appears in *Gendai nihon gikyoku taikei,* vol. 8 (San'ichi shobō, 1972).

The play was performed by Theatre Center 68/70 and was directed by Satoh Makoto.

CAST OF CHARACTERS

Angel Red
Angels 1–5
King of the Birds
Birds 1–4
Grey Winds 1–6
Red Winds 1–6

ACT 1

The inside of the tent is black. At one end stands the "Lunatic Landau," at the other the "Flower Bed," and between them a third performance area.

In the beginning there is darkness. Then, silence. Words on the screen:

THIS IS A DREAM.

The Angels are huddled around two motorcycles that stand near the Lunatic Landau. Bathed in a pale blue light, they sing to the accompaniment of electric guitars.

The Ballad of Fallen Birds[1]

That day the sky was a jaundice yellow
And the last assassination ended.
In a plaza corner of your town,
Two shadows danced, twisting together.
One man's hatchet, one man's brow
That was the end, that was the grand finale.

That day the town was deathly silent
And the last betrayal ended
Your house stood aloof above the plaza
Curtains drawn across its windows
Nobody saw, nobody knew
You just forgot, you lost all recollection.

That day the night was nearly endless
And the last reprisal ended
From the damson plum in your yard
Hung the bloody man, hatchet still in hand
Swinging all alone, making flowers bloom below.
Then came a day when every trace had vanished.

---

[1]The music for the songs in this play may be found in *Concerned Theatre Japan* (Winter-Spring 1971), I(4):107–118.

From that point on?
From that point on?
We'll be all right if we don't dream!
We'll be all right if we don't dream!

As the Angels sing, the following slides flash across the screen:

A DREAM WITHIN A DREAM

WITHIN A DREAM.

THIS IS A DREAM.

THEATRE MUST BE REVOLUTIONARY.

MORAL: IN A CRIMINAL SOCIETY ONE HAS NO
CHOICE BUT TO BE CRIMINAL.

IT IS IMPOSSIBLE FOR THEATRE TO BE REVOLUTIONARY.

THE FIRST REVOLUTION: REVOLUTION WITHIN THE REVOLUTION.

TO TURN ONESELF FROM THE INSIDE OUT.

JULY 13, SATURDAY:

A CALL TO THE PEOPLE OF FRANCE.

SIGNED, JEAN PAUL MARAT.

JEAN PAUL MARAT, A LEADER OF THE ULTRALEFTIST MONTAGNARDS
DURING THE FRENCH REVOLUTION,

WAS ASSASINATED BY THE FANATIC
ANTIREVOLUTIONARY CHARLOTTE CORDAY

ON SATURDAY, JULY 13, 1793.

THEATRE MUST BE OF THE FIRST REVOLUTION.

THESIS: ANY PLEASURE WEAKENS WITH DILUTION!

ANGEL 1 (*shouting*): You! You know I haven't really done anything yet, and you know that I feel now more than ever that I must. But you anticipate, and you're prosecuting me on the basis of that anticipation alone. The honor is more than I deserve. (*Gravely*): I can only hope that some day I will be worthy of the honor you have bestowed upon me, and I pledge myself to the diligent pursuit of that goal. Thank you!

ANGELS (*repeating the refrain of their song, at the top of their lungs*):

We'll be all right if we don't dream!
We'll be all right if we don't dream!
We'll be all right if we don't dream!
We'll be all right if we don't dream!

The headlights of the motorcycles come on. A long scream. Words on the screen:

THIS IS A DREAM.

The Angels mount the motorcycles. They are about to set off, but a figure rises slowly in the glare of their headlights. It is Angel Red, who has been lying prostrate on the ground before them. Angel Red is the victim of an incurable disease and is covered with red spots. Half his hair has fallen out; his movements are slow and painful; his gaze wanders aimlessly in space. With the passage of time, his condition will gradually worsen, and his spots will increase in number and virulence.

Angel Red takes two or three steps, stops, then raises his saxophone to his lips.

ANGEL 2: I'm so fucking cold!

ANGEL 4: It's just your imagination.

ANGEL 2: I feel so damned dizzy!

ANGEL 3: You want some?

ANGEL 2: Yeah.

Angel 3 takes a flask from his pocket and passes it to Angel 2, who

drinks from it greedily.
ANGEL 1: What the fuck . . .
ANGEL 5: You think it's morning?
ANGEL 2: It's so fucking cold! Feels like my heart's going to freeze!
ANGEL 1: I'm going to ask him.
Angel 1 goes to Angel Red. He signals to his companions to kill their engines.
ANGEL 1 (*into Angel Red's ear*): You the one? The one Pluto said to meet on the beach?
Angel Red shakes his head.
ANGEL 2 (*to Angel 1*): Ask him about the long stairway, too. And ask him if the triangular insignia is still on the door to the weatherman's room. And ask. . . .
ANGEL 1: All right! If you're cold it's your own goddamn fault. You're not wearing any fucking clothes, you stupid shit! (*To Angel Red*): Then you're not the one we're supposed to meet?
Angel Red shakes his head. With the exception of Angel 1, the Angels begin to wail.
   Angel 1 removes a pistol from his pocket, turns and fires. Angel 5 screams and falls from the motorcycle.
ANGEL 1: That'll teach you to show some respect.
ANGEL 5 (*raising her head*): But what would you do if I really did die?
   (*She makes a pistol with her fingers and aims it at Angel 1.*) Bang!
The lights dim. The sound of the saxophone continues.
   Words on the screen:

WE ARE INDIFFERENT TO THE PAIN OF OTHERS.

WE CANNOT EXPERIENCE ANOTHER'S PAIN.

THEATRE OF THE FIRST REVOLUTION:

ON THE DOUBLE!

GET THE FIRE EXTINGUISHER!

CAUTION!

Angel 1's voice in the darkness:
ANGEL 1 (*oratorically*): Here is a man who achieved a hero's death. But nothing has ended; it is only the beginning, his first decisive step. He has died and now struggles to be born. He will become the tacit standard for others. His life, indomitable, will blaze on to the very ends of time!
The words on the screen continue:

THE END: 1793/1970

THE END: XXX A.D.

THE CURTAIN SILENTLY FALLS.

MORNING.

THIS IS A DREAM.

BIRDS.

A shaft of light falls on the Flower Bed, revealing the recumbent King of the Birds surrounded by four of his subjects.
KING: It is morning! Report!
BIRD 1: Yes, your majesty. The wind.
BIRD 2: Yes, your majesty. Blowing from two directions.
KING (*signaling with his finger*): Proceed.
BIRDS 3 and 4 (*very slowly*): Dusty and smelling of gun powder—the Grey Wind. Out of the north it blows, from the toothless gums of frostbitten soldiers.
The King of the Birds again signals with his finger.
BIRDS 3 and 4: Feverish, hideous myth. A whirling, suffocating storm of pollen—the Red Wind. Out of the south it blows, from the maggot roar of a sun-struck mare's exploded belly.
KING: Very well. It is morning. Tea!
ANGELS: Monsieur!
The inside of the tent grows light. The Angels sing and dance on the Lunatic Landau.

The Lunatic Landau Rock

Our backs are a superhighway,
A thousand horsepower between our legs.
Crackerjack!
Jelly beans!
Paper balloons!
Pinwheels!
Yeah! Yeah! Yeah!

Outside the tent, a samba rhythm is heard in the distance. There is an orator's voice mixed with the sounds of a crowd. Then from different directions, the Grey Wind and the Red Wind dance their way into the tent.

The Angels and the Winds join in a carnival frenzy that slowly rises to a crescendo.

KING (*shouting*): Very well! More tea!

ANGELS AND WINDS: Monsieur!

The lights dim, leaving only the Flower Bed illuminated.

BIRD 1: There no more, our children . . .

BIRD 2: No longer reflected . . .

BIRD 1: In the mirror on your back . . .

BIRD 2: That faded landscape.

BIRDS 3 and 4 (*singing a children's song*):

Where, oh, where are you from?
Higo, yo.
Higo, where abouts?
Kumamoto, yo.
Kumamoto, where abouts?
The rifles go ba-bang!

KING: That's the spirit! Again!

BIRDS 3 and 4: The rifles go ba-bang!

BIRD 1: There no more, our children . . .

BIRD 2: In the mirror on your back.

BIRDS 3 and 4: The rifles go ba-bang!

KING (*clapping his hands*): Come on, baby, let's see you shake that thing!

BIRDS 3 and 4 (*with all their might*): The rifles go ba-bang!

Blackout.

ACT 2

Words on the screen:

"AH, THE BREACH OF THE LAST EIGHTY YEARS!"

CRIED AUGUSTE BLANQUI IN 1870.

WATCH YOUR LANGUAGE!

PASSION IN 1792. IN 1870 ONLY WORDS.

MODEL: SADE OR DICTATORSHIP?

INDIVIDUAL TERRORISM OR TERRORISM BY THE STATE?

NEITHER IS JUSTIFIABLE AND THUS EACH
JUSTIFIES THE OTHER.

DULY REGISTERED LINE NO. 1:

NO, SIRE, THIS IS NOT A REBELLION, IT IS
A REVOLUTION.

THE END. DEATH. INDIVIDUAL. IN THE EXTREME

WATCH YOUR LANGUAGE!

Voices in the darkness shout, "Watch your language!" and "Off the stage, hack!" At the same time, Red Wind 1 appears on the Lunatic Landau.

RED WIND 1: I am Donatien-Alphonse-François de Sade.
Grey Wind 1, resting in his bath, appears out of the darkness. Angel Red crouches near him.
GREY WIND 1: I am Jean Paul Marat. (*Changing his tone*): Simonne! Simonne!
Grey Wind 6 appears carrying a bucket and bandages. Red Wind 1, his finger to his lips, approaches her and rips bucket and bandages from her hands. Grey Wind 6 is about to speak, but Red Wind 1 forces her from the stage.
RED WIND 1: I am Simonne Evrard.
GREY WIND 1: I am Marat, man of the people. At this moment I am enveloped in a cloud of passion and delusion. My hand has just gripped the quill.
RED WIND 1 (*impassively, as a woman*): Marat, what about our revolution? Marat, we can't wait till tomorrow. We're as poor as ever, Marat. If it's not too much trouble, we'd like the revolution you promised, and we'd like it right away.
GREY WIND 1: A voice, calling from the alleyway, has just faded from my ears. My eyes are fixed on the map of France tacked to the wall before me. Simonne! Simonne!
RED WIND 1: Anon, sir, anon!
Repeating, "Anon, sir, anon!" the Red Wind springs into song. As they are singing, Red Wind 1 goes to Grey Wind 1 and changes his bandages and the water in his bath.

Song of the Master Baiter

Come on, happiness, come on, joy,
Get your sweaty hands off
The hammer-head of my prick!
You are the ones!
You are the ones!
Look at the state you've got us in!
Mun-mun-mun-mun
Mun-mun-mun-mun (*Loud laughter.*)

Come on, Peppermint, come on, Stick,
Come a little faster through

The rye and rosebush dew!
You are the one!
You are the one!
Look at the mess you've got us in!
Mun-mun-mun-mun
Mun-mun-mun-mun (*Loud laughter.*)

GREY WIND 1: Simonne! Simonne! Come quickly, change my water!
RED WIND: Anon, sir, anon!
RED WIND 1: I am Donatien-Alphonse-François de Sade.
Red Wind 1 climbs into Marat's bath. During the following speech, Red Wind 1 artfully charms Grey Wind 1 and arranges their bodies so that Grey Wind 1 mounts him in act of homosexual coitus.

   The Red Wind gathers around them and reacts with jeers and cat-calls.
RED WIND 1: In the name of the free and sovereign people, Citizen Sade wishes herewith to eulogize the great flame of our revolution, Citizen Jean Paul Marat.[2]
RED WIND 6: What are you talking about! Who the hell are you to talk?
RED WIND 4: That's it, man, show him where it's at!
RED WIND 1: Comrade Marat!
RED WIND 3: Nonsense! Eat shit!
RED WIND 1: At an early age you wrote *The Chains of Slavery* and exposed the fallacious theory of absolutism and its concomitant concentration of wealth, as well as the essential deception of religion. You raised high the standard of revolution for our age. Comrade Marat!
RED WIND 3: Nonsense! Eat shit!
RED WIND 1: The painful road of revolution you walked is the path of our people's wisdom, first opened by the illustrious Jean-Jacques Rousseau.
RED WIND 4: That's telling him!

---

[2]This long speech by Red Wind 1 echoes the eulogy Sade actually delivered on September 29, 1793, *Discours prononcé à la fête décernée par la Section des Piques, aux mânes de Marat et de Le Pelletier, par Sade, citoyen, de cette Section, et membre de la Société Populaire.* The full French text is quoted in C. R. Dawes, *The Marquis de Sade: His Life and Work* (London: Robert Holden, 1927), pp. 63–67.

RED WIND 6: Desertion! Treason! Opportunism! Escapism! Defeatism! Indecency!

RED WIND 2 (*to Red Wind 6*): Right on!

RED WIND 1: Comrade Marat!

RED WIND 3: Nonsense! Eat shit!

RED WIND 1: Your uncompromising speeches printed in the *Ami du Peuple* and the *Journal de la republique Française!* What an inestimable contribution they have made to our courage and strength of purpose!

RED WIND 2: I can't hear you!

RED WIND 4: Let's get serious!

RED WIND 1: Comrade Marat!

RED WIND 3: Nonsense! Eat shit!

RED WIND 1: Voices crying aloud! Comrade Marat!

RED WIND 3: Nonsense! Eat shit!

RED WIND 1: Our revolution is now in crisis. The citizens of Paris, nay, the people of France call out to you! Now, more than ever, we need your steadfast leadership, your merciless assaults on our rightist opponents.

RED WIND 6: Get to the point, already! Come on, goddamit, get to the point!

RED WIND 4: It doesn't really matter. Just so there's movement!

RED WIND 1: We need you. Your words aflame, your eyes, beaming the light of reason! Or . . . or your brawny chest. Your moist, passionate lips. Your delicate fingers, gripping your pen. Ah-ah, Comrade Marat!

RED WIND 3: Nonsense! Eat shit!

RED WIND 4: I can feel it! I can feel it!

RED WIND 1: And yet, we stand lost before your corpse! Our ship, tossed on stormy seas, has lost its pilot. Alas!

RED WIND 2: Get out! Get out and stay out! (*Rhythmically*): Get out! Stay out!

RED WIND 6 (*joining in*): Get out! Stay out!

RED WIND 1: Alas! Comrade Marat!

RED WIND 3: Nonsense! Eat shit!

RED WIND 1: That hateful maniac who stole you from us! Shall we forget that pallid girl and her cold steel knife? Shall her blood on the guillotine be met with silence? No! With triumphant shouts of revenge!

RED WIND 4: He's thrusting to the midsection—just like his father!
RED WIND 1: That loathsome maid of Caen—Charlotte Corday!
 There, Marat, Comrade Marat, there . . . there! . . .
RED WIND (*announcing*): The maid of Caen—Charlotte Corday!
Red Wind 1 is locked in a passionate embrace with Grey Wind 1. All at once, the Red Wind swirling around them freeze.
Words on the screen:

THE EMBODIMENT OF MURDER IN THE NAME OF ABSTRACT LAWS.

MODEL: GUILLOTINE OR KNIFE?

THE HEROINE!

Angel Red stands and beats out a fanfare roll on a drum.
KING OF THE BIRDS, BIRD 1, and BIRD 2 (*voices*) : Charlotte Corday!
Called forth by the King of the Birds, two Cordays (Birds 3 and 4) enter to the solemn beat of the drum, attended by Birds 1 and 2. They come to a halt on either side of the bath, which still contains Red Wind 1 and Grey Wind 1.
ANGELS: Charlotte Corday!
Similarly, the Angels appear carrying Angel 5 on their shoulders. Angel 5's Corday is attended by Angel 3. The roll of the drum continues. The Red Wind, not to be left out, raise Red Wind 6 to their shoulders. Her partner is Red Wind 3.
RED WIND: Charlotte Corday!
The four Cordays gather around the bath. Classical music wells up and a minuet begins, danced by the four Cordays and their attendants. When the music stops, the King of the Birds speaks.
KING: Your fingers beat the drum. The sound of sounds is liberated and creates new harmony between men. You take one step and new people rise to move forward. You look behind and there is new love; looking ahead again, new love! Our children sing to you, "Improve our lot! Free us from difficulty! But first do something about the relentless march of time!" The people cry out to you, "The pinnacle of our dreams, the depths of our fate: anywhere will do, just reconcile the two!" You always appear, then go where you will. Shall we have the knife, then?

ANGELS: Monsieur!
The Angels draws knives and begin juggling them. Music.
CORDAYS (*together*): Knife!
RED WIND: Knife!
RED WIND 1 and GREY WIND 1: Knife!
ANGEL RED (*screaming*): Knife!
KING: A real knife! My children, a real knife! A real knife! A real knife!
BIRDS 1 and 2: A real knife!
ANGEL RED (*in a piercing scream*): Knife!
CORDAYS (*together*): Knife!
ANGEL 1: It is like your ambitions, worthless!
RED WIND: Knife!
ANGEL 2: It is like your utopia, empty!
RED WIND 1 and GREY WIND 1: Knife!
ANGEL 3: It is like your chance meeting, pure fantasy!
RED WIND, GREY WIND, and ANGELS: Knife!
ANGEL 4: It is like your diseases, incurable![3]
KING: A knife, a real knife!
BIRDS 1 and 2: A real knife!
ANGELS: I feel nothing, nothing. Nothing at all.
ANGEL RED: Knife!
ALL: Knife!
A large mannequin comes flying into the assembly. An enormous knife is lodged in its back. The butt of the knife glistens white.
Red Wind 6 approaches.
RED WIND 6: Excuse me, please. I would like to purchase a knife.
CORDAYS (*excluding Red Wind 6*): Yes, of course. But tell me, good
  woman, who is it for?
Red Wind 6 does not reply but, smiling, pulls the knife from the mannequin's back.
RED WIND 6: What will this cost me?
Slides flash quickly across the screen with the faces of Patrice Lumumba, Malcolm X, Trotsky, Marat, Che.
  Blackout.

---

[3]These lines paraphrase "Manifeste cannibale Dada" by Francis Picabia (1879–1953). The full text of the original, published in 1920, may be found in Francis Picabia, *Écrits* (Paris: Pierre Belfond, 1975), p. 213.

ACT 3

The Angels sing and play. The male members of the Grey Wind enter carrying baskets overflowing with flowers. They sing and dance to the Angels' music.

The Guillotine Express

Daylight field of flowers
Chestnut eyes wide open
Gentle you and gentle me
Red as beets!
See the tower soaring there and up top
The Cheshire Cat is waving
His smiling flag at us!
Oh my goodness, time to go,
Our transfer bus will pull out if we're too slow!

Let's go, let's go,
The Guillotine Express.
Let's go, let's go,
The Guillotine Express.

Hunting in broad daylight
For girls with legs wide open
How delicious, hit and run: berry hunt!
Dead-end on Third Avenue, and look there,
A funeral pyre erected for someone on the right.
Before we know it, time to go,
Our transfer bus will pull out if we're too slow.

Let's go, let's go,
The Guillotine Express.

Let's go, let's go,
The Guillotine Express.

The music changes. The dancers take bloody heads from their baskets

and begin tossing them back and forth like basketballs. The male members of the Red Wind lift the mannequin corpse to their shoulders, carry it to the Flower Bed, and there go about preparing a guillotine. Grey Wind 6 stands near the bath.
   Words on the screen:

BUS STOP.

SLAUGHTERHOUSE STEAM, CITY STREETS LOST TO VIEW.

Red Wind 6 sings, tightly clutching her knife. Members of the Grey Wind reply to her as a chorus.

RATHER WORSE THAN BETTER, THANK YOU.

RED WIND 6:

> Banks of fog, slaughterhouse steam,
> City streets lost to view.
> Swollen corpses float up to the surface,
> Roll and tumble in the waves, seem warm like me and you,
> But it's only a bad joke: tender flesh, white illusion.
> How are you feeling? How are you feeling?

GREY WIND:

> At the moment rather worse than better, thank you.

RED WIND 6:

> You, leaping sprightly from the bus!
> You, shaking your heads!
> Clapping your hands!
> Rolling your eyes!
>
> Banks of fog, slaughterhouse steam,
> City streets lost to view.

Swollen corpses float up to the surface,
Roll and tumble in the waves, seem warm like me and you,
But it's only a bad joke: tender flesh, white illusion.
How are you feeling? How are you feeling?

GREY WIND:

At the moment rather worse than better, thank you.

RED WIND 6: It won't be long now. I'll be there right away. I'll go up the stairs slippery with blood one step at a time, being careful not to fall. I'll go to join you soon. Don't worry, I'm all right. Ah, yes, it would be best to hide the knife, wouldn't it?

Red Wind 6 conceals the knife between her breasts. Angel Red beats wildly on his drum.

BIRDS: Charlotte Corday, the rosy-cheeked assassin.

ANGELS: She ain't!

Red Wind 6 stands rooted to the ground. Suddenly the Angels have surrounded her. She tries to escape, but the Angels move relentlessly in upon her. Both Red Wind 1 and Grey Wind 1 remain in the bath while Grey Wind 6 stands nearby.

GREY WIND 1: Simonne! Simonne!

GREY WIND 6: Marat! How are you feeling?

GREY WIND 1: At the moment rather worse than better, thanks. This itching is driving me crazy. Bring me some more cold water and change the bandage on my head.

GREY WIND 6: I told you you mustn't scratch so much. You'll tear the skin away. And you really must stop writing.

GREY WIND 1: I scratch because it itches. All I'm asking you to do is shut up and change the water. And besides, I can't stop writing. This is my appeal. I still have appeals to write by the score. (*Reading*): "Saturday, July 13, 1793. A call to the people of France."

GREY WIND 6: Just look! The bath water's turned crimson! How horrible! If you keep on like this you'll do yourself in for sure.

GREY WIND 1: So the water turns red, so what? Think of the bloodbaths still to come! Two days ago I thought taking the heads of a few hundred people would be enough. But yesterday I realized that even several thousand would be too few. And today the numbers soar beyond reckoning. They're everywhere. Everywhere!

Grey Wind 1 suddenly takes Red Wind 1's arm and begins to twist it violently. Red Wind 1 groans with pain.

GREY WIND 1: Everywhere, you hear, everywhere! There! Look, there! Behind the walls, on the rooftops, in the cellars. Vagrants, vandals, looters! Simonne! Simonne! My mind is aflame! It is a raging inferno!

Red Wind 1 is gasping for breath. Grey Wind 1 continues.

GREY WIND 1: I can't breathe! God damn these scabs, this infernal itching! I can't stand it! This wasted, rotting flesh! Simonne, listen! Screaming voices in my breast!

GREY WIND 6: You mustn't scratch. The more you scratch the more you'll itch.

GREY WIND 1: No, I'll scratch all right. I'll scratch and scratch till the skin comes off in strips. Because you see, Simonne, *I* am the revolution. This scab- and pus-ridden revolution, that is who I am!

RED WIND 1 (*painfully*): No you are not! You wouldn't know a revolution from a hole in the ground, Marat!

While this scene is going on, Red Wind 6 is dragged to the ground by the Angels. Her clothes are torn; she is raped and finally discarded like a pile of dirty rags. The Birds blow their whistles violently, scolding the Angels.

ANGEL 2 (*pulling Red Wind 6's head up by her hair*): Come on, let's see if you can stand.

ANGEL 3: Try to walk, once around and back again.

ANGEL 1: Take off her shoes, both of them.

ANGEL 2: "She beat her belly hard against the pavement and broke into tears. She squatted down and, drenched in a cold sweat, thought about the forest."

ANGEL 4: A big smile! See, just like a baby doll—a little girl's gaily smiling face. You must always be smiling, always. Come on.

ANGEL 5: She said smile, you bitch. Something wrong with your ears?

Angel 5 suddenly slaps Red Wind 6 hard across the face.

ANGEL 3: Smile!

ANGEL 2: "Cotton panties. Elastic biting into her waist. She could not even begin to understand how frightened she was."

ANGEL 1: She's okay. Let's go.

The Angels move toward the bath, dragging Red Wind 6. Grey Wind 6 rushes out trying to head the Angels off.

GREY WIND 6: I'm sorry. No visitors. No visitors. No visitors. No visitors! . . .

The Angels beat Grey Wind 6 into unconsciousness and thrust the only semiconscious Red Wind 6 into Marat's bath head first.

GREY WIND 1: What's happened? Simonne! Simonne! Is there someone at the door? Simonne!

RED WIND 1: You have a visitor. Charlotte Corday. She's come to kill you. But don't worry, this is only her first visit. She won't kill you until she's come to your door three times. Then it's a knife in the lungs and good-bye Marat.

The King of the Birds gives a long whistle. Angel Red beats madly on his drum.

BIRDS 1 and 2: Charlotte Corday: The First Visit.

BIRD 3: Corday . . . come now, wake up.

BIRD 4: You must knock, you know. Knock.

BIRD 2: Corday, open your eyes.

The decapitations in the background are rapidly approaching a climax. The Angels beat on the sides of Marat's tub with sticks.

ANGELS: Anybody home? Anybody home? Monsieur Marat? Anybody home? Anybody home? You have a visitor.

RED WIND 1 (*noticing the guillotine*): Shhh! Look!

Everyone gathered around the bath turns to stare at the guillotine. The blade falls and a doll's head thumps to the earth. The Grey Wind let out shrieks of joy.

RED WIND 1 (*speaking directly into Grey Wind 1's ear*): Hey you . . . Jean Paul Marat . . . satisfied? Your instructions have been followed to the letter. You can rest easy in your bath. (*Screaming*): Look! This head will bring the total to three million, no less!

GREY WIND: Nay, m'lord. This chap makes it three million and one.

The Winds laugh raucously. The Angels resume beating on the bathtub and calling out for Marat.

GREY WIND 6 (*facing the guillotine*): You mustn't scratch even if it itches. You must persevere, Jean Paul, you must persevere, you understand?

ACT 4

Words on the screen:

THINKING IS A PLEASURE,
LIKE VIRTUE, LOVE.

REPEAT: ANY PLEASURE WEAKENS WITH DILUTION.

LIFE IS LIMITED.

VIRTUE AND LOVE ARE PREDICATED UPON
ETERNAL LIFE, AS IS LAW.

HOW, THEN, CAN VIRTUE AND LOVE EXIST, OR LAW EITHER?

THEN EVERYTHING IS PERMITTED.

DO WE OR DO WE NOT BELIEVE IN OURSELVES?

FREEDOM IS

EVERYTHING OF WHICH I AM CAPABLE—MY POWER.

THE EXTERNAL BEYOND EXISTS NO MORE
THE INTERNAL BEYOND CONSTITUTES A NEW WAY.

DREAMS FOR DREAMING. REVOLUTION FOR THE REVOLUTION.

X = RETURN TO GO! DO NOT COLLECT $200!

Grey Wind 2's voice is heard overlapping the above.
VOICE: You cannot stop what is happening now. How much have they
had to endure before being capable of this revenge? You gaze upon
the facts before you, wailing, bawling, but you do not understand.
You are responsible. You are the one who made them do it. A man of

belated justice, you mourn the bloodletting. But compared to the sea they have bled for your wars of invasion and implements of torture, the blood flowing here amounts to nothing! Compared to the lives they have had to crush in order to sustain you, the sacrifices being made today do not bear the counting. Compared to your rape of their villages, their ignominious deaths in the gutters, two or three houses pillaged today are not worth noting! Have you but once seen their misery and bellowed in outrage? No, you haven't moved so much as a muscle in their defense! Now your face, your high and mighty face, is twisted with contempt and rage. Who in the name of heaven do you expect to hear your protest?

In the middle of this speech the Flower Bed grows light. Embracing the limbs of the dismembered mannequin, the King of the Birds wails loudly. Grey Wind 2 has delivered the above lines into a microphone, standing beside him.

KING: Tea! Bring me tea! Go ahead, I'll be all right. Bring me tea, I said!
The air is filled with the piercing sound of the Birds' whistles. From the direction of the Lunatic Landau, four Birds approach, this time with real tea carried on a silver platter. Red Wind 1 appears behind them. He enters very slowly, with the gait of an aged man. The whole space of the tent is filled with a soft light. There is no longer anyone on the Lunatic Landau.

The members of the Red Wind exit, passing Red Wind 1, who acknowledges each of them with more fear than propriety. Red Wind 1 stops suddenly. Grey Winds 2, 3, 4, and 5 enter and surround him in a flurry.

GREY WIND 4: And may we inquire as to your age?
RED WIND 1: I will be nineteen in June.
GREY WIND 4: Ho-ho! You look closer to thirty-five or six. And where were you born?
RED WIND 1: In Paris, in the Hôtel de la Bourbon, Rue de la Bourbon.
GREY WIND 3: When did you begin writing?
RED WIND 1: Nineteen-forty-three.
GREY WIND 3: That's strange. If you're nineteen now, that hardly seems possible.
RED WIND 1: I don't understand it myself. It is rather strange, now that you mention it.

GREY WIND 3: Utterly amazing. Of all the people you have met so far, who do you think was the most noteworthy?

RED WIND 1: There are many people . . . take, for example, Dostoevsky.

GREY WIND 3: But if you're not even nineteen yet, you couldn't possibly have met Dostoevsky!

RED WIND 1: I'm sorry if I've said something to offend you, but if you know more about me than I do myself, why do you bother to ask questions?

GREY WIND 3: Just trying to piece things together, that's all.

GREY WIND 2: How exactly did you meet him?

RED WIND 1: One day I chanced to be attending his funeral, you see, and it so happened that he asked me if I wouldn't be more quiet.

GREY WIND 3: What's that? If there was a funeral for him, he must have been dead. And if he was dead, how could he have asked you to be quiet?

RED WIND 1: I really don't know. He always was a rather contrary sort.

GREY WIND 2: I can't make head nor tails of this. According to you, he spoke even though he was dead.

RED WIND 1: I never said he was dead.

GREY WIND 2: Then he wasn't dead!

RED WIND 1: It's matter of some conjecture. Some people say he was dead, and others say he wasn't.

GREY WIND 4: And your opinion?

RED WIND 1: I believe . . . absolutely nothing.

GREY WIND 3: Let's change the subject. What was your first impression when you arrived here?

RED WIND 1: Impression?

GREY WIND 4: Did you see anything?

RED WIND 1: No, nothing at all. (*He suddenly breaks out laughing.*) Shall I tell you the truth? . . . This year I am sixty-seven years old. If you take this year to be 1807.

GREY WIND 3: We've known that all along! From the very first!

RED WIND 1: Just a bit of a joke.

GREY WIND 4: How long will you be here?

RED WIND 1: Let me see. Not so very long, perhaps. It doesn't make much difference where you go, so . . . I suppose . . . .

GREY WIND 5: Your name, precisely speaking?

RED WIND 1 (*puffing out his chest*): Donatien-Alphonse-François de Sade.

Grey Winds 2, 3, 4, and 5 stare at each other in spite of themselves.

RED WIND 1: Is anything the matter?

GREY WIND 3 (*laughing abashedly*): We're terribly sorry. Seem to have the wrong man. Good-bye.

The four members of the Grey Wind exit leaving Red Wind 1 alone. The sound of a guitar. Red Wind 1 speaks, interrupted at intervals by a chorus.

LAST WILL AND TESTAMENT[4]

RED WIND 1: I categorically forbid the dissection of my body for any purpose whatsoever; I must pressingly request that it be kept for forty-eight hours in the room in which I die, in a wooden coffin not nailed down till the forty-eight hours here prescribed have elapsed, after which it shall be nailed. During this time an express messenger shall be sent to M. Le Normand, firewood merchant 101, Boulevard de l'Egalité, Versailles, to request him to come himself, with a wagon, to take my body.

CHORUS:

Remembrances creasing aged lips
And eavesdrop memories, too,
And the times, ah those times,
When my spirit lit darkened skies.
In life's very depths
Symbol of silent ruin,
Oh dimly though it be,
Shine forth just once more for me.

RED WIND 1: Monsieur le Normand shall transport my body in the said firewood wagon to the woods on my Malmaison property in the commune of Émancé near Épernon, where I wish it to be placed, without any sort of ceremony, in the first thicket on the right of

---

[4]This translation of the fifth paragraph from Sade's will is taken from Gilbert Lély, *The Marquis de Sade: A Biography*, tr. Alec Brown (New York: Grove Press, 1970), pp. 460–461.

those woods as you enter past the old manor house by the main drive which divides the estate in two. The grave shall be dug by the Malmaison farmer under M. Le Normand's supervision, who shall not leave my body till he has placed it in the grave.

CHORUS:

> The corners of shadowed moments,
> The sense of days long gone by:
> Carriage traces, stubborn still,
> Fatigued remnants at journey's end.
> In life's very depths
> Symbol of silent ruin,
> All but lost, forgotten,
> The unspoken pledge twixt you and me.

RED WIND 1: Once the grave is filled in, acorns are to be scattered over it, so that in time the grave is again overgrown, and when the undergrowth is grown as it was before, the traces of my grave will vanish from the face of the earth as I like to think memory of me will be effaced from men's minds. Sound in body and in soul, I declare this to be my last will and testament.

Words on the screen:

SIGNED, DONATIEN-ALPHONSE-FRANÇOIS DE SADE.

DULY ACKNOWLEDGED LINE NO. 2.

IT IS NO LONGER POSSIBLE TO PERFORM A WONDERFULLY PERSONAL DEATH.

PERSONAL? DEATH? PERFORM?

ALL THAT REMAINS IS NAMELESS, VALUELESS DEATH.

MODEL: THE IMPASSIVITY OF NATURE OR THE APATHY OF MEN?

HISTORY: HISTORY OF THE REVOLUTION, HISTORY OF THE DREAM, HISTORY OF THE INDIVIDUAL, FOR THE MOST PART.

Red Wind 1 exits. Grey Wind 1 enters followed by the Angels. The Angels prepare their instruments.

ANGELS: Ah, this infernal itch!

GREY WIND 1 (*gaily*): Ah, this infernal itch, infernal itch. . . .

ANGELS: Fever!

GREY WIND 1: Fever races through my brain, ravages my flesh!

ANGELS: Simmone!

GREY WIND 1: Simonne! Change the water in the bath, soak my bandages in vinegar, cool my fevered brow!

Hard, loud music begins. The Angels play with abandon and respond to Grey Wind 1.

SHINING GERMINAL

GREY WIND 1 (*shouting*): Violence in the name of liberty is not necessarily a means to attain liberty. The responsibility we have been assigned is to give direction to spontaneous violence. Weapons are necessary to the revolution, but the power of the revolution is not to be found in those weapons. It is not the ability to take human life that will ensure the people's triumph, but the magnificent determination to defy their own death.

ANGELS and GREY WIND 1:

Vendémiaire
Brumaire
Frimaire
Nivôse
Pluviôse
Ventôse
Shining Germinal

ANGELS: Fevered frozen, your breath, my breath.

GREY WIND 1: For the time being, until the enemies of the people have breathed their last, we are forced to take power ourselves in the name of history. This power of ours is power destined from the very

first to be lost.
ANGELS and GREY WIND 1:

> Vendémiaire
> Fructidor
> Thermidor
> Messidor
> Prairial
> Floréal
> Shining Germinal

ANGELS: Fevered frozen, your breath, my breath.

GREY WIND 1: Anyone who has awakened to his own violence will never be a slave again. We are by no means at the end of our struggle. So long as there are enemies of the people we will maintain power and continue our struggle. We have begun. We are now the ultimate vanguard of the revolution.

Suddenly the Angels stop playing, throw aside their instruments, and close in on Grey Wind 1.

ANGEL 1: Hey, Marat! What happened to our revolution, huh?

ANGEL 4: Give it to us straight, will ya?

ANGEL 1: Come on baby, we just can't wait for tomorrow anymore.

ANGEL 2: Mr. Marat, sir, you get the message? We're hard up, man, and there isn't shit that's changed about us.

ANGEL 3: Come on, how about it?

ANGEL 5: Marat, let's have our revolution. You promised, didn't you?

ANGEL 1: We want it today, right here and now!

ANGEL 2: Let's have it already, motherfuck! Hand over that revolution!

ANGEL 3: How about it, Marat? We get it or don't we?

ANGELS: Give us our revolution, goddamit! Let's have it! Marat! Marat! . . .

The Angels attack Grey Wind 1. A whistle blows. The King of the Birds stands on the Flower Bed, drawn up to his full height. The Angels stare back toward him.

KING: It is morning! What have you done about the tea?

ANGELS: Monsieur!

Birds 1 and 2 move in menacingly on the Angels.

BIRD 1: The Revolution is over.

BIRD 2: It ended long ago—so long ago no memory remains.

KING (*laughing*): It's all right. They want it so badly. All right. We shall grant you what you ask. We'll let you have your revolution, a fine revolution all your own! (*His piercing laughter fills the tent.*)

ANGELS: Monsieur!

KING (*deep into the tent*): Bring him in!

Birds 3 and 4 bodily drag the wasted figure of Angel Red in and throw him to the ground.

KING: There you are. There's your revolution for you!

The painfully rising notes of Angel Red's saxophone. The Winds enter and sing.

WINDS: Shining Germinal Fevered frozen, your breath, my breath.

Blackout. Only the King's piercing laughter remains.

ACT 6[5]

AN EFFECTIVE MEANS TO THE SPIRITUAL MURDER
OF ALL WORDLY POWER:

WRITING.

THE DIALECTIC FOR FORMALIST LOGIC.

THE DIALECTIC.

ESCAPE FROM DUALISM.

ACTING BETRAYS! ACTORS REBEL! IS HELL
REALLY UNDERGROUND?

Two figures appear in the spotlight. Grey Wind 2 and, cowering beside him, Angel Red. As Grey Wind 2 minutely inspects Angel Red's body, he begins to murmur. At first his manner should be utterly composed.

GREY WIND 2: To arms. Fight for your rights. If you don't secure what

---

[5]Scene 5 is titled "A Self-Indulgent Comic Interlude," and it is just that. It was not performed with the rest of the play during the original production, and I have not included it here either because it unnecessarily disrupts the development of the play's major themes. I have translated it, however, and those interested may refer to *Concerned Theatre Japan*, I:4 (Winter-Spring 1971):77–86.

you need now, you will again be doomed to look on for centuries, waiting. They hold their noses because you smell. They heap you with contempt. You must pay them no attention. You must stand. You must stand and move forward ahead of them. You must show them, you hear? You are not yourself alone, you are many. Your number is countless. If but one of you stands. . . .

Suddenly, Angel Red springs to his feet and escapes into the darkness.

GREY WIND 2: Hey, wait! Wait a minute! Wait!

Grey Wind 2's words echo through the tent.

The beams of the spotlights that have been trained on Grey Wind 2 and Angel Red swing away from their targets. Operating the spots are the Angels, who now focus on each other.

ANGEL 5: Wait! Wait!

ANGEL 3: What's wrong? Hey!

ANGEL 2: Don't worry, he won't get away.

ANGEL 4: Point your light more to the right. Yeah, to the right.

ANGEL 2: Ouch! Damn!

ANGEL 4: Hey, take it easy!

Words on the screen:

ESCAPE.

WE ARE NOT NAIVE.

THE PURSUERS GO AHEAD, THE PURSUED FOLLOW BEHIND.

WE ARE CLIQUISH.

AN UNCLOSED CIRCLE.

WE SUCCEED OURSELVES.

RUN!

The lights come up.

ANGEL 1 (*slowly, intoxicated*): Who's going to speak for us? Who? Black fantasies floating in the dark. Who's got the guts to repeat such

nonsense? If there's something to it, let's have it already!
The Winds line up and face off. Red Wind 1 moves forward and points straight ahead.
RED WIND 1: Marat!
RED WINDS: You're wasting your breath!
RED WIND 1: Shall I sing you my sweet lullaby? In the dark of the Bastille, I drove a plaster prick up my ass and shouted and sang with glee. Wouldn't you like to hear, Marat? That was it, my friend. Yes, indeed, that was expression in its purest form.
RED WIND (*groaning*): Aaaaah . . . aaaah!
GREY WIND: You joined the revolution.
RED WIND 1: That is true.
GREY WIND 1: And then betrayed it!
RED WIND 1: Yes! This revolution. Ha! Revolution has only a beginning. It is a flash of light, a splash of dizziness too short to be real. If I betrayed the revolution, it was because I could see where it was going.
RED WIND: Oooo . . . aaaah . . . eeee!
GREY WIND: Liquidate them!
Red Winds 2 and 6 move forward.
RED WIND 6: Some day it will come. Duperret, you are my lover, the one Charlotte Corday adores. Some day. I will be you, inseparably you. I will move boldly out to meet myself.
RED WIND 2: Without strife, part of a sublime order. Corday, though men obey their own desires . . . though they obey their own desires . . . obey . . . desires. . . .
With a long rope, the Angels tie Red Winds 2 and 6 together in an erotic pose. Standing erect, the two gyrate together. At intervals, Red Wind 6 emits small cries of pleasure.
GREY WIND: A storm! Voices whisper, whisper, whisper, whisper . . .
GREY WIND 1: Don't think for a moment that you can destroy them without violence!
GREY WIND: Don't think for a moment.
GREY WIND 1: Even if our revolution is strangled to death!
GREY WIND: Don't think for a moment.
GREY WIND 1: Don't be deceived by their seeming harmlessness, their sweet soft voices!

GREY WIND: Sweet soft, sweet soft, sweesoft, sweesoft, seesoo, seesoo!

GREY WIND 1: Liquidate them! All hedonist elements, all impurity!

GREY WIND: Liquidate them!

RED WIND: Violence is the only recourse with which life has been naturally endowed.

RED WIND 1: In my prison the Bastille, I called forth the ghosts of a dying class. Behind those walls, I sealed a pledge with those unseen figures. I played the country doctor and fondled their wasted genitals. A pleasant change. I chuckled to myself. Before long, lizards and mantises and green caterpillars began to crawl from my rectum. Like a scholarly specialist, I diligently captured each one, pinned it to a card, and made notes among my records. You may call it a bad habit, and that I suppose it was, but in a spray of pleasures, it became my black custom.

RED WIND: Candle's flame. Pokers. A glossy ivory paper knife. Fur. Feathers. Sofa. Morris chair. Mirrors and rocking horses. (*Laughter.*)

RED WIND 1: Beat me . . . if you'd only beat me . . . beat me!

One of the Angels rips Red Wind 1's clothes from his back and strips him naked. The other Angels carry the bound Red Winds 2 and 6 to him. Winds in an uproar.

GREY WIND: Liquidate them! Exterminate them!

GREY WIND 1 (*standing and shouting*): Let them be afraid; let them know the meaning of terror. Warmly wrapped in white blankets, bellies bursting . . . I can hear, I can hear their insidious whispering, their secret laughter, their drip-drip drivel . . .

GREY WIND 6: Marat! Marat! You must be careful. You mustn't get overly excited. Do you hear me? It's not good for you. You'll kill yourself at this rate!

Red Wind 1 laughs loudly. The uproar begins to fade. With the exception of Grey Winds 1 and 6, all eyes focus on Red Wind 1.

RED WIND 1: The beginning of the revolution was magnificent. Orgies of chaos everywhere. Compared to that festival of treason, my fantasy world wasn't worth a fart. Magnificent! Before I knew it, I was in a courtroom. How ironic! To hand counterrevolutionaries over to the executioner was my appointed task.

Red Wind 6 begins to whip Red Wind 1 from her constricted position.

Her blows fall monotonously, and she is expressionless. The Red Wind cries out with each lash of the whip and shrinks with the pain, but slowly this reaction is replaced by one of acute pleasure. One by one, the members of the Grey Wind show the same reaction.

RED WIND 6: Justice of the Revolutionary Tribunal, Marquis de Sade. Correction, Citizen Sade. What did he fail to do? Correction, what was he able to do?

Words on the screen:

MURDER: THE FINAL SOLUTION.

EVERYTHING IS PERMITTED.

RED WIND 1: When the time came, I was incapable of murder. I shut my eyes and allowed the defendants to escape out the back way. . . . Why? Why this nausea? In the streets, in every manner of place, I vomited, vomited ceaselessly.

RED WIND 3: Women came running . . .

RED WIND 4: Manes tossed and tangled in the wind . . .

RED WIND 5: Bearded faces.

RED WIND: Stale breath.

GREY WIND: Oooo . . . aaah . . . eeee!

RED WIND: Penises hacked in chunks . . .

GREY WIND: Oooo . . . aaah . . . eeee!

RED WIND and GREY WIND: Oooo . . . aaah . . . eeee . . . eeee . . . eeee!

RED WIND 1: I bent over and vomited. Perhaps . . . yes, perhaps it gave me pleasure.

GREY WIND 2: The crystal of Monsieur Guillotine's love . . .

RED WIND: Oooo . . . aaah . . . eeee!

GREY WIND 3: Painless . . .

RED WIND: Oooo . . . aah . . . eeee!

GREY WIND 4: Rational . . .

RED WIND: Oooo . . . aah . . . eeee!

GREY WIND 5: Brilliant innovation. . . .

RED WIND: Oooo . . . aaah . . . eeee!

GREY WIND: Oooo . . . aaaah . . . eeee . . . eeee . . . eeee!

RED WIND 1: Several days passed. A procession of carts was formed, overflowing with those to be executed, and the blade of the guillotine rose and fell, rose and fell, rose and fell tirelessly. Revenge had long since lost its meaning. All that remained was individual disease. A slow surge toward uniformity. An annihilation of perception. Self-negation. A mortal weakening. I renounced the revolution. I fled the revolution. I became a spectator, looking on, without a finger lifted; I took in all there was to see. And what enveloped me then was silence.

Red Wind 2, unable to move, manipulating only his hands and feet, whispers continuously to Red Wind 6.

RED WIND 2: Someday. . . some not so distant day, people will be bound together in love. Their bodies will meet indiscriminately. Keys will penetrate keyholes to unlock the darkness of prisons deep within. Etcetera, etcetera.

These words are repeated over and over in a voice of slowly increasing volume. Finally they are spoken clearly in a loud voice. Red Wind 6 claws impatiently and passionately at Red Wind 2 until eventually they fall, one on top of the other. The rest of the company joins them, forming a gently undulating mass. Music. Angel 2 takes Red Wind 6's whip and begins beating people indiscriminately. Grey Winds 1 and 6 are alone.

GREY WIND 1: It's so dark. Simmone . . . I feel as if I'm going to die. I feel like I'm dying. Will I die of the heat or die of the cold? Which will it be?

RED WIND 6 (*deliriously*): I am Charlotte Corday. Charlotte Corday. I have come on my second visit to Jean Paul Marat.

GREY WIND 1 (*preoccupied*): Must write my call . . . I must appeal to the People of France. Where are my pen and paper? Aaaah, why is it so dark?

GREY WIND 6 (*whispering*): It's because the sun has set, Marat. Or perhaps because of the smoke. They're burning a mountain of corpses, you know.

A long pause. The energy of the company slowly wanes. A voice is heard.

ANGEL RED: Bird! Bird! Hello, Bird! Good-bye, Bird! Hello! Hello!

Angel Red appears. He walks unsteadily then stops. The motionless Angels and Winds look like a pile of corpses.

ANGEL RED: Bird! Bird!
He has gone blind. The lights slowly dim.

ACT 7

BIRDS (*voices only, singing a children's song*):

In the cage, in the cage,
Bird imprisoned in the cage,
When, oh, when will you be free?

On the evening of the dawn
The crane and the turtle slipped and fell.
Who is that behind you?

Words on the screen:

WORLD OF THE FLESH.

ALL BODIES ABOUND WITH A FEARSOME POWER.

ALL BODIES ARE ALONE AND RACKED WITH INSECURITY.

MODEL: STOMACH ABOVE GROUND OR MUSCLE BELOW?

OUR MINDS, LIKE OUR BELLIES, SUPPORT
CONFLICTING DEMANDS.

MORNING.

WE MUST HOLD OUR POSITIONS;
WE MUST NOT LOSE OUR PLACE.

A SUDDEN AWAKENING.

Voices repeat the refrain to the song, "Who is that behind you?" several times. The voices belong to the Angels.

WHO IS THAT ... BEHIND YOU?

The image of the King of the Birds seems to hover over the Flower Bed. He is lying on his side as if dead.

KING OF THE BIRDS: It's me ... behind me, looking at my back ... it's me!

Words on the screen:

THE ROAD TO SUPREME PLEASURE CAN BE FOUND
IN THE VILEST PARTS OF CIVILIZED CULTURE.

The Birds and Angels stand in a large circle. Decorated with candles, two motorcycles have been placed to form a kind of altar. Angel Red lies on the altar like a sacrificial offering.

ANGEL RED (*as an incantation*): Agron tetagram vixion stimramaton eroaris retrogressimaton clariolan ikishin moing mephyse notell emmanuel shabot admomy ...

ANGEL 1: Why is it that just when everything's going right an assassin's got to come along? It is an atonement, a recompense of blood. Just when the savage battle is raging between us, the unmurdered multitudes, and the few of them who have somehow gotten away without being killed ... naturally, the blood gets mixed, clouded, congealed. Nevertheless—and this is the important thing —nevertheless, it is clean, pure blood. Bathed in blood, in our own blood alone, we would die a hero's death. That's why we must never become assassins. Instead ...

BIRD 1 (*calmly*): How about this? (*By rote*): "What appears in the thought of visionaries is the dualism of the movement and their own consciousness of it ...."

Angel 5 guffaws.

ANGEL 3: Don't laugh!

BIRD 1 (*continuing*): "All that we have to show the people of this society is why they have been fighting. Then consciousness would be a text which, whether they like it or not, they would have to accept as their own."

The Angels all jump to their feet and shout:
ANGELS: Consciousness!
They immediately sit down again, except for Angels 3 and 5, who separate from the others, arms around each other's shoulders.

MODEL: MASSES OR CONSCIOUSNESS?

BIRD 1: "Therefore our only task is to explain the meaning of the people's own actions to them. We must not arrogate absolute wisdom to ourselves and lead them to create a historical fiction."

CORRECTION—MODEL: THE MASSES' PRACTICAL, CRITICAL ACTION OR CONSCIOUSNESS OF THE BEYOND?

ANGEL 3 (*to Angel 2*): Give me the knife for a second.
ANGEL 2: Sure.
Angel 2 throws Angel 3 the knife. In return, Angel 2 offers Angel 3 his pocket flask. Angel 1 is rolling a joint.
ANGEL 1 (*to 2*): Want some shit?
ANGEL 2 (*raising his flask*): I'll stick with this.
Angel 2 pulls at the bottle of whisky. Angel 1 draws hard on his joint and, holding his breath, passes it on to Angel 4.
ANGEL 1: What if we thought about the problem in reverse? I mean, first there's the assassination. For him everything starts from that point. See what I mean?
ANGEL 2: Then what about the end? Inside his mother's belly? A muddy sea of albumen? The station at the end of the line? The warmth of the grave? Whichever way you look at it, it comes out the same, doesn't it? We just move all the way back to the darkness of ravaged creation, or . . . Oh! I see, a circle! The twisted expanse of space inside a closed circle. But wait a minute . . . can you just ignore historical time like that?
ANGEL 1: In the first place, it doesn't even enter the question. When you come right down to it, history doesn't exist, see? It's enough if there's a beginning. There is no end. The idea of a circle's just a sign of weakness . . . it's an excuse we make to ourselves. A wish for some semblance of order.

Words on the screen:

A MAN IS BORN THREE TIMES.

1. IN THE WOMB: PERFECT SLEEP.

2. IN THE SO-CALLED PRESENT WORLD:
THE COEXISTENCE OF SLEEP AND WAKEFULNESS.

3. IN DEATH: ETERNAL WAKEFULNESS.

THIS NEGATES ABSOLUTE HISTORY.

REPEAT: AN UNCLOSED CIRCLE.

BIRD 1: You know, don't you?

BIRDS 3 and 4 (*simply*): Yes.

BIRD 1: Tell them.

BIRD 3: Yes. Those who create revolutions in this world, those who do good, can only sleep in the grave.

BIRD 4: Continuing. In order for one's principles to triumph, they must lead to morality and happiness. It is therefore necessary that one foreswear all avenues of escape, that one declare one's suicidal intentions publicly in advance.

Break.

BIRD 1: Is that all?

BIRDS 3 and 4: Yes, that is all.

BIRD 2 (*rapidly, as an addendum*): The revolution froze. Every principle was attenuated. All that remained was a world of conspirators and their plotting. Just as strong liquor numbs the palate, the implementation of government by terror rendered people insensitive to crime. In an anarchist age, even virtue unites with crime.

BIRD 1 (*repeating*): Is that all?

BIRDS 3 and 4 (*definitively*): Yes, that is all.

BIRD 1: Oh.

BIRD 2 (*some distance away, to Angel 5*): Assassination is a cause. Revolution is an effect. Assassination, however, is an individual act, while revolution is ineffective without the masses. Today's age is not an age of revolution; it is an age of assassination.

ANGEL 5 (*responding*): This is not an age of revolution; it is an age of assassination!

Words on the screen:

DULY ACKNOWLEDGED LINE NO. 3

TODAY'S AGE.

TODAY! AGE!

IS NOT AN AGE OF REVOLUTION:
IT IS AN AGE OF ASSASSINATION

BIRD 1: That's wrong! Everything is over and done with. Like it or not you have to recognize that. For instance . . . for instance . . .

The Angels dance and sing.

SWEET MACHINE

Rocking to and fro,
Gravel-bellied mama.
Rocking to and fro,
Hung-up head-down papa
Go sweet machine!
Go sweet machine!

Blazing hells afire,
Horse-like fat-assed mama
Blazing hells afire,
Drowned rat sorry puss papa
Go sweet machine!
Go sweet machine!

Both wheels off the ground
Sharp-tongued sassafrass mama

Both wheels off the ground
Wheel-chaired turtle-hared papa
Go sweet machine!
Go sweet machine!
Higher, higher, higher, higher!
Higher, higher, higher, higher!

ANGELS: Consciousness!
Words on the screen:

THE FINAL MISSION.

SECOND MEETING ON THE BEACH.

DREAM AT THE END OF THE DREAM:
REVOLUTION AT THE END OF THE REVOLUTION.

PHYSICAL IMMORTALITY.

In a series of ritualistic gestures, the Angels prepare their motorcycles for departure. Carrying candles, the Birds surround them.
ANGEL 2: Morning. Why has it got to be morning? Why isn't it evening? Christ, it's cold. Cold as the nuts on a brass monkey!
ANGEL 1 (*to Angel Red*): Come on, tell us. Who are we? Where can we go?
ANGEL RED (*slowly, in a low voice*): The knife . . . give me . . . give me the knife.
The Birds blow out their candles. It grows dark.
VOICE (*King of the Birds, repeating*): It's me . . . behind me, looking at my back . . . it's me!
VOICES (*Birds 1 and 2*): The one gazing at your back is you.
VOICES (*Birds 3 and 4*): The rifles go ba-bang!
VOICE (*Angel 1*): All right, let's go!
The motorcycles roar to life. Illuminated by the motorcycles' headlamps, Angel Red can be seen with a knife at the ready rushing toward the King of the Birds. The Birds run after him. Suddenly it is dark.
VOICES (*Birds 3 and 4*): The rifles go ba-bang!

VOICE (*King of the Birds*): Come on, baby, let's see you shake that thing!
The King of the Birds laughs and the other Birds join him. Their laughter grows louder, filling the tent.

ACT 8

Words on the screen:

THE FIRST REVOLUTION.

A BRACING MORNING.

THIS IS A DREAM.

The sound of a storm. Clouds go racing by. The Lunatic Landau has been transformed into a sailing ship tossed about, the plaything of the waves. The Red and Grey Winds are aboard ship, thrown to port and then to starboard.
The Birds and Angels are nowhere to be seen.
Grey Wind 2 is lashed to the mast as a lookout. Grey Wind 1, commander of the vessel, clings to the sides of his bath, placed near the ship's wheel, which is manned by Grey Wind 3. The remaining Winds cling together in a shivering, frightened mass.

GREY WIND 2: You the damned! You who throw yourselves against prison walls! You who try to soar high into the skies on the wings of imagination! You shall be tortured, treated with contempt, and finally thrown helplessly aside. You tried to know the meaning of being human, posing questions to yourselves. What is the soul? What is this mountain of confused reason and insubstantial ideals?

WINDS (*in strangled, suppressed voices*): Marat! We are poor! Our poverty is changeless!

GREY WIND 2: In the end, you demolished the myth of the soul. You concluded that the soul resides in the intellect and that thought is a subject for study.

WINDS: Save us! It no longer matters how! Save us now!

GREY WIND 2: To you the soul is utilitarian, a tool to order the world and rule over it. And then one day you joined the revolution. For one crucial moment, you dreamed that the revolution could change the very bases of our existence!

WINDS: We want our revolution! Marat! We want our revolution! We want it! We want it!

But the Winds remain huddled together in changeless postures.

WINDS (*with sluggish uniformity*): To Marat a crown of laurel! Forward to victory in the name of Marat! Three cheers for the streetlights! Three cheers for the baker! Freedom! Three cheers for freedom!

GREY WIND 4: Boy, would I like some *paté de foie gras*!

RED WIND 1: This is the way it goes, Marat. This is their revolution.

WINDS: My tooth aches! Marat, pull my tooth!

RED WIND 1: If their soup gets burnt, they fly into a rage and demand better soup. If a woman finds her husband wanting, she asks for a better one. A man's shoes are too tight, and his neighbor's look better. A poet can't think of a word to rhyme and, carried away by a fevered torrent searches for new ideas. The fisherman wonders why the fish don't bite. They all come crying to the revolution, believing their wishes will come true. That is their revolution: fish and poetry, new husbands and new wives. Perhaps heroic is the only word to describe their courageous spirit. Knowing no rest, they will march to the ends of the earth. But sooner or later they will realize: everything is just as it was. The soup is burnt, there is no word to rhyme, the same husband lies snoring in bed. Their energy exhausted, they pant clouds of stale breath. To the last, our acts of heroism only see us wallow in the gutter.

GREY WIND 3: Poor Marat, your life is nearing its end. Charlotte Corday creeps stealthily toward you, messenger of death. Poor Marat, perhaps she will sleep past the time, dreaming of the day she will rule the nation. Perhaps your illness will improve, and perhaps Corday will be unable to seek you out. Poor Marat, be brave; forget not that you are the guardian of the people. Through the thin light of sunset, keep careful your watch, for evening precedes the night.

GREY WIND 1: What's that knock? Simonne? Simonne? Simonne, bring more cold water . . . give me my pen. I fervently devoted all my time to my work. Borderless nights and days proved insufficient to my task. Investigating one abuse, like a brushfire it spread out of control. No matter where I stepped, pools of quicksand threatened to consume me. When I wrote I always did so with action in mind and knew that writing was only a preparation. When I wrote I was haunted. I could hear the crash and thunder of the actions my words implied. But almost routinely, they lay in wait for my pronouncements, read them only with hostility, and slandered and defamed them, deprived them of their meaning and their strength. I would finish a pamphlet and then have to rush to the sewers to hide like a rat, half-drowned and starving. They commandeered the cannons, enlisted a thousand men, and surrounded my home. I wait for the sound of knocking at my door. Soon my breast will be pierced by fixed bayonets. I wait. Everything I have said has been the truth, truth thought through and through. All facts proved my point. Then why, why do I doubt? Why does everything sound so wrong?

RED WIND 6: Now is the time! I know the moment when your head leaves your body. At that moment, your hands are tied behind your back. Your head has been shaved. You kneel on the platform, your head placed in the metal opening, and your eyes look into the bloody pan below. There is the sound of the blade being raised, blood still dripping from its slanted edge. Then sliding down from above it severs you in two! Rumor has it that when the executioners lift your severed head high for the crowd to see, your mind still functions, your eyes still see, your tongue still moves, your arms and legs still twitch and flail about.

It has grown dark. At some point Angel Red has crawled in amongst the Winds. A plague is slowly spreading among them.

RED WIND 2: Charlotte, awake from your reverie. Wake up, Charlotte! Look there, at the stand of trees, at the rose-colored sunset. Fill your soft breast with the fresh air of evening. Isn't that better? There is nothing to worry about. Forget your worries and take a deep breath of warm summer air. What . . . what's that you're hiding? A knife! Why? Throw it away immediately. A knife! Come, hurry, throw it away this instant.

RED WIND 6: A knife to protect myself, not to inflict pain on others.

RED WIND 2: Nobody's going to harm you, Charlotte. Throw the knife away. And let's go home to Caen.

RED WIND 6: Look at this city! Its prisons overflow with our friends. Just now, if only for a moment, I was with them in my dreams. Those people, packed painfully together in their cells, listen through ceiling grates to their keepers discuss the executions. The jailers talk as if they're considering a gardener burning a pile of fall leaves. I heard them. With bureaucratic precision the names of the doomed are one by one checked from the top of the list. And when the list grows short new names are added to the bottom. I was with them, and with them I waited for my name to be called.

RED WIND 2: Charlotte, what are you trying to do?

RED WIND 6: What manner of city is this? What collection of roofs and walls is this? Who could have invented this hateful machine, this instrument of murder? Who will judge? Who will distinguish people one from the other? And who will pronounce sentence?

RED WIND 2: Charlotte, what are you doing standing in this doorway? Do you know who lives here?

RED WIND 6: He does. I have come here for him.

RED WIND 2: Him? Who, Charlotte? Come, let us return to Caen. Come, Charlotte.

RED WIND 6: I have work to do. Go ahead. Leave me alone!

GREY WIND 1: I am correct! I must write once more. Simonne, my pen! I have an urgent appeal!

RED WIND 1: Marat, look at her. What are your pamphlets and speeches compared to her? She is standing there, wanting to meet you, kiss you, embrace you. Marat, the unsullied virgin offers you her body. Look at her smile. See how her teeth glisten, how she sweeps back the long black strands of her hair. Marat, forget everything. There is not a creature on earth who has transcended the flesh. She is standing there. Beneath that thin layer of gauze, her breasts are naked, moist. Her knife is warm with the warmth of her nakedness. Stand, Marat, stand and welcome her.

RED WIND 6: I have come to meet Marat. Is anyone at home?

GREY WIND 1: Simonne! Simonne! Someone's at the gate. Simonne! Simonne! Go and see who it is.

Red Wind 6, with much effort, stands and takes two or three steps. But to no avail. She stiffens, falls to the floor, and dies. All around her the

Winds, swept by the plague, crawl along the ground, making animal sounds of suffering. Some of their number are already stiff and immobile. Only two of those present remain able to stand, Grey Wind 1 and Angel Red.

KING OF THE BIRDS (*voice only*): It is morning! Tea! It is time for morning tea!

ANGEL RED: Monsieur!

On the Flower Bed, wrapped in a golden light, the Birds are seen dozing around the central figure of the King. The storm passes and dim rays of dawn light illuminate the Lunatic Landau.

GREY WIND 1: Who is that in the doorway?

BIRD 1: It is Charlotte Corday. She has come from Caen to visit you.

GREY WIND 1: Come in.

BIRD 2: Tell him.

BIRD 3: Yes. Marat, I want you to know the names of my friends.

BIRD 4: Continuing: But it will do no good, Marat. For you are already dead.

The legends that have been projected on the screen since the beginning of the play (with the exception of those from scene five) begin flashing across the screen again in their original order.

Angel Red slowly moves toward Grey Wind 1.

GREY WIND 1: Speak more clearly. I can't understand you. Come closer. Who are you? Come closer, closer.

BIRD 3: I have come, Marat.

BIRD 4: But you can't see me, can you, Marat? After all, you're already dead.

RED WIND 1 (*groaning*): Alone, as if left to die on a field of pebbles washed round by the sea. Listening to the ceaseless whispering of lips, I was shut behind thirteen bolted doors. Fetters bound my legs. Openings! All over the body! Openings to penetrate, poke, probe! That is all! . . .

GREY WIND 2: Listen! Listen to me! You are the ones who killed Marat! You are the ones! You are the ones who killed him!

RED WIND 1: Marat, the prison of the heart is far more terrifying than the prison of mortar and stone. Where are the openings? Marat, your revolution . . . your revolution, too . . . a revolution in chains!

GREY WIND 1 (*standing and screaming*): Saturday, July 13, 1793. A Call to the People of France!

Grey Wind 1 collapses. Not one of the Winds remains moving. Angel Red drops his knife to the floor, then turns and bows deeply to the Birds. The King of the Birds applauds . . . alone. On . . . and . . . on. Words continue to flash across the screen. Angel Red exits. Music.

One entire side of the tent suddenly opens onto the outside world. The Angels come roaring out of the distance on their motorcycles and drive into the tent in a cloud of exhaust smoke and dust. They are clothed completely in white. They dance and sing.

The Lunatic Landau Rock

Our backs a superhighway
A thousand horsepower between our legs.
Crackerjack!
Jelly beans!
Paper balloons!
Pinwheels!
Yeah, yeah, yeah!

The dance ends.

ANGELS: Monsieur!

BIRD 1 (*to the Angels*): After the weatherman rabbit!

BIRD 2: Lie in wait on the beach!

BIRDS 1 and 2: That's an order!

ANGELS: Monsieur!

Angel 1 picks up the knife Angel Red has dropped.

ANGEL 1: I'll take this with me. We'll do the job with this.

Bird 1 nods.

BIRDS 3 and 4: The rifles go ba-bang!

The King of the Birds blows on his whistle for what seems an eternity.
   Blackout.
   Words on the screen flash on and off, on and off.

THIS IS A DREAM.

Music. The entire company sings.

So Long For Now

So long for now.
It's the day that all begins,
The day for us to
Bid you a fond farewell.

Into the openings
Down to the deepest depths
There is a rainbow,
There is a rainbow there
Sweet and soft as
Cotton candy
A delicious world lies in store.

So long for now.
On the day that things begin,
That's the day we'll
All be dead and gone.
So long for now!
So long for now!

Criticism:
Tsuno Kaitarō and the
Post-Shingeki Movement

In the late 1960s and early 1970s, Tsuno Kaitarō (1938-) was the
leading theoretician in Theatre Center 68/71. He was by no means the
only critic whose views helped to shape the self-understanding of the
post-shingeki movement, but the seminal importance of his contribution is widely acknowledged.[1] His books *A Critique of Tragedy*[2] and
Theatre Beyond the Gate[3] did more than any other critical writings to
explicate the post-shingeki movement; and as editor-in-chief of the
publishing firm Shōbunsha, he issued many of the basic texts of the
movement, including the plays of Arnold Wesker, Satoh Makoto, and
the complete works of Walter Benjamin. Tsuno's views have deeply
influenced my understanding of the post-shingeki movement, and a
presentation of his thinking here may clarify some of the ideas presented in this book.

The Trinity of Modern Theatre

Tsuno's most fundamental insight is that what we call "modern theatre" is a structurally unique entity with identifiable characteristics.
Shingeki is the Japanese version of this unique "modern theatre." It
developed, as "modern theatre" had in Europe, as a result of the
modernization process.[4]

In order to make the problem more manageable, Tsuno reduces the complex relationship between modern theatre and modernity to three elements that he calls collectively "the trinity (*sanmi-ittai*) of modern theatre."

> What we refer to as modern drama is drama supported by the universalistic doctrine of humanism, with tragedy as its sole mode, presented in a theatre divided in two by means of a curtain.[5]

Of the three components of Tsuno's trinity of modern theatre, the theatre building equipped with a proscenium arch and divided in two by a curtain is the most concrete and therefore the most basic. It is a shorthand expression for urbanization, rationalism, and bureaucratization, in fact the entire range of phenomena known collectively as modernization.[6] Tsuno has written a full-length study of the modern theatre building since its appearance in the sixteenth century and has argued that its spread was accompanied by a steady enervation of the theatrical imagination.[7]

The second component of the trinity of modern theatre is humanism. Tsuno shares Ōe's disaffection with humanism, which he understands as "the sole ideology of the modern bourgeoisie."[8] According to this ideology, all human beings are "free individuals" with their own "inner truth" and an equal potential to participate in "history." Tsuno appreciates the past attraction of these ideas, but in the modern theatre building he experiences them as a limiting, pernicious dogma enforced through numerous prohibitions, legal and customary, explicit and implicit, all symbolized by the omnipresent "no smoking" sign.[9]

> As soon as modernism [was] established in theatre, it was systematized and made a matter of custom. Cursing to ourselves we came to accept any number of its prohibitions. . . . When they came to be guarded by innumerable red lamps, visible and invisible, not only those reading "no smoking," then "the free individual," "inner truth," and "the egalitarian spirit"—in fact modern humanism, which encompasses them all—most conspicuously lost their former attraction.[10]

Tsuno reverses Robbe-Grillet's dictum that tragedy is the last invention of humanism.[11] In Tsuno's view, tragedy is responsible for the ideology of humanism.[12] Tragedy for Tsuno is not classical tragedy but tragedy in its modern guise, which originates with Hegel. Tsuno supports the concatenation of humanism and tragedy with a quotation from Hegel himself:

> To genuine tragic action it is essential that the principle of individual freedom and independence, or at least that of self-determination, the will to find in the self the free cause and source of the personal act and its consequences, should already have been aroused.[13]

I pointed out in the introduction to this volume that shingeki was profoundly influenced by Christianity and Marxism. In fact, these two are linked in Hegel's philosophy, and therefore Tsuno's rejection of Hegelian modern tragedy was a rejection of the fundamental assumptions underlying the shingeki movement. As one authority has written,

> Hegel's all-comprehensive philosophy requires, not "religion" but Protestant Christianity. His left-wing disciples require, directly Hegel's "modern world," and indirectly, the Christianity that is part of it. In short, Hegel preserves Christianity, his left-wing followers destroy it, but both require it.[14]

Hegel's concept of "genuine tragedy" is the very heart of the historical process according to both (Protestant) Christianity and Marxism, only in Christianity that process is a spiritual one while in Marxism it is political and economic. Free, self-conscious individuals come into conflict with the movement of history as it approaches its ultimate goal and are "tragically" sacrificed. This dialectic, the encounter of the free individual with history, provides history's motive force. At the same time, through the mechanism of tragic irony, the individual's sacrifice unites him with the ineluctable movement of history, makes his life meaningful, and thus (ironically) ensures his salvation.[15]

At the core of modern tragedy as Tsuno understands it, then, is "the dialectical 'cognizance' of the fact that ... individualism was to be trampled beneath the fated totality called history and that only by thus being trampled could man achieve humanity."[16] In other words, modern tragedy habituates the theatre to the conviction that there is a homogeneous and ineluctable historical process, and that only through the dialectical encounter with, defeat by, and assimilation to that process can the theatre (and life) be meaningful.

Tsuno stresses the interdependence of humanism, tragedy, and the modern theatre building: the modern theatre building enforces the tragic conception of history in the guise of the ideology of humanism. "Each of these three essential elements comprising modern drama," he writes, "stipulates the existence of the others and is bound to them in an organic whole. . . ."[17]

The Problem of Shingeki

As the Japanese version of modern theatre, shingeki manifests the trinity of modern drama in Japan. Tsuno agrees with Saeki Ryūkō, a fellow critic in Theatre Center 68/71, that the work of Japan's postwar playwrights, particularly those descended from Kubo Sakae, such as Miyamoto Ken, Kinoshita Junji, and Fukuda Yoshiyuki, amounts to nothing less than an attempt to rewrite the history of modern Japan as an enormous modern tragedy.[18]

The act of interpreting modern Japanese history as a modern tragedy has been a highly self-conscious process. As Eric Gangloff has written of Kinoshita Junji, for example,

> For Kinoshita, drama is inseparable from interpretation of history. The nucleus of his plays is that point where a single character meets with and is defeated by the historical events which surround him.[19]

Tsuno believes that underlying this self-conscious rewriting of history as a modern tragedy has been the acceptance of the universalistic doctrine of humanism and the need, felt by the entire spectrum of postwar shingeki dramatists, to depict the tragic interplay of Japanese particularity and the universal, ineluctable process of history, which is construed as the history of the West. Tsuno points out that Kinoshita, Miyoshi Jūrō, Fukuda Tsuneari, and Kishida Kunio, very different playwrights on the surface, all wrote books on what it means to be a Japanese in the modern world; and he implies that their acceptance of modern tragedy has been their way of coming to terms with Japan's encounter with the Western world. The ideologies of humanism and modern tragedy explain and legitimize Japan's modern experience for them.[20]

In short, therefore, while it is a generic description of modern theatre, Tsuno's "trinity" is also a formulation of the particular state of Japanese modern drama as it was being written around 1960.

Post-Shingeki

According to Tsuno and Saeki, what post-shingeki troupes did in rejecting shingeki was to reject this trinity of modern theatre. Performing in tents and other nontheatre spaces, their rejection of the modern theatre building and its attendant bureaucratic apparatus was obvious; but their rejection of tragedy and humanism were equally unequivocal. Saeki's critique of Saitō Ren's 1967 play *Red Eyes*[21] makes the attitude of the entire movement explicit:

> The dramatic method of the play, to describe an entire situation or history by describing a single individual's struggle to protect his inner "something," is the fundamental pattern of postwar Japanese situation theatre, which begins with Kinoshita Junji. . . . *The greatest fault of this dramatic method is that it almost totally dichotomizes external history and the individual inner world.* The individual, driven by some idiosyncratic logic, runs haphazardly into the wall of history or is trapped in some circumstantial cul-de-sac, whereupon he explodes in one great flash of self-destructive light. As members of the audience, the only thing that supports this mad dash and explosion, gives us a glimpse of the situation behind it all, and suggests that all is as it should be is our emotional acceptance of the "something" unfolding on stage. With incredible ease the characters shoulder history, suffer under its burden, and give way to despair. The fact that most such plays end either in a second departure, in the ultimate depths of despair, or in total madness, i.e., in clean, uncomplicated tragedy, is due not to the weight of the history or circumstances depicted on the stage, but to the fact that because the role forced on the individual was too great, he was unable from the first to bear it. Thus he rids himself of the unbearable contradictions of his role through emotional catharsis. Only his cosmic rage remains for eternity, and *history is reduced to the very Hegelian simplicity we have hoped to escape.*[22]

The post-shingeki movement rejected both modern tragedy and the humanistic concept of "the free individual" so central to it. It also rejected the underlying obsession of shingeki dramatists with the West. It denied their implicit acceptance of the notion of Western universalism and Japanese particularity, the concept that the West somehow constitutes the mainstream of history and Japan, if not exactly an aberration, little more than a special case.

Waiting for Godot

Tsuno views Samuel Beckett's *Waiting for Godot* as the ultimate modern drama. Waiting for someone or something that never appears is, argues Tsuno, the essence of modern drama. From Chekhov's three sisters, waiting for the day when they can leave for Moscow, to Clifford Odets' taxi drivers in *Waiting for Lefty*, and Bertolt Brecht, waiting for the Red Army, modern theatre is filled with people who are waiting. In each case, there is the understanding that the awaited someone or something will never arrive; and the peculiar pleasure the modern audience derives from the theatre is watching the ingenious ways people find to kill time.[23]

If there has been a developmental process in modern drama, it has been a steady degeneration culminating in *Waiting for Godot*, where hopeless, meaningless waiting is given its ultimate expression.[24] *Waiting for Godot* is the ultimate modern drama because in it all pretense has been stripped away. There is not the slightest suggestion that Vladimir and Estragon, who wait endlessly for Godot, can expect to be saved through tragic irony, through unification with some transcendent historical or natural logic that will make their waiting and their inevitable, empty death meaningful. Indeed, this endemic incapacity is so all-encompassing that Tsuno concludes,

> It is not possible to attribute "Godot" to one intelligence, that of [Samuel] Beckett. That is, what produced "Godot" was not Beckett personally but the totality of the dramatic sensibility of the age that stretches from Chekhov to Beckett and includes Brecht.[25]

Thus, for Tsuno,

> the location of the problem is clear. It is how to release theatrically the diverse and ambiguous meanings and relationships imprisoned in the ruined euphemisms of modern drama, from Chekhov's "a distant sound is heard that seems to come from the sky" [in *The Cherry Orchard*] to Beckett's "Godot."[26]

How is this to be done? As I detailed in the Introduction, Tsuno suggests a dialectical return to the past as a means to transcend the limitations of the present. He argues that the point of the post-shingeki movement is to use the premodern popular imagination as a negating force to transcend the modern.

An Alternative Dramaturgy

Tsuno feels that the multidimensionality of post-shingeki plays and their "symbolistic" method are the key to the post-modern dramaturgy he has been seeking:

> Multidimensionality is not a manageable thing like an onion, whose skin can be peeled away one layer at a time; it is accompanied inevitably by the dislocation of one time sequence being forced into another, one space being forced into another. This dislocation is concentrated in the site of one [metamorphosing] person. In other words, metamorphosis is none other than the mode of existence of human beings who live in multidimensional time and space. And as I write this, I at last feel that I have begun to grasp another prototypical paradigm different from *Waiting for Godot*: To give expression to the recognition that, beside the time and space to which we have become accustomed—where everything is deemed to be self-evident—there are any number of other dimensions of time and space that we have either forgotten or are pretending to forget. And in the very midst of that multidimensionality, the waiters metamorphose into the awaited. This is what happened in plays from *Find Hakamadare!* to *My Beatles*, and it is the alternative paradigm I believe I have grasped. By creating the conditions where "waiting for Godot" and "being Godot" can be the same thing, Vladimir and Estragon metamorphose into "Godot" of their own accord. Other than this, there is no way to make "Godot" appear. . . .[27]
>
> What sort of space is it that is permeated by multidimensionality? Put in the simplest terms, it is the space of symbolism. *Symbolism brings into proximity by virtue of their very distance from each other two irreconcilably divorced entities, plus and minus poles, irresolvable contradictions, and raises their opposition to a higher level of truth. That is an impossible task in either the naturalistic or allegorical theatre.*[28]

By "symbolism," Tsuno was not referring to the symbolist literary movement but the symbolism of the mystic, the man unrestrained by "the dialectic" or any conventional logic, who transcends history and intuits a hidden reality in an all-encompassing "now."[29]

Tsuno hoped that with this mystical method, the post-shingeki movement could produce a new mythological formulation to animate a new movement in politics and the arts and replace the monolithic myth of tragic historical progress proposed by shingeki.

Something similar was happening in the West at this time. A disaffection with Hegelianism and a desire to recapture the premodern imagination as a means to transcend the paralysis and impotence symbolized by Godot was also taking place in France in particular. As George Steiner wrote of structural anthropologist Claude Lévi-Strauss,

> Lévi-Strauss does not see history as a case of linear progression (this is the crux of his debate with Hegelianism and Sartre's dialectical historicism). By making of history a transcendental value, a concealed absolute, Sartre excludes a major part of past and contemporary humanity from the pale of significant experience. Our sense of history, with its dates and implicit forward motion, is a very special arbitrary reading of reality. It is not natural but culturally acquired. Chronology is an ever-changing code. The grid of dates we use for prehistory is based on the entirely different scheme of values and admissible data than the grid we use to conceptualize the period from, say, 1815 to the present. It is the essence of primitive thought to be *intemporelle* (timeless, untimely), to conceive of experience in simultaneous and partial *imagines mundi*.[30]

This is, of course, precisely what the post-shingeki movement was about: it was an attempt to recapture "timeless primitive thought" (the premodern Japanese imagination), to place on the stage "simultaneous and partial *imagines mundi*" (multi-dimensionality) in order to transcend Hegelianism and the monolith of historical materialism.

Notes

1. See, for example, Kan, *Sengo engeki*, Asahi sensho 178 (Asahi shinbunsha, 1981), p. 214; and Senda Akihiko, "Kaisetsu," *Gendai nihon gikyoku taikei*, vol. 8 (San'ichi shobō, 1972), pp. 422-424.

2. *Higeki no hihan* (Shōbunsha, 1970).

3. *Mon no mukō no gekijō* (Hakusuisha, 1972).

4. Eric Bentley has written, "Realism was not the result of an itch for the new at all costs. It was the result—or concomitant—of the urbanization and mechanization of life, which, it is appraised, cannot be ignored. It was the result—or concomitant—of the rise of the physical sciences which aimed at controlling nature by knowing its pro-

cesses." (Eric Bentley, *The Playwright as Thinker* [New York: Harcourt, Brace & World, 1946, 1967], p. 3.)

5. *Higeki no hihan*, p. 227; "The Trinity of Modern Theatre," *Concerned Theatre Japan* (Summer 1970), I(2):88–90.

6. John Whitney Hall and Richard K. Beardsley, *Twelve Doors to Japan* (New York: McGraw-Hill, 1965), p. 167. Hall offers a comprehensive list of the characteristics of modernity in this essay on the historical dimension of the Japanese experience.

Tsuno of course is aware of the variety of theatre architecture and the fact that contemporary productions often dispense with the curtain and with the proscenium stage. His point is that the proscenium stage constitutes the normative form of modern theatre, and he contends that theatres-in-the-round and other production modes are merely an admission that "the special mode of dramatic imagination called for by that separation which has been the sine qua non of modern theatre has lost its magic, its charm, its majesty, its power." (*Higeki no hihan*, pp. 221–223; "The Trinity of Modern Theatre," pp. 87–88.)

7. *Pesto to gekijō* (Shōbunsha, 1980).

8. "Poor European Theatre," *Concerned Theatre Japan*, II(3–4):15.

9. Tsuno was playing on Brecht's notion of a "smoking theatre." Brecht had written: "I even think that in a Shakespearean production one man in the stalls with a cigar could bring about the downfall of Western Art." (Quoted in John Willett, ed., *Brecht on Theatre* [New York: Hill and Wang, 1964], pp. 8–9.)

10. *Higeki no hihan*, pp. 223–224; "The Trinity of Modern Theatre," p. 88.

11. "Tragedy may be defined, here, as an attempt to 'recover' the distance which exists between man and things as a new value; it would be then a test, an ordeal in which victory would consist in being vanquished. Tragedy therefore appears as the last invention of humanism to permit nothing to escape: since the correspondence between man and things has finally been denounced, the humanist saves his empire by immediately instituting a new form of solidarity, the divorce itself becoming a major path to redemption." (Alain Robbe-Grillet, *For a New Novel: Essays on Fiction*, tr. Richard Howard [New York: Grove Press, 1956], p. 59.)

12. *Higeki no hihan*, p. 224; "The Trinity of Modern Theatre," p. 88.

13. *Higeki no hihan*, p. 225; "The Trinity of Modern Theatre," p. 89. Tsuno quotes from the Japanese translation of Raymond Williams, *Modern Tragedy* (Stanford: Stanford University Press, 1966), p. 33.

14. Emil L. Fackenheim, *Encounters Between Judaism and Modern Philosophy* (New York: Basic Books, 1973), p. 137.

15. Raymond Williams, *Modern Tragedy*, pp. 35–36, 61–84 and *passim*; Emil L. Fackenheim, *The Religious Dimension in Hegel's Thought* (Bloomington: Indiana University Press, 1967), pp. 160–222 and *passim*.

16. *Higeki no hihan*, p. 225; "The Trinity of Modern Theatre," pp. 88–89.

17. *Higeki no hihan*, p. 227; "The Trinity of Modern Theatre," p. 90.

18. Saeki suggests that plays like Kinoshita's *Fūrō* (Turbulent Times), Miyamoto's *Meiji no hitsugi* (A Coffin for Meiji), and Fukuda's *Majo densetsu* (Legend of a Witch), which deal with the Meiji period (1868-1912); Miyamoto's *Utsukushiki mono no densetsu* (Legend of the Beautiful), which concerns the Taishō period (1912-1926); and Fukuda's *Nagai bohyō no retsu* (A Long Row of Tombstones), which deals with the prewar years of the Shōwa period (1926-), laid end-to-end constitute episodes in the history of modern Japan rewritten as a Hegelian tragedy. In each play, a young hero is

sacrificed to history only to be resurrected in the next to struggle, fail, and be sacrificed again. (Saeki Ryūkō, *Ika suru jikan* [Shōbunsha, 1973] pp. 79–87; Tsuno, *Mon no mukō no gekijō*, p. 57.)

Hotta Kiyomi's *The Island* also conforms to this pattern. See my discussion of the play in *After Apocalypse: Four Japanese Plays of Hiroshima and Nagasaki* (New York: Columbia University Press, 1986), pp. 16–17.

19. Eric J. Gangloff, "Kinoshita Junji: A Modern Japanese Dramatist" (Ph.D diss., University of Chicago, 1973), p. 425.

20. *Higeki no hihan*, pp. 49–59; *Mon no mukō no gekijō*, pp. 49–58.

21. *Akame*, tr. David G. Goodman, *Concerned Theatre Japan*, 2(1–2):45–109. Saitō's play recasts *Find Hakamadare!* in the tragic mode Fukuda had tried to escape.

22. *Ika suru jikan*, pp. 76–77; "The Eternal Recanter," *Concerned Theatre Japan*, vol. II(1–2):112. Emphasis added.

23. *Mon no mukō no gekijō*, pp. 9–25 and *passim.*

24. *Higeki no hihan*, pp. 27–29 and *passim.*

25. *Mon no mukō no gekijō*, p. 35. Maurice Valency makes basically the same argument in *The End of The World: An Introduction to Contemporary Drama* (New York: Schocken Books, 1983).

26. *Mon no mukō no gekijō*, p. 102.

27. *Mon no mukō no gekijō*, p 114.

28. *Mon no mukō no gekijō*, pp. 154–155. Emphasis added.

29. According to Gershom Scholem, "If allegory can be defined as the representation of an expressible something by another expressible something, the mystical symbol is an expressible representation of something which lies beyond the sphere of expression and communication, something which comes from a sphere whose face is, as it were, turned inward and away from us. A hidden and inexpressible reality finds its expression in the symbol. If the symbol is thus also a sign or a representation it is nevertheless more than that. . . . The symbol 'signifies' nothing and communicates nothing, but makes something transparent which is beyond all expression. Where deeper insight into the structure of the allegory uncovers fresh layers of meaning, the symbol is intuitively understood all at once—or not at all. . . . It is a 'momentary totality' which is perceived intuitively in a mystical *now*—the dimension of time proper to the symbol." (Gershom Scholem, *Major Trends in Jewish Mysticism* [New York: Schocken Books, 1961], p. 17.)

Also compare Tsuno's statement about symbolism and the reconciliation of irreconcilably divorced entities with the following statement by Martin Buber: "*It is only when reality is turned into logic* and A and non-A dare no longer dwell together, that we get determinism and indeterminism, a doctrine of predestination and a doctrine of freedom, each excluding the other. According to the logical conception of truth, only one of two contraries can be true, but in the reality of life as one lives it they are inseparable. The person who makes a decision knows that his deciding is no self-delusion; the person who has acted knows that he was and is in the hand of God. The unity of the contraries is the mystery at the innermost core of the dialogue [between man and God]. (Martin Buber, "The Faith of Judaism," *Israel and the World*, 2nd ed. [New York: Schocken Books, 1963], p. 17.)

30. Steiner, *Language and Silence* (Harmondsworth, Middlesex, England: Penguin Books, 1969), p. 253.

Postscript:
The Legacy of the 1960s

The post-shingeki movement of the 1960s revolutionized Japanese modern drama, and subsequent developments in the theatre arts were profoundly influenced by the precedents set during this period. An account of how the legacy of the 1960s played itself out in the 1970s and 1980s is beyond the scope of this volume, but it is possible to give a few examples of the way the return of the gods affected Japanese drama.

Post-Shingeki Dramaturgy and
Liberation Theology

In 1979, the English-language quarterly *Ampo* (named for the 1960 anti-Security Treaty demonstrations) published a special double issue entitled "Theater as Struggle: Asian People's Drama."[1] With a lead article by Tsuno Kaitarō, the issue contained scripts of four Asian plays, including *The People's Worship*, a play from the Philippines by Reverend J. Elias.[2]

The special issue of *Ampo* grew out of the activities of the Black Tent Theatre 68/71. After spending the years 1972 to 1976 producing Satoh Makoto's trilogy, *The World of Shōwa: A Comedy*,[3] the Black Tent Theatre turned its attention to Asian "people's drama," becoming deeply involved with the Philippines Educational Theatre Association (PETA), a group founded in 1967 and based in Manila. The relationship between the Black Tent Theatre and PETA was a fruitful one, and in 1982 the two troupes cooperated to produce a Festival of Asian People's Drama in Tokyo.

PETA was profoundly influenced by the movement within the Roman Catholic Church known as "liberation theology," which proposes that "the religious instinct be defined as a revolutionary urge, a psycho-social impulse, to generate a new humanity";[4] and although it was not originally performed by PETA, *The People's Worship* typifies the movement of which PETA is a part. The play clearly demonstrates how liberation theology reinterprets Christian faith out of the experience of the poor and interrelates spiritual redemption and social revolution.

Tsuno and the Black Tent Theatre were attracted to Asian people's drama as a logical extension of their own theatre activities, which, as we have seen, sought to redefine the concept of political revolution by replacing it in its theological context. That Tsuno and the Black Tent Theatre should have identified with the PETA is thus not surprising, for, following their own uniquely Japanese and necessarily tortuous route, Tsuno, Satoh, and the rest of the Black Tent company had combined aspects of Marxism and Judeo-Christian theology in a new dramaturgy that shared much in common with Philippine liberation theology.[5]

Suzuki Tadashi and the Shrine of Toga-mura

In 1976, Suzuki Tadashi led the Waseda Little Theatre (*Waseda shōgekijō*) out of Tokyo to take up residence in Toga-mura, an isolated farming village in Toyama prefecture, eight hours by train and bus from Tokyo. Known today as the Suzuki Company of Toga (SCOT), the Waseda Little Theatre originated at Waseda University during the 1960 anti-Security Treaty demonstrations.[6] In the 1960s, the troupe played an important part in the post-shingeki movement, producing a series of important works, including Betsuyaku Minoru's *The Elephant* (1962), an early version of Satoh Makoto's *My Beatles* (1966), and Kara Jūrō's *Virgin Mask* (*Shōjo kamen*, 1969).[7]

After Betsuyaku left the troupe in August 1969, Suzuki began directing *Concerning Things Dramatic* (*Gekiteki naru mono o megutte*), a series of three highly original collages composed of great scenes from Western and Japanese drama. After successful performances in Europe in 1972 and 1973, the troupe began producing Greek tragedies—*The Trojan Women* in 1974, *The Bacchae* in 1978, and *Clytemnestra* in 1983—using the unique style of acting the troupe had begun to develop by adapting nō and kabuki techniques to the modern stage.[8]

Shortly after the move to Toga, a rumor began to circulate in Tokyo that Suzuki intended to register the Waseda Little Theatre as a religious organization (*shūkyō hōjin*), presumably for the preferential tax treatment that would result. I spoke with Suzuki in May 1981 and asked him if there was any truth to the rumor. He replied:

> That was a joke, of course, because no matter how you look at it we're a theatre troupe, not a religious organization. But what we're doing is close to a religious activity. Every year at the same time in a predetermined space we go through a certain ritual. The form of the place is predetermined, and in that space, the same group performs. It's a prescribed space where the unchanging, the eternal can be introduced, where a changeless something can be performed. That's why we established our theatre in Toga: we wanted to create a fixed, ritual space. That was clear and explicit. As in nō, although we're different from nō, the idea was to create our own unique fixed space, our own sacred, purified space, where the continuous memory of the ensemble could work. This is religious. Our idea was to create a religious shrine [*honzan*]. Shingeki isn't doing anything like this. So the idea that we would register ourselves as a religious organization is ridiculous, but I think it would be safe to say that of contemporary theatre groups, as far as the way theatre is produced is concerned, the Waseda Little Theatre is the most "religious" among them.

The eight-hour journey from Tokyo to Toga is nothing less than a pilgrimage to "a religious shrine" where "the unchanging, the eternal" appears. Toga is a sacred space, a *temenos*, to which the gods released by the post-shingeki movement can return and where the faithful can go to meet them.

The Butoh Movement and the Return of the Gods

Maro Akaji played the role of Miss Safety in the Tokyo production of *John Silver: The Beggar of Love*. In 1972, he left the Situation Theatre to found his own dance company, *Dai Rakuda Kan* (The Great Camel Battleship).

Maro had lived for three years (1965–1968) with Hijikata Tatsumi. Hijikata (1928–1986) was an iconoclastic dancer-choreographer from the Tōhoku region whose debut in May 1959 with an adaptation of the homosexual theme from Mishima Yukio's 1951 novel *Forbidden Colors* (*Kinjiki*) had caused a scandal. According to Mark Holborn,

> The whole dance was performed without music. Ohno [Kazuo]'s son, Yoshito, who was still a young boy, enacted sex with a chicken squeezed between his thighs and then succumbed to the advances of Hijikata.[9]

Holborn writes that "Japanese Dadaists, who were pioneering Performance Art in Tokyo in the 1960s, greatly admired Hijikata's theatrical techniques";[10] but Hijikata's dance derived from the same impulses that motivated the post-shingeki movement, not some generalized quest for novelty. As he declared in 1985, in what is certainly the definitive expression of his philosophy of dance,

> To make gestures of the dead, to die again, to make the dead reenact once more their deaths in their entirety—these are what I want to experience within me. A person who has died once can die over and over again within me. Moreover, I've often said although I'm not acquainted with Death, Death knows me.[11]

Hijikata defined himself shamanistically, as a medium for the appearance of the dead on the stage. Through him, the Japanese gods, the immortal dead, could manifest themselves in the world of the living.

Maro Akaji integrated the perspective of the post-shingeki movement into Hijikata's *butoh* dance form. It was Maro and his troupe that first introduced *butoh* to America and with it post-shingeki dramaturgy. As Anna Kisselgoff wrote in her review of Dai Rakuda Kan's New York City debut: "Haunted implicitly by the horrors of The Bomb, obsessed with themes of creation and destruction, Butoh pieces bank on the grotesque in their concertedly primeval imagery."[12] The abiding influence of the atomic bomb experience, the fascination with eschatological issues, the aggressive embrace of anomaly, and the dialectical return to the premodern—the main characteristics of post-shingeki dramaturgy are all unmistakable in Kisselgoff's description. One need only look at Ethan Hoffman's recently published photographs of Dai Rakuda Kan and other *butoh* groups to understand that, white-faced, arms extended, faces up-turned, eyes vacant, they are ghosts incarnate, that with them the gods have returned to the Japanese stage.[13]

*   *   *

The new mythological formulation that made it possible for the gods to return to the Japanese stage in the 1960s profoundly influenced subsequent developments in the Japanese performing arts. From Asian people's drama to *butoh*, it has been interpreted and articulated in diverse ways and has opened an extraordinary range of possibilities to Japanese theatre.

Notes

1. *Theater as Struggle: Asian People's Drama, Ampo* (1979), 11:2–3. *Ampo* is published by the Pacific-Asia Resources Center (PARC) in Tokyo.
2. The other three plays are *Chinogi* by Korean dissident poet Kim Chi Ha, *Ugly JASEAN* by Areeya Mitrasu of Thailand, and *The House of Man* by Chinen Seishin of Okinawa.
3. I describe *The World of Shōwa* in "Satoh Makoto and the Post-Shingeki Movement in Japanese Contemporary Theatre" (Ph.D. diss., Cornell University, 1982), pp. 278–346.
4. These are the words of Sri Lankan theologian Aloysius Pieris, quoted in Phillip Berryman, *Liberation Theology* (New York: Pantheon, 1987), p. 167.
5. Tsuno's firm Shōbunsha also published the Japanese translation of Paulo Freire's *The Pedagogy of the Oppressed*, one of the most influential texts of the liberation theology movement, under the title *Hiyokuatsusha no engeki*, literally "The *Theatre* of the Oppressed."
6. Nobuko Albery's *Balloon Top* (New York: Pantheon, 1978) is a *roman à clef* that presents a first-hand, albeit self-serving, rendition of theatre activities at Waseda at the time of the 1960 demonstrations.
7. For details regarding Suzuki Tadashi and the Waseda Little Theatre, see my comments in *Theatre Companies of the World*, ed. William C. Young and Colby H. Kullman (Westport, CT: Greenwood Press, 1986), pp. 119–122.
8. See *The Way of Acting: The Theatre Writings of Tadashi Suzuki*, tr. J. Thomas Rimer (New York: Theatre Communications Group, 1986).
See also James R. Brandon, "Training at the Waseda Little Theatre: The Suzuki Method," *The Drama Review* (December 1978), 22(4):29–42; and Suzuki Tadashi, "The Sum of Interior Angles," tr. Frank Hoff and David G. Goodman,

Canadian Theatre Review (Fall 1978), 20:20-27.

9. Mark Holborn, "Tatsumi Hijikata and the Origins of Butoh," in Ethan Hoffman et al., *Butoh: Dance of the Dark Soul* (New York: Aperture, 1987), p. 11.

10. Holborn, "Tatsumi Hijikata and the Origins of Butoh," p. 11.

11. Hijikata Tatsumi, "Kazedaruma," in Ethan Hoffman et al., *Butoh*, p. 127.

12. "Dance: Dai Rakuda Kan's '5 Rings,'" *New York Times*, April 10, 1987.

13. Ethan Hoffman et al., *Butoh*.

Contributors

Akimoto Matsuyo is the doyenne of Japanese playwrights. Born in 1911, she began her playwriting career after World War Two with the encouragement of dramatist Miyoshi Jūrō. Her work has received, among others, the Tamura Prize (1964), the Mainichi Prize (1969), and the Yomiuri Prize (1975). A three-volume collection of her plays was published in 1979.

Fukuda Yoshiyuki was born in 1931. He graduated in French literature from Tokyo University, where he was active in the Tokyo University Theatre Study Society (*Tōdai gekiken*). Originally an enthusiastic supporter of the Japanese Communist Party, he later rebelled, setting an important example for his younger contemporaries. His influence reached its peak in the early sixties as leader of the Youth Art Theatre (*Seigei*), where he worked with Satoh Makoto, Kara Jūrō, Betsuyaku Minoru, and many others. Fukuda was strongly influenced by dramatist Kinoshita Junji and later by the work of Bertolt Brecht. Collections of his plays include *Sanada fūunroku* (Chronicle of the Sanada Uprising, 1963), *Majo densetsu* (Legend of a Witch, 1969), and *Yakeato no onna* (Woman in the Ruins, 1974).

David G. Goodman has been involved in modern Japanese theatre since 1968. From 1969 to 1973 he edited *Concerned Theatre Japan*, an English-language theatre journal. He is the editor-translator of

After Apocalypse: Four Japanese Plays of Hiroshima and Nagasaki (Columbia University Press, 1986); *Land of Volcanic Ash* (Cornell East Asia Papers, 1986); and, with J. Thomas Rimer and Richard McKinnon, *Five Plays by Kishida Kunio* (forthcoming). In addition, he has written three books in Japanese. Goodman teaches Japanese and comparative literature at the University of Illinois, Urbana-Champaign.

Kara Jūrō (born 1940) graduated from Meiji University, where he was active in *Jikken gekijō*, the student Experimental Theatre. He founded *Jōkyō gekijō* (The Situation Theatre) in 1963 after a brief apprenticeship with the Youth Art Theatre. Kara is a prolific writer, and a six-volume collection of his plays was published in 1979–80. Kara is recognized as one of Japan's leading writers, having won not only the Kishida Prize (1969) and the Izumi Kyōka Prize (1978) for his plays, but also the coveted Akutagawa Prize for a novel in 1983. Kara continues to write, direct, and perform with the troupe he founded, today occasionally performing in theatres as well as the company's red tent.

Born in 1942, **Katō Tadashi** has been a member of the Black Tent Theatre 68/71 since its inception. He has been active as both an actor and a playwright. Characterized by punning and slapstick comedy, his plays include *Shūrearisuto sengen* (The Surrealist Manifesto, 1973) and *Amerika* (1983).

Saitō Ren was born in Pyongyang, Korea, in 1940. He majored in Russian literature at Waseda University but withdrew before graduating and joined the Actors' Theatre Training School (*Haiyūza yōseijō*), where he met Satoh Makoto, Kushida Kazumi, Yoshida Hideko, and others with whom he founded *Jiyū gekijō* (The Freedom Theatre) in 1966. He helped found Theatre Center 68 but left the troupe in 1971, after the production of *The Dance of Angels Who Burn Their Own Wings*. In 1980, Saitō won the twenty-fourth Kishida Prize for *Shanhai bansukin* (*Welcome, Shanghai!*), which was subsequently made into a feature film.

Born in 1943, **Satoh Makoto** is the product of a complex intellectual background. A grandnephew of Anami Korechika (1887–1945), the fanatical war minister who committed *hara kiri* at the time of Japan's World War Two defeat, Satoh has long been concerned with the legacy of Japanese imperialism and ultranationalism. His early education, through the fifth grade, was in Christian schools. He showed an early interest in philosophy, particularly in the thought of St. Augustine and Søren Kierkegaard, whose complete works he read in high school. Satoh graduated from the Actors' Theatre Training School in 1965 and joined the Youth Art Theatre, where he assisted Fukuda Yoshiyuki in directing the company's final production. Satoh was a founding member of both *Jiyū gekijō* and Theatre Center 68. In 1970 he won the Kishida Prize for Playwriting for *Nezumi Kozō: The Rat.* He continues to write and direct for the Black Tent Theatre 68/71, the name by which Theatre Center 68 is currently known.

Yamamoto Kiyokazu was born in a working class section of Tokyo in 1939, and although he graduated with a degree in educational psychology from the elite Tokyo University, he has continued to write about working class environments like the one where he grew up. While in college, Yamamoto met Saeki Ryūkō and other members of the Tokyo University Theatre Study Society and went on to found *Rokugatsu gekijō* (the June Theatre) with them. Today he is affiliated with the Black Tent Theatre 68/71. A collection of his plays, *Sayonara Makkusu* (Good-bye, Max), appeared in 1980.